European Union and its Neighbours in a Globalized World

Volume 30

The series publishes monographs and edited volumes in the field of European and international law and policy. A special focus is put on the European neighbourhood policy, current problems in European and international law and policy as well as the role of the European Union as a global actor. The series supports the publishing and distribution of research results of cross-border research consortia. Besides renowned scientists the series is also open for publication projects of young academics. The series emphasizes the interplay of the European Union and its neighbouring countries as well as the important role of the European Union as a key player in the international context of law, economics and politics.

Bernardo Calabrese
Editor

Legal Perspectives for a Sustainable Circular Economy

Springer

Editor
Bernardo Calabrese
Università degli studi di Verona
Verona, Italy

ISSN 2524-8928 ISSN 2524-8936 (electronic)
European Union and its Neighbours in a Globalized World
ISBN 978-3-032-07794-3 ISBN 978-3-032-07795-0 (eBook)
https://doi.org/10.1007/978-3-032-07795-0

This work was financed in the context of European Union funds - Next Generation EU, component M4C2, investment 1.1, project PRINPNRR2022 titled "Empowering Citizens for Circular Economy: a HUMAN-centred law model" (ECCE-HUMAN), CUP: B53D23032500001, project code: P20225JRCM.

This Springer imprint is published by the registered company Springer Nature Switzerland AG
The registered company address is: Gewerbestrasse 11, 6330 Cham, Switzerland

Foreword

The most often cited source for the concept of "sustainability," the Brundtland Report envisaged (rather than defined in the strict sense) this phenomenon as "meeting the needs of the present without compromising the ability of future generations to meet their own needs." The beauty of this sentence is that we might read anything into it. Is sustainability a right or a privilege? Does it impose any obligation on any entity, be they humans, corporations, nations, or supranational organizations? Is it enforceable? I am not convinced that sustainability could easily be defined. My pitch is similarly far from being a definition, but a purely pragmatic understanding: sustainability, in the broadest sense, shall cover any human acts that contribute to the lessening of negative impacts, including social, technological, or economic stress, on our environment. Such a pragmatic approach allows any and all interested parties—including researchers—to come up with environmentally conscious ideas and solutions.

It looks like there is another great output on the interpretation of sustainability: the present book offers a timely, in-depth, and interdisciplinary review of corporate and consumer law vis-à-vis sustainability. No doubt, corporations and consumers are the engines and the steam of our consumer society—they are mutually responsible for the deterioration of our environment.

Hence, I agree with Francesca Bianconi, who argued in her chapter that there is space "for the direct involvement of legal instruments typical of company law" in this discourse. Other authors of the volume reimagined consumers' rights and obligations in the same vein. Similarly, Federica Pasquariello's chapter on workers' buyouts evidences that a sustainable circular economy might mean both "economic sustainability" and the "economy of sustainability." The overall goal of a sustainable circular economy must be therefore two- (or probably even mani-)fold: it shall contribute to the decrease of negative effects on our environment, but also to evade any future/potential negative effects. This might be true for workers' buyouts, even though Pasquariello herself warned on the limits of any such hope: "[i]t should also be considered, on the other hand, that empirical evidence shows that companies, although restructured or likely to be restructured, may still be unattractive to third party investors, be they financial or industrial."

Overall, the regulatory intervention to tackle the negative environmental repercussions caused by the consumer society is inevitable. Any such intervention might necessitate a clear vision on at least three distinct grounds. First, the level, the actual steps and the scope, as well as the actual field of law of such intervention shall be clearly decided. This volume takes a clear stand in all the three issues. First, it recommends a layered approach by intervening at the national level (in the instant case, predominantly in Italy, the country of domicile of the authors), as well as regional (the European Union) and international level. Second, it reimagines and extends existing frameworks, as well as offers bold proposals. Third, the book focuses on corporate law and consumer law, but extends well beyond that by addressing some constitutional law, EU law, intellectual property law matters, as well as touching upon other disciplines like sociology and economics.

To do so, the book follows a tripartite logic (or quadripartite if you count the introductory remarks separately): the questions are elaborated separately at national, regional, and international levels. Indeed, in its first part on Italian corporate/consumer law, the chapters represent a clear-cut structure by focusing on corporate leadership and social (consumers) responsibility for sustainability within and outside of corporations.

All five chapters in this part are straightforward in their message: existing frameworks are no longer appropriate. Corporate leaders shall do more, and consumers shall be granted more flexibility to partake in environmentally crucial decisions. For that purpose, Anna Genovese argues for holding corporate leaders "liable for non-compliance with sustainability obligations, for declared but disregarded sustainability commitments, and for management decisions taken without abiding by sustainability principles." Andrea Caprara recommends allowing "active stakeholders" to contribute to in-house decision-making. Francesca Bianconi looks at the principle of proportionality as a tool and reviews how it might be applied more effectively to make more environmentally conscious decisions at the corporate level. Federica Pasquariello discusses workers' buyouts as a case study to see how individuals can contribute to lessening the negative impacts of consumericsm on our society via business crisis law. Finally, Bernardo Calabrese broadens the scope of corporate sustainability to external/consumer-centered solutions, especially the recently accepted repairability right. As he puts it, "[o]n the one hand, against an excessive reverence to intellectual property, it is maintained that the pursuit of public interest underlying repair could well entail a 'due prejudice' to private business rights, limiting their prevalence to abuse cases. On the other hand, against the biased presumption that servitization is always beneficial for the circular economy, it is maintained that the consumer shall instead enjoy the right to freely turn to an open competitive market for repair, in order to counteract the relevant foreclosure effects of this contract model." These topics are equally relevant—though fragmented—steps toward a more sustainable economic environment.

The book then transitions from Italian case studies to a broader perspective, focusing on the European Union (EU). There is not only a growing need but also a clear rationale to "weaponize" consumer protection law by embedding rules that promote more sustainable practices. The EU has rightly recognized the need to intervene and establish a regulatory framework that empowers consumers—who have traditionally been relatively powerless players in the circular economy. However, any such framework must be carefully constructed.

Consumers, after all, are the ones who ultimately consume—and as such, they directly contribute to the overwhelming burden on our landfills. If companies are to be blamed for overproduction and the sale of short-lived goods, then consumers, too, might be held accountable for accepting these practices and choosing convenience over consciousness. While these may seem like harsh words directed at consumers—the "humans" in the system—and no one enjoys being blamed, such frankness may be necessary to underscore the urgent need to shift consumer mindsets.

Consequently, any successful regulatory intervention in this field must rely not on punitive measures, but on a combination of education and incentives. Consumers must be empowered to change not only certain aspects of the economy but also their own thinking.

Whether this can be achieved through flexible interpretation of existing norms, the creation of new rules, or a complete overhaul of the status quo remains a difficult question. The book offers examples of all three approaches.

In his contribution, Francesco Deana explores how literacy and rights/responsibilities can be effectively combined. He advocates for consumer education and examines consumer rights related to product longevity and repairability—areas where the EU has already taken significant steps, demonstrating that sustainability can be meaningfully addressed at a regional level. Yet, the real work lies ahead. Whether and how consumer repair habits or authorized repair services contribute to a sustainable economy—that is, whether they reduce net environmental harm—requires empirical investigation.

Undoubtedly, in order to maximize the positive effects of such rights, the other essential component—consumer literacy—must be emphasized. I fully agree with Deana, who pays close attention to how information is visually conveyed to consumers. As he aptly notes, "The growing attention to product life cycles—from design to disposal—necessitates the adoption of tools such as sustainability labelling and environmental footprint indicators. These instruments would standardize information on key sustainability factors such as carbon footprint, energy efficiency, reparability, recyclability, and overall lifecycle impact." In today's society, visual tools appear to be among the most effective ways to inform consumers, raise awareness, and facilitate the sharing of important messages.

To strengthen such consumer rights, a clear and effective enforcement mechanism is essential. The level and form this mechanism should take is another intriguing issue. Currently, a variety of options are available, from traditional court proceedings to alternative dispute resolution methods (e.g., arbitration or mediation) and, more recently, platform-based in-house dispute mechanisms—some of which are mandated by EU e-commerce regulations, particularly the Digital Services Act.

This book also contributes to the systematic review of these mechanisms. Elisabetta Bergamini's chapter addresses the efficiency of internal consumer-to-consumer dispute resolution processes. Her work goes further, advocating for the strengthening of consumers' rights—both in scope and depth—especially concerning extrajudicial avenues for enforcing their interests.

Is the current legal framework equipped to serve these purposes? More broadly, is the constitutional framework of the EU—and its Member States, such as Italy—adequate to protect consumer interests in the context of sustainability? Alessia-Ottavia Cozzi argues that the EU and its Member States may approach this issue differently. The EU has already "constitutionalized" environmental protection through the TEU and the Charter of Fundamental Rights, whereas Member States like Italy have not necessarily followed suit. In such cases, environmental concerns remain "external" constraints on their economies. Cozzi believes these perspectives are not inherently incompatible. In one of the boldest claims in the book, she calls for a revision of the EU's existing social contract to enable a new paradigm for a sustainable circular economy.

Whether the EU can take the necessary and sufficient steps to advance sustainability—and to realize its ambitions under the Green Deal—remains to be seen. But the book rightly emphasizes that efforts must not stop there. "Greening" our economy demands international cooperation as well. Three additional chapters explore this global dimension in compelling ways.

Claudia Candelmo reminds readers that the EU is not alone in seeking a more sustainable world—and indeed, it may not even be leading the way. Her chapter presents a rich overview of actions taken by the United Nations and four global regions: Africa, Latin America, Asia, and the Pacific. I wholeheartedly support this comparative approach, and I urge readers to explore Candelmo's chapter for at least two reasons. First, it reinforces the importance of comparative research in all areas, including sustainability regulation. Second, my own research on upcycling—a creative and timely sustainable practice—confirms her findings. People in these regions often devise the most innovative solutions to reduce humanity's carbon footprint. In some ways, this is not surprising: many of these countries are net importers of waste. Consider the landfills in Africa, South America, and Asia filled with discarded clothing and e-waste from exporting nations like those in North America and Europe. From this, we can draw two important conclusions: Europe is far from perfect—we must do better—and we must open our minds to learn from the Global South.

Finally, two chapters by Sara Dal Monico and Sara De Vido bring the discussion into the realm of international legal and sociological frameworks. Dal Monico returns to the book's central theme—"consumer"—and bridges it with the discipline of sociology. She argues that current consumer law is still too "eco-centric" rather than "human-centric" and calls for a fundamental rethinking of international legal norms. Her vision includes recognizing consumer rights as human rights and promoting robust information rights that allow consumers to make more rational and sustainable decisions.

The book's climax—and perhaps its boldest proposal—comes from Sara De Vido, who advocates for legally recognizing the environment as a rights-bearing entity. To be candid, this idea pushes the limits of actual (legal) reality. Yet, it lingers in the mind. How profoundly would we need to rewrite the international human rights framework to effectively combat climate change, overconsumption, and environmental degradation? While I cannot answer this with certainty, I align with De Vido's view: we may indeed need a new social contract on an international scale.

Szegedi Tudományegyetem
Szeged, Hungary

Péter Mezei

Acknowledgment

Financed in the context of European Union funds—NextGenerationEU, component M4C2, investment 1.1, project PRINPNRR2022 titled 'Empowering Citizens for Circular Economy: a HUMAN-centred law model' (ECCE-HUMAN), CUP: B53D23032500001.

Contents

Introduction to Legal Perspectives for a Sustainable Circular Economy

Bernardo Calabrese

The paradigm shift towards a Sustainable Circular Economy (SCE) is at the core of the EU policy agenda, aiming at revolutionizing the whole economic productive model that characterizes our contemporary society. The main features of this new paradigm, which is intended to tackle the environmental (and indeed systemic) crisis that affects our age and jeopardizes our future, have been for some time at the heart of the debate, so that such features can be considered as already well known. In essence, SCE can be appreciated in its challenging the socio-economic 'linear' model of 'take-make-dispose'—or, from a specular perspective, 'buy-use-toss'—in favour of a new 'circular' one that lies on reuse, repair and recycle.

If properly understood, it should be considered neither in a reductive way as returning to (wise but minor) traditional good practices of recovery and savings, nor in an ideological way as indulging (provocative but antihistorical) degrowth temptations: in fact, the challenge is to reconcile an advanced and innovative economy, such as that of today's global and digital market, with objectives of socio-environmental sustainability, so that the values already circulating in the market become a resource that feeds on itself, to the benefit of all. From this perspective, innovation is traditionally seen as bringing about greater entropy, with inevitable negative social and environmental repercussions, almost as if it were a necessary price to be paid for achieving progress. However, the novelty of this paradigm rests precisely on its discontinuity with previous models of progress, internalizing sustainability as its cardinal principle.

Such a radical change would have a major impact on current production and consumption patterns, which in turn would revolutionize not only the economy, but also society as a whole. In this sense, the lessons of modern philosophy remind us that we cannot rely exclusively on economic rationales and techno-science, in their

B. Calabrese (✉)
Università degli studi di Verona, Verona, Italy
e-mail: bernardo.calabrese@univr.it

B. Calabrese (ed.), *Legal Perspectives for a Sustainable Circular Economy*, European Union and its Neighbours in a Globalized World 30,
https://doi.org/10.1007/978-3-032-07795-0_1

fallacious promise of infinite progress, but we must look to humanity to fairly orient the evolution of society. In the context of SCE, this is expressed by the idea of the so-called 'human-centered' approach: that is, the endeavour to decouple economic growth from environmental degradation placing at the center the human needs, in terms of well-being of individuals as aware human beings that, as such, take care of the world they live in.

Accordingly, it should be exactly the mission of the legal order to be in charge of protecting and promoting individual needs and rights, according to human solidarity, in all socio-economic fields. Yet, the legal dimension of individuals is often underestimated in the SCE framework. It is true that many reforms have been enacted and many others are expected to come, as will be duly reported in this research: but most of this legislative intervention is mainly done with a mindset of adapting old legal solutions, which, in fact, have proven to be unsatisfactory in assuring proper answers and remedies against the interests of global economic forces. Then, the risk is not negligible for the system to remain incomplete without a clear set of rights, duties and prerogatives recognized to the benefit of people together representing the public community.

Therefore, it is decisive that the legal dimension of SCE, and so the regulation of the market and the society on which it impacts, is designed consistently with the same innovative human-centered approach, in order to achieve effectively the indicated objectives of progress. This means, first and foremost, not limiting oneself to uncritically assimilating schemes of economic convenience, but asking oneself how to shape the new model with a change of paradigm that should necessarily invest the existing legal order as well. This research intends to fill this 'legal gap' in the realization of SCE.

In this regard, the need for innovation also arises at the legal level. Actually, as said, the system cannot resort to old schemes if it wants to respond properly to new challenges, and this is all the more true for the ones deriving from such a paradigm shift. That is why this research intends to promote a general reconceptualization of existing legal configurations, exploring new perspectives to strengthen the role of 'human' individuals in the socio-economic system, so that they can become the point of reference in governing the transition to SCE.

In this sense, this research develops a profound rethinking of the role of market and institutional actors in our society, as well as those of individuals, understood primarily as persons in the holistic 'human' sense mentioned above, and not as mere 'economic' consumers. This requires not only a careful analysis of the state of the art and its relevant criticalities, but also the effort to formulate innovative proposals that try to break traditional barriers in order to avoid the repetition of long-standing faults. Such a constructive and innovative effort, at least as a genuine attempt, is the little ambition that moved this project.

Admittedly (and obviously), it would have been impossible to cover all the possible profiles and issues that concern the legal dimension of SCE, especially in light of the multifaceted condition of the individual as citizen-consumer-user in our contemporary society. Therefore, this research focuses on selected legal perspectives that are considered key in such context, due to their primarily commercial and systemic relevance, which is mostly characterizes on a structural level an economic model that stands as a new paradigm (as SCE is supposed to be).

Such an oriented approach to economic reality can be found in the order of the single chapters. In figurative terms, it can be said that the book presents the different legal perspectives as a zoom-out: it starts from the main economic actors involved in the market system (i.e. corporate enterprises) and then it expands to the overall economic environment (considering the other relevant subjects, i.e. workers, competitors and consumers); furthermore, it looks more widely from a legal policy height at this set of economic relationships, firstly from a contextual constitutional framework, and then moving even beyond to the global international dimension.

According to this prevalence for a concrete approach, the book opens with a sociological analysis, which anticipates the legal investigation that follows and that constitutes the core of the research. This specific sociological perspective, carried out by Michele Marzulli (Chap. 1), aims to present the relevant framework by means of the analysis of its key concepts, issues and actors. In particular, it highlights the social complexity implied in the regulation of SCE, because of the multidimensional nature of such sustainable circular practices. In this sense, any policy initiative that places people at the centre (following the aforementioned 'human-centred' approach) must consider at least a sort of duplicity, i.e. the dialectic between the macro dimension (the global scenario) and the micro dimension (social action understood as individual action). These difficulties can explain—to some extent—why 'green' policies seem recently to be in crisis, but the same difficulties represent also the unavoidable starting point for formulating viable solutions, including for the present research.

Then, the proper legal analysis begins, starting as said from the profiles more specifically related to corporate enterprises. In this regard, due to the peculiarity of this sector, the analysis of EU law is substantially integrated by a specific national perspective where such harmonized rules are put into practice: in particular, for reasons of proximity, Italian company law will be used as a case study. However, this focus mirrors the intention to offer a more concrete example, without any self-referentiality, but rather having in mind how the national dimension represents the ultimate moment of appreciation of the very same EU level.

More precisely, different issues of corporate governance arise. Respectively, Anna Genovese (Chap. 2), deals with corporate sustainability reporting, as the new legal framework where corporate ESG information has been transformed, going beyond the mere financial dimension of investors and other corporate-related addresses. If mandatory reporting about sustainability is apparently meaningful for establishing a concrete transition towards SCE, such informational obligations are still to be verified in their effectiveness. In this sense, the analysis explores the admissibility and practicability of corporate liability for non-compliance with sustainability obligations, also in terms of management implications.

Furthermore, Andrea Caprara (Chap. 3) investigates the possible role of citizens as stakeholders actively engaged in corporate governance, bringing within business companies the societal interests that are relevantly fostered in SCE. In particular, and with the same concrete approach, the analysis focuses on the viable solutions that could be developed in practice, considering the categories of admissible statutory clauses and also other atypical cases of involvement within the scope of managerial discretion. In this regard, it is underlined how the relevant profiles of legal protection should be based on the fundamental arrangement of an appropriate corporate organization, in which active involvement is integrated consistently with the proper management of the lucrative enterprise itself.

In addition, the theme of corporate governance in the new paradigm framework of SCE is tackled in terms of management duties by Francesca Bianconi (Chap. 4). Here the analysis pursues the idea of finding within the legal system possible instruments to govern the discretion of directors, and it claims for an extension of the general principle of proportionality to the business context as a relevant criterion for concretizing and reviewing directors' management choices. This innovative application is claimed to transform sustainability into a concretely enforceable and verifiable managerial duty, while maintaining the profit-making purpose typical of companies, in line with the inherent spirit of SCE.

Moving beyond corporate governance, Federica Pasquariello (Chap. 5) considers business companies not in their physiological status, but when facing insolvency or crisis. In this regard, the paradigm shift towards SCE spurs the research for possible models for 'regenerating' the value that persists in such companies. Following that human-centered approach that goes beyond a purely capitalist logic, the model of Workers' Buyout (WBO) stands out, by virtue of the significant role that workers can play not only for preserving business continuity, but also for the relevant spillovers to the benefit of the local community. Such a model of cooperative enterprise is then appreciated in its applicative profiles, including the possible means of support that appear necessary in practice.

Still looking at the commercial system, but from a larger market perspective, is the analysis carried out by (myself) Calabrese Bernardo (Chap. 6) about the so-called 'right to repair'. The actual possibility of repairing products by individuals as end-users is one of the pillars of SCE, and this is testified by an international movement that is pushing for this kind of regulation across the world. Not by chance, the EU legislator intervened very recently with a specific Directive on this point, which, however, other aspects aside, shows two main issues concerning intellectual property and servitization. Hence, the analysis tries to overcome these obstacles, not limiting to critical review, but also offering possible interpretative solutions within the enacted normative text in order to ensure effectiveness to repair as a building block of such a paradigm shift.

The market is also the framework of the analysis by Francesco Deana (Chap. 7) about the role of consumers in the paradigm transition towards SCE. This chapter focuses on the relevant empowerment of consumers who, by means of their informed decisions, can implement sustainable practices. However, in a reality affected by information overload and complexity, consumer education becomes decisive for supporting an effective decision-making power that can shape the market. Moreover, consumer awareness about sustainability becomes the lens through which understanding new business obligations, like in terms of product longevity and repairability, so to redefine the relevant market relationships (including the respective responsibilities) in light of the public policy objectives characterizing SCE.

In a complementary and too often neglected perspective then comes the analysis by Elisabetta Bergamini (Chap. 8) about private international law. In particular, this chapter assesses the adequacy of conflict-of-law and jurisdiction rules applicable to 'circular' transactions in the EU market. In this sense, the increasing selling from consumers to consumers in the context of online intermediary platforms raises new challenges that should be appropriately tackled in order to promote economic practices that are fundamental for SCE. Along this line, special attention is given also to alternative dispute resolution systems, as usually offered by the same platforms, reviewing their effectiveness for consumer protection and the possible innovative solutions that could be envisaged within the EU legal acquis.

Following the zoom-out metaphor as described above, the research then moves to more systemic aspects that frame the paradigm shift towards SCE. This further level of analysis is opened by Alessia-Ottavia Cozzi (Chap. 9), whose research investigates the constitutional foundations of circular economy and sustainability in general. Comparing the EU and national levels (using again Italy as a case study), this chapter explains how possible different approaches lead to not-so-distant solutions: actually, either if respect for the environment is internalized in the constitutional economic model or if it is posed as an external limit, the contradiction is only apparent, by virtue of the strong integration that forms the relevant environmental policy in the interconnection between the two institutional levels concerned.

The EU system is the starting point for Claudia Candelmo (Chap. 10) in extending the research beyond this horizon. In particular, this chapter explores the global landscape for the promotion of models equivalent to SCE, looking at other meaningful continental and international experiences. In this sense, the role of the EU as a frontrunner is appreciated in a wider context where also other important actors are pushing in the same direction, giving rise to a truly global effort that, political contingencies aside, is trying to drive such a paradigm change.

A global approach is also shared by Sara Dal Monico (Chap. 11) in dealing again with the figure of consumers, but from an international law perspective. In particular, this chapter tries to reshape the notion of 'sustainable' consumers around the funding principles of SCE in order to foster such a paradigm shift. Following the aforementioned human-centered approach, the analysis offers an innovative conceptualization of consumer rights as human rights: this legal possibility is investigated especially about a right of access to information, considered as the backbone of consumers' power of choice and, consequently, as one of the most important instruments for achieving globally—as global is nowadays the economy—environmental protection and sustainability in the market.

Finally, the international dimension is further explored by Sara De Vido (Chap. 12), who challenges some critical prejudices that affect the existing model and, to some extent, also the same new paradigm. In particular, this chapter highlights how a real change can be achieved only if 'human nature' is intended in a better and superior dimension, embracing the whole of nature itself with all its living creatures. In legal terms, this founding role of the environment for a proper SCE is transposed in the innovative construction of the environment itself not as a mere resource, but as an autonomous legal entity, enjoying special rights that could be opposed against unsustainable economic interests.

This last perspective allows the present research to come full circle, matching in a certain sense the first sociological perspective on the human-centered approach. Such an approach, if more profoundly understood, demonstrates how a sensible model of SCE must imply an overcoming of the static convictions that have characterized the excesses of the past. And this proves true also for the legal dimension, as the present research has tried to address.

This brings to a conclusive consideration: this project certainly does not have the ambition to solve every legal issue related to SCE, but nevertheless wants to stimulate the relevant debate and offer its contribution to support—and in its own small way suggest improvements to—a necessary change of paradigm, whose urgency seems to be reinforced by increasing political turmoil and, above all, by a systemic environmental crisis that unfortunately shows no sign of abating.

'*Ubi societas ibi ius*': Centering a Sustainable Circular Economy from a Sociological Perspective

Michele Marzulli

Abstract The transition to a Sustainable Circular Economy ('SCE') represents a fundamental shift from the linear 'take-make-dispose' model to a regenerative system focused on reuse, recycling and resource recovery. The SCE is an economic model that aims to eliminate waste while increasing resource efficiency and promoting social equity. It is not just one technological improvement among others, but a paradigm that moves away from conventional production-consumption systems to a circular model that prioritizes sustainability at all levels. This chapter aims to present the framework and to analyse its key concepts, issues and actors, as well as the challenges for regulating this transformation process. Regulating SCE is complex because of the multifaceted nature of circular practices. The law and policymaking process must balance the interests of different stakeholders while ensuring global cooperation, particularly through international supply chains. In particular, any policy initiative that places people at the centre ('human-centred' model) must confront a sort of duplicity, i.e. the dialectic between the macro dimension (the global scenario) and the micro dimension (social action understood as individual action). These difficulties can explain why recently the green policies seem to be in crisis. Solutions must aim to promote equitable access, ensuring that all individuals, regardless of their background, can benefit from the SCE. The chapter try to reshape the fundamental issues in the SCE and aims to be a call for responsibility of all social actors.

M. Marzulli (✉)
Università Ca' Foscari, Venezia, Italy
e-mail: michele.marzulli@unive.it

B. Calabrese (ed.), *Legal Perspectives for a Sustainable Circular Economy*,
European Union and its Neighbours in a Globalized World 30,
https://doi.org/10.1007/978-3-032-07795-0_2

1 Introduction: Toward an Inclusive and Equitable Transition

The concept of a Sustainable Circular Economy ('SCE') has emerged as a transformative paradigm that challenges traditional linear economic models and their multifactor implications in the twenty-first century. This approach represents a fundamental shift from the conventional 'take-make-dispose' economic system to a regenerative framework that prioritizes values as resource conservation, social equity, and environmental sustainability[1].

The global significance of SCE has become increasingly apparent as societies face mounting environmental challenges and resource constraints. The prevailing concern regarding global warming has prompted scientists and supranational institutions, as the United Nations, the European Union, and the OECD, to acknowledge the imminent threat humanity faces if no immediate adjustments are made to the current course. Understanding these dynamics is crucial for developing inclusive and effective circular and sustainable economy strategies that can address both environmental and social challenges.

In this introductive chapter, the SCE paradigm will be analysed under a sociological perspective since it can offer unique insights into how this economic transformation affects social structures, human behaviour, and institutional dynamics. Recent research has showed that the transition to a circular economy requires not only technological innovations but also profound social, normative and cultural changes[2]. The success of circular initiatives depends heavily on social acceptance, behavioural adaptation, an adequate law infrastructure, and the restructuring of established consumption patterns.

From a theoretical standpoint, the SCE framework integrates various sociological concepts, including social practice theory, institutional theory, and theories of social change. These foundations help explain how circular economy practices are adopted, normalized, and institutionalized within different social contexts, as is getting in the European context. The interplay between individual agency and structural-normative constraints becomes particularly relevant when examining the implementation of SCE principles across diverse societal settings.

The most relevant points in analysing SCE in this sociological perspective lie in several areas. First, this approach moves beyond purely economic or environmental considerations to examine how economic practices interact with social systems and cultural/legal norms. Second, it introduces a framework for understanding how social networks and communities can facilitate or hinder the adoption of circular practices. Third, it helps to identify social inequalities and power dynamics emerging in the transition to a circular economy.

Someone might say that if the lawmakers forget such aspects, they might run into trouble, as can be seen in the process of the so-called 'green transition'. Indeed, the

---

[1] Rashid and Malik (2023).

[2] Nikolaou and Stefanakis (2024).

year 2024 will be remembered as a time of significant political transformation and a re-evaluation of several pro-environmental policies. This shift in perspective can be attributed to two major factors: the European elections in June 2024 and the US presidential elections in November 2024, both characterized by scepticism towards the issue of reducing climate change. The result of these developments has been the initiation of some changes in previously established policies. In particular, the European Green Deal ('EGD')—approved by the European Commission in 2019 and ratified by the European Parliament in 2020—seems to be challenged by the new European parliamentary majority and, above all, by the Commission itself. In fact, the political debate seems to have come to the highly controversial conclusion that the EGD is excessively ideological and potentially harmful to industries and public welfare.[3]

At this juncture, it is not pertinent to engage in a debate concerning these sentiments. The present moment is of paramount importance, as it needs a comprehensive understanding of the factors that can impede the efficacy of an environmental policy and the measures that can be implemented to circumvent such failures in the future. A complex and transdisciplinary approach, following Edgar Morin's philosophy,[4] which encompasses a variety of complex issues—including sociological concerns—can facilitate the comprehension of the challenges associated with a novel circular and sustainable economic model.

This perspective also highlights the importance of social justice and equity in the transition to a circular economy. Indeed, SCE initiatives can exacerbate existing social inequalities, depending on how they are implemented and governed. This understanding is crucial for developing inclusive policies that ensure the benefits of circular economy practices are distributed equitably across society. The European debate during the Parliament general election phase in 2024, and the partial change in the European Commission strategy of the Green Deal represent a clear wakeup call for policymakers to pay more attention to the consequences of policy decision-making process.[5]

In a such scenario, the current state of global circular and sustainable practices reveals a complex landscape of initiatives, policies, and social movements. While some regions have made significant progress in implementing circular economy principles, others face substantial challenges related to infrastructure, social acceptance, and economic feasibility. The variation in adoption rates and success levels across different societies underscores the importance of considering local social contexts in circular economy implementation.

This sociological analysis of SCE contributes to the broader field of sustainability studies by providing new frameworks for understanding how economic transformations interact with social systems. Understand such issues can help to suggest several promising directions for future investigation: how adapt to circular economy

[3] Catarinella et al. (2025).

[4] Morin (2022).

[5] Cunningham et al. (2024)

practices, the role of social networks in promoting sustainable behaviours, and the potential social impacts of various circular economy policies and initiatives.

In conclusion, the sociological perspective on SCE offers valuable insights into how societies can successfully transit to more sustainable economic models, while highlighting the importance of considering social factors in sustainability initiatives.

2 Individuals and Social Change: Beyond Unlimited Consumption

It has been asserted that the political and social framework is intricate, particularly in the context of the pressing challenge of climate change. Notwithstanding the inherent uncertainties of politics, there are factors, principally related to the warming of the atmosphere and the ever-increasing cost of raw materials, that are precipitating a reconsideration of the development model. However, the complexity of action is further compounded by the multifaceted challenges inherent in today's interconnected society[6]. Indeed, the networked society is characterised by an increase in problems (complexity) and individual citizens find themselves caught between environmental protection regulations, the desire to preserve nature, but also material needs related to the lack of employment and growing consumption needs. The crux of the issue, therefore, is to comprehend that any policy initiative that places people at the centre (human-centred model) must confront this duplicity, i.e. the dialectic between the macro dimension (the global scenario) and the micro dimension (social action understood as individual action). This can be expressed differently by considering the intersection between agency and social structure.

In the domain of sociology, the role of the individual within the social system has been a subject of extensive debate. The issue is one of freedom and necessity, of social constraint and the individual's ability to intervene in the social structure[7]. In classical theory, the maturation process of the individual is defined as a process of individual adaptation to the social structure. In Talcott Parsons' classical systemic theory, socialisation is said to be successful when individuals learn the norms and values of society.[8] The process of learning social norms is heavily reliant on the system of (social) rewards and sanctions that the individual receives. The reward is linked to conformity to the social norm, and the sanction is the form of sanction for deviating from the norm. In this sense, the legal system can be regarded as a system that sanctions deviance from the established social norm.

This interpretation signifies a landmark in comprehending the fundamental process of social reproduction, defined as the phenomenon through which a society

[6] Castells (2010).

[7] Parsons (1937).

[8] Parsons (1964).

perpetuates itself over time. Since its genesis, this interpretation has undergone numerous revisions, particularly within the domain of critical theory. A notable example of this evolution can be seen in the work of Bourdieu, a prominent French sociologist. Bourdieu's contributions, particularly his concept of the *habitus*, have challenged the notion that social conditions inevitably determine individuals' actions and thought processes: instead, he has argued that individuals have the capacity to resist societal influences and, thereby, engender change[9].

It is imperative to emphasise that, particularly in a contemporary society characterised by complexity and differentiation, subject to influences of diverse (though not necessarily conflicting) values, it is no longer feasible to conceptualise the development of individuals (the outcome of the socialisation process) in a linear manner. The notion that society functions through more complex processes has also become firmly accepted within the social sciences. The role of the mass media in shaping public opinion, a phenomenon that has been in existence for at least a century, is a pertinent example of this. These influences can often contradict the traditional social norms proposed by family and educational institutions. A similar observation can be made with regard to the role of new media and social networks, which have been shown to have a significant impact on the lives of individuals (for example, about family relationships)[10]. In a society as dynamic as today's, these influences have become increasingly evident. That is, the norm evolves in relation to an ever-changing society. Individuals, as a result, follow and interpret the changes in which they are immersed. This is the concept of reflexivity, as postmodern sociology conceptualises it, and signifies that individuals cannot be defined exclusively as economic agents or as predetermined by their community of origin[11]. People are capable of interacting with the social system, even going so far as to modify it, at least in part. One may consider, for example, Touraine's reflection on collective movements as a form of shared social action[12]. Or otherwise stated: Blau argued for a dialectical social theory in which structure was reproduced and transformed by the individual in the course of social exchange, so that 'structural change, therefore, assumes a dialectical pattern'[13].

This fact becomes even more relevant when one considers the scenario of evolution, but also of uncertainty, in which the change of the society is taking place: in a society increasingly exposed to risk and the complex interdependence of the global context, the actions of individuals seem to be increasingly intertwined with those of

[9] Bourdieu (1977).

[10] Over the past few decades, social research has provided some evidence that traditional institutions (school, family, and religion) are in decline, partly as a result of the modernization process. Consequently, novel institutions are emerging to assume the role of shaping beliefs and convictions among new generations. In particular, new media and social media are playing an increasing role (Pattaro 2015).

[11] Giddens (1991).

[12] Touraine (2000).

[13] Blau (1964), p. 338.

others[14]. At the turn of the century, following Luhmann's reflection on complexity, sociologists such as Ulrich Beck demonstrated how generalised risk and the loosening of social relations appear to have a significant impact on individuals' choices[15]. Confronted with global challenges that appear to overwhelm individuals, the formidable task of responding to global social issues on an individual basis seems insurmountable. In this sense, Bauman emphasises the impossibility of living in an unequal, polluted and armed world that asks the individual to 'act morally in an immoral world'[16].

While the situation appears complex, with individuals facing changes that are beyond their control, a further dimension emerges that is relevant to the present paper. Indeed, when individuals are regarded as consumers, that is, as market actors, two discrete and antithetical tensions come to the fore, reflecting the overarching paradigm of action and structure. Indeed, consumers represent an essential component of a system in which consumption is the ultimate objective of every economic transaction. When consumption diminishes, a nation's economy enters a state of crisis. The phenomenon of consumerism in the global era, as posited by Bauman, has been shown to represent a pernicious trap from which it is difficult to extricate oneself. Indeed, the Polish sociologist has asserted that consumption has become inextricably intertwined with the very identity of the individual: this phenomenon can be understood as a result of the societal pressure for continuous consumption, which is driven by the need to avoid feelings of frustration, loneliness, and personal inadequacy[17]. It can thus be argued that the prevailing social structure (in this case, the economic structure) exerts a significant degree of pressure on individuals to perpetuate consumption. However, unlimited consumption poses a threat to the survival of society, and individuals also recognise the finite nature of resources.

Consequently, the challenge of constructing a people-centred (human-centred) regulatory framework for the economy must acknowledge the intricacies of the prevailing pressures, both individual and structural, which render choices progressively arduous.

3 Natural Resources and Human Responsibility: The Origin of Sustainability

In an attempt to establish a suitable framework for illustrating the multifaceted nature of an SCE system, it is useful to begin by delineating the two most pertinent concepts. The first aspect is the issue of sustainability and how it emerges in the economic context; the second aspect concerns the idea of a circular economy. In the

[14] Beck (1992).
[15] Beck and Beck-Gernsheim (2002).
[16] Bauman (2001), p. 175.
[17] Bauman (2001).

SCE model, these two notions are interconnected, and it can be posited, as a preliminary proposition, that the circular economy can be conceptualised as a facilitating condition for any sustainability. It is important to add that sustainability implies a different economic model to the waste model, i.e. the linear system. Consequently, the subsequent discussion will proceed with a distinct definition, with the objective of establishing the fundamental principles of the ensuing reflection and elucidating analytically several pivotal concepts.

3.1 *Sustainability as an Ecological and Social Model*

The notion that the prevailing economic model is no longer viable in the face of the planet's dwindling resources has only recently emerged as a salient theme in the public discourse, notwithstanding its genesis in the 1960s.[18] The climate crisis has become global and has worsened enormously over the last decade: over the last 10 years, the evidence suggests that the climate crisis has intensified at an accelerated rate. The predictions about the greenhouse effect and the resulting global warming have proven to be true: moreover, since the twenty-first century, this issue has become increasingly salient for the populations of Western countries, who have borne the brunt of its consequences.[19]

The acceleration of climate change, marked by increasingly protracted summers across both hemispheres, has had a profound impact on public opinion and the global political agenda. This shift has been particularly influenced by the actions of supranational institutions (in particular the United Nations and the European Union). The political agenda, in recent times, seems to be very discordant and the policies of the most industrialised countries of the West seem, in some cases, to be faltering.[20] Nevertheless, the ecological issue has become a global concern, partly due to the pressure on public opinion from environmental scientists and researchers, but also from collective movements for environmental protection. A seminal finding in this regard pertains to the 2024 European Citizens' Survey, which revealed a pervasive sense of concern among the European populace for environmental issues. In particular, 78% of Europeans believe that environmental issues have a direct impact on their daily lives and health, 84% believe that EU environmental legislation is necessary to protect the environment in their country, and 92% believe that companies should bear the costs of cleaning up pollution.[21]

---

[18] Oosthoek and Gills (2013).

[19] Eurobarometer (2024).

[20] Think about the turn that Donald Trump's second presidency may have on these policies: if election promises are kept, the US will exit all global environmental agreements (US Presidential Actions, 'Putting America first in international environmental agreements', 20 January 2025, https://www.whitehouse.gov/presidential-actions/2025/01/putting-america-first-in-international-environmental-agreements/)

[21] Eurobarometer (2024).

After a not linear and not ever easy pathways, starting about in the 1992 at Rio Conference,[22] the UN countries established the Paris Agreement in the 2015. This is a historic agreement, which came into force in 2016, and important because, for the first time, all countries have committed themselves with a legal constraint to act and combat climate change: to limit global warming and concretely address its effects.[23] An even more binding step forward was defined by the 27 countries of the European Union, which in 2019 committed themselves, again legally not only with declarations of intent, to combat climate change by switching to a climate-neutral economy, with zero net greenhouse gas emissions, by 2050. This commitment was subsequently formalised by the European Commission through the European Green Deal ('EGD'). This strategy is predicated on two principles: firstly, that the planet is facing a climate crisis, and secondly, that this new programme represents an economic opportunity for European countries.

Such concern for the environment prompts consideration of both the present state of the ecosystem and the future of subsequent generations: what planet is being prepared for the next generations? Furthermore, will the availability of resources be sufficient to sustain an adequate standard of living? The central question guiding such inquiry is whether the world will remain habitable, if current standards of living and security are to be sustained.

However, recent political milestones such as the EGD were preceded by many years, at least four decades, of thinking about the environmental sustainability of the production system. In the mid-1980s, with the future of new generations in mind, the United Nations Commission on Environment and Development produced a document called 'Our Common Future', also known as the 'Brundtland Report' by the name of the first signatory. This document defines sustainability as a form of development that meets the needs of the present without compromising the ability of future generations to meet their own needs.[24] The principle is universal and concerns the possibility of continuing to enjoy a scarce resource.

The Brundtland Report is a milestone in the history of global environmental policy, not least because it clearly declares that the way out of the environmental crisis is through the model of sustainability. This model is based on the integration of three subsystems that interact and influence each other: the social, the environmental and the economic. These subsystems are interdependent and strengthen or

[22] In 1992, representatives of 172 countries gathered at the 'United Nations Conference on Environment and Development, UNCED' in Rio de Janeiro to try to solve problems such as poverty, the growing disparity between industrialised and developing countries, as well as growing social, economic and environmental difficulties, by laying the foundation for sustainable development worldwide. The participating countries signed three non-binding international agreements (Agenda 21, the Rio Declaration, the Declaration of Principles for Sustainable Forest Management) and two legally binding conventions (the Framework Convention on Climate Change and the Convention on Biological Diversity).

[23] For its institutional presentation see the relevant UN website (https://www.un.org/en/climatechange/paris-agreement); however, as anticipated, the US administration announced in 2025 to withdraw from the Paris Agreement (see footnote above).

[24] WCED, Report 'Our Common Future' (1987), para. 51.

weaken each other. For this reason, sustainability has increasingly become part of institutional policy agendas, not only as an environmental policy, but as a complex development model[25].

It is nevertheless crucial to remember that the challenge was not only environmental, but also economic. Indeed, a few decades earlier, MIT in Boston had commissioned a group of young scholars, known as the Club of Rome, to produce a report expressing a concern that had not been adequately addressed at the time. The economists gathered around this working group did indeed publish a report, intended primarily for their peers, which for the first time challenged a linear and tendentially positivist view of the development of the market economy. The document, entitled 'The Limits to Growth',[26] placed the question of the existence of limits to industrial development at the centre of the debate at a time when it was difficult to foresee them. The political aim of the document was, in fact, to challenge the West's complacent view that it had achieved the maximum possible development of humanity. The report was based on a simulation carried out with a computer of the time, which aimed to predict the possible development of the world economy if consumption continued at the same rate. The report focused in particular on some key issues: population, food, industrial production, non-renewable resources and pollution. The report came to two conclusions: if we continued to consume and pollute at the same rate, the planet would face a crisis (reduction in population and industrial capacity) within a century. Furthermore, it was possible to achieve ecological stability by adopting a sustainable economic model. The authors therefore wrote that it was necessary to accept the idea of the finiteness of the planet and its resources, but also that it was possible to take certain actions to manage this finiteness. These actions required a real paradigm shift and they even spoke of a 'sustainable revolution'.

It should be noted that one of the objections raised against the report was that technology (and thus the improvement of the whole industrial production apparatus) would avoid the greatest risks. However, the authors countered this objection with Jevons' paradox,[27] using the example of the fish fauna. Intensive fishing, ever-increasing consumer demand and the use of sophisticated fishing techniques had indeed led to a sharp decline in fish stocks, as was the case in the Mediterranean.[28] It was also due to the fact that one of the report's predictions came true very quickly with the economic crisis of 1973–1974, the so-called 'oil shock'.

[25] Geissdoerfer et al. (2017).

[26] Meadows et al. (1972).

[27] It is the insight that technological improvements that increase the efficiency of a resource may, however, increase the consumption of that resource, rather than decrease it (Alcott 2005).

[28] FAO (2023).

3.2 *The Crisis of the Linear Economic Paradigm*

The most intellectually relevant element of this passage is that, even today, it seems very difficult for much of public opinion (from politicians to business, and hence civil society itself) to accept the idea that industrial progress can have limits. The reason for this lies in the origins of industrial modernity itself and its ability to change the fate of humanity as a whole, at least since the mid-1700s. In fact, the current system of exploitation of natural resources has its roots in the Scientific Revolution and then the Industrial Revolution, between the 17th and 18th centuries: a path that effectively led to the era of greatest economic development and prosperity in human history.

It is a path that sociologists call 'modernisation' and that invests various aspects of social life: at the economic level, industrial development; at the political level, the affirmation of democratic institutions; and at the cultural level, the growing secularisation that goes hand in hand with the expansion of individual freedom of choice in social relations. Last but not least, there is the issue of urbanisation, with the consolidation of large urban centres as places of industrial production and mass consumption. The ideological assumption, sometimes explicitly expressed, was that nature, creation, had been given to humankind as an instrument for building its own well-being. In essence, this approach was born with the idea of an unlimited expansion of development due to the availability of unlimited natural resources.

With the second phase of industrialisation, in the nineteenth century, the search for natural resources led the major Western powers to extend their influence over the rest of the planet by creating large colonial empires, the essential feature of which was to have (once again unlimited) access to the resources of the subjugated countries. Note that this is the main reason why, in the international climate agreements mentioned above, the most industrialised countries are asked to contribute more than the others. This is not only because they have more economic resources, but also because of a kind of assumption of responsibility in relation to the colonial and neo-colonial era, in which the resources of the colonised countries were extracted to build the wealth of the colonising countries.

This is the root of the current crisis of the ecological system and by far the most worrying aspect of this beginning of the third millennium, since the acceleration of climate change calls into question the very maintenance of human life on earth. It is therefore essential to reflect on how to re-establish a correct balance between human beings and the environment, through a critical reading of the social and economic processes that have accompanied modernity. Indeed, one of the foundations of sustainability can be found in the reflections of the German philosopher Hans Jonas, who states that the disproportionate success of technology in 'subjugating nature for the sake of human happiness'[29] risks becoming a potential threat to human life itself because of the heterogony of ends. This threat therefore calls for a way of thinking capable of developing a new way of acting based on the principle of responsibility:

[29] Jonas (1984), p. 16.

'act in such a way that the consequences of your actions are compatible with the permanence of authentic human life on earth'[30].

To understand how we came so close to ecological disaster, we need to start by re-reading the *'trente glorieuses'* [31], the long period of peace and prosperity that followed the end of the Second World War and ended abruptly in the mid-1970s. This period was characterised by a unique and, in some respects, unrepeatable dynamic. From an economic point of view, following the Bretton Woods agreements of 1944, which regulated the future international financial landscape, and thanks to the effects of the Marshall Plan, there was unprecedented economic growth; industrial production grew exponentially and was reorganised on the basis of the Taylorist-Fordist model. From a social point of view, the welfare system took shape, albeit following very different strategies in the various Western countries. One of the most interesting aspects is the fact that this was accompanied by significant changes in culture and habits, such as access to mass consumption, the development of the media system and the increasingly decisive role of advertising: this gave rise to the consumer (*homo consumens*) [32], voracious for goods that were often disposable but necessary to define one's own status and gain social recognition.

The sense that things could change only began to emerge in the mid-1970s, when the welfare system that had guaranteed prosperity in Europe and the United States began to go into crisis (the end of the said 'thirty glorious years'): the expansionary phase of the economy had come to an end and the countries of the South of the world, which had become independent, began to demand a different use of natural resources and raw materials[33]. Above all, the oil crisis made two things clear: that the world economy was now globalised (Wallerstein's world-economy model)[34] and that resources were not at the unlimited disposal of Western countries. In fact, the Club of Rome's report was basically a Malthusian economic model in which the main problem is that resources become scarce. That was basically the main concern of those economists: to cope with the scarcity of available goods.

It is in this context that economists begin to talk about sustainability. Here, once again, is a reflection with a different moral approach. It is not so much a question of the accessibility or scarcity of natural resources, but of 'responsibility' towards future generations. While it is clear that resources are in principle sufficient and that scarcity can be the subject of negotiation between different nations, it is becoming increasingly clear at the end of the twentieth century that it is by no means guaranteed that future generations will have the resources available to them that previous generations have had. The idea of paying attention to the development model and the consumption of resources therefore takes on a tone that is not exclusively

---

[30] Jonas (1984), p. 16.

[31] Fourastié (1979).

[32] Bauman (1998).

[33] The demands of this part of the world today are notoriously gathered around the idea of the 'Global South' and/or the so-called BRICS countries. On such aspects see in general Duggan et al. (2022).

[34] Wallerstein (1984).

economic (rational use of a scarce resource), but rather moral: what planet will be left to future generations? It is therefore not only a question of thinking about a sustainable economic model, in the sense of a model that allows the current inhabitants of the planet to continue consuming as they have always done. Rather, it is a model that can ensure that others, those who do not yet exist, have the same opportunities. It is therefore a projection into the future, a question of responsibility, the guiding principle that Hans Jonas spoke of.

4 The Circular Economy as an Alternative

The traditional economic model is rooted in past manufacturing production and global trade. It is called 'linear' because it is based on a process that can be divided into three main stages: (i) resource extraction, (ii) production and consumption, (iii) creation and disposal of waste[35].

The process, which dates back to the dawn of the Industrial Revolution, typically begins with the extraction of raw materials and is highly dependent on natural resources. Once extracted, these are transformed into products through the manufacturing process. The products then reach the public for consumption, and consumers contribute to economic growth by purchasing the final goods. This fuels a process that leads to increased demand for goods and thus the need to produce and extract more of them.

When analysing this process, it should first be noted that in the past little attention has been paid to one of the stages, the last one, i.e. the end of the life cycle of products, where they are disposed of, typically in landfills or incinerators. Indeed, in recent decades, many durable products have been replaced by disposable or short-lived products because they are cheaper and easy to use (and then discard). Finally, with globalisation, one of the developments of this model has been the shift of production from the economically more advanced countries to those less advanced (i.e. the South of the world or, on our continental scale, the East of Europe). In these latter countries, labour and raw materials are cheaper, so the production and waste model is less expensive for consumer countries, allowing companies to maximise profits[36]. Moreover, the extraction, production and disposal phases not only generate large quantities of waste, but also emissions of substances (such as CO2) that contribute to accelerating global warming and climate change. This is a trap in which the global division of labour often ends up rewarding the consuming countries and further penalising the countries where the raw materials are processed and where the production waste itself often ends up.

Another implication, secondly, concerns a consequence implicit in this model: namely that consumption, and hence its mass practice (consumerism), is an

---

[35] Ellen MacArthur Foundation (2013).

[36] Morseletto (2023).

essential part of the business cycle pursuing growth without limits. Serge Latouche, one of the critics of this model, argues that society has condemned itself to growth: from the pension system to the labour market and all public spending, the system can only sustain itself if the growth cycle continues. And this is a problem that affects not only the industrialised countries, but also the developing countries, which are often forced to produce in order to pay the interest on the debts they have contracted with the more economically developed countries[37].

The extreme consequence of Latouche's critique is a conscious decision to reduce the levels of production and consumption and the role of markets and trade in social organisation[38]: what Latouche defines as 'degrowth'[39]. The theorists of this proposal openly criticise the idea of sustainability, which in their view does not solve the problem of the global crisis at its root. However, it is clear that the hypothesis of eliminating the market as the main regulator of the economy does not seem to be within reach, and instead the model of sustainability and circularity attempts to provide a realistic answer to the problem of resources and waste.

The alternative to crisis and degrowth may therefore lie precisely in circularity. It is based on the balanced integration of three spheres that interact and influence each other: the social, the environmental and the economic. These three pillars are interdependent and mutually reinforcing. As mentioned above, the current linear production model poses serious sustainability problems because it consumes a disproportionate amount of available resources. Environmental impact can be calculated on the basis of three factors: population, consumption and technology[40]. In other words, the environmental impact of human activity is a function of population, wealth (understood as the level of consumption) and the level of technological development. In order to reduce this impact, the idea of the Circular Economy ('CE') emerged around the 1970s, which addresses both technology and consumption[41].

The contemporary elaboration of the concept is based on the analysis of available natural resources[42] and the environmental sustainability of the economic model, influenced by the work of Kenneth Boulding[43]. This economist described the Earth as a closed circuit with a limited assimilative capacity. For this reason, he proposed a 'spaceship' economic model to describe a model that is self-sufficient because it uses the available resources efficiently and is able to guarantee the regeneration, or at least the stability, of the existing natural capital[44]. In more contemporary terms,

---

[37] Latouche (2009).

[38] Sekulova et al. (2013).

[39] Latouche (2009).

[40] da Silva et al. (2021).

[41] Geissdoerfer et al. (2017).

[42] Pearce and Turner (1990).

[43] Boulding (1966).

[44] Cardoso (2018).

perhaps the simplest interpretation is of CE as a deliberately restorative and regenerative industrial system[45].

The CE is based on three fundamental principles: the elimination of waste and pollution, the circulation of products and raw materials, and the regeneration of nature. At its core is a circular (closed) cycle, which involves using the same raw materials and energy in several stages of production, rather than just one.

This is the meaning of the three 'R' of the CE: Reuse, Refurbish, Remanufacture. 'Reuse' means to use the product again without consuming new resources, e.g. by donating the product or reselling it through second-hand channels[46]. 'Refurbish' means to restore the product using new resources but keeping the original object: only the worn parts of the product are replaced. 'Remanufacture', finally, means to dismantle the product into its essential components, inspect them one by one and reuse them to restore the product to its maximum performance level. To illustrate the difference between the last two terms, consider a piece of technological hardware: restoration extends the life of the product, but it may not perform as well as a new one, while remanufacture creates a device with the same capacity as a new one, thus reducing the demand for new resources.

This cycle is therefore developed through a series of processes aimed at minimising negative externalities. This is possible thanks to various ways: first of all, as far as non-renewable resources are concerned, and starting from the initial production phase, goods must be designed to be durable and repairable[47]; finished products can then be reused by redistribution; finally, waste can be recycled, i.e. at least partially returned to its original form of raw material, and finally reintroduced into other production processes.

Through practices such as reuse, remanufacturing and refurbishment, CE extends the life cycle of products and thus consumes fewer resources and less energy, making it more economically and environmentally viable than both the linear economy and the traditional recycling process. According to circular logic, used products should first be reused, repaired or refurbished as far as possible, then remanufactured and only then recycled into new raw materials. Only after all these reuse attempts have been made should incineration for energy be considered, followed by landfill. In this way, the maximum value can be extracted from all the raw materials used and the end products, while at the same time reducing waste and making the production process more efficient[48].

The CE model has also entered supranational legislation[49], like with the European Commission's Communication 'A new Circular Economy Action Plan. For a cleaner

[45] Ellen MacArthur Foundation (2013).

[46] For the issues faced by consumers in such reselling markets at the level of private international law see Bergamini (Chap. 8).

[47] Lofthouse and Prendeville (2018).

[48] Korhonen et al. (2018).

[49] See Candelmo (Chap. 10).

and more competitive Europe'[50]. The document, within the framework of the EGD, aims to accelerate the CO2 reduction path with specific actions[51]. In particular, an extension of the scope of the eco-design rules, empowering consumers for the green transition and the sustainable textiles strategy[52]. This is followed by other regulatory measures such as reducing packaging, improving its design, providing clear labelling and encouraging reuse and recycling[53]. Also, it includes a shift to bio-based, biodegradable and compostable plastics[54].

It is worth noting that these measures have been taken after measuring the amount of waste produced in the Union, the world's largest market for goods. First on the list of waste produced in the Union is electronic and electrical waste, which is the fastest growing waste stream; then food and water (it is estimated that 10% of all food produced in the EU is lost or wasted); packaging (it is estimated that in 2021 the average amount of packaging waste produced by each individual in the EU will be 189 kg); and finally, there is waste that cannot be recycled at all (the EU produces around 2.1 billion tonnes of waste per year and exports to third countries such as Turkey and India will reach 32.1 million tonnes in 2022)[55].

These last passages make it possible to combine once again the macro dimension (in this case, the cycle of production of goods) and the micro dimension, i.e. the behaviour of individual consumers. However, as is evident, it must be stressed at once that it is understood that the behaviour of individuals (agency) cannot be considered predominant in relation to the economic structure, that is, the social system. In fact, it is the production model (extraction of raw materials, production and consumption, and then waste) that causes the destruction of the natural environment. In the past, environmental movements have also placed great emphasis on individual responsibility. However, it should be clear from the discussion so far that empowering citizens as consumers is only one part of the overall change. Consider one of the most important issues: the right to repair purchased products. It is clear that the regulation is only partly directed at the behaviour of individuals, but rather at the design of products and the discouragement of behaviour by manufacturers that hinders the possibility of repair[56]. Responsibility therefore lies with producers, consumers and the public authority itself in its role as regulator through legislation.

---

[50] European Commission, Communication 'A new Circular Economy Action Plan For a cleaner and more competitive Europe', COM (2020) 98 final.

[51] Side by side with such 'production' regulations are the 'information' ones, as for corporate sustainability reporting, on which see Genovese (Chap. 2).

[52] See Regulation (EU) 2024/1781 establishing a framework for the setting of ecodesign requirements for sustainable products, about which see Deana (Chap. 7).

[53] For example, Directive (EU) 2024/1799 on common rules promoting the repair of goods, about which see Calabrese (Chap. 6).

[54] Commission Regulation (EU) 2022/1616 on recycled plastic materials and articles intended to come into contact with foods.

[55] See again European Commission, Communication 'A new Circular Economy Action Plan For a cleaner and more competitive Europe', COM (2020) 98 final.

[56] Specifically on such aspects see Calabrese (Chap. 6).

In addition, it has to be considered that the environmental efficiency of production processes (which is the result of the CE itself) does not necessarily coincide with sustainability[57]. Eco-efficiency is simply a management method that consists of a process that achieves the ability to produce goods and services at competitive prices that meet human needs and improve quality of life, while progressively reducing environmental impacts and resource intensity throughout the product life cycle, in line with the estimated carrying capacity of the planet. However, eco-efficiency alone does not necessarily mean sustainability. It is therefore an indispensable indicator for achieving sustainability itself and can be used for improvements along the value chain of a production process[58]. This is why the SCE system seems to respond most appropriately by fulfilling the two principles: responsible management of the production process, but also conservation of resources for future generations.

In summary, therefore, it is not enough to change production processes in order to make policies and regulations effective and efficient for the implementation of a circular economy model that is also sustainable. This is, of course, an indispensable step, but it is also appropriate to clarify the more complex social dynamics of such a change, as will be done in the conclusion of this chapter.

5 Conclusions: Actors and Policy in the SCE

It has been pointed out that in a complex system characterised by global uncertainty and interdependence (echoing the ideas of Beck and Bauman), it is necessary to take into account all the social subjectivities involved and the complex relationships between them. The environmental crisis, which at times seems to herald an imminent ecological catastrophe, cannot therefore be tackled solely with a technical solution (improving production processes) or a technological solution, perhaps based on the latest innovations, forgetting that the subjugation of nature to technology is at the root of the problem of sustainability itself[59]. Then, the social dimension—understood as the ability to guarantee acceptable conditions of well-being (security, health, education, democracy, participation, justice, etc.) and a fair distribution of resources between continents and between the different social groups within them—therefore becomes strategic.

The main issues in this context can be summarized in three perspectives: individual, normative and equity. The role of the individual in SCE goes beyond the traditional consumer market view. People are simultaneously (i) consumers, whose purchasing power influences market trends; (ii) users, whose interactions with

[57] Korhonen et al. (2018).

[58] Gusmão Caiado et al. (2017).

[59] Jonas (1984); furthermore, along this line of understanding the 'human' essence as intimately related to the living environment see De Vido (Chap. 12).

products determine sustainability outcomes; (iii) contributors, who engage in recycling, upcycling, and other sustainable practices; moreover, they are (iv) citizens, individuals who have social responsibilities and actively participate in shaping community sustainable policies and efforts. In this regard, it is important to involve citizens in the process of change. They cannot be seen simply as consumers. This is what we have tried to make clear in the previous pages, arguing that the market cannot be the sole regulator of change, relying once again on the so-called 'invisible hand'.

In fact, environmental pollution is a phenomenon not limited to national borders[60], it is transnational and aggravates the crisis of governability experienced by nation states, imposing the need to rethink the relationship between economic prosperity and environmental concerns, giving more room for action to citizens as stakeholders[61]. Actually, lifestyles can be understood as material expressions of individual identities[62], which in the consumer society are largely determined by consumption itself. In this sense, consumption becomes the space in which citizens can make their voices heard in the public debate on issues traditionally discussed in the sphere of political citizenship. The decision to buy products that are characterised by ethical values can be seen as a form of political consumerism, as reflected in the notion of consumership[63]. It reduces the focus on the purely individual dimension of consumer choices, instead highlighting their political significance and strengthening the link between consumption and citizenship[64]. Consumption is first and foremost a form of communication and not an activity that is carried out solely for the purpose of pleasure and satisfaction. In this way, the ecological crisis and the need to legislate to meet social demands for protection intersect with the crisis of governability that nation states themselves have been facing since the dawn of the age of globalisation[65]. As postmodern sociology has clearly shown, nation states are declining because they are no longer able to respond to issues that arise elsewhere, beyond national borders, but whose consequences spill over within those borders. The decision to implement socially responsible local policies, as envisaged by transnational regulations, thus becomes crucial. The problem remains how to deal with decision-making processes in this complex era.

For this type of participation, it is indeed necessary to design policies inspired by models of complex policy-making: models in which all stakeholders, including citizens and their representative organisations, are involved. In fact, recent models of

---

[60] Ulrich Beck's reflection defining our age as a 'risk society' stems from the accident at the Chernobyl nuclear power plant and the discovery that the consequences of a catastrophe are no longer confined to national borders (Beck 1992).

[61] For a specific focus on citizens as stakeholders in corporate governance see Caprara (Chap. 3).

[62] Sobel (1981).

[63] Blättel-Mink (2014).

[64] This presupposes also a proper level of consumer education, on which see more extensively Deana (Chap. 7)

[65] In this sense, about the possible configuration of consumers' rights' as human rights in the international legal framework see Dal Monico (Chap. 11).

participation have recognised not only that the bureaucratic model of decision-making is outdated. But also that participation in the form of consultation alone is insufficient, if not counterproductive, for citizens. The example of the EGD should serve as a warning to legislators, at least on the European continent. More fruitful, however, are approaches that seek to act on a different way of looking not only at the present, but above all at the future. It will be recalled that in the previous pages we have insisted that the SCE differs from other models of economic development in its moral tension towards the new generations. This is why it looks to the future. It is precisely in this sense that the defined organisational approach to the management of potentiality is addressed[66].

The scenario in which decisions are made today is one in which the speed of change creates a distance between what we imagine the future could be, based on expectations linked to past experience (for which we define strategies and act) and what it will actually be (i.e. the unpredictability of changes). Working on potentiality (on what only seems possible today, *in potentia*) means knowing how to make use of uncertainty and the future. It requires the ability to negotiate and to develop horizontal governance processes (integration with other sectors, as in the WHO 'Health in all policies' model, for example[67]), through the construction of new spaces that define common social interests.

In short, the legislation that accompanies this change cannot be constructed by the bureaucratic apparatus alone in collaboration with manufacturing companies. On the contrary, it can open up new deliberative arenas in which to try to build shared solutions. And this is not an absolute novelty, given that the UN's 2030 Agenda for Sustainable Development itself explicitly calls for the involvement of all components of society, from private companies to the public sector, from civil society to information and cultural operators[68]. From a regulatory perspective, it is clear that a human-centred standard—in the terms clarified above—is a possible solution that is certainly appropriate to support and promote sustainable development[69].

There is still a final step to be taken: the inequalities that, as we have seen, characterise the traditional model of resource extraction. The problem is complex because economic evolution seems to indicate that societies where inequality is greatest and wealth remains concentrated in the hands of a few are also those where

---

[66] Andersen and Pors (2016).

[67] It is a framework defined as: 'an approach to public policies across sectors that systematically takes into account the health and health systems implications of decisions, seeks synergies, and avoids harmful health impacts, in order to improve population health and health equity' (WHO 2013).

[68] United Nations, A/RES/70/1 'Transforming our world: the 2030 Agenda for Sustainable Development' (2015), whose goal 17 is to 'revitalize the global partnership for sustainable development'.

[69] This conclusion gives a sense of the purpose of this sociological premise with respect to the substantial part of the research in the following Chapters, which are dedicated to the actual legal perspectives in support of the paradigm shift towards SCE.

environmental neglect is greatest, where there is more pollution and less recycling[70]. It therefore seems impossible to solve the environmental problem without addressing the issue of redistribution of resources.

Addressing the issue of sustainability today therefore means not only tackling the problem of resource scarcity and redefining human impact on the environment but also addressing the phenomena of exclusion and social vulnerability. It should not be forgotten that in recent years inequality in the world has increased everywhere, especially in North America, China, Russia and India, and more moderately in Europe[71]. The situation is particularly acute in Africa. The inequitable distribution of the wealth produced in many of the continent's countries, combined with a sharp increase in population, is creating an explosive mix[72]. Moreover, as the discussion of the 'Limits to Development' report and the 'Brundtland' report shows, this increase in inequality did not start with the recent economic crises (such as the one that erupted in the United States in 2008), but began in the 1970s, albeit in different ways and with different dynamics worldwide. Between 1980 and 2016, the share of wealth held by the richest 1% of the population rose from 10% to 12% in Europe, and from 22% to 39% in the US, mainly due to educational inequalities in the US, the introduction of less progressive taxation and the privatisation of state assets[73]. The redistribution of responsibilities between North and South on a global scale is therefore a crucial element, but inequalities within countries must not be forgotten. Only in this way can citizens play a role in defining priorities and processes of change.

However, the problem of inequality does not end with the redistribution of income; on the contrary, the increasing availability of individual data in recent years has made it possible to extend the concept of inequality to various areas of non-material well-being, such as health status, education and gender. From a sociological perspective, this means a renewed recognition of the interdependence between biographical trajectories and major environmental, economic and social transformations (the agency-structure relationship). For this reason, even the idea of what means 'well-being' is beginning to change, taking into account environmental, economic and social aspects (such as the 'Equitable and Sustainable Well-being Framework' in Italy[74]), with the aim of understanding social dynamics, but above all to enable the adoption of policies aimed at guaranteeing people's quality of life.

Responsible environmental policies, changing production processes, participatory processes at local and global level: this seems to be the framework within which a serious SCE policy can produce regulations which are 'human-centred' in the right sense of this notion.

---

[70] Wilkinson and Pickett (2009).

[71] Chancel et al. (2021).

[72] Milanovic (2016).

[73] Chancel et al. (2021).

[74] Blazey et al. (2022).

References

Alcott B (2005) Jevons' paradox. Ecol Econ 54(1):9–21. https://doi.org/10.1016/j.ecolecon.2005.03.020
Andersen NÅ, Pors JG (2016) Public management in transition: the orchestration of potentiality. Bristol University Press, Bristol
Bauman Z (1998) Work, consumerism and the new poor. Open University Press, Buckingham
Bauman Z (2001) The individualized society. Polity, Cambridge
Beck U (1992) Risk society: towards a new modernity. Sage, London
Beck U, Beck-Gernsheim E (2002) Individualization: institutionalized individualism and its social and political consequences. Sage, London
Blau PM (1964) Exchange and power in social life. Wiley, New York
Blazey A, Lelong M, Giannini F (2022) The equitable and sustainable Well-being framework in Italy: an action plan for its use in policy and budget decision making, OECD work papers on public governance, 56. OECD Publishing. https://doi.org/10.1787/4f48c504-en
Blättel-Mink B (2014) Active consumership as a driver towards sustainability? GAIA Ecol Persp for Science and Society 23(3):158–165. https://doi.org/10.14512/gaia.23.S1.3
Boulding KE (1966) The economics of the coming spaceship earth. In: Jarrett H (ed) Environmental quality in a growing economy. Johns Hopkins University Press, Baltimore, pp 3–14
Bourdieu P (1977) Outline of a theory of practice. Cambridge University Press
Cardoso JL (2018) The circular economy: historical grounds. In: Delicado A, Domingos N, de Sousa L (eds) Changing societies: legacies and challenges. The diverse worlds of sustainability. ICS Universidade de Lisboa, Lisboa, pp 115–127. https://doi.org/10.31447/ics9789726715054.04
Castells M (2010) The information age: economy, society and culture, 1. The rise of the network society. (2nd). Wiley Blackwell, Oxford
Catarinella P, Kram S, Colombo O, Husain MA (2025) Unveiling the path forward: Eu green policies post-June 2024 elections. Int J Res Inn Soc Sci 9:2. https://doi.org/10.47772/IJRISS.2025.9020204
Chancel L, Piketty T, Saez E, Zucman G (eds) (2021) World inequality report 2022. World Inequality Lab. https://wir2022.wid.world/
Cunningham K, Hix S, Dennison S, Learmonth I (2024) A sharp right turn: a forecast for the 2024 European Parliament elections. ECFR Policy Brief 523
da Silva BA, Constantino M, de Oliveira OS, de Moraes PM, Lima dos Santos SA, Kulevicz RA, Porfírio G, da Costa RB (2021) Econometric analysis of IPAT-e: a new tool for the environmental impact assessment of publicly traded companies. Env Impact Ass Rev 89. https://doi.org/10.1016/j.eiar.2021.106586
Duggan N, Hooijmaaijers B, Rewizorski M, Arapova E (2022) Introduction: 'The BRICS, global governance, and challenges for South–South cooperation in a Post-Western World'. Int Politi Sci Rev 43(4):469–480. https://doi.org/10.1177/01925121211052211
Ellen MacArthur Foundation (2013) Towards the circular economy. Vol. 1: an economic and business rationale for an accelerated transition. https://www.ellenmacarthurfoundation.org/towards-the-circular-economy-vol-1-an-economic-and-business-rationale-for-an
Eurobarometer (2024) Attitudes of Europeans towards the environment. https://europa.eu/eurobarometer/surveys/detail/3173
FAO (2023) The state of Mediterranean and Black Sea fisheries 2023. Special ed. General Fisheries Commission for the Mediterranean, Rome
Fourastié J (1979) Les Trente Glorieuses ou la révolution invisible de 1946 à 1975. Fayard, Paris
Geissdoerfer M, Savaget P, Hultink EJ, Bocken NM (2017) The circular economy. A sustainable paradigm? J Clean Prod 143:757–768. https://doi.org/10.1016/j.jclepro.2016.12.048
Giddens A (1991) Modernity and self-identity: self and Society in the Late Modern age. Polity Press, Cambridge

Gusmão Caiado RG, de Freitas DR, Mattos LV, Gonçalves Quelhas OL, Filho WL (2017) Towards sustainable development through the perspective of eco-efficiency–a systematic literature review. J Clean Prod 165:890–904. https://doi.org/10.1016/j.jclepro.2017.07.166
Jonas H (1984) The imperative of responsibility: in search of ethics for the technological age. University of Chicago Press, Chicago
Korhonen J, Honkasalo A, Seppälä J (2018) Circular economy: the concept and its limitations. Ecol Econ 143:37–46. https://doi.org/10.1016/j.ecolecon.2017.06.041
Latouche S (2009) Farewell to growth. Polity Press, Cambridge
Lofthouse V, Prendeville S (2018) Human-Centred Design of Products and Services for the circular economy. A Review. Design J 21(4):451–476. https://doi.org/10.1080/14606925.2018.146816 9
Meadows DH, Meadows DL, Randers J, Behrens W (1972) The limits to growth. Potomac Associates, New York
Milanovic B (2016) Global inequality. A new approach for the age of globalization. Harvard University Press, Cambridge
Pattaro C (2015) New media & youth identity. Issues and research pathways. Italian J Sociol Educ 7, 1:297–327. https://doi.org/10.14658/PUPJ-IJSE-2015-1-12
Morin E (2022) The challenge of complexity: essays by Edgar Morin. Liverpool University Press, Liverpool
Morseletto P (2023) Sometimes linear, sometimes circular: states of the economy and transitions to the future. J Clean Prod 390:3–4. https://doi.org/10.1016/j.jclepro.2023.136138
Nikolaou IE, Stefanakis AI (2024) The circular economy concept: a new or an old, refreshed concept? In: Stefanakis AI, Nikolaou IE (eds) Circular economy and sustainable development. Circular Economy and Sustainability. Springer, Cham, pp 1–12. https://doi.org/10.1007/978-3-031-66007-8_1
Oosthoek J, Gills BK (eds) (2013) The globalization of environmental crisis. Routledge, London
Parsons T (1937) The structure of social action. The Free Press, Glencoe
Parsons T (1964) Social structure and personality. Collier-Macmillan, London
Pearce DW, Turner RK (1990) Economics of natural resources and the environment. The John Hopkins University Press, Baltimore. https://doi.org/10.2307/1242904
Rashid S, Malik SH (2023) Transition from a linear to a circular economy. In: Bandh SA, Malla FA, Hoang AT (eds) Renewable energy in circular economy. Circular economy and sustainability. Springer, Cham, pp 1–20. https://doi.org/10.1007/978-3-031-42220-1_1
Sekulova F, Kallis G, Rodriguez-Labajos B, Francois S (2013) Degrowth: from theory to practice. J Clean Prod 38. https://doi.org/10.1016/j.jclepro.2012.06.022
Sobel M (1981) Lifestyles and social structure: concepts, definitions, analyses. Academic, New York
Touraine A (2000) Can we live together? Equality and difference. Stanford University Press, Stanford
Wallerstein I (1984) The politics of the world-economy, the states, the movements and the civilizations. Cambridge University Press, Cambridge
Wilkinson R, Pickett K (2009) The Spirit level: why more equal societies almost always do better. Allen Lane, London
World Commission on Environment and Development (WCED) (1987) Our common future. Oxford University Press, New York
World Health Organization (WHO) (2013) 8th WHO global conference on health promotion. http://www.healthpromotion2013.org/health-promotion/health-in-all-policies

Corporate Sustainability Reporting and Commitments: Effectiveness and Enforceability from EU to National Law

Anna Genovese

Abstract The chapter examines the legal framework surrounding corporate sustainability reporting, as mandated by EU law and, in its relevant transposition, national law. It focuses on the transformation of corporate ESG information, both for internal purposes and for the market, from non-financial reporting to corporate sustainability reporting framework. Specifically, the chapter underlines that the objectives of mandatory corporate sustainability reporting extend beyond merely enhancing the quantity and quality of ESG information available to investors and corporate financiers: its goals are also non-financial. Mandatory corporate sustainability reporting requirements speak to both financial and non-financial stakeholders while aligning with corporate and broader societal interests. Hence, the sustainable transition of companies is not left solely to the discretion of shareholders or lenders (duly informed about ESG factors). However, the effectiveness and enforceability of mandatory corporate sustainability reporting vary depending on the nuances of national regulations on corporate governance. From this perspective, the chapter will explore Italian law as a case study in order to verify if and to what extent relevant claims can be brought with regard to mandatory corporate sustainability reporting. In particular, it questions whether companies could be held liable for non-compliance with sustainability obligations, for declared but disregarded sustainability commitments, and for management decisions taken without abiding by sustainability principles.

A. Genovese (✉)
Università degli studi di Verona, Verona, Italy
e-mail: anna.genovese@univr.it

B. Calabrese (ed.), *Legal Perspectives for a Sustainable Circular Economy*,
European Union and its Neighbours in a Globalized World 30,
https://doi.org/10.1007/978-3-032-07795-0_3

1 Introduction. Subject Matter

The Corporate Sustainability Reporting Directive—Directive (EU) 2022/2464, hereinafter 'CSRD'—had only been transposed by a few Member States within the deadline.[1] Italy was among the States that complied with this deadline, by means of Legislative Decree no. 125/2024.[2]

The CSRD introduces amendments to various European legal sources (EU Directives and Regulations) on corporate reporting and disclosure.[3] Its transposition therefore brings in significant changes to company law in Member States.

The CSRD replaces the rather loose and flexible approach of the Non-Financial Reporting Directive—Directive (EU) 2014/95, hereafter 'NFRD'—regarding environmental and social sustainability reporting. It establishes sustainability reporting as a hetero-regulated corporate disclosure obligation, which is mandatory for certain European public limited companies, reinforcing its overall importance.[4]

This chapter will present and evaluate a number of reconstructive hypotheses concerning the effectiveness and efficiency of the national provisions implementing the CSRD. Using Italian Law as a case study, the analysis aims to ascertain 'whether' and 'how' corporate transparency on ESG factors contributes to sustainable development, in particular regarding the essential role of the circular economy.[5]

The initial Sections 2 and 3 will describe the transition from the previous transparency model of Non-Financial Report (hereinafter "NFR"), governed under

[1] France was the first Member State to transpose the CSRD. Ordonnance No. 1142 of 6 December 2023 transposes the CSRD based on the delegation contained in Law No. 171 of 9 March 2023. A subsequent decree (Decree No. 1394 of 30 December 2023) detailed and supplemented specific provisions of the Ordonnance. On Ordonnance No. 2023–1142 and Decree No. 2023–1394, which entered into force on 1 January 2024, see Stevignon (2024) and Tirel (2024), p. 34. But the majority of Member States have not yet transposed the CSRD. The European Commission sent a formal letter of notice to 17 states (Belgium, Czechoslovakia, Germany, Estonia, Greece, Spain, Cyprus, Latvia, Luxembourg, Malta, the Netherlands, Austria, Poland, Portugal, Romania, Slovenia and Finland) in October 2024.

[2] Legislative Decree no 125/2024, of 6 September 2024, adopted on the basis of Delegation Law no 15/2024, of 21 February 2024.

[3] The CSRD amends Directive (EU) 2013/34, as well as Directive (EC) 2006/43, Directive (EC) 2004/109 and Regulation (EU) 537/2014. On the scope of the CSRD see Palmieri (2023), p. 273, Rota and Scalzini (2023), Genovese (2023a), p. 88, and also Krasodomoska, Zarzycka and Zieniuk (2024), p.1 and Fornasari and Traversi (2024), p. 117.

[4] According to the CSRD timeline, from 1 January 2025, all large shareholding companies and large groups will be involved. From 1 January 2026, all listed companies and issuers of market-traded securities will be involved (excluding only micro-companies). From 1 January 2028, some large non-EU companies will also be affected. Commission Delegated Directive (EU) 2023/2775, published in the OJEU on December 21, 2023, updated (and raised) the size thresholds at which CSR obligations are triggered: on the perimeter of obligated companies see Caprara (2025), p. 21.

[5] The circular economy, which reduces the consumption of scarce resources, is as instrumental to the EU plans for the Green Deal of 2019 (Commission Communication, 11 December 2019, COM (2019) 640 final) as to those for the Clean Industrial Deal (Commission Communication, 26 February 2025, COM (2025) 85 final).

Italian Law by Legislative Decree no. 254/2016, to the new framework introduced by Corporate Sustainability Report (hereinafter "CSR"), implemented by Legislative Decree no. 125/2024. The subsequent Sections 4 and 5 will examine the compliance safeguards of CSR, and some reconstructive hypotheses will be formulated in the following Sections from 6 to 10 regarding the managerial relevance of CSR: both 'upstream' and 'downstream', internal and external, and for financial and non-financial stakeholders. Finally, Section 11 will provide a commentary on the overall findings of the research.

At the outset, however, a specific caveat should be made. On 26 February 2025, the European Commission published legislative proposals to amend, defer, and relax the prescriptive scope of the CSRD. Therefore, if the proposals of the European Commission are endorsed by the co-legislators (the EU Parliament and the Council) in the coming months, the EU regulatory framework for corporate transparency on sustainability will undergo significant changes. Such amendments could have significant repercussions also for the domestic laws of Member States such as Italy, who have already transposed the CSRD. However, the present research remains nonetheless useful, also in the perspective to better understand the future developments in light of the legal framework currently in place.

2 Disciplines Compared. The Continuity Profiles Between the CSR and the NFR

A comparison between the relevant Italian norms in the transition from NFRD and CSRD, i.e., Legislative Decree no. 254/2016 and Legislative Decree no. 125/2024, reveals traits of both continuity and discontinuity.

The most notable point of discontinuity in the new discipline concerns the significant expansion of the scope of companies required to submit reports. Estimates suggest that the number of companies obligated could increase from approximately 200 under the NFR framework to around 5000 under the CSR framework.[6] The comparison also reveals that, for the (few) Italian companies previously subject to the NFR, some of the consequences of Legislative Decree no. 125/2024 could have a small impact. This is because Legislative Decree no. 254/2016, which was repealed by Legislative Decree no. 125/2024, had already established content obligations as well as internal and external control obligations for sustainability transparency that were not so dissimilar, on closer inspection, from those envisaged under the CSR regulation. In this sense, Legislative Decree no. 254/2016 held directors and auditors responsible for transparency compliance, mandated professional assurance of the non-financial reporting, was supplemented by the Taxonomy Regulation

[6] See CERVED (2023). The figures are significant, although estimates circulating vary (other estimates report 4000 companies in scope: see Bianchini and Bianchi (2023).

(EU) 2020/852,[7] and entrusted CONSOB (the relevant Italian National Authority) with the administrative supervision of the compliance of non-financial information.

There are thus some elements of continuity between the last NFR reports published in 2024, under Legislative Decree no. 254/2016, and the first CSR to be published by the same companies in 2025. Nevertheless, significant new features also emerge.

3 (Following) and What's New in CSR

The first notable change is the obligation to include the CSR within the management report, an annex to the financial statements (referred to as an "appendix") in Art. 2428 Italian Civil Code. Under Art. 5, Legislative Decree no. 254/2016, the inclusion of the NFR in the management report was instead optional and little practiced. Between 2018–2023, only a small percentage of NFRs—around 16%—were included in companies' management reports.[8] Most companies that had this choice opted rather to publish the NFR as a separate document.

Hence, the transition from NFR to CSR has significant implications for the content and regulation of the management report. Similarly, for companies subject to CSR requirements, the regulation of the management report—both under Italian Civil Code (Art. 2428) and sector-specific rules (for listed companies: Art. 154-*bis* of Legislative Decree no. 58/1998, hereinafter referred to as the 'TUF')—plays a crucial role in corporate disclosure on ESG factors. Consequently, flaws in the form or substance of the CSR could potentially and theoretically impact the validity of the shareholders' resolution approving the financial statements.[9]

Other changes concern the contents of the report. Legislative Decree no. 125/2024 requires the CSR to provide all material information as well as some specific company information that is presumed to be 'material' unless proven otherwise. Notably, the legislation requires detailed transparency on the company's plans, including implementation actions and related financial investment plans, to ensure that the company's business model and strategy are compatible with the transition to a sustainable economy and the limitation of global warming to 1.5 °C, in line with the Paris Agreement under the United Nations Framework Convention on Climate

[7] Taxonomy Regulation (EU) 2020/852, entered into force on 1 January 2022, and was supplemented by delegated regulations. Delegated Regulation (EU) 2021/2139 and Delegated Regulation (EU) 2021/2178, as amended in particular by Delegated Regulation (EU) 2023/2485 and the Delegated Regulation (EU) 2023/2486. On the provisions referring to taxonomy see Cossu (2023a), p. 558, Genovese (2023b), p. 74.

[8] According to data published on CONSOB's website https://www.consob.it/web/area-pubblica/storico - elenco - dnf

[9] The thesis of the relevance of defects in the management report for the invalidity of the resolution approving the financial statements is supported by Strampelli (2016), sub art. 2348 of the Civil Code. The thesis of irrelevance is instead supported by Cian (2024), p. 645.

Change by 2050 as set out in Regulation (EU) 2021/1119 of the European Parliament and the Council.[10]

From this perspective, the transparency provisions extend beyond merely addressing information asymmetries in ESG investing. The provisions presuppose specific duties of sustainable and eco-sustainable management on the part of the directors. The nature and importance of these duties will be examined in greater detail in the following Sect. 6. Another key innovation of the CSR framework is the obligation to adhere to specific EU-defined reporting standards, unlike under the NFRD framework, which allowed companies to select a preferred reporting standard.

The first set of European Sustainability Reporting Standards (hereinafter 'ESRS') was adopted by the European Commission on 31 July 2023 and made binding through Delegated Regulation (EU) 2023/2772. Additional ESRS are in the process of being adopted.

The discontinuity between the NFR and the CSR is particularly evident in the reporting standards. The forecasts defined by the ESRS are, in fact, notably precise and highly detailed.

4 CSR Compliance Safeguards

The compliance safeguards of the CSRD are fundamental to the overall effectiveness of the discipline.[11] In this sense, Legislative Decree no. 125/2024 provides for various safeguards depending on whether the CSR is produced by a listed or unlisted company. Certain safeguards are of general application, while others are sector-specific and apply exclusively to the CSRs of listed companies.

One generally applicable safeguard is the responsibility assigned to directors, as provided for in Art. 10, Legislative Decree no. 125/2024. This provision states that the directors of companies that are subject to CSR obligations must 'ensure' compliance with the report. Additionally, it specifies that directors must fulfil the obligations of Legislative Decree no. 125/2024 'with professionalism and diligence'. In cases of non-compliance, directors can be held liable to the company, its creditors, shareholders, and third parties as generally established by Arts. 2392, 2394, and 2395 Italian Civil Code.[12]

The liability of directors is combined, where the prerequisites are met, with that of members of the controlling body[13] and of the company itself.

---

[10] See Articles 19-bis and 29-bis of Directive (EU) 2013/34, as amended by the CSRD and then transposed by Articles 3 (2) and 4(2) of Legislative Decree no. 125/2024.

[11] See Hopt (2023), p. 29 and p. 44.

[12] On this regulation, see Sanfilippo (2024), p. 544 and, regarding the procedural profiles of liability, Dongiacomo (2024), p. 1.

[13] See following Sect. 4.5.

The directors' liability towards the company and creditors (Arts. 2392 and 2394 Italian Civil Code) presupposes that the non-compliant CSR has caused damage to the company's assets. The directors' liability, however, also extends (and is in addition to the company's liability) towards shareholders, third parties, and non-financial stakeholders. Several passages in the CSRD explicitly refer to such parties as users of the CSR.[14] The legal regime of the external liability of directors is defined in Art. 2395 Italian Civil Code. Hence, damage to the company is not a prerequisite for this liability. What matters is the direct damage to the shareholder or third party and the causal link between the event (in this case, the non-compliant CSR) and the resulting damage caused.

Other generally applicable safeguards include the professional assurance (external audits) of CSR compliance. Art. 9, Legislative Decree no. 125/2024, specifies that the assurance must be entrusted to an auditing company or an auditor, depending on whether the company is listed or unlisted. Audit professionals tasked with the audit are subject to both civil and administrative liability for the accuracy of their assurance. In the event of damage, the civil liability of these professionals is contractual with respect to the company, and non-contractual with regard to shareholders, creditors, and third parties.

Further safeguards of general applicability could be of a criminal and administrative nature. Specifically, presenting a non-compliant CSR could potentially be included in the list of false corporate communications and classified as a criminal act under Arts. 2621 and 2622 Italian Civil Code. Similarly, the failure to publish the CSR (whether by failing to publish the management report or failing to include it in the published management report) could be considered an administrative offense under Art. 2630 Italian Civil Code, concerning the failure to publish the CSR in the Company Register.

The possibility of criminal liability appears to be reinforced by the provision of Art. 193 TUF: the administrative sanctions applicable to the non-compliant CSR of listed companies apply 'unless the act constitutes a crime'.[15]

The scope of all the safeguards, both general and sectoral, must be related to the compliance status of the CSR. Indeed, the NFR regulation was assisted by the same effectiveness safeguards.[16] With Legislative Decree no. 125/2024, however, the

---

[14] Specifically in Recitals 9, 14 and 39 CSRD.

[15] Delving into such an aspect would lead too far, involving issues related to the regulation of the corporate governance report as an annex to the financial statements and also the mechanisms of the cumulation, or mutual exclusion, between criminal and administrative sanctions. The topic is widely debated regarding market abuse conduct and the ne bis in idem principle: see Alvaro and Bianconi (2023), as well as the role of criminal law in the system of supervision of financial operators, Mucciarelli Fr (2023), p.162.

[16] See Rolli (2020), p. 127, Montalenti (2021a, b), p. 671, Genovese (2023b), p. 161, and Riolfo (2024), p. 180.

importance of the safeguards changes. The importance increases because the CSR compliance constraints are more significant.[17]

4.1 *The Compliant CSR. The Handling of Information (Forward-Looking, Financial, or Confidential)*

Generally speaking, for compliance purposes, all (and only) information necessary to understand the impact of the company (Art. 3(1), or the group (Art. 4(1), Legislative Decree no. 125/2024) on sustainability issues (from an inside-out perspective) must be included in the report and, therefore, must be produced and collected. The report must also include information that enables stakeholders to understand how sustainability issues affect the company or group (from an outside-in perspective). More specific indications apply to individual fields of activity and certain types of information.

The application of compliance safeguards, therefore, needs an assessment of the legal requirements of reporting. This implies an analysis that takes into account the thematic fields that are subject to transparency, the types of information required (e.g., historic, forecast, financial or confidential, etc.), and any opacities that could compromise information transparency (such as omissions, falsehoods or biased information). Numerous interpretative questions arise from this. Without claiming to be exhaustive, this research will focus on limited thematic fields—ecological transition plans, physical and regulatory climate risks, innovation and competition—and especially on three distinct types of information: a) forecast, b) financial, c) confidential.

Corporate transparency on ESG factors necessitates the inclusion of forward-looking information in certain subject areas. As previously mentioned, Legislative Decree no. 125/2024 mandates transparency concerning the company's energy transition and CO2 emission reduction plans. The fundamental nature of this field of information and the materiality of the associated data are presumed. Typically, the inclusion of this information is essential for ensuring CSR compliance. Information on transition plans is based on forecasts, so there may be deviations between the original forecasts and actual data from one CSR to the next. Forward-looking information, however, should not be judged as compliant or non-compliant based on the magnitude of the deviation that has occurred but rather on the ex-ante processing and the (foreseeable or unforeseeable) causes of the deviation. Forward-looking information should be judged to be compliant 'as of now', based on the reasonableness of the underlying processing criterion.

[17] Regarding individual and consolidated sustainability statements, see Treu and Candotti (2025), p. 51.

Information on the environmental commitments declared by the company[18] may be different. In this case, the company's liability could depend on the mode of voluntary disclosure, the reasons for failing to comply with the commitment, and the merits of the interest asserted by the injured party.

In certain specific areas, sustainability transparency requires the disclosure of financial information. Legislative Decree no. 125/2024, for example, requires that the CSR disclose information on the physical and regulatory environmental risks to which the company is exposed. This information has financial relevance and must be provided based on financial materiality. With regard to this type of information, Legislative Decree no. 125/2024 also lays down provisions for consolidation and cross-referencing between the CSR and the management report.[19] The conformity of the financial information in the CSR has to be verified together with the corresponding accounting information.

Climate information, which is subject to the specificities of financial statements and sustainability reporting, is doubly relevant and is subject to a coordinated transparency regime. Typically, climate information that meets CSR compliance requirements—particularly regarding the physical and regulatory impacts of climate change on the company (the outside-in impact) is also pertinent to financial statements, and vice versa. Consistency and alignment between the information in the CSR and that in the financial statements is therefore essential.[20] Discrepancies in the treatment of this information and other opacities relating to this matter can result in the invalidation of both financial statements and sustainability reports. Both non-compliant CSRs, which include information that is inconsistent with financial statement data, and non-compliant CSRs containing information that is consistent with incorrect, untrue, or unreliable financial statement data, are possible. The latter would give rise to a formal concurrence of offenses (non-compliant financial statements and non-compliant CSRs), with cumulative civil and, where appropriate, also administrative and criminal remedies.

Transparency on sustainability could have a significant impact when addressing information that is confidential or that is sensitive for competition reasons. According to Arts. 3(5) and 4(5), Legislative Decree no. 125/2024, transparency on ESG factors does not allow for the omission of confidential information, save for exceptional cases. This does not mean, however, that for the CSR to be complete, the company's business secrets must be revealed. In this matter, Legislative Decree no. 125/2024 must be interpreted alongside the ESRS Regulation. An integrated reading of both sources leads to the conclusion that CSR compliance does not require confidential information to be revealed, provided that the protection of the corporate

[18] On the relevance of any commitments declared in the NFR, see Briguglio (2022), p. 193. Generally, on the possibility of holding companies accountable for their sustainability claims, see Bertelli (2025), p 291.

[19] See Art. 3(12) and Article 4(11) and (12), Legislative Decree no. 125/2024.

[20] This need for consistency also emerges from CONSOB's Attention Reminder no. 2 of 2024, issued on 20 December 2024.

secrets does not render the CSR opaque or incomplete.[21] The solution, therefore, lies in the balancing of different forms of protection. Thus, the compliance regulation of CSR revolves around the technicalities of trade secrets that are pertinent to ESG principles. It imposes secrecy, qualified by specifically appropriate organisational arrangements. Secrecy can maintain the CSR's production and implementation activities but does not compromise the possibility of detecting and tracking information 'substituting' the one which is confidential: that is, substitute information that can be disclosed without (actively) compromising confidentiality, or (omissively) compromising the 'overall relevance of the disclosure' of sustainability.[22] Therefore, the possibility can be excluded that information susceptible to exploitation as trade secrets is essential for CSR compliance.

4.2 *The Compliant CSR and the Duties of the Directors*

Art. 10, Legislative Decree no. 125/2024 states that the responsibility for the conformity of the financial statements (either individual or consolidated) lies with the directors. The directors must act professionally and diligently in this regard.

This replicates the provision of Art. 3(7), Legislative Decree no. 254/2016, referring to compliance with the NFR. Legislative Decree no. 125/2024, however, introduces some key innovations. The traits of professionalism and diligence in management imposed on directors by Legislative Decree 125/2024 differ due to the distinct and hetero-regulated compliance requirements of the NFR.[23] With the introduction of Legislative Decree no. 125/2025, the likelihood of non-compliant CSR resulting in liability increases, as the potential for causing damage grows in tandem with the expanding regulatory and economic significance of sustainability information.

Consequently, directors, when ensuring compliance with the financial information, must act with the professionalism and diligence required to comply with a legal obligation that carries significant internal and external implications.

In general, the directors must, in accordance with the board's competencies and divisions of responsibility, oversee and evaluate (Art. 2381 Italian Civil Code) the administrative and organisational structures of the company (or group) as an appropriate 'means' to produce a compliant CSR. Internal board delegations play a significant role in this context. The responsibility for overseeing the organisational structures lies with the delegating administrative bodies, while those of managing the organisational structures are responsibility of the delegated administrative body. This division of responsibility is subject to the provisions of Article 2392 Italian Civil Code regarding the internal allocation of duties.

[21] On this subject, refer to Genovese (2025), p. 83.

[22] See para. 7.7. of the annex to the ESRS regulation.

[23] See Sect. 4.1.

Overall, however, the civil liability of directors for an inadequate organisation cannot be envisaged in such terms.[24] For liability to exist, in fact, there must be conduct that implements the organisational structures and damage. Hence, both the publication of the non-compliant accounts as well as the damage must be evident. In the case of a listed company, if no damage is identified, the liability of the directors would potentially be only administrative in nature.[25]

4.3 CSR Compliance and Auditor Supervision

Art. 10, Legislative Decree no. 125/2024, also contains provisions on the supervisory tasks of the company's internal control body. The provision, as previously mentioned, states that the control body, within the framework of the performance of the functions assigned to it by law, shall supervise compliance with the provisions laid down in this decree and shall report on this in its annual report to the shareholders' meeting. This provision also replicates the content of the corresponding rule in Legislative Decree no. 254/2016. The provision, however, outlines new supervisory tasks connected to the new legal requirements of the CSR.

The Statutory Auditors' duties regarding the supervision of the CSR derive from their duties to verify the lawfulness of the company's acts and the adequacy of the organisational, internal control, and risk management structures. The duties involved are those established, in general, by Article 2403 Italian Civil Code and, for listed companies, by Article 149(1)(c) TUF.

Art. 10, Legislative Decree no. 125/2024 does not mention auditor liability. It is, however, included in the rationale of the norm, entitled 'Liability and Sanctions', which clearly assigns the company's internal control body tasks to which these responsibilities correspond. The liability will generally fall on the members of the company's control body. The statutory auditors are, therefore, jointly and severally liable with the directors for compliance with the CSR towards to the company, the shareholders, and third parties within the terms, limits, and for the effects established by Article 2407(2) Italian Civil Code.

4.4 CSR Compliance and CONSOB Supervision

In the case of listed companies, compliance safeguards with a general application nature are sided by those with a sector-specific application. In this case, administrative sanctions for non-compliant CSRs are provided for and introduced explicitly in

[24] See Ferri and Rossi (2024), p. 27.

[25] See Sect. 4.4.

TUF through Legislative Decree no. 125/2024. The competent authority responsible for the imposition of such sanctions in Italy is CONSOB.[26]

Legislative Decree no. 254/2016 also entrusted CONSOB with the task of supervising the compliance of the NFR. CONSOB's sanctioning powers were contained in Art. 8, Legislative Decree no. 254/2016. However, it does not appear that these sanctioning powers have ever been exercised.

Legislative Decree 125/2024 introduces some key changes to the administrative and supervisory controls on CSR compliance concerning both the perimeter of these controls and their content.

The scope of public supervision on CSRs is now limited to those of listed companies. CONSOB's supervision of the CSRs is part of the administrative oversight on market information provided by issuers. Supervision will be conducted on a risk assessment basis, following ESMA's specific 'common supervisory priorities' set annually for the National Competent Authorities (NCAs) and supervised entities.[27]

Further innovations are also evident. While Legislative Decree no. 254/2016 provided for a system of supervision and sanctions that were separate from TUF, with Legislative Decree no. 125/2024, administrative compliance safeguards regarding the CSR are set out specifically in TUF.

Overall, Legislative Decree no. 125/2024—by means of its Art. 12—makes multiple changes on TUF.

Article 118-*bis* TUF, as amended, includes the subject of sustainability reports among those on which CONSOB has secondary regulatory powers.[28]

Article 154-*bis* TUF, as amended, regulates the assurance of the CSR, as well as the duties of the directors and the manager in charge.

Article 154-*ter*(1-*quater*), as amended, regulates CSR as part of the contents of the management report.

Finally, in terms of sanctions, Article 154-*ter*(7-*bis*), as amended, provides that CONSOB, where it has ascertained that the CSR information does not comply with the rules governing its preparation, may require the issuer to disclose this circumstance and to publish the additional information necessary to restore correct market information.

---

[26] CONSOB is called upon, where appropriate, to cooperate with other supervisory authorities and competent public administrations (see Art. 11, Legislative Decree no. 125/2024).

[27] ESMA's latest European Common Enforcement Priorities (ECEPs) were published on 24 October 2024 and refer to the supervision of the financial materiality of sustainability information and compliance with EU taxonomy and ESRS: see https://www.esma.europa.eu

[28] See Delibera Consob no. 23463 of March 12, 2025, in Gazzetta Ufficiale no. 67 of March 21, 2025, with amendments to the secondary legislation implementing Legislative Decree no. 125/2024.

5 CSR Compliance Safeguards and Corporate Transparency on ESG Factors

In Italy, CSR compliance is safeguarded by a complex system of sanctions and liabilities. The safeguards provided for in Legislative Decree no. 125/2024 are designed to ensure the effectiveness of transparency regulations. This effectiveness must be commensurate with the importance of the interests involved, which, in this case, is high, considering the critical role sustainability information can play in economic, social, and market dynamics. The importance of such information has increased hand in hand with the rise in demand for transparency from stakeholders and the expansion of regulations on sustainable and transitional investments. Additionally, the increasing prioritization of environmental, human, and labour rights issues has been influential.

The need for appropriate safeguards is crucial. There is, in fact, an—unintended—correlation between sustainable finance measures and greenwashing. Provisions referring to sustainable finance facilitate companies' access to green finance resources and establish a link between sustainability and competitiveness. The same rules that steer development towards sustainability goals and the circular economy push companies to undertake and publicise sustainable activities, financial investments, and business supply to the market. Rules on finance for sustainable development may, however, incentivize opportunistic behaviour. Regulation, therefore, must also address the risks of greenwashing that it has helped to fuel.

That being said, the risks of non-compliance with sustainability transparency obligations within the reporting system are high. These risks are particularly elevated when CSR non-compliance involves inflated information, information omissions, or, more broadly, information that is not in line with the standards (the ESRS).

The apparatus of sanctions and liabilities contained in Legislative Decree no. 125/2024 should, therefore, be assessed as a system of safeguards necessary to counter harmful opacity practices that weaken EU policies for sustainable development: both those that leverage market supply and demand, and those that aim to hold the largest and most influential companies accountable.

From this point of view, CONSOB's administrative supervision of the CSRs of listed companies appears justified, and the failure to provide for administrative supervision of the CSRs of unlisted companies, on the other hand, is puzzling. Although this choice of Legislative Decree no. 125/2024 aligns with the precise direction of its Delegation Law no. 15/2024, it nevertheless appears questionable. It seems to overlook the fact that, among unlisted companies, there are also large companies and issuers who are active on the capital markets, as well as potentially EIPRs (unlisted banking and insurance companies), whose NFRs, until 2024, were supervised by CONSOB, as provided for by Legislative Decree no. 254/2016.

Conversely, entrusting the supervision of CSR compliance of unlisted companies only to internal corporate controls, assurance services, and civil (or possibly criminal) sanctions risks resulting in broad but loose supervision, since it is purely reactive and entirely entrusted to the ordinary judicial authority. There is a risk that the supervision becomes random, occasional, and uncoordinated.[29]

It can also be noted that the system of effectiveness and efficiency entrusted to sanctions in the broad sense should be complemented by a system based on incentives and support policies. The regulation should encourage the production of reliable sustainability information by as many companies as possible. The transition to sustainability could be hindered not only by CSRs that are non-compliant due to inflation but also by CSRs that are too cautious and reticent. The term 'greenhushing' has been coined to describe this phenomenon, which refers to the choice made by companies that are genuinely committed to sustainability not to communicate their sustainability initiatives in order to avoid false accusations of greenwashing.[30] Hence, if the system of greenhushing were to result in overcaution, it would benefit neither the effectiveness and efficiency of sustainability transparency, nor sustainable development and the circular economy.[31]

6 Corporate Sustainability Transparency and Sustainable Corporate Governance

Let us move on to consider the managerial implications of CSR. As previously mentioned, transparency on ESG factors has clear managerial implications related to company compliance. It is debatable, however, 'whether' and 'how' this discipline introduces additional managerial duties and, if so, 'which' ones.[32]

The critical issues pertain to the integration of CSR within the corporate governance system, i.e. within the organisational statute of joint-stock companies. These challenges, in my view, are not significantly different from those encountered in relation to the NFR. The discussions surrounding Legislative Decree no. 254/2016 remain relevant with the entry into force of Legislative Decree no. 125/2024. However, they now carry greater significance due to two key factors: the substantial

[29] See ASTRID Comments, by Anna Genovese, Mario Libertini, Luigi Donato, and Rosa Rota, to the public consultation launched by the Italian Ministry of Economy and Finance in February 2024 on the proposal of the legislative decree transposing the CSRD: https://www.dt.mef.gov.it/ir/dipartimento/consultazioni_pubbliche/direttiva_20222464UE/html

[30] See Guarnieri (2023), p. 401.

[31] On the relationship between sustainable finance objectives and the enforcement of such provisions, see Trovatore (2024), p. 616.

[32] See Campobasso (2024), p. 1; Onza (2023), p. 757, Cian (2021b), p. 1131. More generally, on the complex relationships between sustainability and corporate governance, see Stella Richter jr (2024), p. 1081.

increase in the number of companies required to adhere to transparency legislation,[33] and the pervasive regulating scope of the legislation itself.[34]

Managerial implications of CSR raise several reconstructive challenges, directing interpreters towards broader and often contentious systematic issues. These challenges pertain to the substance of management performance, which remains a subject of debate, as well as the precise meaning of the adjective 'sustainable' that is intended to qualify it.

In particular, while the notion of 'management of the shareholding company'—is defined as a set of powers and duties that are the exclusive responsibility of the company's directors for the pursuit of the company's objectives, following the bylaws and the guidelines expressed by relevant shareholders and the shareholders' meeting[35]—is generally agreed, the same cannot be said for the concept of 'management duties' nor for that of environmental and social 'sustainability'.

Overall, the subject appears to be lacking in stable reconstructive approaches. Nevertheless, the managerial implications of CSR must also be considered when evaluating the effectiveness of corporate sustainability transparency. In the discussion that follows, a number of considerations will be made regarding the role of CSR within the corporate governance system. However, coping with the scope and purpose of this analysis, an exhaustive examination of the functions and rules of corporate governance cannot be undertaken here. The management implications of CSR will, therefore, be evaluated at two levels only. Firstly, the 'upstream' administrative tasks, which refer to the organisational arrangements for producing a compliant CSR (Sect. 6.1), and secondly, 'downstream' managerial performance regarding the use of the information included in the compliant CSR (Sect. 6.2). The implications connected to these two levels will not only be derived from the transparency regulations in Legislative Decree no. 125/2024. They will be drawn also from the rules relating to management performance that influences the areas of business that the CSR monitors. Since the Italian legal system does not provide for

---

[33] However, it must be considered that in the Commission's so-called *Omnibus Simplification Package*, published on February 26, 2025, concerning the CSRD, it is proposed to reduce the scope of the CSRD to large companies with more than 1000 employees (i.e. companies that have more than 1000 employees and either a turnover above EUR 50 million or a balance sheet above EUR 25 million). Companies outside the scope of CSRD (companies with up to 1000 employees) may choose to report voluntarily on the basis of a simplified voluntary standard to be adopted by the Commission, based on the voluntary standards for SMEs (VSME) developed by EFRAG. The Commission estimates that the proposal will reduce the number of companies in scope by 80%.

[34] On the lack of effectiveness of the NFRD, see Ahern (2016), pp. 599–630; Ghoogassian (2015), p. 361; La Torre, Sabelfeld, Blomkvist, Dumay (2020), p. 701; and Cuomo, Gaia, Girardone, Piserà (2024), p. 726. On extra-EU experiences of corporate transparency on ESG factors, see Iannou and Serafaim (2017), p. 100, and Jebe (2020), p. 233.

[35] Statutory clauses can dictate the direction management should take: see Angelici (2021), p. 213. On the prerogatives of statutory autonomy and direction of shareholders and the shareholders' meeting, see Cian (2021a), p. 475; Malberti (2023), p. 1. Guidance may also be conveyed by policies on the remuneration of managerial performance: on this topic see Capelli (2023), p. 755, as well as Ballerini and Sacchi (2023), p. 1463.

specific dedicated norms on this matter,[36] the interpretation will refer, on the one hand, to the general provisions on the directors' duties towards the company (Sects. 6.1, 6.2, 6.3.) and, on the other hand, from Italian Constitution and the general clause on civil tort liability (Sect. 7).

6.1 The 'Upstream' Management Transparency Tasks

When a company is subject to the CSR obligation, 'upstream' tasks related to the organisational structures of the company clearly fall under the responsibilities of the directors. The company's organisational structures must be designed and maintained to effectively produce a compliant (individual or group) sustainability report. This includes accounting for the specificities of the various fields addressed by transparency requirements, as well as the types of information necessary to fulfil this obligation.

These tasks lie 'upstream' of transparency and are instrumental to ensuring the conformity of the accounts. They concern, first and foremost, the establishment of adequate organisational structures which the company, individual or group, must have in place. These requirements are grounded in the provisions of Arts. 2086 and 2380-*bis*(1), Italian Civil Code, as well as in the specific indications derived from Legislative Decree no. 125/2024 and the relevant EU Directives. As such, the conduct expected from directors consists of the diligent and professional structuring of corporate functions responsible for the production, collection, and monitoring of the sustainability information that must be included in the CSR. This obligation applies both to 'internal' corporate information and 'external' corporate information, in terms of value chain.

The 'upstream' sustainable management tasks include the diligent structuring of the internal control functions on CSR compliance,[37] the liaison functions between the company bodies and the corporate functions involved in sustainability reporting, as well as the professionals (auditors and auditing firms) entrusted with the assurance of the report.[38] In the case of group consolidated reporting, the tasks include structuring the relationship between the corporate functions of the parent company, which receives and consolidates the information, and the corporate functions of the subsidiaries and branches, which produce and transmit it.[39]

---

[36] In France there is a law on the duty of the company to monitor the impacts of its value chain (Law no. 399/2017; see, for initial information, Tirel (2023) p. 34); Germany also has legislation on the subject: see Kindler (2022), p. 1605, Bordiga and De Maria (2022), p. 971, as well as Vicari (2023), p. 757.

[37] Including the verification function of the delegated administrative bodies: see Article 154-bis(5-ter) TUF.

[38] See Bessone, Landriani and Pozzoli (2025), p. 103.

[39] See Guerrera (2024), p. 224.

The CSR obligation, therefore, has significant implications for the management duties related to the company's organisational structures. These implications are connected to providing the conditions necessary for the company to produce a compliant CSR. While linked to compliance obligations (i.e. the publication of a compliant CSR), these implications extend beyond merely establishing a corporate function with compiling tasks. CSR goes beyond simply 'mechanical' compliance and entails discretionary choices regarding the selection and processing of information. These decisions must take into account the standards of completeness and accuracy of transparency reporting, the fields of activity subject to disclosure, and the type of information (quantitative or qualitative, forward-looking or historical, public or confidential, etc.) that is needed to produce the report. As a result, 'upstream' CSR management tasks include both discretionary choices and managerial duties. It is on these choices and responsibilities that further attention must be focused.

As is widely recognized, the exact nature of managerial duties referring to appropriate organisational arrangements is a topic of ongoing debate.[40] For the purposes of this research, without entering into the broader dispute, it can be argued that the discretion involved in the 'upstream' sustainable management of the CSR is technical in nature and entrusted to the diligence and professionalism of the directors.[41] The law requires directors to diligently and professionally track, retain, and periodically disclose information that must be 'complete, neutral and accurate' as defined by ESRS.[42]

6.2 *The 'Downstream' Management Transparency Tasks*

In addition to the CSR's 'upstream' administrative tasks, there are those that can be categorised as 'downstream'. In this context, the duty of the directors of a joint-stock company—Società per azioni, S.p.a., in the Italian system—to act in an informed manner (Art. 2381(6) Italian Civil Code) obliges them to use the information provided in the individual CSR and the historical series of the company's CSRs.[43] It is, therefore, necessary to delineate the specific contents of this management duty.

---

[40] The comparison concerns the possibility of invoking the business judgment rule to affirm, as a matter of principle, the unquestionability of the adequacy of a company's organisational arrangements: in favour see Benedetti (2019), p. 425; against, among others, see Amatucci (2016), p. 648 and Brizzi (2015), p. 362. For more articulated positions distinguishing levels and spheres of organizational arrangements, see Montalenti (2021b), p. 11 as well as Di Cataldo and Arcidiacono (2021), p. 69.

[41] Following the specific wording of Art. 10, Legislative Decree no. 125/2024.

[42] Para. QC5, Commission Delegated Regulation (EU) 2023/2772; on such aspects see the writings collected in Tettamanzi (2023).

[43] See Denozza and Stabilini (2020), p. 225.

The duty, in this case, pertains to the importance of the sustainability issues outlined by the CSR for the orientation and implementation of the company's strategic, commercial, and financial plans. Accordingly, the 'downstream' performance of CSR relates to the company's strategy and the role that the company handbook assigns to the CSR function in the company's strategic, commercial, and financial planning process, either at individual company level or across a group of companies. Management performance, therefore, encompasses multiple management choices, including those made at the senior management level.

While the discretion of 'upstream' tasks is largely technical,[44] that of "downstream" tasks appears, to a large extent, more 'entrepreneurial'. Entrepreneurial discretion, however, does not exclude the existence of managerial duties. As is well known, the discretionary powers of directors are always functional.[45]

The functional orientation of discretionary management services is debated. The primary disagreements revolve around defining the social interest and scope of the so-called business judgment rule. That said, the transparency of sustainability information could influence the functional orientation of managerial performance.[46] The critical issue to be resolved is whether the principles—whatever they may be—that govern the company's management performance define (deductively) the functions of the power/duty to use the information contained in the CSR, or whether this power/duty entails (inductively) an evolution or adaptation of these functional principles.[47]

In this regard, the answer cannot be uniform for all 'downstream' CSR management functions. It will have to be grounded in the regulatory functions of CSR and be adapted according to the distinct requirements of financial and non-financial tasks, such as sustainability transparency tasks.

6.3 *The Financial Functions of the CSR*

The regulatory functions of the CSR are derived from its framework and requirements. Overall, these regulatory functions differ significantly from those of the NFR. Unlike the NFR, the CSR moves beyond the framing of sustainability information as 'non-financial' information and strengthens the financial dimension of transparency on ESG factors. The CSR, however, is not solely intended to supplement financial statement information for the benefit of the company's (current and

[44] See before Sect. 6.1.

[45] Costi (2023), p. 503.

[46] On this topic, see Morini and Castellini (2023).

[47] See Maugeri (2019), p.992, and Cossu (2023b), p. 783. To the contrary, Boggio and Pinto (2024), p. 1241.

potential) shareholders and financial stakeholders. The regulatory functions of CSR are both financial and non-financial.[48]

The outside-in perspective of transparency shows the financial functions of the CSR. From this standpoint, the information contained in the CSR supports the engagement and decision-making prerogatives of the company's financial stakeholders, including creditors, external shareholders, and potential investors. The financial functions of the CSR are further reinforced by the placement of the CSR within the management report.

In the financial sphere, CSR enables those who provide risk capital or financing to the company to gain an insight—both in advance and throughout the relationship—into the risks and opportunities the company faces with regard to certain sustainability-related factors (both exogenous and endogenous).[49] Directors, therefore, must use CSR financial information in the exclusive interest of the company, regardless of how this is defined.[50] As a consequence, regardless of the shareholders' varying levels of 'sensitivity' to sustainability issues, directors are obligated to incorporate sustainability transparency into the company's strategic plans, seizing related opportunities and mitigating its criticalities.

From this point of view, it can be said that monitoring the ESG factors of the business is useful for all companies and all enterprises.[51] However, for companies with a CSR obligation, this usefulness does not fall within the discretion of directors or shareholders: CSR is part of the directors' mandatory accountability to shareholders, society, and creditors.[52]

It can, therefore, be concluded that the financial functions of CSR in the 'downstream' managerial performance tasks restrict the entrepreneurial discretion of directors in the assessment and management of ESG factors.[53]

6.4 *The Non-Financial Functions of the CSR*

The inside-out perspective of transparency shows instead the non-financial functions of CSR. In this context, the information contained in the CSR facilitates mechanisms of engagement and self-reliance of non-financial stakeholders and third parties in general.[54] The non-financial function of CSR aligns with the goals of the Green Deal. The CSR obligation forms part of the measures aimed at mitigating systemic risks arising from the misalignment between highly significant and

[48] See Genovese and Rossi (2023), p. 703.

[49] In this sense, Fortunato (2020), p. 185.

[50] On this point Strampelli (2022), p. 145.

[51] In line with Art. 2086 Italian Civil Code: see Sanfilippo (2022), p. 1000.

[52] See La Torre, Sabelfeld, Blomkvist and Dumay (2020), p. 701.

[53] See Lenzi (2019), p. 244., and Sanfilippo (2022), p. 933.

[54] About citizens as stakeholders see Caprara (Chap. 3).

influential corporate strategies and public policies in support of the Green Deal. The transparency subordinates certain negative societal externalities to broad internal and external scrutiny. Without overestimating the effectiveness of regulation based on information,[55] it can be said that CSR performs analogous functions on the non-financial side as it does on the financial side. It shifts choices that would otherwise be within the perimeter of technical discretion, and as such challengeable, to options that would otherwise be unquestionably within the perimeter of business discretion or, possibly, the policy prerogatives of shareholders' general meeting.[56]

Hence, the principles applicable to other management areas subject to prescriptive regulation also apply to the fields and informational content of CSR. Certain obligations are mandatory for the general interest, which is greater than that of the parties directly involved. In the case of CSR, the general interest is essential not only for the smooth functioning of business activities but also for the widespread control of certain negative externalities linked to the economic results of such activities.

6.5 CSR as a Tool for Controlling and Guiding Economic Initiatives

The foregoing analysis leads to include Legislative Decree no. 125/2024 among the control measures envisioned by Art. 41(3) of the Italian Constitution, which—after the recent reform—aims to guide economic initiatives towards socially and environmentally valuable goals.[57] Sustainability transparency introduces process controls on the results of specific companies and their environmental and social impact. These controls are pertinent to both 'upstream' and 'downstream' management duties, though their implications vary in scope.

With regard to 'upstream' management, the normative scope is substantial, including room for specific judicial protection. This includes the remedy provided for in Art. 2409 Italian Civil Code, which may be invoked by a 'socially responsible' investor or, in the general interest, by the public prosecutor when the (obligated) company's structures are manifestly inadequate for producing a compliant CSR.[58] This form of protection seems difficult to envisage for the 'downstream' management of the CSR. In this sphere, the liability of the directors predominantly governs their management duties.

Therefore, in my opinion, the directors' liability—towards the company, individual shareholders, creditors, and third parties, under Arts. 2392, 2394, and 2395

[55] See Conac (2024), p. 29.

[56] In this sense Kuntz (2024), p. 67.

[57] Cozzi (Chap. 9).

[58] See Sanfilippo (2022), p. 1016. In general, on the ex-ante justiciability of the adequacy of the organizational structures of the joint stock company, see Benedetti A M (2023), p. 979.

Italian Civil Code—extends not only to damage resulting from the publication of a non-compliant sustainability statement (e.g. containing incomplete, incomprehensible, unreliable, or false information) but also for damage arising from negligence or incorrectness in using the information provided (or that should have been provided) in the report.

However, the scope of this additional liability needs to be defined. It is essential to identify, by contrast, the management conduct that can mitigate or avoid such liability towards the company, financial stakeholders, and third parties. From this point of view, it is equally important to clarify the relationship between Legislative Decree no. 125/2024 and Article 41(2) of the Italian Constitution.

7 Sustainable Management, Corporate Interests, and 'Alien' Interests

The valorisation of the regulatory functions of CSR in the context of the sustainable management of a company is a controversial reconstructive step. In this regard, the debate on the relationship between NFRs and sustainable management can partially intersect with a similar discussion on the relationship between CSR and sustainable management. However, a distinction must be made between the current and the actual facets of the debate, given the emphasis placed on the regulatory or self-assessment components of NFR and CSR.

Regarding the self-assessment components of transparency, part of the doctrine argued that the non-financial function of the NFR, within the 'downstream' management, could, at most, enhance the convenience of socially responsible conduct (in terms of "corporate social responsibility").[59] However, this function was always tied to the valorisation of the company's shareholdings, meaning it was relevant only insofar as the company's 'conscientious' choices were associated with positive economic results, at least in terms of forecasts. Moreover, it is inevitable that in some contexts, there may be minimal tension between initiatives aimed at improving the ESG profile of the business and its communication, and those initiatives aimed at enhancing the efficiency and profitability of the business.[60] Undoubtedly, there are multiple ways to achieve the goal of profitability for the company.[61]

This approach could be used to redefine the perimeter and normalize the managerial prominence of the regulatory functions of CSR. It would uphold managerial performance, including the sustainable management of the company (whether individual or group), while ensuring that ESG transparency obligations remain anchored

[59] See Angelici (2018), p. 3; Rossi (2021), p. 99, Portale (2022), p. 947, Barcellona (2022), p. 201 and Id (2023), p. 123.

[60] See d'Alessandro (2022), p. 409 highlights, in this sense, the risk of encouraging the transformation of 'business ethics' into the 'business of ethics' or sustainability.

[61] See Cian (2021b), p. 1131.

to corporate contractualism and the principles of shareholder value theory.[62] The basic assumption would be that the 'downstream' implications of sustainability transparency must always, in the public interest, aim at maximizing shareholder value.

Other authors,[63] on the other hand, have linked the regulatory functions of the NFR to the regulatory components of the framework. Building on this connection, these authors argued that the NFR obligation had specific 'downstream' sustainable management implications. The authors maintained specifically that the NFR had implications for the duties of corporate fairness (e.g. eco-sustainability) of the directors towards the company, shareholders, and creditors, as well as for parallel duties of business fairness (again in terms of eco-sustainability) of the companies and their directors towards third parties.

This interpretation did not attribute the sustainable 'downstream' management—or the hypothetical duties associated with it—solely to the rules on transparency. Instead, it ascribes such duties and obligations to higher-ranking rules (the constitutional norms of Arts. 9 and 41(2) and (3) of the Italian Constitution) as well as rules of general relevance (including fairness in terms of civil tort liability, under the general clause contained in Art. 2043 Italian Civil Code). However, a pivotal role was assigned to the NFR. This role is twofold: first, to substantiate the eco-sustainable character of the conduct imposed on directors towards the company, shareholders, and creditors, on the one hand, and to third parties on the other; and second, to delineate the purpose of the corporations obligated to such compliance.[64]

Two forms of objection have been raised against this interpretation.[65] It is my belief that these objections miss the mark, both when they argue that it would not be correct to derive duties and obligations of management from transparency regulations[66], and when minimizing the importance of the limits within which economic initiative is free. In fact, they rely on the shareholder value theory as an inescapable

[62] See for all Maugeri (2019), p. 994.

[63] On this topic, regarding the NFR, see Bruno (2018), p. 974, Sfamemi (2020), p. 197, Marchegiani (2021), p. 105, Rescigno (2022), p.165 and Id (2023), p. 630; Genovese (2023b), p. 115; Lenzi (2022), p. 193. With particular reference to the consolidated NFR see Guerrera (2024), p. 224, and Scognamiglio (2024), p. 1279

[64] On the subjective scope of application of the CSR obligation, see Caprara (2025), p. 21.

[65] See Di Marcello (2023), p. 619.

[66] Di Marcello (2023), p. 620, points out that the taxonomy does not set environmental criteria or mandatory environmental performance levels but provides tools to cleanse market information flows of greenwashing practices, facilitating comparisons between companies and investments. It also notes that the sustainability category is irrelevant to liability since: "if there is a legally relevant damage, it will be necessary to identify those responsible, without any need to refer to sustainability; if, on the other hand, legally relevant damage is missing, there is nothing to answer for and the negative impact cannot be transformed into significant damage merely because in the concrete case it would have been possible to adopt a decision with less or no environmental impact". Along the same lines Boggio and Pinto (2024), p. 1241.

principle of corporate governance,[67] a principle that then discourages consideration of alternative models.

The argument that corporate transparency obligations cannot be transformed into management duties seems to be outdated in the terms mentioned above. All the more so in view of the differences between the highly stringent transparency regulation of the CSR and the partially flexible regulation of the NFR.[68]

Other arguments seem more relevant. The idea that the general limits of Art. 41 of the Italian Constitution (if not translated into mandatory rules) does not count for anything more than efficiency and the maximization of shareholders' profits for the socially useful purposes of economic initiative has undeniable theoretical entanglements. It also poses a potentially topical objection to the regulation and relevance of CSR. All in all, such an objection, as previously mentioned, does not seem convincing: its analysis, however, needs a brief digression.

7.1 The Profit Purpose and the Social Utility

As is widely known, Milton Friedman famously argued that within a market economy, the only corporate social responsibility is to generate profits.[69] His analysis has strongly influenced the debate on corporate governance. As a result, a significant body of thought exists that can be drawn on to criticize any reconstructive proposal that deviates from the shareholder value theory model and Friedman's positions.

Any alternative management model—other than that entrusted to specialized managers who are obligated to maximize company and shareholder profits—would, from the point of view of the general interest, be suboptimal.[70] Consequently, even the management performance associated with 'downstream' transparency obligations on sustainability should be interpreted in alignment with the shareholder value theory. Any deviation is considered illegitimate. In fact, any other model of company management would be deficient in comparison from the standpoint of the general interest and the competitiveness.

[67] Boggio and Pinto (2024), p. 1241, state that management duties cannot result from international disciplines that are not directly applicable to private individuals, without mediating the legislative and political choices necessary to balance the different needs. They add that: "devolving, on the other hand, to the judicial authority the power to scrutinize the programs of corporations in the field of sustainability—environmental, social, etc.—even when there is no breach of specific legal prescriptions, would expose the indispensable balance between sustainability and the functionality of the economic system to the risk of being altered by uncoordinated judicial pronouncements, which would not be part of a unified and coherent strategy". The model would also be incompatible with the reservation of law that is explicit in paragraph 3 of Article 41 of the Italian Constitution but implicit in paragraph 2 of the same provision.

[68] See Ioannou and Serafeim (2017).

[69] See Friedman (1970).

[70] See, among others, Brescia Morra (2022), p. 78, d'Alessandro, (2022), p. 413, Barcellona (2022), p. 123, and Id (2023), p. 123.

These arguments aim to mitigate the risks of the 'uneconomic' shifts arising from the alleged mainstream on sustainability. Such concerns are not entirely unfounded. The political and economic issues involved in ecological transition are vast and, one might say, have not been adequately addressed.

However, in my view, based on the relevant principles, it cannot be asserted that the general interest and social utility—as referred to in Article 41(2) and 41(3) of the Italian Constitution—are fulfilled solely in the case that economic initiative increases allocative efficiency and productivity (along with the profits of the shareholder of the profit-driven company). The question of the relationship between interests and powers in large joint-stock companies, in particular, is far more intricate. Today, large corporations play a role in economic development that competes, and in some cases surpasses, that of States.[71]

In general, the various proposals regarding the sustainable or responsible management of the joint-stock company, as the archetype of the large enterprise, cannot all be regarded on equal footing. A clear distinction must be made between the theses that critique the principle of maximising shareholder value *per se*,[72] those advocating stakeholderism and (weak) institutionalism in place of (strong) contractualism,[73] and the theses aimed at reconstructing the normative framework of sustainability—or eco-sustainability—in relation to management.[74]

From this point of view, for companies subject to CSR, it does not appear that the principles of economic freedom can be validly invoked against such obligations. Specifically, reliance on the fundamental freedom of economic initiative laid down in Art. 41 of the Italian Constitution seems unfounded, regardless of the overall formulation of the provision; the same is true for European law and its many regulatory acts that functionalise freedom of enterprise as a power.[75] Similarly, I remain unconvinced by the reasoning of those[76] who disregard the significance of the general principle of *neminem laedere* unless interpreted as a specific imperative rule for certain categories, such as directors of joint-stock companies.

In my opinion, in general matters of economic initiative, the question should not be limited to whether such initiatives are efficient (within a given horizon of time and space) but also whether it is right (i.e., in line with the legal system, its principles and general clauses[77]) to oblige the management of a joint-stock company to

[71] The focus on contemporary crises, and the role played in them by large joint-stock companies, is the starting point for numerous treatises on corporate governance: see, also for bibliographical references, Tombari (2019), passim; Id. (2022), p. 135; Genovese (2023b), p.15 and Hopt (2023), p. 40. From an interdisciplinary perspective, see the writings collected by Caterino and Ingravallo (2020).

[72] See Denozza, (2023), p. 587.

[73] See Montalenti (2021b), p. 671 and Libertini (2014), p. 669.

[74] See Alpa (2021), p. 721, Libertini (2023), p. 54, Genovese (2023b), p. 129, Rimini (2024), p. 285.

[75] See Libertini (2019), p. 255.

[76] In this sense Barcellona (2023), p. 123.

[77] See Marchetti (2024), p. 9. On the role of principles and general clauses in commercial law and critical jurisprudence, see Libertini (2018), p. 1.

take the risks (as well as the opportunities) of sustainability into account; or to expect a company to make reasonable efforts to reduce the risks of human rights violations[78] or disproportionate and avoidable damage being done to the environment within its value chain.[79]

In this sense, no legal principle, not even fundamental principles such as economic freedom, the protection of the market, competition, and efficiency, is absolute, and they cannot be considered as such in legal discourse.[80]

I see no reason, therefore, to deny that regulatory and interpretative developments aimed at admitting challenge to decisions that were previously entrusted to the business judgment rule are both practicable and desirable. Efforts to enhance the sustainability of the management of shareholding companies—those that are most influential—already take into consideration the public interest involved in their activities and have strong historical and regulatory underpinnings.[81]

Closing the digression, the question remains as to how far the management implications of the CSR obligation can be extended.

7.2 The Significance of 'Alien' Interests

In essence, the remainder of the discussion focuses on determining 'whether' and 'how', in the 'downstream' performance of the CSR, the directors' discretion should encompass the non-financial functions of the CSR and certain 'alien' interests. Indeed, these interests could pertain only to the company itself, as it is within the scope of the director's duties to use the information periodically provided in the CSR[82] in the company's interests. On the other hand, the directors' general loyalty duties are owed exclusively to the principals and the corporation.

The uncertainty lies not only in shaping managerial performance to account for the protection of 'alien' interests, but also in the definition of such 'alien'—or extra-corporate—interests that may be relevant for these purposes.

On this point, the rules are somewhat ambiguous. Legislative Decree no. 125/2024 requires that certain extra-corporate interests be 'taken into account' and that the company be equipped to report on the impact of the company on those interests (following the inside-out perspective). However, the ultimate purpose of this consideration is not indicated. Moreover, Legislative Decree no. 125/2024

---

[78] De Vido (Chap. 12).

[79] Dal Monico (Chap. 11)

[80] Although orthodox neo-liberal economics theorises corporate profit and efficient production processes as constraints on economic regulation, and not the other way around: see d'Alessandro (2022), p. 443.

[81] Hopt (2023), p. 44 recalls that the original joint-stock company came into being by concession of the state and when a specific public interest was associated with the economic activity. On this subject, see Fleischer (2022), p. 37.

[82] In these terms also Di Marcello (2023), p. 621 and Boggio and Pinto (2024), p. 1242.

contains no specification of the duty for the company or its directors to satisfy or protect 'alien' interests affected by sustainability transparency.

In this, Legislative Decree no. 125/2024 is similar to Legislative Decree no. 254/2016. The regulation refers to safeguards that the company must prepare and transparently declare in order to 'contain' the environmental impact of its activity.[83] However, it does not introduce any obligation of this nature. Consequently, it lacks the instruments for stakeholders or third parties to truly encourage the company to adopt sustainable behaviours (in whatever sense this is understood).

It could, therefore, be concluded that, in terms of 'downstream' negligent management practices, Legislative Decree no. 125/2024 counteracts only conduct those places 'excessive' or 'undeclared' environmental or social risks on the company, shareholders and creditors. It seems to disregard managerial conduct that fuels such risks or that causes (either environmental or social) externalities that are disproportionate and unnecessary.[84] This conclusion is possible but, in my opinion, is not particularly convincing.

Legislative Decree no. 125/2024 certainly differs from Directive (EU) 2024/1760 on a company's due diligence for sustainability (hereinafter also: CSDDD) in that it does not introduce duties to protect 'alien' interests.[85] However, such duties could derive from the duty of 'fairness' in management performance.[86]

7.3 (Following) and What Are 'Alien' Interests?

The first question to be addressed is whether the CSR framework contains a definition of potentially significant extra-corporate interests in 'downstream' CSR management activities. I believe the answer to this question is affirmative, as the CSR framework provides just such a normative basis. Legislative Decree no. 125/2024 is aligned, as Legislative Decree no. 254/2016, with the EU Taxonomy related to environmentally sustainable economic activities and with inviolable human rights along the value chain. The EU Taxonomy Regulation is directly applicable in national legislation and Article 9 identifies six environmental impacts (climate change mitigation, climate change adaptation, the sustainable use and protection of water and marine resources, the transition to a circular economy, pollution prevention and control, the protection and restoration of biodiversity and ecosystems) that qualify in terms of environmental sustainability. Based on the Taxonomy Regulation, economic activity can, therefore, be considered sustainable if it contributes to one or more of these environmental sustainability objectives without causing significant

[83] See Articles 19-bis and 29-bis of Directive (EU) 2013/34, as amended by the CSRD and then transposed by Articles 3 (2) and 4 (2) of Legislative Decree no. 125/2024.

[84] Thus, Di Marcello (2023), p. 621 and also Boggio and Pinto (2024), p. 1242.

[85] See Marchetti (2024), p. 9.

[86] See Mucciarelli Fe (2023).

harm to anyone (DNSH criteria of Article 3 EU Taxonomy Regulation) and it is carried out in compliance with the OECD Guidelines and the United Nations Guiding Principles on Business and Human Rights (in line with Article 13 EU Taxonomy Regulation).[87]

Having defined 'alien' interests, another critical question emerges: should directors, 'downstream' of the CSR, be obligated merely to 'take into account' certain 'alien' interests, or do they also have a duty to 'satisfy' or 'protect' those interests? This question applies both to the management of the company and, with all the complexities of the case, to the hetero-direction of a group of companies.[88] The issue lies in determining the position that managerial discretion must adopt when using the information provided in the CSR (whether individual or consolidated), which identifies these 'alien' interests. Should these interests be protected?

This question is crucial in evaluating the effectiveness of corporate transparency as a tool to steer economic development in the direction of sustainability.

The question can be answered in the affirmative within the context of the CSDDD.[89] However, as of today, the CSDDD has a different scope of application than the CSRD and, at the national (Italian) level, the relevant Legislative Decree no. 125/2024. Under these regulations, the perimeter of companies subject to sustainability transparency and those subject to sustainability due diligence are currently different: the perimeter delineated by the CSDDD is narrower than that of the CSRD.[90] As a result, the CSDDD cannot provide a unitary normative answer to the question of the management implication of 'alien' interests within the context of the CSRD.

In any event, the debate on the systemic scope of CSDDD or CSRD for the interpretation of general management clauses could transcend the boundaries of the scope of application of these two pieces of legislation.[91]

The debate on the relationship between sustainable management and 'alien' interests only partly coincides with that concerning shareholder value and the primacy of shareholder interests over stakeholder interests, or with that concerning the procedural structure of the dialogue between directors and stakeholders.[92] It refers to directors' duties towards those subjects with whom the company comes into con-

---

[87] On the provisions of EU Taxonomy Regulation about environmental impacts, DNSH and Human Rights, see Gortsos and Kyriazis (2024), p. 505, and Linciano, Cafiero, Ciavarella, Di Stefano, Levantini, Mollo, Nocella, Santamaria and Taverna (2021) pp. 80, 106 and 117. With a different perspective, on the relationship between UE Taxonomy and sustainable corporate governance, see Pacces (2021), p. 12316.

[88] See Rondinone (2020), p. 305, Guerrera (2024), p. 228, and Scognamiglio (2024), p. 1279.

[89] See Scognamiglio (2024), p. 1279; Stabilini (2023), p. 731, Saavedra Servida (2024), p. 1, Laus (2024), p. 913, Mosco and Felicetti (2022), p. 185, Latella (2023), p. 115, Habersack and Zickgraf (2023), p. 533.

[90] Although Recital 7 of the CSDDD also states that all companies are responsible for respecting human rights, the scope of application of the Directive's provisions refers to large corporations.

[91] See Marchetti (2024), p. 9, and Libertini (2023), p. 56.

[92] See Caprara (Chap. 3).

tact or in conflict (interests of non-financial stakeholders and, in general, the company's involuntary creditors). It relates to management choices concerning, for example, innovation, restructuring, relocation, supply and value chain policies, and responsibility in multinational group companies. It involves, in general, the precautionary principle, and the space and function of civil tort liability (*neminem laedere*) in the management of a joint-stock company (whether individual or a group).

These issues surrounding sustainable management, which have already been analysed in the context of Legislative Decree no. 254/2016, resurface with even greater force following the introduction of Legislative Decree no. 125/2024. In simplified terms, it can be said that, also in this case, the debate revolves around two opposing theses: one that minimizes the managerial significance of 'alien' interests, and another that emphasizes their importance.

7.4 Sustainable Management that Minimizes the Significance of 'Alien' Interests

The thesis that minimizes the significance of 'alien' interests, in essence, normalizes it. It assumes that such significance corresponds to the duty and power of directors to 'take into account' such 'alien' interests. From this perspective, the consideration of 'alien' interests may even stretch beyond compliance with the environmental and social regulation of the relevant jurisdiction, where this is beneficial to the company. Mitigating certain negative impacts of their activity or strategy to a greater extent than is strictly necessary may, in certain circumstances, open up new commercial and financial opportunities related to sustainable development, as well as the protection of the company's reputation. This leads to the possible (but not obligatory) consideration of 'alien' interests in discretionary management choices, within the limits set down by the interests of the company.[93] This could be defined as 'sustainable management', but it does not contradict the logic of shareholder value. In fact, in terms of the orientation of managerial performance, nothing changes: it remains aimed at maximizing the company's profits and the efficiency of production. Therefore, according to this reconstruction, the concrete managerial choices—in terms of risk assessment and risk management, as well as of impacts and benefits with regard to environment, society, innovation, supply chain and group—of companies subject to CSR, would continue to be directed only by the interests of the company (or possibly of the group) and not by balancing these interests with duties of protection (fairness) towards certain "alien"' interests.

This reasoning could be corroborated by observing that sustainability transparency, while regulated, does not (and in fact cannot) change the legal obligations on environmental and social compliance that the company (individually or as a group) must fulfil. As a result, it does not change the responsibilities of the company and its

[93] See Giannelli (2020), p. 257.

director. It could be argued that only legal obligations, in the event of a breach, would give rise to the liability of the company and its directors towards the injured third parties. Furthermore, it is only legal obligations that could justify the exit from the market of the marginal company that is unable to comply with them.[94]

This thesis is highly conservative. It aligns the managerial consideration ('downstream' of CSR) of the 'alien' interests that are drawn into the perimeter of managerial performance by sustainability transparency with the precepts of corporate contractualism and shareholder value theory. There is room, at most, for openness towards what is termed enlightened shareholderism or a long-term approach (long-termism), as an alternative to short-termism.[95] This, for example, is the consideration within which the 2020 Corporate Governance Committee of Borsa Italiana's Self-Regulatory Code allows certain 'alien' interests (those closest to the social interest) to be held in the context of a management that pursues the sustainable success of the company (defined as: creation of value in the long term for the benefit of shareholders, taking into account the interests of relevant stakeholders).[96]

This thesis is only partially convincing. I agree with the assertion that directors of a shareholding company today must cultivate sustainability opportunities, and mitigate risks, for the benefit of corporation. The directors of every company must conduct ESG assessments and take into consideration the 'alien' interests impacted by the business in their management strategies, acting in the interest of the company, especially when the company is subject to CSR obligations. However, I do not believe that this fully captures the managerial significance of 'alien' interests identified through CSR (whether mandatory or voluntary).

7.5 Sustainable Management Enhancing the Importance of 'Alien' Interests

I am not convinced that the managerial consideration of 'alien' interests identified through CSR should be limited to those shaped by a (regulatory and market) context which, in certain parts of the world, might render specific investment strategies or business choices—for example, ecological or eco-sustainable practices—economically advantageous. While the EU regulatory environment undoubtedly incentivises and contributes to making certain sustainability practices (such as climate mitigation and adaptation) worthwhile, these practices can, in fact, facilitate access to

[94] This line of thought, generally defended, among others, by d'Alessandro (2022), p. 413 and by Barcellona (2022), p. 201, Id (2023), p. 123, in the debate on the managerial relevance of corporate transparency on ESG factors is taken up by di Marcello (2023), p. 607, and by Boggio and Pinto (2024), p. 1235.

[95] See Zammitti (2021), p. 255. However, there has been no lack of critical remarks on the risks of a "long-term" management orientation: see Stella Richter jr (2021), p. 16.

[96] See https://www.borsaitaliana.it On the relevance of sustainability for governance and the role of self-regulation, see Calvosa (2024), p. 3.

credit (in the capital markets or the banking system), as well as improve resilience and positively impact the company's profit and loss account. In this sense, such practices may be owed to the company, the shareholders and the 'downstream' creditors of the CSR. However, the scope of regulation of ESG transparency is, in my opinion, broader than this.

Sustainable management driven by market preferences—such as those of the capital markets, the end customers, institutional investors, or shareholders—represents only one side of the coin.[97] The other side lies in the prominence of the issues at stake. These issues include the relationship between the conduct of certain joint-stock companies (those that, either by obligation or choice, produce CSR reports in accordance with ESRS) and the climate crisis, the violation of human rights, and the destruction of ecosystems and biodiversity. In the Italian[98] and EU[99] legal framework, these issues do not have only economic relevance. They touch upon the very foundations of the social contract and the principle of solidarity, including intergenerational solidarity.[100] Therefore, market-driven responses, which may be delayed as well as quantitatively or qualitatively inferior to what is needed, are not the only responses that need to be contemplated.

If these analyses are accepted, it can be concluded that the publication of the CSR may also have sustainable management implications with regard to the protection of certain 'alien' interests. In particular, it could impact the liability of the company and its directors towards these kinds of interests. Management performance rendered 'downstream' of the CSR, even when compliant with the relevant environmental and social regulations, does not always shield the directors and the company from liability if damage is caused. It would not exclude liability in cases where avoidable and disproportionate negative externalities emerge (or which should have emerged from a compliant CSR) and are therefore unlawful. In this sense and within these limits, sustainable management that, 'downstream' of the CSR, provides reasonable and proportionate protection to the 'alien' interests identified is, in my opinion, required by the legal order.

8 Sustainable Management and Entrepreneurial Fairness of the Company

The analysis above leads to the conclusion that certain strategic or operational, management or hetero-directional choices must be considered dutiful in the strategic and industrial plan or in the company or group handbook, even when they do not

[97] Like the 'sustainable' choice for a production policy more open to repair in order to meet consumers' market preferences: on such topic see Calabrese (Chap. 5).

[98] See Arts. 2, 9, and 41(2) and 41 (3) of the Italian Constitution.

[99] See Art. 3 TEU.

[100] See Cerrato (2022), p. 63, and Milazzo (2024), p. 91.

have a positive impact on the profit and loss account or even when they have a negative impact, provided that it is bearable, i.e., such that it does not jeopardise the economic sustainability of the company (whether individual or group).

The source of the duty, however, is not the CSR obligation per se, but the regulatory framework for the correct use of the sustainability information that the report contains. With reference to the Italian legal system, this framework is outlined, as far as 'alien' interests are concerned, in Arts. 9 and 41(2) of the Italian Constitution, and Article 3 TEU, which are also pertinent for the purposes and effects of Art. 2043 Italian Civil Code.[101] These provisions, as I see it, sanction duties of entrepreneurial correctness of the company and, therefore, of its directors with respect to certain "alien" interests.[102] Interests that, having been identified in the CSR, are relevant to 'downstream' management and are protected by the general principle of *neminem laedere*. Moreover, the civil liability of a joint-stock company (as a legal entity) requires the unlawful conduct be attributable to it. In this case, it presupposes a management, strategic or implementation choice—at the level of organisational structures—that was unlawful under the given circumstances and for which the directors, pursuant to Art. 2395 Italian Civil Code, are also liable to third parties.[103]

This interpretation places certain rules of constitutionalised private law (relating to the duties of solidarity and fairness and to the limits of economic initiative) on a level above the freedom of economic initiative.[104] It also takes into account the clear link established by the reform between Art. 41(2) and (3) and Arts. 2 and 9 of the Italian Constitution, on the one hand, and the EU regulation on sustainable economic development, on the other hand.[105]

There are, therefore, normative foundations for attributing to the directors of the company producing the CSR a duty to reasonably protect the 'alien' interests identified in the CSR. The robustness of this theory, however, must be critically examined on two profiles: a) with regard to the limits of such duties; and b) with regard to the safeguards needed to enforce these duties.

---

[101] Libertini (2023), p. 71 argues that, after the constitutional reform of 2022, Art. 41(2) of the Italian Constitution, in relation to Art. 9 thereof, should no longer be read as an indication of principle with implicit reservation of law: the protection of the environment is indicated as having an immediate value as a binding legal principle, and as such must also be taken into consideration in the application of the general clauses contained in the legislation. It may therefore be recalled—for example—in the reconstruction of the notion of economic public order and the assessment of the merits of the interests pursued by acts of private autonomy, as well as in the application of the general clause of *neminem laedere*. More broadly on the significance of such constitutional reform see Cozzi (Chap. 9).

[102] Without prejudice to the liability set forth in Art. 2497 Italian Civil Code.

[103] See Sambucci (2015), p. 453. On the relationship between Arts. 2043 and 2395of Italian Civil Code, in relation to the NFR, see Riolfo (2024), p. 357.

[104] See Cariello (2022), p. 413 and Capo (2023), p. 81.

[105] See Angei (2024), p. 730, Cerrato and Sartoretti (2024), p. 1201. More specifically see again Cozzi (Chap. 9).

9 Tightness Test. Business Propriety and Directors' Duties

The theory that directors have duties that also relate to the proper use of sustainability information, including those of taking into consideration or protecting 'alien' interests, may face several objections. The main problem could result from the constrained nature of the management duty for which the directors are responsible.[106] In this context, the scenarios that could arise where the director needs to make decisions—whether organisational or operative—that provide reasonable protection to certain 'alien' interests (those identified in the CSR) could be numerous. A number of these cases should be considered in more detail.

Let us consider the case in which the directors of a large for-profit shareholder company have to choose between business plans, business models, organisational structures, and value chains that, net of regulatory compliance, have a different ESG impact and a different forecast profitability for shareholders (residual creditors). Imagine a profitability forecast that is positive but that decreases in line with the reduction of the negative ESG impact. In this scenario, a distinction must be made. If the decision alone that provides reasonable protection of 'alien' interests causes losses that threaten the company's financial equilibrium, the director who takes this decision could be revoked and called to account for his conduct vis-à-vis the company, shareholders and creditors. However, if the director is able to prove that he or she caused the loss in order to prevent serious harm to the environment or human rights, they should not be held liable even if they have jeopardized the company's business continuity.[107] An exception to this would be if negligent conduct on the side of mandatory ESG assessment and management emerges as a precondition.

If, on the other hand, the director's decision does not cause a serious loss but rather results in a limited, temporary, and moderate reduction in profits, there is no basis for liability. There could, however, be a resolution of the shareholders' general meeting to revoke their mandate. This would, however, be a revocation without due cause (and therefore would be indemnified). Where the company structure is oriented towards extracting the maximum profit from the investment, there is a greater likelihood that the mandate of the director would simply not be renewed. This scenario clearly relies on there being other directors ready to replace the person whose mandate has been revoked, who are instead willing to indulge the profit expectations of shareholders/investors in the presence of CSRs.[108]

In my view, this brief analysis shows that corporate law and corporate governance principles limit (through balancing), but do not preclude, a managerial style

[106] See Onza (2023), p. 757.

[107] The relationship between directors' duties, sustainable management and crisis is complex, both in terms of the balance between business continuity and sustainability, e.g. environmental sustainability, and in terms of the various possible solutions for overcoming or defining an ascertained business crisis: see Stanzione (2023); Fauceglia (2023); Palmieri (2024), p. 209; Ballerini (2023), p. 486. With specific focus on Workers Buy-Out as a possible model in line with the principle of sustainability see Pasquariello (Chap. 4).

[108] Save the possible direct liability of directors under Art. 2395 Italian Civil Code.

that offers reasonable protection of 'alien' interests that have been identified as such in the CSR.[109]

10 Entrepreneurial Fairness and Civil Tort Liability Protection of 'Alien' Interests

As a matter of principle, I believe that general civil tort liability, as under Art. 2043 Italian Civil Code, can offer third parties the tool to demand certain conduct of entrepreneurial fairness from the company publishing the CSR (i.e., the reasonable mitigation of negative externalities). In fact, this general norm permits the qualification of damage that harms a protected interest as unfair if that damage is disproportionate and concretely avoidable.

Civil liability, therefore, emerges as a remedy that is, in theory, capable of giving effect to the 'downstream' sustainable management implications of CSR, also with regard to the protection of 'alien' interests. However, liability as a general clause remains an instrument that is dependent on the prudent discretion of judges. When applied to business conduct that leads to negative externalities, it raises challenging questions, even in cases where the protected interests and the perimeter of protection are ostensibly delineated by primary legislation and, in particular, through Legislative Decree no. 125/2024.

Non-contractual liability protection against social or environmental externalities, such as those addressed in Legislative Decree no. 125/2024, faces significant reconstructive challenges. These challenges include determining the subjective situation that may serve as a basis for establishing the interest in bringing an action,[110] the imputation of liability within chains and groups (either national or transnational), the identification of the indemnifiable damage, and defining the form and extent of compensation.[111] While some solutions could come from the framework of class actions,[112] the complexities of these matters should not be underestimated.

---

[109] See Turner (2020), p. 245.

[110] See Guerra and Mazza (2022), p. 3, Fontanarosa (2020), p. 1.

[111] See Riolfo (2024), p.257. Possible profiles of the external relevance of sustainability obligations, and of the liability of the company and the directors, are also put forward (with concern) by Guerrera (2024), p. 233: And indeed, from the duty of care of the directors (and the parent company) towards individual or collective stakeholders external to the company (and the group), but affected by the business activity, to a liability based, rather than on the breach of fiduciary duties on the 'social contact' and on the 'duties of protection' of the managers of the company—a protection that would extend, that is, beyond the boundaries of the protection ensured by the mandatory rules and by bargaining (individual and collective, private and public) and would be based on the mere consideration of the negative externalities of the exercise of the activity—the step risks being very, perhaps too, short. On such issue see also Caprara (Chap. 3).

[112] See Rolli (2020), p. 155, Renna (2022), p. 537, and Riolfo (2024), p. 299. Concerning experiences from other national systems, see Remédio Marques (2020), p. 343.

Italian case law is currently addressing questions related to the theoretical existence, rather than the concrete structure, of civil law protections for fundamental personal rights connected to the environment. These rights are being asserted against companies that, while not violating any mandatory norms, are factually responsible for high pollution.[113] However, this litigation does not take into account (in part due to the timing of the action) the role of corporate transparency provisions on sustainability within the broader context of the various relevant international and national sources. Nonetheless, the outcome of this litigation will reveal the orientation of the Italian courts towards this new frontier of liability.

11 Some Problematic Conclusions and a *de Iure Condendo* Proposal

Some conclusions can be drawn at this point regarding the scope, effectiveness and enforcement of corporate transparency obligations on sustainability, focusing on Italian law as a case study.

The transition from the NFRD to the CSRD, and from the NFR to the CSR, has accentuated the prominence of the managerial implications of sustainability transparency without facilitating its reconstructive arrangement. Transparency regulations have, in the terms I have tried to illustrate, implications for the principles of fair management concerning both 'upstream' and 'downstream' duties. The implications are manifold, both with regard to (internal) corporate fairness and (external) business fairness.

Some of these repercussions pertain to the 'upstream' administrative tasks of the CSR,[114] while others involve the "downstream" tasks and various aspects of management performance. The focus is on the components of performance tied to the relevant duty. On the one hand, this concerns the duty of the directors to take into account the interests of the stakeholders, also in the interests of the company[115]

[113] There is no shortage of EU precedents, although they are of varying signs: see Bianchini (2024), p. 781. One interesting case is the comparison between the Hague District Court's 26 May 2021 Royal Dutch Shell ruling (granting protection to the claimants) and the High Court of London's 12 May 2023 Shell Plc ruling in Boggio and Pinto (2024), p. 1237 (dismissing the application). Moreover, the Dutch decision of 26 May 2021, was reformed on appeal (Hague Court, 12 November 2024) with rulings of law that are in the sense of the obligation of emission reduction initiatives also on the part of companies, but the absence of predetermined reduction parameters: for initial information see Johannsen, Kotzé and Macchi (2025), p. 1, and Pagni and Rota (2024). In Italy, the first climate case was brought against Eni S.p.A. in 2023. Information on this case can be found on the company's website, where it can be read that on 9 May 2023, the NGOs Greenpeace Onlus and Recommon APS and several private plaintiffs filed a writ of summons with the Civil Court of Rome against Eni S.p.A, Cassa Depositi e Prestiti S.p.A and the Ministry of Economy and Finance in what they call a 'just' lawsuit: see in ENI web site https://www.eni.com/it

[114] Sections 4, 4.1, 4.2, and 6.

[115] Sections 6.2 and 6.3.

(including by means of dedicated organisational safeguards).[116] On the other hand, it involves the duty of the directors to ensure the reasonable protection of certain extra-corporate interests,[117] where this is compatible with the interests of the company and does not impose excessive and disproportionate sacrifices.[118]

In my view, CSR confers managerial significance on certain 'alien' interests and the duty of the company (and hence its directors) to monitor, rather than encourage negative externalities that could be avoided given a reasonable technical and/or economic effort. In terms of general civil tort liability (under Art. 2043 Italian Civil Code), injury to a protected interest is not considered unlawful if it is necessary and proportionate, but rather if it is unnecessary and disproportionate.

The sustainable management implications of CSR are various in nature. They do not all have the same influence or prominence.

The management implications stemming from the framing of Legislative Decree no. 125/2024, as part of the legal provisions not only directly transposing CSRD, but systemically implementing Article 41(3) of the Italian Constitution, are significant. They include implications regarding the organisational structures on which CSR compliance depends and those on the use of the sustainability information contained in the report for the interest of the company, creditors and shareholders.[119] In contrast, the implications based on the further systemic framing of Legislative Decree no. 125/2024 within the legal provisions implementing Article 41(2) of the Italian Constitution are weaker and more nuanced. These pertain to the fairness imposed on the company (and its directors) for the protection of the 'alien' interests outlined by the CSR.[120]

Such implications are particularly weak when reliant on the general clause for civil tort liability. Such a legal remedy proves challenging to apply in practice and requires an extended period of case law development and refinement.

However, starting from the problematic aspects of these conclusions, I would like to make a *de jure condendo* proposal.

The CSDDD addresses the issue of safeguards to ensure the effectiveness and efficiency of the regulation. It provides for a public enforcement framework and dedicates some provisions to private enforcement. The private enforcement provisions enshrine the civil liability of the company for damages that sustainability diligence is intended to prevent. These provisions outline special identification and extraterritoriality criteria for liability that may arise in the case of international groups and supranational value chains.[121]

---

[116] See Della Tommasina (2022), p. 782; and Maugeri (2021), p. 1351.

[117] See Sections from 6.4 to 8.

[118] More broadly, on the proportionality principle in such fields, see Bianconi (Chap. 6).

[119] Section 6.5.

[120] Sections from 7 to 10.

[121] See Article 29 of the CSDDD and on this provision see Boschiero (2023), p. 661. However, it must be considered that in the Commission's so-called *Omnibus Simplification Package*, published on February 26, 2025, with reference to the CSDDD, it is proposed to postpone the entry into force for 1 year, to reduce due diligence obligations along the chain of activities to direct partners only

The rules on corporate sustainability reporting do not contain such provisions, either at EU level or at the level of Italian transposing legislation. This does not mean, as has been argued here, that civil liabilities of a similar type cannot be envisaged for the company and its directors. It only means that the regime of these liabilities would remain entrusted to the general principles and rules of tort, in this case under the before mentioned Article 2043 Italian Civil Code. The regime would, therefore, remain uncertain, at least until the establishment of a stable case law on the subject.

I therefore think, and with this I conclude, that in Italy (as well as in other Member States with an analogous situation), when transposing the CSDDD, in addition to the civil and administrative liabilities of the companies (whether individual or as part of a national or international group) to which that Directive applies, it would be appropriate to regulate also the liabilities of other companies that—due to corporate sustainability reporting and commitments—may face similar challenges and liability actions.

The proposal might appear overly ambitious and potentially detrimental to competitiveness. However, the question is not whether measures aimed at steering the management of some of the largest and most influential companies towards more sustainable or eco-sustainable practices should exist in theory, or whether those introduced in the EU and Italy are sufficient to prevent or slow the melting of glaciers or prevent the exploitation of workers or the environment within the global capitalist supply chains. The critical question is whether such measures are among those that are essential in systems that aim to protect the environment and people in the face of economic initiative and the competition it fuels. And whether the safeguards for the effectiveness of such measures should be those of general civil tort liability or those with a more specific nature.

References

Ahern D (2016) Turning up the heat? EU sustainability goals and the role of reporting under the non–financial reporsting directive. ECFR 13(4):599–630

Alpa G (2021) Responsabilità degli amministratori di società e principio di "sostenibilità". Contr e impr 37(3):721–732

Alvaro S, Bianconi A (2023) L'apparato sanzionatorio. In: Ventoruzzo M (ed) Diritto delle società quotate e dei mercati finanziari. Giappichelli, Torino, pp 513–534

Amatucci C (2016) Adeguatezza degli assetti, responsabilità degli amministratori e Business Judgment Rule. Giur comm 43(5):643–670

Angei S (2024) Sostenibilità e libertà di iniziativa economica. Limiti costituzionali e sovranazionali. NGCC 40(3):II/730-736

Angelici C (2018) Divagazioni sulla «responsabilità sociale» d'impresa. Riv soc 63(1):3–19

Angelici C (2021) A proposito di «shareholders», di «stakeholders» e di statuti. Riv dir comm 119(2):213–224

and to eliminate harmonized EU conditions for civil liability so that the prerequisites for this will be delegated to the legislators of each of the Member States.

Ballerini G (2023) La sostenibilità nel diritto della crisi: problemi e prospettive. Rivista ODC 2:486–527
Ballerini G, Sacchi R (2023) Profili ESG e politiche di remunerazione. NLCC 46(6):1463–1485
Barcellona E (2022) Shareholderims versus Stakeholderism. La società per azioni contemporanea dinanzi al «profitto». Giuffrè Francis Lefebvre, Milano
Barcellona E (2023) Scopo della società per azioni e interessi degli stakeholders nelle proposte di direttive euro—unitarie: i limiti all'internalizzazione del "bene comune". Dir cost 3:123–166
Benedetti A M (2023) Gli «assetti organizzativi adeguati» tra principi e clausole generali. Appunti sul nuovo art. 2086 c.c. Riv soc 68(5–6):964–982
Benedetti L (2019) L'applicabilità della business judgment rule alle decisioni organizzative degli amministratori. Riv soc 64(2–3):413–452
Bertelli F (2025) Pratiche commerciali scorrette. Le asserzioni di sostenibilità e la Dir. 2024/825/UE. In: Genovese A (ed) La trasparenza societaria per lo sviluppo sostenibile Il decreto legislativo n. 125/2024 sul rendiconto di sostenibilità. Passigli, Firenze, 291–324
Bessone M, Landriani L, Pozzoli S (2025) Attestazioni interne e servizi di attestazione sulla conformità della rendicontazione di sostenibilità: articoli 8, 9 e 12 del decreto legislativo 6 settembre 2024, n. 125. In: Genovese A (ed) La trasparenza societaria per lo sviluppo sostenibile. Il decreto legislativo n.125/2024 sul rendiconto di sostenibilità. Passigli, Firenze, 103-142
Bianchini M (2024) Doveri fiduciari degli amministratori e climate change. In: Marchetti P G, Rossi S P, Strampelli G, Urbani F, Ventoruzzo M (ed) La s.p.a. nell'epoca della sostenibilità e della transizione tecnologica. Atti del Convegno internazionale di studi per il 70 anni della Rivista delle Società, Venezia, 10–11 novembre 2023. Giuffré Francis Lefebvre, Milano, II/781–804
Bianchini M, Bianchi M (2023) Le principali novità della direttiva e il ruolo dell'EFRAG. Forum ASSONIME Report di sostenibilità (10 marzo 2023)
Boggio L, Pinto M (2024) Sostenibilità e responsabilità degli amministratori. Giur it 5:1235–1252
Bordiga F, De Maria A (2022) Tutela dei diritti umani nelle catene di approvvigionamento nell'ordinamento tedesco: la Lieferkettensorgfaltspflichtensgesetz. Riv soc 67(4):971–984
Boschiero N (2023) L'extraterritorialità della futura direttiva europea sul dovere di diligenza delle imprese ai fini della sostenibilità, tra diritto internazionale pubblico e privato. Diritti umani e Diritto internazionale 17(3):661–705
Brescia Morra C (2022) Chi salverà il Pianeta. Lo stato o le grandi corporation? ESG: una formula ambigua e inutile. Supplemento Riv trim dir ec 4:78–99
Briguglio A (2022) Riflessioni sulla natura giuridica della dichiarazione non finanziaria. Corp Gov 1:193–219
Brizzi F (2015) Doveri degli amministratori e tutela dei creditori nel diritto societario della crisi. Giappichelli, Torino
Bruno S (2018) Dichiarazione «non finanziaria» e obblighi degli amministratori. Riv soc 63(4):974–1020
Calvosa L (2024) La sfida della sostenibilità. RDS 1:3–18
Campobasso M (2024) Gli amministratori, il successo sostenibile e la pietra di Spinoza. Banca, borsa e tit cred 77(1):1–19
Capelli I (2023) Le politiche di remunerazione degli amministratori nelle società quotate tra massimizzazione del valore per gli azionisti e il perseguimento della sostenibilità ambientale e sociale: un percorso ancora agli inizi. Rivista ODC 3:755–782
Capo G (2023) Libertà d'iniziativa economica, responsabilità sociale e sostenibilità dell'impresa: appunti a margine della riforma dell'art. 41 della Costituzione. Giust Civ 1:81–104
Caprara A (2025) I soggetti tenuti alla rendicontazione di sostenibilità (individuale o consolidata). In: Genovese A (ed) La trasparenza societaria per lo sviluppo sostenibile. Il decreto legislativo n.125/2024 sul rendiconto di sostenibilità. Passigli, Firenze, pp 21–50
Cariello V (2022) Per un diritto costituzionale della sostenibilità (oltre la "sostenibilità ambientale"). Rivista ODC 2:413–447

Caterino D, Ingravallo I (eds) (2020) L'impresa sostenibile. Alla prova del dialogo dei saperi, Euriconv, Lecce
Cerrato S A (2022) Appunti per una via italiana all'ESG. L'impresa costituzionalmente solidale (anche alla luce dei nuovi artt. 9 e 41, comma 3, Cost.). Age 1:63–114
Cerrato SA, Sartoretti C (2024) Fattori ESG: profili costituzionali e riflessi applicativi diretti. Giur it 5:1201–1211
CERVED (2023), CSRD: la direttiva europea che cambio lo scenario ESG (8 novembre 2023) (www.cerved.com)
Cian M (2021a) Clausole statutarie per la sostenibilità dell'impresa: spazi, limiti e implicazioni. Riv soc 66(2–3):475–507
Cian M (2021b) Sulla gestione sostenibile e i poteri degli amministratori: uno spunto di riflessione. Rivista ODC 3:1131–1148
Cian M (2024) La documentazione dell'attività sociale. In: Cian M (ed) Diritto commerciale III–Diritto delle società2. Giappichelli, Torino, pp 626–650
Conac PH (2024) Verifica dell'efficacia dell'informazione non finanziaria: i limiti della regolamentazione dei comportamenti attraverso l'informazione. Banca, impresa, società 1:29–49
Cossu M (2023a) Sostenibilità e mercati: la sostenibilità ambientale dell'impresa dai mercati reali ai mercati finanziari. Banca borsa e tit cred 76(4):558–598
Cossu M (2023b) Stakeholders theory, obiettivi ESG e interesse sociale. Rivista ODC 3:783–804
Costi R (2023) Sostenibilità e scopo della società. Banca, impresa e società 3:503–508
Cuomo F, Gaia S, Girardone C, Piserà S (2024) The effects of the EU non-financial reporting directive on corporate social responsibility. Eur J Financ 30(7):726–752
d'Alessandro F (2022) Il mantello di San Martino, la benevolenza del birraio e la Ford modello T, senza dimenticare Robin Hood (divagazioni semiserie sulla c.d. responsabilità sociale dell'impresa e dintorni). Riv dir civ 68(3):409–461
Della Tommasina L (2022) Sustainability-related disclosures in financial services and dialogue policies. Listed Companies ECFR 19(5):782–827
Denozza F (2023) Consumer Welfare e Shareholder Value: le comuni radici, i limiti e i difetti di due teorie neoliberali, in Rivista ODC (3): 587–629
Denozza F, Stabilini A (2020) Informazione non finanziaria e Stakeholder Empowerment. In: Marchetti PG, Ghezzi F, Sacchi R (eds) Il caleidoscopio dell'informazione nel diritto societario e dei mercati. In ricordo di Guido Rossi, Giuffré Francis Lefebvre, Milano, pp 225–252
Di Cataldo V, Arcidiacono D (2021) Decisioni organizzative, dimensione dell'impresa e business judgment rule. Giur comm 48(1):69–99
Di Marcello T (2023) Strategia europea sulla finanza sostenibile, informazione societaria e possibili riflessi sulla gestione della società. Giur comm 50(4):607–623
Dongiacomo G (2024) Il giudizio di responsabilità nei confronti degli amministratori di società di capitali2. Giuffrè Francis Lefebvre, Milano
Ferri G, Rossi M (2024) Assetti dell'impresa e responsabilità degli amministratori. Riv dir comm 122(1):27–36
Fleischer H (2022) Klimaschutz im Gesellshcafts — Bilanz — und Kapitalmarktrecht. Der Betrieb 1-2:37–45
Fontanarosa F (2020) Climate change damages, Una analisi comparativa del diritto al clima tra ipotesi di responsabilità e fattispecie risarcitorie. CELB 2:1–70
Fornasari T, Traversi M (2024) The impact of the CSRD and the ESRS on non—financial disclosure. Symphonya. Emerging Issues in Management (synphonia.unicusano.it) 1:117–133
Fortunato S (2020) Parole, simboli e diritti nell'informazione societaria. Verso una cultura della comunicazione d'impresa responsabile e sostenibile, in Caterino e Ingravallo (a cura di), L'impresa sostenibile. Alla prova del dialogo dei saperi, EuriConv Lecce:183–196
Friedman M (1970) The social responsibility of business is to increase its profits, The New York Times Magazine, 13 settembre 1970
Genovese A (2023a) L'armonizzazione del reporting di sostenibilità delle imprese azionarie europee dopo la CSRD. Contr e impr 39(1):88–111

Genovese A (2023b) La gestione ecosostenibile dell'impresa azionaria. Fra regole e contesto, Il Mulino, Bologna
Genovese A (2025) Rendiconti di sostenibilità e segreto. In: Genovese A (ed) La trasparenza societaria per lo sviluppo sostenibile Il decreto legislativo n.125/2024 sul rendiconto di sostenibilità. Passigli, Firenze, 83-101
Genovese A, Rossi S (2023) Considerazioni conclusive sulle funzioni dell'informazione non finanziaria. Rivista ODC 3:698–710
Ghoogassian C (2015) Evading the transparency tragedy: the legal enforcement of corporate sustainability reporting. Hast Bus Law J 11(2):361–384
Giannelli V (2020) L'impresa (in)sostenibile: responsabilità, tutele, rimedi. In: Caterino D, Ingravallo I (eds) L'impresa sostenibile. Alla prova del dialogo dei saperi, EuriConv, Lecce, pp 253–267
Gortsos CV, Kyriazis D (2024) The taxonomy regulation and its implementation. In: Busch D, Ferrarini G, Grünewald S (eds) Sustainable finance in Europe. EBI Studies in Banking and Capital Markets Law, Palgrave Macmillan, Cham, pp 505–561
Guarnieri D (2023) Pratiche commerciali sleali e dichiarazioni ambientali: la sottile linea verde tra pratiche ecologiche virtuose e greenwashing. In: Raffaelli EA (ed). XV Conferenza. Antitrust fra diritto nazionale e diritto dell'Unione europea, Bruylant, pp 401–414
Guerrera F (2024) Assetti organizzativi di gruppo, forme di eterodirezione e regimi di responsabilità. RDS 2:205–241
Habersack M, Zickgraf P (2023) Sorgfaltsplichten und Haftung in der Lieferkette als Regelungsmodell. Rabels Zeitschrift fur auslandisches und internationales Privatrecht 87(3):532–607
Hopt H (2023) Corporate purpose and stakeholder value–historical, economic and comparative law remarks on the current debate, legislative options and enforcement problems. ECGI Working Paper 690
Iannou I., Serafaim G (2017) The consequences of mandatory corporate sustainability reporting. Harvard Business School Research Working Paper No. 11-100
Jebe R (2020) Sustainability reporting, and new Governance: South Africa Marks the path to improved corporate disclosure. Cardozo J Comp Law 23:233–293
Johannsen B, Kotzé L J, Macchi Ch (2025), An empty victory? Shell v. Milieudefensie et al 2024, the legal obligations of carbon majors, and the prospects for future climate litigation action. RECIEL: 1
Kindler P (2022) I gruppi di società nella nuova legge tedesca in materia di due diligence nelle catene di approvvigionamento (Lieferkettensorgfaltspflichtengesetz), in Aa. Vv. Governance e mercati. Studi in onore di Paolo Montalenti. Giappichelli, Torino, II/1605-1616
Krasodomska J, Zarzycka E, Zieniuk P (2024) Exploring multi—level drivers of accountants' opinions on the changes introduced by the corporate sustainability reporting directive, accountig in Europe: https://doi.org/10.1080/17449480.2024.2382205
Kuntz T (2024) How ESG is weaking the business judgment rule. In: Kuntz (ed) Environmental, social and corporate governance, UK. Edward Elgar Publishing, UK, pp 67–94
La Torre M, Sabelfeld S, Blomkvist M, Dumay J (2020) Rebuilding trust: sustainability and non-financial reporting and the European Union regulation. Meditari Account Res 28(5):701–725
Latella D (2023) ESG initiatives and directors' fiduciary duties. In: Spataro L, Quirici MC, Iermano G (eds) ESG integration and SRI strategies in the EU. Challenges and opportunities for sustainable development. Pelgrave Macmillan, Switzerland, pp 109–128
Laus F (2024) Corporate Sustainability Due Diligence e amministrazione del rischio. Le società 8-9:913–929
Lenzi D (2019) La gestione del rischio di danno ambientale per le società di capitali. In: Cerrato SA (ed) Impresa e rischio. Profili giuridici del risk management, Giappichelli, Torino, pp 233–273
Lenzi D (2022) Sostenibilità delle imprese e dichiarazioni non finanziarie. Corp Gov 1:159–192
Libertini M (2014) Ancora in tema di contratto, impresa e società. Un commento a Francesco Denozza, in difesa dello "istituzionalismo debole". Giur comm 41(4):669–697

Libertini M (2018) Ancora a proposito di principi e clausole generali, a partire dall'esperienza del diritto commerciale. Rivista ODC 2:1

Libertini M (2019) Sulla nozione di libertà economica. Contr e impr 35(4):1255–1286

Libertini M (2023) Gestione "sostenibile" delle imprese e limiti alla discrezionalità imprenditoriale. Contr e impr 39(1):54–87

Linciano N, Cafiero E, Ciavarella A, Di Stefano G, Levantini E, Mollo G, Nocella S, Santamaria R, Taverna M (2021) La finanza per lo sviluppo sostenibile. Tendenze, questioni in corso e prospettive future alla luce dell'evoluzione del quadro regolamentare nell'area euro, Roma, Quaderno CONSOB

Malberti C (2023) ESG e clausole statutarie: dallo scopo di lucro al successo sostenibile. Dialoghi di diritto dell'economia 12:1

Marchegiani L (2021) Riflessioni su informazione non finanziaria, comunicazione d'impresa e fiducia degli stakeholders. Osservatorio del diritto civile e commerciale (1):105-136

Marchetti PG (2024) Dal Convegno del 1966 ad oggi evoluzione della società per azioni. In: Marchetti PG, Rossi SP, Strampelli G, Urbani F, Ventoruzzo M (eds) La s.p.a. nell'epoca della sostenibilità e della transizione tecnologica. Atti del Convegno internazionale di studi per il 70 anni della Rivista delle Società, Venezia, 10–11 novembre 2023. Giuffré Francis Lefebvre, Milano, Tomo I, pp. 9–31

Maugeri M (2019) Informazione non finanziaria e interesse sociale. Riv soc 64(5–6):992–1031

Maugeri M (2021) Sostenibilità ed Engagement degli azionisti istituzionali. Riv soc 66(5–6):1350–1371

Milazzo P (2024) ESG and the reformed Italian constitution: toward a constitutionally oriented Reading of corporate sustainability. In: Bernini F (ed) Creating value through sustainability. Springer, Cham, pp 91–103

Montalenti P (2021a) Assetti organizzativi e organizzazione dell'impresa tra principi di corretta amministrazione e business judgment rule: una questione di sistema. Il nuovo diritto delle società 1:11–32

Montalenti P (2021b) La società per azioni: dallo shareholder value al successo sostenibile. Appunti. In: Costa C, Mirone A, Pennisi R, Sanfilippo P, Vigo R (ed), Studi di diritto commerciale per Vincenzo Di Cataldo, Impresa, società e crisi d'impresa, Giappichelli, Torino, vol. II, Tomo II, pp 671–686

Morini A, Castellini B (2023) ESG: impatto sulla governance societaria e doveri degli amministratori, in XIV Convegno annuale dell'Associazione dei professori Universitari di Diritto Commerciale, Orizzonti del Diritto Commerciale, Imprese, mercati e sostenibilità. Nuove sfide per il diritto commerciale, Roma, 26/27 maggio 2023

Mosco GD, Felicetti R (2022) Prime riflessioni sulla proposta di direttiva UE in materia di Corporate sustainability due diligence. AGE 1:185–211

Mucciarelli Fe (2023) Interesse sociale e sostenibilità: un falso problema, in XIV Convegno annuale dell'Associazione dei professori Universitari di Diritto Commerciale, Orizzonti del Diritto Commerciale, Imprese, mercati e sostenibilità. Nuove sfide per il diritto commerciale, Roma, 26/27 maggio 2023

Mucciarelli Fr (2023) Supervisione finanziaria e sistema sanzionatorio: la prospettiva penalistica. Riv soc 68(1):162–173

Onza M (2023) "Attività funzionale" ed "interessi degli altri" nella gestione dell'impresa "entificata": annotazioni dalla direttiva (UE) 2022/2464. Banca, borsa, tit. cred 76(5): 757-768

Pacces AM (2021) Will the EU taxonomy regulation Foster sustainable corporate Governance? Sustainability 13:12316

Pagni C, Rota M (2024) Climate change: shell assolta, ma le emissioni vanno ridotte. (www.DB.it) 22 novembre 2024

Palmieri M (2023) L'informazione non finanziaria e il bilancio di sostenibilità. Rivista ODC 1:273–302

Palmieri M (2024) Crisi dell'impresa e responsabilità sociale. In: Barachini F (ed) La crisi d'impresa nel nuovo codice: problemi e prospettive. Giappichelli, Torino, pp 209–215

Portale GB (2022) La corporate social responsibility alla ricerca di effettività. Banca borsa e tit cred 75(6):947–957
Remédio Marques JPF (2020) La class action a garanzia dell'impresa armoniosa e sostenibile nel diritto portoghese. In: Caterino D, Ingravallo I (eds) L'impresa sostenibile Alla prova del dialogo dei saperi. EuriConv, Lecce, pp 343–354
Renna M (2022) Attività d'impresa, sostenibilità ambientale e bilanciamento tra diritto alla salute e iniziativa economica privata. Contr e impr 38(2):537–563
Rescigno M (2022) Note sulle regole dell'impresa sostenibile. Dall'informazione non finanziaria alla informativa sulla sostenibilità. Age 1:165–184
Rimini E (2024) Sostenibilità e nuova governance delle imprese azionarie nel diritto interno e comunitario tra realtà, criticità e prospettive. Giur comm 51(2):285–301
Riolfo G (2024) L'impresa "sostenibile". La rilevanza esterna degli obblighi e delle responsabilità degli amministratori, Cedam, Milano
Rolli R (2020) L'impatto dei fattori ESG sull'impresa. Modelli di governance e nuove responsabilità, Il Mulino, Bologna
Rondinone N (2020) Interesse sociale vs. interesse "sociale" nei modelli organizzativi di gruppo presupposti dal d.lgs. 254/2016. In: Marchetti PG, Ghezzi F, Sacchi R (eds) Il Caleidoscopio dell'informazione nel diritto societario e dei mercati. Milano, Giuffré Francis Lefebvre, pp 269–312
Rossi S (2021) Il diritto della Corporate Social Responsibility. Rivista ODC 1:99–134
Rota R, Scalzini S (2023) Implementazione della Direttiva Corporate Sustainability Reporting Directive 2464/2022 a livello europeo e suo recepimento in Italia. I contenuti della direttiva. Rassegna Astrid 381(16)
Saavedra Servida B (2024) Sostenibilità ambientale, autonomia privata e private regulation. Dialoghi di diritto dell'economia 3:1
Sambucci L (2015) Art. 2395 c.c. In: Gabrielli E (ed) Commentario Codice Civile. Giuffrè Francis Levfebre, Milano
Sanfilippo P (2022) Tutela dell'ambiente e «assetti adeguati» dell'impresa. Compliance, autonomia ed enforcement. Riv dir civ 68(6):933–1026
Sanfilippo P (2024) Gli amministratori. In: Cian M (ed) Diritto commerciale III—Diritto delle società, 2nd edn. Giappichelli, Torino, pp 476–570
Scognamiglio G (2024) Gruppi di imprese e sostenibilità. In: Marchetti PG, Rossi SP, Strampelli G, Urbani F, Ventoruzzo M (eds) La s.p.a. nell'epoca della sostenibilità e della transizione tecnologica. Atti del Convegno internazionale di studi per il 70 anni della Rivista delle Società, Venezia, 10–11 novembre 2023. Giuffré Francis Lefebvre, Milano, Tomo II, pp 1279–1306
Sfamemi P (2020) Disciplina dell'informazione a carattere non finanziario e mercati regolamentati. Problemi e prospettive. In: Caterino D, Ingravallo I (ed) L'impresa sostenibile. Alla prova del dialogo dei saperi, EuriConv, Lecce, 197–225
Stabilini A (2023) La futura direttiva sulla corporate sustainability due diligence: profili di diritto societario, in Diritti umani e Diritto internazionale (3): 731-743
Stanzione D (2023) Liquidazione dell'attivo e interessi degli stakeholders. Esi, Napoli
Stella Richter M Jr (2021) Long termism. Riv soc 66(1):16–52
Stella Richter M Jr (2024) Sostenibilità e doveri, poteri e diritti degli amministratori. Riflessioni sul diritto societario dell'antropocene. Riv soc 69(6):1081
Stevignon A (2024) Transposition de la CSRD: les derniers détails sont désormais fixés, in Dalloz Actualité (https://www.dalloz-actualite.fr)
Strampelli G (2016) Art. 2428. Relazione sulla gestione. In: Abbadessa P, Portale G B (dir) Le società per azioni. Giuffrè Francis Lebfevre. Milano, I, sub 2348 c.c
Strampelli G (2022) L'informazione non finanziaria tra sostenibilità e profitto. Age 1:145–164
Tettamanzi P (2023) (ed) Sostenibilità, Impresa e Stakeholder. Profili manageriali, finanziari e operativi del bilancio sostenibile, Giuffrè Francis Lefebvre, Milano
Tirel M (2024) RSE et droit des sociétés. Dr sociétés 1:34

Tombari U (2019) «Poteri» e «interessi» nella grande impresa azionaria. Giuffrè Francis Lefebvre, Milano
Tombari U (2022) Riflessioni sullo statuto organizzativo dell'impresa sostenibile, tra diritto italiano e diritto europeo. Age 1:135–144
Treu T, Candotti A (2025) Contenuti e ambiti della rendicontazione di sostenibilità: articoli 3, 4 e 5 del decreto legislativo 6 settembre 2024 n.125. In: Genovese A (ed) La trasparenza societaria per lo sviluppo sostenibile. Il decreto legislativo n.125/2024 sul rendiconto di sostenibilità, Passigli, Firenze, pp 51–82
Trovatore G (2024) Sull'enforcement degli obblighi di sostenibilità nel mercato finanziario. Giur. comm 51(3):616–622
Turner S J (2020) Corporate law, directors' duties and ESG interventions: Analysing pathways towards positive corporate impacts relating to ESG issues. JBL 4:245–264
Vicari A (2023) Risikoanalysis e Risikomanagement nella LkSG: spunti in tema di assetti adeguati nella "catena di fornitura". Giur comm 50(5):757–776
Zammitti M V (2021) Long—termism e short—termism nella ricerca di strategie di sostenibilità. Rivista ODC 1:255–274

Citizens as Active Stakeholders in Corporate Governance

Andrea Caprara

Abstract This chapter will examine whether subjects who are outside of the enterprise but who bear interests potentially harmed by the enterprise's activity—like citizens—can intervene to protect supra-individual prerogatives in the organization and activity of profit-making companies. In particular, the possible role of such 'active' stakeholders in corporate governance will be explored on the basis of admissible statutory clauses or through spontaneous openings of the directors within the scope of managerial discretion. The analysis will focus on the hypothesis of joint-stock company under Italian Law—'Società per azioni' (S.p.a.)—as a case study of possible European relevance.

1 Premise

In a regulatory context inspired by the circular economy[1], the involvement of stakeholders tends to be solicited sometimes by the legislature (limiting the discretion of directors), sometimes by institutional investors[2]: however, it remains a strategic choice that must be shared with the shareholders[3], then requiring the identification

---

[1] Kujala et al. (2023).

[2] Stakeholders engagement was stimulated also by the *Study on directors' duties and sustainable corporate governance*, prepared for the European Commission by Ernst & Young in 2020 (https://op.europa.eu/en/publication-detail/-/publication/e47928a2-d20b-11ea-adf7-01aa75ed71a1/language-en); such a study suggests requiring boards of directors to involve external stakeholders in the decision-making process to identify, prevent, and mitigate sustainability risks, as highlighted by Mucciarelli (2022) p. 186.

[3] Campobasso (2024) 11.

A. Caprara (✉)
Università degli Studi di Verona, Verona, Italy
e-mail: andrea.caprara@univr.it

B. Calabrese (ed.), *Legal Perspectives for a Sustainable Circular Economy*,
European Union and its Neighbours in a Globalized World 30,
https://doi.org/10.1007/978-3-032-07795-0_4

of stakeholders (or at least the criteria for selecting them) and the procedures for involving them.

This chapter will examine whether, and if so by what means, 'citizens' can intervene as active stakeholders in the organization and activity of the profit-making enterprise to protect supra-individual prerogatives or interests potentially harmed in its exercise. In particular, the focus will be on the form of joint-stock company under Italian Law—'Società per azioni' (S.p.a.)—as a case study of possible European relevance[4]. In this sense, the research will consider legal norms, statutory clauses and operative solutions for such company type that could encourage the adoption of profit-making strategies with the involvement of citizens as stakeholders in certain management choices.

In the absence of legislative indications of general scope, there is a preliminary need to define the meaning of the relevant concepts ('citizen', 'active', and 'enterprise') with the aim of setting a useful taxonomy for the present work. Only after that can the subject of the research be circumscribed in more precise terms, and with it also its object and objectives.

1.1 A Preliminary Definition to Delimit the Object of the Research: The Notion of 'Active Citizen'

The term 'citizen' alludes to a category of stakeholders (i.e., a *species* of the *genus* stakeholders) that is inevitably very extensive, but evidently heterogeneous and blurred[5]. For an initial conceptual delimitation, it may be useful to refer to some normative indications from Italian and EU law governing company profiles of organization and activity.

A first normative indication can be drawn from the regulation of so-called benefit corporations ('*società benefit*')[6]. Such companies, unlike social enterprises ('*imprese sociali*') regulated by the Italian legal system[7], are (profit-making or mutualistic) corporations that, in addition to the purpose of profit, pursue one or more purposes of common benefit and operate in a responsible, sustainable and transparent way

[4] The question concerns issues on which the doctrine in Italy has already begun a very heated debate: among many, see Calvosa (2024) p. 5; Mucciarelli (2022) p. 193; Denozza (2023) p. 301; Tombari (2023) p. 338.

[5] The elasticity of concepts and the progressive extension of sustainability is confirmed by ECHR Court, 9 April 2024, *Verein KlimaSeniorinnen Schweiz and Others v Switzerland*, where an association, in order to safeguard the fundamental rights of its members and, in particular, the right to life and health, obtained a ruling from the Court establishing a direct link between human rights and climate, founding obligations for States to take action. See Reich (2024) p. 1; Savaresi (2024) p. 1.

[6] Zoppini (2022) p. 1098.

[7] As of now, EU law lacks a clear model for this category, while there are some relevant national examples: see Felicetti (2018) p. 221.

towards people, communities, territories and the environment, cultural and social goods and activities, bodies and associations and other stakeholders[8]. The Italian legislator in that context provides also a definition of those 'other stakeholders', as the subjects or groups of subjects affected, directly or indirectly, by the activity of the benefit corporation, such as workers, customers, suppliers, lenders, creditors, public administration and civil society[9].

A second normative indication can be found in the context of the domestic transposition of the so-called Shareholders Rights Directive II (SRD-II)[10], which introduced into Italian Law regulations applicable to institutional investors and asset managers[11]. Namely, the law requires them to adopt and disclose to the public a commitment policy describing how they integrate the commitment as shareholders into their investment strategy[12]. The subject referred to by the legislator is, again, very general: in fact, the 'public' can coincide with all possible stakeholders and, therefore, not only with the institutional investor's shareholders, but also with the issuer's shareholders as well as the manager's clients.

With regard to EU law, it is sufficient to recall, on the one hand, the so-called Corporate Sustainability Due Diligence Directive (CSDD)[13], and, on the other hand, the European Sustainability Reporting Standards (ESRS)[14].

The former identifies as stakeholders the company's employees, the employees of its subsidiaries, trade unions and workers' representatives, consumers and, in general, those (individuals, groupings or communities) whose rights or interests are affected, even if only potentially, by the products, services and operations of the company and (among others) its subsidiaries[15]. Moreover, as will be better seen, the CSDD Directive tends to delimit this general category, imposing a proceduralization of the dialogue between the company and its stakeholders that, inevitably, leads the company to select the most representative categories in relation to the activity carried out and the interests or rights even potentially affected by it[16].

The latter—approved by the European Commission on the basis of a technical opinion prepared by European Financial Reporting Advisory Group (EFRAG)—will have to be adopted by companies subject to mandatory reporting on impacts, risks and opportunities in accordance with the respective Corporate Sustainable

[8] Art. 1(376), Law no. 208/2015.

[9] Art. 1(378)(b), Law no. 208/2015.

[10] See Directive (EU) 2017/828, as presented in general terms by Hooghiemstra (2020) p. 1; Van Marcke (2023) p. 1; furthermore, from the Italian perspective at hand see Denozza (2022a, b) p. 97; Strampelli (2018) p. 187; Tedeschi (2020) p. 557.

[11] Legislative Decree no. 49/2019, as a transposition of the cited SRD-II in modification of so-called 'TUF' (Legislative Decree no. 58/1998); in particular see Della Tommasina (2022) p. 39.

[12] Art. 124-quinquies(1) TUF.

[13] Directive (UE) 2024/1760.

[14] Commission Delegated Regulation (EU) 2023/2772.

[15] Art. 3(n), Directive (UE) 2024/1760.

[16] Art. 13, Directive (UE) 2024/1760.

Reporting Directive (CSRD)[17]. Such standards, in the section devoted to stakeholders and their relevance to the materiality assessment process, provide a definition of stakeholders as 'those who can affect or be affected by the undertaking', distinguishing two groups: (i) 'affected stakeholders' (i.e., those who are or may be affected by the activities of the enterprise) and (ii) 'users of sustainability statements' (which include, among others, investors, lenders and creditors, including potential ones, and, more generally, other users of sustainability statements, such as business partners and social partners)[18].

In conclusion, both Italian and EU regulatory references indicate interested third parties which are not attributable to a unitary category of subjects. In fact, the Italian norms refer to very broad and heterogeneous lexical figures ('subjects external to the company', 'stakeholders', 'public'), capable of including both the individual and the local community, both organized entities (from committees to the public administration) and groups without a structure but identified as a result of the business activity.

At the EU level, the choice of a positive definition makes the situation more interesting. However, stakeholders are defined not only (again) in very broad terms, but also from a perspective which is at the same time procedural, for the identification of those with whom the company must dialogue in the management of risk from liability in value chains and, functional, for the consideration of those to whom the sustainability information might be useful[19].

The lack of sufficiently clear normative and doctrinal references does not exempt from delimiting the figure of the citizen as a category of stakeholders, moving from some basic considerations[20].

First, an excessively broad and heterogeneous figure of current or potential stakeholders does not seem in itself useful in terms not only of substantive configuration, but also of the possible protections that can be provided. The different types of stakeholders within the general category of 'public' may in fact have access to different regimes of 'participation' and, therefore, benefit from different informative means or different reactive tools.

Second, different categories of subjects that make up the 'public' may carry interests in conflict with each other[21]. Consider, for example, the different approach that non-shareholder investors (or potential investors) and workers might have when faced with a decision to relocate production in order to increase the sustainability of

[17] Directive (UE) 2022/2464; see Strampelli (2023) p. 828; Calvosa (2024) p. 16; Mezzanotte (2024) p. 925; Ahern (2023) p. 1; Hummel and Jobst (2024) p. 1.

[18] Para. 22, ESRS 1—General Requirements, Annex I, Commission Delegated Regulation (EU) 2023/2772.

[19] More broadly about corporate sustainability reporting see Genovese (Chap. 2).

[20] In addition, for a sociological perspective of citizens as individuals in the research framework at hand see Marzulli (Chap. 1).

[21] See Stella Richter jr (2021) p. 33.

the enterprise policy, or with respect to a proposed acquisition of the majority of the corporate equity following a takeover bid[22].

Third, the notion of sustainability, whose ambiguity has been vastly criticized[23], is far from unitary with respect to both the function it performs in the pursuit of the common good, and the ways of representation and interaction of its different constitutive profiles (social, environmental, governance).

All this being said, for the purposes of this research, it is useful to embrace a broad, but not indeterminate, and generally 'elastic' definition of citizen, selecting stakeholders on the basis of a twofold criteria: positive and negative.

Positive, in the sense that we must deal with legal subjects (natural or legal persons) who are, with various roles (such as, for example, creditors and financial stakeholders, or local communities and more generally non-financial stakeholders), affected by the activity carried out by the enterprise, in terms of legal or factual relationships capable of producing adverse consequences that are legally relevant.

Negative, in the sense that it will be considered only those categories of stakeholders who—regardless of their nature (public or private) and organizational structure (natural or legal person)—do not have access to appropriate tools to intervene on enterprise choices by participating directly in corporate governance.

The difficulty in elaborating a unitary and fixed definition is due to the fact that both EU and national law do not operate a hierarchy among stakeholders' interests: rather, there is a debate on the degree of involvement of directors, i.e. whether they—always in the collegial framework of the board[24]—could restrict themselves to take stakeholders' interests in consideration, or should carry out a more penetrating duty of balancing them with shareholders' interests, when making management decisions[25].

Leaving aside such disputes, it is necessary to examine the hypothesis that such a category include citizens, understood as a stakeholder who does not necessarily have a formalized relationship with the company, but could nonetheless suffer from adverse effects of the enterprise activity. Here derives the hypothetical *a priori* claim, on the one hand, of citizens to be actively involved in the management and so to influence enterprise choices that could even only potentially affect them and, on the other hand, of the enterprise to involve citizens in order to prevent subsequent litigation or news that adversely affects its reputation.

The 'active' attribute that qualifies the 'citizen' among stakeholders relates to the means by which he or she interacts with and/or impact on enterprise choices: actually, it is on such means that a legal protection can be provided. The attribute 'active' also has a specializing character, in the sense that it circumscribes the field within which to identify the 'citizen' as a stakeholder, which tends to be a subject covered

[22] In this regard, Art. 3, Directive (EC) 2004/25 provides that the board of directors of the offeree company must take into account 'the effects of implementation of the bid on employment, conditions of employment and the locations of the company's places of business'.

[23] See Tombari (2023) p. 340 and 345; Rimini (2024) p. 285; Hopt (2023) p. 1.

[24] Calvosa (2024) p. 11.

[25] In these terms, specifically, Calvosa (2024) p. 10; see also Barcellona (2022a) p. 6 and 29.

by a variety of disciplines. In other words, the relevant stakeholder for the present research is only the one who in the given set of disciplines has a legal instrument to condition management choices. However, since this discipline has yet to be reconstructed, the notion of citizen in this phase needs to be elastic and susceptible to individuation by progressive approximation.

The set of instruments for exercising citizen 'activism' and the reactive tools available to the same must be tested in the field of the enterprise, that is, economic activity, organized in the form of a joint-stock company under Italian law (*Societa per azioni*, S.p.a.) as a case-study. As such, the reference is to an enterprise that operates durably in the competitive market and to which is essential—and therefore unavoidable—the profit goal[26]: an enterprise whose persistence then expresses the defense of the market and the defense of sociality, and their reconciliation in the social market economy[27].

Therefore, for the purposes of this research, the active participation of stakeholders remains a phenomenon in objective terms, that is, concerning the relationship between the enterprise and the socio-economic context in which it operates. This will make it possible, on the one hand, to develop the analysis on the same level (the objective one) of such a relationship[28] and, on the other hand, to disregard accordingly the debate on the purpose of the company and the opposition between shareholderism and stakeholderism. This means also to confine to special laws the forms of necessary interaction between these visions, like for business activities of general interest carried out not for profit, but for civic, solidaristic and socially useful purposes[29].

1.2 Object, Purpose, Methodology and Structure of the Research

From the above, the structure of this chapter can be outlined as follows.

Right here, the object of the research can be better defined by adopting a residual definition (i.e., one that is intended to operate only in the absence of a different legal or statutory indication) of 'active citizen': namely, that particular category of stakeholder composed of subjects who are potentially affected in negative terms by the business activity, and, as such, have legal and/or statutory means of contributing to certain management decisions, but without being part of company bodies[30].

[26] In Italian Law, the debate about enterprise goals is quite intense: see Tombari (2023) p. 348; Calvosa (2024) p. 4; Barcellona (2022a) p. 25; Genovese (2023) p. 26; Libertini (2023) p. 54.

[27] Literally, Gentili (2024) p. 349.

[28] Also referring to the so-called 'double relevance' within the meaning of Directive (EU) 2464/2022.

[29] Art. 1, Legislative Decree no. 112/2017.

[30] This clarification is especially relevant in light of the views that highlight the role of institutional investors in facilitating the control of the sustainability policies of the companies in which they

Accordingly, also the purpose and method of the present work can be better specified. The purpose is to ascertain whether organizational models are conceivable, and if so in what terms, in order to make citizens contributing to business management decisions, and what might be the legal protection available to them to make such participation effective. All this without prejudice to the orientation of productive activity toward profit goals.

The method will consist, firstly, in ascertaining the legal hypotheses in which forms of interaction between directors and third parties are configurable, and then in understanding whether they can be interpreted analogically or are rather exceptional provisions.

Such a methodological analysis will be carried out immediately afterwards (Sect. 2), with some intermediate conclusions to follow (Sect. 3). As a result, it will be necessary to investigate the limits within which statutory participation clauses may possibly be elaborated, as well as the further atypical cases of active involvement and the relevance of the unquestionability of managerial choices (respectively, Sects. 4 and 5). Then, it will be elaborated a reconstruction of the possible legal powers that can be exercised by citizens in order to effectively realize their rights of active participation (Sect. 6), followed by some final conclusive remarks (Sect. 7).

2 Some Italian and European Legal Assumptions of Citizens' Participation (or Necessary Involvement) in the Enterprise

As anticipated, Italian and EU law provides for very heterogeneous forms of stakeholder participation in the enterprise. The analysis of some of them is useful to see if it is possible to identify elements that can be traced to a common underlying rationale.

2.1 Citizens' Participation in Italian Legal Norms

A first normative core can be identified with regard to so-called 'third sector' entities, especially associations, which may also carry out an instrumental business activity[31], as well as social enterprises. In particular, this can be seen in two distinct, though partly overlapping levels: the appointment of management bodies, and the relevant involvement of stakeholders.

invest: see Denozza (2023) p. 301.

[31] Under Art. 6, Legislative Decree no. 117/2016, third sector entities may engage in activities other than those of general interest (provided for in Article 5 of the same Decree), if 'secondary and instrumental'. See Fusaro (2022) p. 157.

In the former level, the law generally provides that the appointment of directors is responsibility of the associates' meeting[32]. However, special provisions are also added. On one side, the deed of incorporation or bylaws may provide that one or more directors be chosen from among members of the different categories of members[33]; on the other side, the deed of incorporation or bylaws may assign the appointment of one or more directors to third-sector or non-profit entities, civilly recognized religious entities, or to workers or users of the entity[34]. In any case, there is the mandatory ultimate limit that in any case, the appointment of the majority of directors is reserved to the associates' meeting[35].

Furthermore, in social enterprises, the regulatory framework is quite similar: the only real difference is that it is not indicated which are the types of external parties that can compete in the appointment of the (minority of the) directors[36]. If there is a reason for such a difference, it is probably due to the fact that in (social) enterprises the identification *a priori* of stakeholders categories can be more articulated and therefore far from simple, so it is more appropriate to leave the matter to the bylaws or deed of incorporation[37].

In the latter level, there are significant provisions for the involvement of stakeholders in the regulation of social enterprises, according to the so-called multi-stakeholder approach. In fact, it is stated that the enterprise adopts 'management methods' aimed, among other things, at encouraging the involvement of workers, users and other stakeholders in the enterprise activities[38]. In addition, appropriate forms of involvement must be provided for in the statutes of social enterprises, which must consist of a consultation or participation mechanism through which workers, users and other stakeholders directly affected by the activities are placed in a position to exert influence on the decisions of the social enterprise itself[39].

Moreover, another normative reference concerns the regulation of professional sports clubs, where it is provided that the memorandum of association shall establish an advisory body that shall provide, with mandatory but non-binding opinions, for the protection of supporters' interests. This advisory body must be heard whenever 'specific interests of supporters' are considered: a broad and generic formula that statutory autonomy is free to determine with a wide margin of discretion in selecting the relevant matters, but subject to the constraint of supporters' consultation[40].

---

[32] Art. 26(1), Legislative Decree no. 117/2016, except for the first directors who are indicated in the deed of incorporation (and subject to the rules and principles applicable to associations with at least five hundred members under Art. 25(2) of the same Decree).

[33] Art. 26(4), Legislative Decree no. 117/2016.

[34] Art. 26(5), Legislative Decree no. 117/2016.

[35] See Cian (2023a, b) p. 484.

[36] Arts. 7 and 11, Legislative Decree no. 112/2017.

[37] See again Cian (2023a, b) p. 488.

[38] Art. 1, Legislative Decree no. 112/2017.

[39] Art. 11, Legislative Decree no. 112/2017.

[40] Article 13(7), Legislative Decree no. 36/2021.

A second normative core pertains to so-called benefit corporations. For such companies, legal obligations do not actually concern stakeholders' involvement in decision-making, but more a duty on directors to balance the interest of shareholders, the pursuit of the purposes of common benefit, and the interests of people, communities, territories, environment, cultural and social assets and activities, entities and associations[41].

A third normative core concerns bank law. As is well known, cooperative banks were established to collect savings and grant credit to households and small businesses operating in a specific territorial context. The issue of territoriality has retained undoubted relevance for such a business model. Albeit with specific reference to cooperative credit banks, the Bank of Italy's Supervisory Instructions give prominence, in addition to mutuality, also to the localism that characterizes the nature of these banking enterprises, that should be reflected in the relationships between the bank on the one hand and the members, customers and the territory on the other. The member's benefit is ensured by the fact that the activities of cooperative credit banks must be directed primarily in favour of the members and respond on the whole to the collective interest of its social base[42]. Membership access as well as the banking activity area are both dependent on the relevant territory.

Actually, territoriality and localism are concepts essentially related to mutuality, not to sustainability. However, in such cases, they too require (by law) that certain stakeholders must be taken into account in the management of the enterprise.

2.2 *Relevant Indications in EU Law*

The norms recalled so far in some cases precede, in others follow, and in any case are nowadays part of a broader systematic pattern that characterizes EU law: here, the participation (in its broadest sense) of stakeholders seems to have strong roots in the sustainability discipline with inevitable repercussions also on corporate governance[43]. Such discipline—which presupposes the dissemination of a corporate culture of sustainability[44]—rests on three main pillars closely related to each other (outlined by additional disciplines)[45], consisting of:

- investments, with rules 'for financial market participants and financial advisers on transparency with regard to the integration of sustainability risks and the consideration of adverse sustainability impacts in their processes and the provision

[41] Art. 1(380), Law no. 208/2015.

[42] See Banca d'Italia, Istruzioni di Vigilanza, Titolo VII, Cap. 1, Sez. 1, para. 1; on this subject see Fauceglia (1995) p. 66.

[43] See Ferrarini (2023) p. 327.

[44] See Calvosa (2024) p. 4.

[45] Further indications in this sense can be drawn from 'Greenwashing' Directive (EU) 2024/825, as well as 'Green Claims' Directive Proposal COM/2023/166 final.

of sustainability-related information with respect to financial products'[46], as well as 'criteria for determining whether an economic activity qualifies as environmentally sustainable for the purposes of establishing the degree to which an investment is environmentally sustainable'[47], so obliging companies to offer also relevant 'non-financial' information;
- sustainability reporting[48], now strengthened to increase the numbers and quality of sustainability reporting with respect to non-financial reporting[49];
- the aforementioned due diligence, where participation through stakeholder dialogue is specifically regulated[50]: in particular, while it is left to the company the identification of the stakeholders to be involved, such stakeholders once involved have precise rights to interact with the company, for example, by submitting 'a reasoned request for additional relevant information'[51], in addition to intervening in the different moments of the company's activity[52].

This latter regulatory source is particularly interesting from a systemic point of view, because it closely correlates due diligence, enterprise risk management and dialogue with stakeholders as means to fulfill such new obligations.

3 An Intermediate Conclusion: Citizen Involvement as a Way of Organizing and/or Exercising Enterprise Even Apart from Sustainability

From the methodological approach of analyzing the normative provisions of interaction between enterprises and third parties, some indications can be drawn regarding both their systematic relevance and their legal nature. In addition, some other indications about the relationship between managerial discretion and citizen participation seems to emerge[53].

---

[46] Art. 1, Regulation (EU) 2019/2088. See Hooghiemstra (2020) p. 1.

[47] Art. 1(1), Regulation (EU) 2020/852 (so-called Taxonomy Regulation).

[48] See Directive (EU) 2022/2464, which can, with good reason, be considered the main pillar: in these terms Rimini (2024) p. 292, Rescigno (2022) p. 172; see also Mähönen and Palea (2024) p. 1; Strampelli (2023) p. 829, who specifically notes that although the Directive only poses information (disclosure) obligations, it is in reality also intended to affect the organizational structure of companies.

[49] See specifically Genovese (2023a, b) p. 95 and furthermore Genovese (Chap. 2). This is true considering the discipline of Directive (EU) 2013/34 (on non-financial information) and the references made to (and received from) the other European sources already in force and awaiting approval, but which, in turn, intervenes in the groove traced by the Taxonomy Regulation: in this sense Genovese and Scalzini (2023) p. 3 and footnote 11.

[50] Art. 13, Directive (EU) 2024/1760.

[51] Art. 13(2), Directive (EU) 2024/1760.

[52] Art. 13(3), Directive (EU) 2024/1760.

[53] See further Sect. 5.

Firstly, in the domestic and EU discipline of joint-stock companies there are different hypotheses of stakeholders' participation in the enterprise, which are realized in different operative modes:

- 'passive' interaction, imposed mostly in subsequent terms, that is of mere communication or publicity of information with typical content, as for the example of sustainability matters, or atypical content, as for the epitome of profits heterodestination[54];
- 'dialogic' interaction, regulating confrontation with certain categories of interested parties[55], who are identified in general terms by law or selected by the company on the basis of relevant criteria or interests[56];
- 'active' interaction, when the law mandates the involvement of certain categories of stakeholders, while still leaving room for statutory autonomy[57].

Secondly, with regard to the legal nature of the provisions referred to, it emerges that there is no contradiction with the principles governing the enterprise. Consequently, there are no indications to conclude that they should be considered as exceptional. Therefore, if passive interaction does not contain useful elements for theorizing forms of active citizen involvement, dialogic interaction and active interaction can instead be meaningful in this sense. Save their different means and techniques, such hypothesis can represent models for elaborating, even (but not only) by way of statute, applicative solutions for involving citizens in certain management choices.

Starting from this aspect, it can also be set up the reasoning about managerial discretion and citizens involvement, especially in the absence of a specific statutory clause.

In this regard, it can be preliminarily stated that active participation is not a necessary and exclusive corollary of sustainability, nor of the common benefit pursued by benefit corporations. While the doctrine has already demonstrated that such pursuit of common benefit and sustainability do not overlap[58], the previous Section highlighted the reasons why also active participation and sustainability should not be overlapped. This conclusion is particularly significant on a systemic level, because it allows to continue the analysis regardless of the debate about the strong or weak conception of sustainability as a source of obligations for directors[59].

---

[54] See Cian (2021) p. 485.

[55] Just think at 'users of the sustainability statement', as defined by para. 3.1(b), Commission Delegated Regulation (EU) 2023/2772 on sustainability reporting standards.

[56] This is the case of supporters' specific interests under Art. 13(7), Legislative Decree no. 36/2021.

[57] In the case of the social enterprise, for example, it is prescribed that company regulations or bylaws shall provide for appropriate forms of involvement of workers and users and other persons directly affected by their activities (Art. 11, Legislative Decree no. 112/2017), while in Art. 13, Directive (EU) 2024/1760 it is provided that consultation with stakeholders takes place at different stages of the process of implementing the due diligence obligations.

[58] Cian (2021) p. 482 and 484.

[59] Barcellona (2022b).

Therefore, the reasoning can proceed just on the level of the (legal and statutory) discipline of enterprise organization and management.

Moreover, for ordinary profit-making companies, recent developments in EU law show two key profiles:

- solutions for enterprise organization (or management planning) that are permissible in purely for-profit companies in terms of active involvement, must not go as far as radically imply the involvement of all stakeholders[60];
- the positive role of the principle of proper administration and the duty to provide the company with adequate arrangements for risk management operates in two directions: as a possible source of obligations, and as a limitation of statutory autonomy and management choices[61].

In essence, it should be noted that the composition of interests realized by the board of directors for the proper pursuit of the purpose of the enterprise will have to be implemented differently than in the past[62]. It is agreed in doctrine that the board of directors is a body that operates a composition between sometimes conflicting interests[63], but until now we have been reasoning about internal interests, that is, belonging to shareholders or share classes, or even financial instruments or creditors (bondholders or otherwise)[64]. However, EU law applicable to large companies as well as—in cascading terms but in accordance with the principle of proportionality[65]—to all market operators[66], requires directors to take increasingly and effectively account also of other interests.

The aforementioned profiles will be decisive to identify the legal protections available and the subjects who can legitimately claim them, using the case study of Italian joint-stock company (*Società per azioni, S.p.a.).*

---

[60] Denozza (2023) p. 315 and footnote 23.

[61] In Italian Law, see Art. 2086 Civil Code; at EU level, see Directive (EU) 2019/1023; Commission Recommendation (EU) 2014/135/EU.

[62] See: Salvioni and Almici (2020) p. 1; Buhmann (2023) p. 150–155.

[63] See already Stella Richter jr (1995) p. 277.

[64] In Italian Law, the issue emerged with more relevance in the context of the reform in 2003, especially regarding the composition of potentially conflicting interests deriving from the mixed financial structure of S.p.a.: in this regard Tombari (2004) p. 1082.

[65] More broadly about the principle of proportionality and its relevance in this context see Bianconi (Chap. 4).

[66] Directive (UE) 2024/1760 expresses the idea of exploiting the instrument of contractual assurances in order to ensure compliance with codes of conduct, so to give prevalence to interaction with business partners in value chains rather than termination of relevant relationships (see in particular Recitals 46, 48, 49 and 50).

4 Statutory Clauses for Citizens' Participation: Categories of Cases and Limits to Their Admissibility

Statutory clauses, which may favour or require involvement of active citizens, can be abstractly classified into four categories to be examined separately:

- clauses aimed at encouraging not merely information obligations, but dialogue between directors and citizens;
- clauses that allow citizens to nominate a member of the board of directors;
- clauses that, following citizens' resolutions, impose managerial constraints on directors in a twofold sense, both negative (right of veto) and positive (binding opinions to which directors must then comply);
- clauses for the mandatory involvement of citizens, according to the special models of 'social enterprises' or sports enterprises.

4.1 Clauses Regulating the Dialogue with Citizens

A first category of clauses is the one that establishes the autonomous (i.e. not imposed by law) formation of committees, in order to deal with citizens' interests possibly affected by the enterprise.

In order to assess the legitimacy of such a clause, it may be useful to refer not so much to the national law that evokes dialogue as a stakeholder involvement technique, but rather to EU law. More precisely, in the framework of sustainability due diligence, it can be found a specific norm which is emblematically indexed as 'meaningful engangement with stakeholders'[67]. There, it is provided that Member States, in transposing the harmonized discipline, shall 'ensure that companies take appropriate measures to carry out effective engagement with stakeholders', taking into account indications already present in EU law itself[68]. In this regard, it is particularly meaningful the specification that consultation with stakeholders must take place at the stages where due diligence comes into consideration, and thus: i) the gathering of information necessary to assess actual or potential adverse impacts; ii) the development of prevention and corrective action plans; and iii) the decision to take appropriate measures to remediate adverse impacts[69].

Between the normative lines, relevant elements can be spotted for reconstructing in general—so beyond the application of the due diligence Directive—the possible content of a statutory clause on citizens' active involvement in S.p.a,.

---

[67] Art. 13, Directive 2024/1760.

[68] Art. 13(1), Directive 2024/1760.

[69] Art. 13(3), Directive 2024/1760.

Firstly, there are no reasons against clauses that establish such a dialogue, at least not in the form of atypical bodies[70], but rather through stable ways of confrontation between directors and stakeholders.

Secondly, such a clause should indicate the composition of the committee, the requirements of its components, and the appointment and removal of such components as stakeholders affected by the exercise of business activity. Nothing precludes that the composition may be heterogeneous (i.e. with subjects bearing different interests in order to try to settle, in that forum, possible contrasts), even to the point of contemplating different committees in relation to the type of operation or interest involved[71]. While also external experts can be included in such committees, it is not considered permissible instead for members of the board of directors to participate with voting rights: the decision of the board of directors must, in any case, be subsequent to and distinct from that of the committee, which then the board of directors must take into account (with the effects that will immediately be discussed)[72].

Thirdly, such clauses should clearly circumscribe the subject matter, i.e. the issues or situations which impose the activation of the dialogue by the directors, in order to prevent the risk of too generic formulation[73].

Moreover, additional profiles such as time and effects of the committee's resolution should also be taken into account.

Regarding time, it is believed that in order to fulfill the role that citizens should play with respect to management, the committee should be able to operate not only at crucial moments, but also with a preventive character with respect to decision-taking, so to prevent the harm of their protected interest. In other words, the directors should make their decision subject to previous discussion with stakeholders so that, from a different point of view, the proceduralization of confrontation with citizens must embody the adequacy of the company's organizational arrangements.

Regarding effectiveness, there is the question of whether the committee's resolution is binding or non-binding for the subsequent decision by the board of directors. The doctrine has argued for the validity even of resolutions with a binding character: in particular, it has been observed that while nothing precludes shareholders from reserving the right to ask authorizations and opinions[74], it could well be expected that such authorizations or opinions would be provided, on specific matters, by different parties representing from time to time the interests involved in the specific decision[75]. Therefore, albeit with certain cautions directed at not eliminating directors' management power or compressing the minimum prerogatives of

---

[70] See Cian (2023a), p. 361 and 366.

[71] Cfr. Irrera and Scarabelli (2023) p. 1583.

[72] Cfr. Cian (2021) 499.

[73] Cfr. Cian (2023a) 364; see the position A.B. (*ESG e clausole di sostenibilità*), by Notary Council, Interregional Committee Tre Venezie (2024); Ventoruzzo (2024) p. 129.

[74] In the relevant normative context of S.p.a, see Art. 2364, no. 5, Italian Civil Code.

[75] Cfr. Cian (2023a) 368 and 370.

shareholders, admissibility can be recognized to statutory clauses that attribute a binding character to the resolutions of committees composed of persons unrelated to management[76].

4.2 Clauses Reserving the Appointment of a Member of the Board of Directors in Favour of Citizens (and the so-called 'Board Observer')

The legitimacy of clauses reserving the appointment of a member (or at most the minority of total members) of the board of directors in favour of a center of interests outside the shareholders' meeting is a very complex issue. Considering the case of S.p.a., Italian law allows exceptions to the rule of appointment by the shareholders' meeting only for the first members of the board of directors and control bodies at the time of incorporation, if it is a company participated by the State or other public bodies[77], as well as for holders of financial instruments, who are precluded from voting in the general shareholders' meeting[78]. Thus, the clause reserving the appointment of a member of the board of directors to third parties does not seem admissible[79]. However, nothing precludes shareholders from giving themselves criteria for identifying the members to be elected, the rules on the appointment procedure or also the definition of the requirements that such candidates must possess. In fact, one can imagine the use of voting list mechanism, with the adoption of criteria for the composition of the lists that presuppose the consultation of stakeholders or even—if the binding nature of the resolutions by relevant committees were assumed—indicate the name of the person to be included in the list. In addition, it can be provided professional requirements and business guidelines that the proposed person should follow.

It is clear that if it were admitted such a board of directors, i.e. with an articulated composition representing also stakeholders outside the company, this corporate body would be converted from a purely technical one into a political one (broadly speaking)[80].

From this point view it emerges also the figure of the so-called 'board observer', i.e. an observer who attends board meetings to bring the interests' of stakeholders directly to the board's attention, but without voting rights[81]. Even if it operates on a different level, this figure could be very useful in verifying the proper taking and

[76] See Cian (2023b) p. 381.

[77] In accordance with the criterion of proportionality in the recently amended Art. 2449 Italian Civil Code; see again Bianconi (Chap. 4).

[78] Art. 2383 Italian Civil Code.

[79] See Cian (2021) p. 498.

[80] See Denozza (2019) p. 625.

[81] In these terms Calvosa (2024) p. 13; Geslevich Packin and Alon-Beck (2024).

implementation of strategic decisions on sustainability. In fact, although the board observer does not exercise voting rights, it can represent institutional investors pursuing an ESG investment policy, so such an observer could directly exert political pressure (again broadly speaking) on the directors[82].

4.3 Clauses Imposing Limits and Constraints on Enterprise Management

As known for joint-stock companies, in the case of S.p.a. the managerial power is reserved by law in the hands of the directors. In particular, they are entrusted with the exclusive management of the company, and at the same time they have the burden to carry out the operations necessary for the implementation of the corporate purpose[83].

However, it is true that there are normative indications that can support the introduction—by means of statutory clauses—of not only constraints, but also obligations on directors, thus affecting the business activity.

Preliminarily, it is clear that the perimeter of the corporate purpose also becomes relevant in order to identify the interests potentially affected by the same corporate action[84].

Secondly, the clauses in question cannot go so far as to introduce an obligation for the directors to put in place an ideal activity (i.e. non-profit and non-compliant with the economy principle) in order to achieve merely altruistic and solidaristic ends[85].

Thirdly, it is necessary to consider the profile of managerial choice—in terms of how the enterprise is managed—and, in particular, the possibility of placing limits and constraints on directors' decisions. In this sense, the doctrine has relied on specific norms. On one side, the reservation of authorizations and opinions by shareholders in the articles of incorporation[86]. On the other side, the unenforceability of limits imposed by shareholder on agency powers[87]. In particular, this latter provision could imply that limits on directors' managerial choices (constraints of a negative nature) are legitimate, but perhaps also the imposition of rules of conduct obliging directors to adopt certain choices (constraints of a positive nature) are legitimate as well[88]. In this perspective, among the procedural methods by which to

[82] Actually, this role was originally established in the practice of capital markets: see Packin and Alon-Beck (2024) p. 1.

[83] Art. 2380-bis Italian Civil Code.

[84] Such a methodological approach emerges literally from Art. 8, Directive (EU) 2024/1760.

[85] Cfr. Cian (2021) 489.

[86] Article 2364, no. 5, Italian Civil Code.

[87] Article 2384 Italian Civil Code.

[88] See Cian (2021) p. 489.

acquire information on the interests potentially affected by the enterprise activity, it could be imagined not only the consultation with stakeholders, but also, in the case where it is not possible to institutionalize such a dialogue, the request of experts' opinion[89].

Finally, save its merely persuasive nature, it must be considered lawful a clause aimed at connecting directors' remuneration to the outcomes of periodic evaluations carried out by a group of independent experts regarding the company's environmental or social performance[90].

4.4 Clauses for the Mandatory Involvement of Citizens

As mentioned above, there are special norms for the mandatory involvement of stakeholders in the enterprise[91]. Then, it should be seen if such a model could be extended also to ordinary profit-making companies, regardless of their possible purpose of common benefit or general interest.

In the case of social enterprises, Italian law requires that the statute contemplates cases and modalities of stakeholders participation in the associates' general meeting, plus, in larger enterprises, the appointment of at least one member of both the administrative body and the control body[92]. In the relevant guidelines, three modes were outlined for the application of this norm: information, consultation and participation[93]. Especially for the last two modes, guidelines refer to general principles: from proportionality (appropriate measures with respect to the purpose pursued) to regularity and effectiveness (as the concrete suitability of the measure to achieve participation)[94]. Thus, the guidelines constitute a non-binding way of operating 'appropriate forms of involvement' as required by law[95]. It follows that such measures (and the legal basis that makes them mandatory) are to be considered as special, but not as exceptional: this means that it should not be prevented their transposition to purely profit-making business, as long as the (profit-making) purpose of the corporate model and the relevant interpretative construction of the business organization is not contradicted.

[89] The normative model of reference is Art. 13, Directive (EU) 2024/1760.

[90] See the position A.B.5 (S.p.a.—*valutazione della performance degli amministratori* - pubb. 10/23—motivato 10/23) by Notary Council, Interregional Committee Tre Venezie.

[91] See before Sect. 2.1.

[92] Article 11, Legislative Decree 112/2017, dedicated to the involvement of workers, users and other stakeholders in the social enterprise activities.

[93] See Guidelines by Italian Ministry of Work and Social Policies, 7 September 2021, for identifying ways to involve workers, users and other stakeholders directly affected by the activities of the social enterprise.

[94] Once more about proportionality principle in this context see Bianconi (Chap. 4).

[95] Within the meaning of Article 11(1), Legislative Decree no. 112/2017.

5 The Atypical Cases of Citizens' Active Involvement and the Limits to the Reviewability of Management Choices

While it is true that clauses by which shareholders limit managerial discretion or introduce relevant rules of conduct for directors are legitimate, the question remains whether directors can make decisions with citizens' direct involvement in the absence of particular statutory rules.

In the absence of legal or statutory prescriptions, it is difficult to identify means by which directors can incorporate interests other than those of the shareholders into the purpose of corporate management[96]. In fact, directors are subject to certain conditioning factors of normative relevance, arising from shareholder activism, sustainable finance leverage and reputational leverage[97]. In any case, given that the pursuit of profit does not coincide with the maximization of profit, and that the ways in which directors pursue profit are inherent in the strategy they arrange, it can be affirmed that:

- it is not forbidden, but remains within the discretion of the directors, to involve citizens in the definition of policies or actions that affect interests other than those of the shareholders;
- equally, it remains within the discretion of the directors to regulate the possible involvement of citizens in structural terms[98] or occasionally[99], also in terms of subjects, modality[100] and objects[101] to be established on a case-by-case basis: in essence (and as noted above) stakeholders' participation should be proceduralized[102];
- with the growing space that socially relevant purposes are occupying in corporate strategies, it is reasonable to expect the affirmation of the so-called 'stakeholder capitalism', meaning that stakeholders will cease to be mere beneficiaries of actions put in place by others, but they will and assume the role of actors

[96] See Campobasso (2024) p. 11, footnote 17.

[97] See again Campobasso (2024) p. 12.

[98] For example, pre-definition of an internal regulation of the board of directors, or adoption of a code of ethics.

[99] For example, depending on the type of decision and its impact on a certain community.

[100] For example, episodic survey to acquire information with a view to taking resolutions impacting the interests of citizens, up to the institutionalization of committees.

[101] For example, a particular type of choice to be taken such as relocation, divestment or the establishment of a production line, as well as a periodic discussion of strategic and management choices.

[102] See Calvosa (2024) p. 8; such a conclusion is imposed by the principle of adequacy of business arrangements that can be derived from Art. 2086 Italian Civil Code, but also by the principles of precaution and proportionality); moreover, it can be facilitated by the use of technological tools and artificial intelligence: see Santagata (2022) p. 312.

capable of orienting business policies towards ESG values, through the exercise of their voice power within the enterprise organization[103];

- in the absence of directors appointed by external stakeholders other than shareholders, independent directors could play an important role in order to make the board permeable to such 'other interests'[104], also in terms of their legal protection, as it will be immediately shown.

6 Profiles of Legal Protection

The effectiveness of such tools for citizens' involvement is closely linked to their relevant legal protection, i.e. the reactive means that stakeholders can activate in case their prerogatives are denied or harmed.

In addition to the general remedies related to the alteration of the competitive dynamic[105], private and public enforcement protections can be distinguished.

About the former, the possibility of bringing actions for damages is generally rejected[106]. However, a recent (and convincing) interpretation maintains that it can be reconstructed a non-contractual liability of directors, as a breach of their duties when management choices do not conform to sustainability and affect third parties' interests[107].

Moreover, it cannot be ruled out also a special form of contractual liability, especially where there are statutory clauses that circumscribe rather precisely the categories of stakeholders involved in the management of the company, in terms of 'social contact'[108]. In such cases, especially if the directors' wrongdoing consisted in the violation of the duties of stakeholder involvement, injunctive protection could also be recognized[109].

Besides, sustainability due diligence imposes the provision of complaints mechanism to which certain categories of persons may have access if they 'have legitimate concerns regarding actual or potential adverse impacts with respect to the companies' own operations, the operations of their subsidiaries or the operations of their business partners in the chains of activities of the companies'[110]. Given that this provision relates to the way in which the company is organized, nothing precludes

[103] Specifically Calvosa (2024) p. 12.

[104] Denozza (2022b) p. 607.

[105] Cian (2023b) p. 361.

[106] See Barcellona (2022a) p. 49.

[107] Recently Riolfo (2024), but see also the different opinions by Scognamiglio (2023) p. 88 ss. and, with particular reference to workers, Maresca (2023) p. 105.

[108] More specifically, again, Riolfo (2024) p. 292.

[109] As provided for in Article 840-sexsiedecies Italian Civil Procedure Code, as well as, when the company is subject to due diligence obligations, by Arts. 13, 14 and 29(3)(d), Directive (EU) 2024/1760.

[110] Art. 14, Directive (EU) 2024/1760.

such a procedure from being provided for in the articles of association even regardless of the applicability of the new discipline, as long as it complies with the principles of proper administration and adequacy of organizational arrangements.

Furthermore, stakeholders' prerogatives may cause the invalidity of acts taken by corporate bodies in violation of the relevant duties towards (e.g. consultation). In this sense, two profiles must be taken into account: the illegitimacy of the act and the standing for the invalidity claim.

Regarding the illegitimacy of the act, two further issues must be reflected upon: i) the non-conformity of the board's decision with the committee's resolution, and ii) the source providing for the establishment and operation of the stakeholder committee.

The validity of such clauses will have to be measured against compliance with the organizational adequacy of the company and the principles of good administration. The establishment of committees should not represent an unnecessary procedural and bureaucratic burden, but rather an appropriate way of managing business risk in order to make thoughtful decisions that also avert possible litigation between the company and stakeholders. Then, the committee's resolutions represent a way of carrying out the necessary preliminary activity with respect to the board's decisions involving citizens' interests. It follows that board's decisions that deem to deviate from the committee's resolutions should be justified and explained, even if the latter are not binding.

Regarding the validity of committee resolutions, it is necessary to start from the legal nature of such committees (and consequently of the resolutions taken by them): committees cannot be qualified as bodies or offices of the company, nor can those decided by them be considered legal acts. In fact, these are measures having exclusively internal value in a procedural sense, to be placed within the framework of the preliminary activity implemented by the board of directors with respect to the decisions to be taken by the same. Any irregularity of the committee's resolutions (due to illegitimate composition, or the absence of a structural quorum) cannot have autonomous relevance, but it may, at most, affect the validity of the board's decision.

However, for the purpose of identifying the protection that can be afforded, the source allowing or obliging the establishment of the committee is also relevant. Violation of provisions requiring consultation does not always imply the invalidity of the non-compliant act. It has been held that, for example, if the provision for forming external committees were governed by a decision or regulation adopted by the board of directors on its own initiative, its violation would not constitute a relevant 'defect of compliance'[111]. At the same time, this conclusion is not persuasive insofar as, even assuming that board regulations are an expression of the relevant power of self-organization, their unreasonable disregard could represent a violation of the principles of proper administration[112].

---

[111] Under Art. 2388 Italian Civil Code; see Cian (2023b) p. 362.

[112] Due to inadequate preliminary investigation or contradiction with other decisions taken previously, in terms of excess of powers: see Caprara (2021) p. 332.

Another issue concerns the standing to challenge the validity of relevant enterprise decisions, taken by shareholders' general meeting or the board of directors. In addition to the fact that standing is reserved by law only to certain subjects, there is also the ancillary issue of access to documentation, in order to collect evidence about the said invalidity. Such question cannot be duly analyzed here, but it could be assumed that the regulations establishing the stakeholders committees would provide for a right of access to the documentation relating to the resolution in which citizens' interests are considered[113]. Failing this, it could be useful the intervention of the independent director, who, as such, is entitled to challenge the decisions of the board of directors, could be useful, and the same is true for the board of auditors.

Further profiles of protection concern so-called public enforcement.

Special administrative pecuniary sanctions were provided for failure to file the non-financial declaration with the commercial register or for its non-compliance with certain requirements[114]. But the duties concerned by this provision do not imply the failure to implement forms of active involvement, and, in any case, the relevant norm fell with the transposition of the Corporate Social Responsibility Directive[115].

However, a major sanction profile could relate to non-compliance with due diligence obligations in value chains. Although it needs to be understood how each Member State will transpose the relevant Directive, actually the European legislature imposes the provision of 'dissuasive, proportionate and effective penalties for infringements,' which 'should include pecuniary penalties and a public statement indicating the company responsible and the nature of the infringement if the company fails to comply with a decision imposing a pecuniary penalty within the applicable timeframe'[116].

7 Concluding Remarks

In light of the above considerations, an attempt can now be made to answer the questions posed at the beginning of this research: namely, the identification of the cases of citizens active participation and the safeguards that may be provided to make such claims effective. With regard to the cases, once the figure of the citizen has been defined by outlining the different types of interactions (active, passive and dialogic) envisaged by domestic and EU law, it is possible to move in two directions out of the (specific but not exceptional) legal hypotheses: the statutory level and the management level. The former implies the provision of special statutory clauses defining the time, manner and object of the interaction between shareholders and/or

[113] Along the lines of Art. 2545-bis Italian Civil Code for members of cooperatives.

[114] Art. 8, Legislative Decree no. 254/2016.

[115] Art. 10, Legislative Decree no. 125/2024.

[116] Recital 76, Directive (EU) 2024/1760.

directors and citizens. The latter excludes a specific statutory provision and operates as a way of implementing a precise management strategy. In both cases, shareholders' adherence to management choices or agreement on fundamental strategic lines between shareholders and management is decisive.

Furthermore, relevant profiles of legal protection must be reconstructed on the basis of general principles, analogical extension of non-exceptional rules, and extensive application of special rules operating on the side of public and private enforcement.

Finally, there remains one basic fact that permeates the whole issue of citizens' active participation in the management of the enterprise, understood as an organization for the detection and management of risks for its enduring permanence in the competitive market: such participation presupposes the provision of an appropriate organization in which active involvement is integrated and which does not preclude the directors from being able to manage the enterprise in pursuit of the lucrative end.

References

Ahern DM (2023) The sustainability reporting ripple: direct and indirect implications of the EU corporate sustainability reporting directive for SME actors (https://ssrn.com/abstract=4517356)

Barcellona E (2022a) La sustainable corporate governance nelle proposte di riforma del diritto europeo: a proposito dei limiti strutturali del c.d. stakeholderism. Riv soc 67(1):1–52

Barcellona E (2022b) Shareholderism versus Stakeholderism. Giuffrè, Milano

Buhmann K (2023) Human rights, business and meaningful stakeholder engagement. In: Bonnafous-Boucher M, Rendtorff JD (eds) Encyclopedia of stakeholder management. Edward Elgar, Cheltenham, pp 150–155

Calvosa L (2024) La sfida della sostenibilità. RDS 1:3–18

Campobasso M (2024) Gli amministratori, il successo sostenibile e la pietra di Spinoza. Banca, borsa e tit cred 77(1):1–19

Caprara A (2021) I principi di corretta amministrazione. Struttura, funzione e rimedi. Giappichelli, Torino

Cian M (2021) Clausole statutarie per la sostenibilità dell'impresa: spazi, limiti e implicazioni. Riv soc 66(2–3):475–507

Cian M (2023a) Amministrazione degli enti del terzo settore e coinvolgimento di soggetti esterni. Riv dir civ 69(3):482–500

Cian M (2023b) I comitati rappresentativi degli stakeholders e l'organizzazione societaria. Banca, borsa e tit cred 76(3):I/356-384

Della Tommasina L (2022) L'attività di reporting negli emittenti quotati: governo societario e politiche non finanziarie. In: Donativi V (ed) Trattato delle società, IV. Utet giuridica-WKI, Torino, pp 139–179

Denozza F (2022a) La Direttiva Shareholders' Rights II e il ruolo degli investitori istituzionali. In: Montalenti P, Notari M (eds) La nuova società quotata: tutela degli stakeholders, sostenibilità e nuova Governance, Giuffrè, Milano, pp 97–124

Denozza F (2022b) Due concetti di stakeholderism. Rivista ODC 1:37–67

Denozza F (2023) Sostenibilità e corporate governance: dagli investitori agli stakeholder. Riv soc 68(2–3):301–316

Fauceglia G (1995) Esiste ancora il localismo delle banche popolari? Bancaria 51(11):66–68

Felicetti R (2018) L'impresa sociale negli altri ordinamenti. Age 1:221–254

Ferrarini G (2023) Lo scopo delle società tra valore dell'impresa e valore sociale. Riv soc 68(2–3):317–337
Fusaro A (2022) Gli enti del terzo settore. Giuffrè, Milano
Genovese A (2023a) La gestione ecosostenibile dell'impresa azionaria. Fra regole e contesto, Il Mulino, Bologna
Genovese A (2023b/1) L'armonizzazione del reporting di sostenibilità delle imprese azionarie europee dopo la CSRD. Contr e impr 39(1): 88–111
Genovese A, Scalzini S (2023) Il d.lgs. n. 254 del 2016 di recepimento della non financial reporting directive (NFRD) 2014/95/UE e la corporate sustainability reporting directive (CSRD) 2464/2022 a confronto. Astrid Rassegna 383:1–10
Gentili A (2024) Le fonti del diritto d'impresa: un tentativo di sistema. Contr e impr 40(2):342–359
Geslevich Packin N, Alon-Beck A (2024) Board observers. Illinois Law Rev (forthcoming). (https://ssrn.com/abstract=4745278)
Hooghiemstra SN (2020) The ESG disclosure regulation–new duties for financial market participants & financial advisers. (https://ssrn.com/abstract=3558868)
Hopt KJ (2023) Corporate purpose and stakeholder value–historical, economic and comparative law remarks on the current debate, legislative options and enforcement problems. ECGI Working Paper No. 690/2023
Hummel K, Jobst D (2024) An overview of corporate sustainability reporting legislation in the European Union. Account Eur. https://ssrn.com/abstract=3978478
Irrera M, Scarabelli BM (2023) I comitati di sostenibilità nella governance delle società quotate: tra funzioni gestorie e di controllo. Il nuovo diritto delle società 11:1583–1623
Kujala J, Heikkinen A, Blomberg A (eds) (2023) Stakeholder engagement in a sustainable circular economy theoretical and practical perspectives. Palgrave Macmillan imprint, Cham
Libertini M (2023) Gestione 'sostenibile' delle imprese e limiti alla discrezionalità imprenditoriale. Contr e impr 39(1):54–87
Mähönen JT, Palea V (2024) Analyzing double materiality through the lens of the European political constitution: implications for interoperability and standards-setting. University of Oslo Faculty of Law Research Paper No. 2024–05, Nordic & European Company Law Working Paper No. 24–03. (https://ssrn.com/abstract=4731089)
Maresca A (2023) I profili lavoristici della riforma dell'art. 2086 c.c. In: Alvino I, Imberti L, Romei R (eds) La gestione dei rapporti di lavoro nelle crisi di impresa. Milano, Giuffrè, pp 105–112
Mezzanotte FE (2024) Examining the reasons for impact materiality in EU corporate sustainability reporting. Euro Bus Law Rev 35(7):925–946
Mucciarelli FM (2022) Perseguire un diritto societario 'sostenibile': un obiettivo sincero? In: Callegari M, Cerrato SA, Desana ER (eds) Governance e mercati. Studi in onore di Paolo Montalenti, Giappichelli, Torino, pp 182–193
Notary Council, Interregional Committee Tre Venezie (2024) A.B. ESG e clausole di sostenibilità. Riv soc 69(1): 153–158
Packin NG, Alon-Beck A (2024) Board observers. Illinois Law Rev (forthcoming) (https://ssrn.com/abstract=4745278) https://doi.org/10.2139/ssrn.4745278
Reich J (2024) KlimaSeniorinnen and choosing between imperfect options: incorporating international climate change law to maintain the ECHR's relevance amid the climate crisis. (https://ssrn.com/abstract=4800443)
Rescigno M (2022) Note sulle regole dell'impresa sostenibile. Dall'informazione non finanziaria all'informativa sulla sostenibilità. Age 1:165–184
Rimini E (2024) Sostenibilità e nuova governance delle imprese azionarie nel diritto interno e comunitario tra realtà, criticità e prospettive. Giur comm 51(2):I/285-301
Riolfo G (2024) L'impresa 'sostenibile'. La rilevanza esterna degli obblighi e delle responsabilità degli amministratori. Cedam-WKI, Milano
Salvioni D, Almici A (2020) Circular economy and stakeholder engagement strategy. Symphonya. Emerging Issues in Management (symphonya.unicusano.it). (https://ssrn.com/abstract=3716266)

Santagata R (2022) Intelligenza artificiale, adeguatezza degli assetti 'tecnici' e principio di precauzione nell'amministrazione delle società quotate. Riv dir impr 2:307–332
Savaresi A (2024) Verein KlimaSeniorinnen Schweiz and Others v Switzerland: making climate litigation history. (https://ssrn.com/abstract=5039605)
Scognamiglio G (2023) Il nuovo art. 2086 c.c.: la prospettiva del diritto commerciale. In: Alvino I, Imberti L, Romei R (eds) La gestione dei rapporti di lavoro nelle crisi di impresa. Giuffrè, Milano, pp 73–103
Stella Richter M Jr (1995) La collegialità del consiglio di amministrazione tra ponderazione dell'interesse sociale e composizione degli interessi sociali. In: Libonati B (ed) Amministrazione e amministratori di società per azioni. Giuffrè, Milano, pp 277–310
Stella Richter M Jr (2021) Long-termism. Riv soc 66(1):16–52
Strampelli G (2018) Knocking at the boardroom door: a transatlantic overview of director-institutional investor engagement. Law and practice. Virginia Law Bus Rev 12(2):187–241
Strampelli G (2023) ESG, disclosure di sostenibilità e stewardship, degli investitori istituzionali. Riv soc 68(4):828–846
Tedeschi C (2020) La direttiva shareholder rights II e il nuovo ruolo degli investitori istituzionali nelle società quotate: dall'attivismo all'engagement nella prospettiva di efficienza e di continuità dell'impresa. Riv dir comm 118(4):II/557-589
Tombari U (2004) La nuova struttura finanziaria della società per azioni (Corporate Governance e categorie rappresentative del fenomeno societario). Riv soc 59(5):1082–1104
Tombari U (2023) Lo 'scopo della società': significati e problemi di una categoria giuridica. Riv soc 68(2–3):338–351
Van Marcke L (2023) Who is the shareholder? The (Ir)Relevance of Introducing An EU-Harmonised Definition of 'Shareholder' in the Context of the SRD II Review Process. (forthcoming in) Tijdschrift voor Rechtspersoon en Vennootschap–Revue pratique des sociétés (TRV-RPS) (4) (https://ssrn.com/abstract=4448719)
Ventoruzzo M (2024) Osservazioni sulle conseguenze applicative dell'adozione di clausole statutarie (e di autodisciplina) sul 'successo sostenibile'. Riv soc 69(1):129–152
Zoppini A (2022) Le società 'benefit' e le società 'imprese sociali'. In: Donativi V (ed) Trattato delle società, IV. Utet giuridica-WKI, Torino, pp 1089–1106

The 'Proportionally Sustainable' Management of Companies in the Context of a Sustainable Circular Economy

Francesca Bianconi

Abstract After reconstructing the sustainable business paradigm that emerges from the multiple sources that introduce obligations towards sustainability and the circular economy, this chapter analyses the principle of proportionality in the context of company law. Focusing on the Italian legal system as a case study, this principle is investigated as a tool that could arguably become a criterion guiding the discretion of directors in making decisions that impact on sustainability issues. This analysis thus attempts to demonstrate how the proportionality criterion applied to corporate governance can contribute to the paradigm transition to a fully 'human-centred' model of sustainable development.

1 Introduction

Sustainability in its multiple meanings currently inspires the reflections of scholars in every field of knowledge. It has become such a crucial theme in political, economic and social debate that it could be defined as one of the key words of the present age. In this context, an increasingly prominent role is played by circular economy as one of the possible forms that sustainability can assume. This 'circular' and 'sustainable' revolution has also taken on a purely normative dimension. It has been included in European and national legislation aimed at fostering the transition towards a more sustainable model of economic development. In the Italian context, it has found expression also in constitutional law, with the constitutional principle

F. Bianconi (✉)
Università degli Studi di Verona, Verona, Italy
e-mail: francesca.bianconi@univr.it

B. Calabrese (ed.), *Legal Perspectives for a Sustainable Circular Economy*,
European Union and its Neighbours in a Globalized World 30,
https://doi.org/10.1007/978-3-032-07795-0_5

of the protection of the environment, biodiversity and ecosystems also in the interest of future generations.[1]

The economic paradigm shift calls for redirecting the way economic activities are conducted and governing the impact they have on both the environment and the relationships they create. It therefore calls for the direct involvement of legal instruments typical of company law. From this point of view, the debate on sustainability has been focused on three main topics: the measures to carry out effective engagement with stakeholders; the forms of reporting the results of corporate performance, also from a non-financial perspective; the duties and responsibilities of directors. In this research we will not deal specifically with sustainability reporting nor with citizens' participation in the management of companies, to which two different chapters of this volume are dedicated.[2] We will rather focus on the study of the duties of directors in relation to circular economy and to sustainability in general, using the relevant applicative framework of the Italian legal system as a case study.

Actually, the consideration of social and environmental concerns of companies in their business operations and in their relations with third parties is not new to corporate law. Indeed, the concept of corporate social responsibility (CSR) has a long history and it has been specifically investigated by scholars during the twentieth century, especially since the 1950s.[3] However, the topic has revived in the context of sustainability regulations, which have abandoned the purely voluntarist approach of CSR towards the implementation of solutions that induce companies to adopt sustainable practices.[4]

[1] See Arts. 9 and 41 of the Italian Constitution, as reformed by Constitutional Law no. 1/2020. In this sense see Cozzi (Chap. 9).

[2] See respectively Caprara (Chap. 3) and Genovese (Chap. 2).

[3] In international literature see Carroll (1999), p. 268; Latapí Agudelo et al. (2019); as well as Pollman (2021), p. 662–672, who examines the shifting debate and landscape of CSR, ESG, and their connection to compliance. In the Italian literature see Libertini (2013), p. 3–4, who traces the origin of the concept back to the 1980s in response to the absolutisation of the shareholder value theory.

[4] For an overview on the relevant legislation on sustainability within the framework of European policies see, in the most recent Italian debate, Riolfo (2024), p. 24; Montalenti (2024), p. 1190. In international literature see Busch et al. (2021), p. 19; Gortsos (2025), p. 552; Di Majo (2024), p. 207.

The evolution of the regulatory framework at the national level, following the primary input of the European legislative agenda, raised the fundamental question of how sustainability goals impact on profit-oriented management and what responsibilities result for managers. The question that animated the doctrinal debate was then whether and how the multiple pressures towards the transition to a model of (eco)sustainable development impact on the managerial duties of company directors, in particular in the conjugation of speculative objectives with 'other' interests in the strategic choices of management, and whether, therefore, all this entails a transfiguration of the traditional profit-oriented conception of the corporate purpose.[5] These fundamental questions have thus ended up reviving the wider debate on the interpretation of the corporate interest,[6] which has involved an impressive number of authoritative Italian scholars questioning whether the traditional contractualist conception of corporations should be overtaken in favour of a stakeholderist vision.[7]

We enter this debate with a very precise and much more limited focus: the principle of proportionality, as the main instrument for balancing competing interests. Through that canon of action typical of the public administration, we attempt to provide directors with an effective and objective instrument to guide them in the weighing of interests. In this sense, it could arguably act as an intermediate mechanism responding to the need to identify enforceable and binding provisions that could restrict the 'free in-sustainability'[8] of productive activities. Moreover, in this analysis, sustainability will be referred to the social and environmental profiles of companies' actions: for this reason, profiles relating to economic and financial sustainability will not be addressed.[9] Furthermore, we will deal with managerial discretion and not technical-organisational discretion,[10] since we will consider proportionality as a criterion for reviewing the company's strategic choices, in order to make them somehow 'enforceable'. Instead, we do not look at proportionality of the administrative and accounting organisational structures, where it is frequently

[5] Within the Italian debate, see for all Cian (2022), p. 101.

[6] With a certain mixture of the concepts of corporate purpose and interest. For a distinction between them see Tombari (2023), p. 348.

[7] The bibliography on the topic is now boundless. See, *ex multis*, Cerrato (2022), p. 77–83; Barcellona (2022a), p. 1–52; Id. (Barcellona 2022b), p. 87–99; Costi (2023), p. 503; Daccò (2022), p. 374–376; Tombari (2021), p. 1; *Id.* (2023), p. 338; Stanzione (2022), p. 1023; Denozza (2023), p. 308–309. One of the most famous theories advocated in literature, is the 'neo-institutionalism' or 'weak institutionalism', developed by Montalenti (2004), p. 244–245 and then revived in recent times in relation to ESG factors. It combines the 'ultimate' purpose of the company, still conceived as a profit-making purpose for the benefit of the community of shareholders, with the stakeholder perspective typical of the older institutionalist approach and brought back to attention in ESG policies. For a definition see Montalenti (2018), p. 319.

[8] The expression—as a translation of 'libera insostenibilità'—is quoted from Cian (2022), p. 103.

[9] The distinction is outlined in particular by Stella Richter jr (2021), p. 29–32.

[10] On the difference between the two concepts see Caprara (2021), p. 155.

referred to in the Commercial Law debate as a criterion implicitly stated in the duty to establish adequate organisational structures.[11]

However, this chapter is part of a broader research question aimed at identifying instruments that would contribute to the transition to a truly 'human-centred' development model.[12] From this point of view, the use of the principle of proportionality proposes to strengthen the position of stakeholders, making management decisions fully accountable. Although it does not grant instruments of direct enforcement, it could contribute to giving prominence to the position of people as such, whose needs can finally find objective consideration in management's strategic decisions.

To meet the objectives of this research, we will first summarise the main sources at European and national level that meet the requirements of the circular economy and sustainability. From this point of view, both the regulatory sources (Sect. 2) and the constraints potentially arising from self-regulation and business practices (Sect. 3) will be considered. The analysis of the regulatory context that, from a purely legal point of view, foster a sustainable development model will be functional to reconstructing both the paradigm of the sustainable corporation and the role that sustainability currently plays in the management of companies (Sect. 4). The analysis will then turn to the principle of proportionality as such, in order to clarify the meaning and practical application of this methodological criterion (Sect. 5). Building on such principle, the applicability of a proportionality criterion to guide management's discretionary decisions in the implementation of sustainable solutions and its consequences will then be illustrated (Sect. 6). Then, some considerations will be proposed relating to the impact that the proportionality principle can have from a 'human-centred' perspective (Sect. 7), followed by final conclusive remarks (Sect. 8).

[11] Referring to 'organisational' proportionality, see Luciano (2018), p. 1520–1521; Di Cataldo and Arcidiacono (2021), p. 81–82; as well as Meruzzi (2016), p. 55–59, to whom we owe, to date, one of the most in-depth and precise reflections on the application of the principle of proportionality in the configuration of the organisational, administrative and accounting structures of companies. Recognising in the principle of proportionality the operational parameter that must guide the judge in balancing the various constitutionally protected interests, the author identifies in the same principle the criterion that should guide the judge in the concrete determination of the content of the general clause of the adequacy of the structures, as suitable to allow the balancing between the interest in the freedom of economic initiative (Art. 41 of the Italian Constitution) of those who exercise the entrepreneurial activity and the interests—of equal constitutional standing, as subsumed under Arts. 41 and 47 of the Italian Constitution—of shareholders, creditors and third parties, whose protection is served by the duty to establish adequate structures.

[12] For a general review of this approach see Marzulli (Chap. 1).

2 Sustainability and Circular Economy Duties

Firstly, among the most relevant duties that European regulation has placed on the circular economy, Regulation (EU) 2024/1781 can be mentioned as one of the most important sources for the circular economy. Through this so-called 'Eco-design' Regulation, the European Union establishes a framework for setting eco-design requirements for sustainable products, moreover through a 'strong' regulatory instrument—a Regulation, as said—which prove the need for maximum and immediate harmonization of the matter. The abovementioned Regulation repeals Directive (EC) 2009/125, extending to the widest possible range of products those eco-design requirements which were initially established by the Directive with reference to energy-related products only.[13] It first outlines the regulatory framework for determining the eco-design requirements that products must meet in order to be placed on the market or put into service, leaving it to the Commission to adopt delegated acts containing technical specifications according to the nature and purpose of the product. These requirements are intended to improve the environmental sustainability characteristics of products, such as durability, reusability, reparability, energy efficiency, recyclability, and limitation of materials that pollute or damage health. The requirements must also be 'transparent, objective, proportionate and in compliance with international trade rules'.[14] The Regulation also provides for information requirements, again referring the adoption of the relevant detailed rules to the Commission, and establishes the so-called 'digital product passport'.[15] In addition, the Regulation contains provisions to avoid the destruction of unsold consumer products. The general principle is introduced whereby 'economic operators shall take necessary measures which can reasonably be expected to prevent the need to destroy unsold consumer products'.[16] This provision is particularly interesting in the context of the present analysis. In fact, unlike the previously mentioned provisions of the Regulation, it does not postulate the adoption of detailed technical rules, but introduces a general clause of necessity-adequacy that calls into question an assessment, clearly discretionary, by the economic operator itself on which measures are appropriate for the purpose. However, despite the differences that can be found among specific duties and general provisions, the whole set of regulatory acts that

[13] See Recitals 5 and 13, Regulation (EU) 2024/1781. The Regulation applies to any physical goods placed on the market or put into service, including components and intermediate products, with the exception of those listed in Art. 1(2) of the same Regulation.

[14] See Recital 16, Regulation EU 2024/1781.

[15] See Arts. 7 and 9, Regulation EU 2024/1781.

[16] See Art. 23 Regulation EU 2024/1781; furthermore, the following Art. 24 introduces a duty of transparency regarding the volumes of unsold and destroyed products, with an indication of the reasons for disposal and the measures taken and planned to prevent it. It should be noted that the economic operator is defined in Art. 2(46) of the same Regulation as 'the manufacturer, the authorised representative, the importer, the distributor, the dealer and the fulfilment service provider'.

concretise the European effort on circular economy prescribes new constraints and obligations towards the 'sustainable' action of companies.[17]

Indeed, from this point of view, it might be recalled that EU legislation itself defines a precise relationship between circular economy and sustainability, through the provisions of the Regulation (EU) 2020/852, known as the Taxonomy Regulation.[18] The Regulation is part of the action plan to finance sustainable growth, launched by the European Commission in 2018 and aimed inter alia at directing capital flows towards sustainable investments.[19] The Taxonomy Regulation sets out 'the criteria for determining whether an economic activity qualifies as environmentally sustainable for the purposes of establishing the degree to which an investment is environmentally sustainable'.[20] It has a fundamental systematic value within the framework of the rules on sustainable finance, because it introduces a common concept of environmentally sustainable investment, which should be adhered to by Member States and the European Union, from a regulatory point of view; by financial market participants and issuers, in order to label financial products or corporate bonds traded as environmentally sustainable; as well as by companies subject to the obligation to publish a declaration (including a consolidated declaration) of a non-financial character, which shall include 'information on how and to what extent the undertaking's activities are associated with economic activities that qualify as environmentally sustainable'.[21]

Therefore, this Regulation in itself is part of the framework of sustainable finance and sustainability disclosure. However, it ultimately displays a much broader function. In fact, it identifies the environmental impacts on which the eco-sustainable feature of an activity or investment is based. In its taxonomy can thus be found the

---

[17] It is not possible to mention here all the EU legislation, which consists of a multitude of regulations imposing circularity and sustainability duties. Among the most recent and discussed interventions there is Directive (EU) 2024/1799 (regarding the so-called 'Right to Repair'), establishing common rules promoting the repair of goods, whose scope and effectiveness about the relevant critical issues of intellectual property and servitization is specifically reviewed by Calabrese (Chap. 6). Furthermore, there is Directive (EU) 2024/825 (so called 'Greenwashing Directive'), which places constraints and limits on the use of labels, sustainability marks and environmental and sustainability claims in general: this aims to protect consumers from misleading marketing practices and to help them make more informed purchasing choices, save some systemic critics to its underlying approach as highlighted by De Vido (Chap. 12); in a certain sense, it can be said that the Greenwashing Directive is complementary to the reporting obligations concerning sustainability, in order to empower consumers and involve them in the green transition, guaranteeing them access to correct information regarding the environmental and social characteristics of products and business activities: for a wider analysis of the EU legal framework about corporate sustainability reporting, in addition to what will be cited after, see extensively Genovese (Chap. 2).

[18] Regulation (EU) 2020/852, on the establishment of a framework to facilitate sustainable investment.

[19] European Commission, Action Plan: Financing Sustainable Growth, COM(2018) 97 final.

[20] Art. 1(1), as well as Recital 6, Regulation EU 2020/852. On the crucial role of the Taxonomy Regulation in the framework of EU law following the 2018 action plan see Genovese (2023b), p. 78 where she defines it as the cornerstone of the relevant EU regulatory action.

[21] Art. 8, Regulation EU 2020/852, whose normative scope is generally clarified in its Art. 1(2).

legal reference to the objectives that confer a normative qualification of eco-sustainability to economic activities that pursues them.[22]

This is even more relevant in the context of this investigation, because in establishing the unified classification system of eco-sustainable activities, it draws a link between sustainability and circular economy. In fact, it draws up a list of environmental objectives (six altogether) that are instrumental in determining the eco-sustainability of a given economic activity. The six environmental objectives covered by the regulation are, specifically: 'climate change mitigation; climate change adaptation; the sustainable use and protection of water and marine resources; the transition to a circular economy; pollution prevention and control; and the protection and restoration of biodiversity and ecosystems'.[23] In the taxonomy outlined by the Regulation, the transition to the circular economy is stated as one of the environmental objectives that economic activities can pursue in order to qualify as 'environmentally sustainable'. It then represents the connection between circular economy and sustainability, identifying the relationship—from means to end—that links the two concepts. Thus, an enterprise (and the investment in the enterprise) that substantially contributes to the transition to the circular economy, without significantly harming any other of the environmental objectives, can be considered environmentally sustainable.[24]

Broadening our view to the more general aspects of sustainability, we can then recall the Union's first (and perhaps most relevant) line of action, concerning sustainability reporting. The guiding regulation is currently set by the Corporate Sustainability Reporting Directive, Directive (EU) 2022/2464 ('CSRD'), on corporate sustainability reporting, in force since 1 January 2024. The latter replaced the non-financial reporting governed by the Directive (EC) 2014/95 (Non-Financial Reporting Directive, 'NFRD'), introducing several and significant innovations. The new form of reporting shows a broader scope of application, now involving not only larger companies, but also the SMEs that are 'public-interest entities'.[25] In addition, the Directive provides for the possibility of voluntary subjection for unlisted SMEs, which are themselves not obliged to this form of reporting.[26] Moreover, unlike its predecessor the CSRD identifies a uniform European reporting standard,

---

[22] See expressly Genovese (2023b), p. 86, who concludes that the Taxonomy Regulation can be considered as the real EU source of the normative standards for eco-sustainability of productive activities.

[23] Recital 23, then reproduced in Art. 9(d), Regulation EU 2020/852.

[24] Provided that the activity is carried out in compliance with the minimum guarantees of Art. 13, Regulation EU 2020/852, and complies with any technical screening criteria specified by the Commission.

[25] Art. 2(1), Directive (EU) 2013/34 as amended by Directive (EU) 2022/2464. However, the new obligations will apply gradually, starting with large public interest companies and extending to smaller companies at a later stage, in compliance with the spirit of proportionality.

[26] Recital 21, Directive (EU) 2022/2464. In this case, the simplified standards for SMEs are applied according to the principle of proportionality. See Genovese (2023a), p. 103; Riolfo (2024), p. 45–46 and 51.

overcoming the drawbacks of the absence of a uniform standard in the drafting of the non-financial report.[27]

The most relevant aspect for our aim concerns the content of the report, which includes what is necessary to illustrate the undertaking's impact on sustainability matters, as well as conversely how sustainability issues affect the undertaking's development, performance and position (so-called dual materiality). Thus, reporting requires transparency as to the policies adopted and actions taken to assess, monitor, manage and mitigate the negative impacts of their activities. This issue is particularly important from the perspective of the proportionality test, given that the parameters to be taken into account in the proportionality assessment are embodied in these profiles.

While the CSRD (as well as the Taxonomy Regulation) focuses on disclosure issues,[28] true behavioral duties are imposed by Directive (EU) 2024/1760, so-called Corporate Sustainability Due Diligence Directive ('CSDD'). It was finally adopted after a long legislative process, which was characterized by multiple revisions and rethinks.[29] The Directive targets larger firms and it is expected to begin to apply gradually starting in 2027, unless further extensions are granted.[30] As the European Commission underlines, 'the aim of this Directive is to foster sustainable and responsible corporate behaviour in companies' operations and across their global value chains. The new rules will ensure that companies in scope identify and address

[27] See Recital 13, Directive (EU) 2022/2464. The first set of European Sustainability Reporting Standards (ESRS) developed by EFRAG were adopted by Commission Delegated Regulation (EU) 2023/2772. For a general overview see Ponzio and Carlino (2024); Zaniboni and Caristia (2024); Verrascina and Pecoraio (2024).

[28] See Recital 3, Directive (EU) 2014/95. Transparency obligations only indirectly orient corporate management towards the adoption of specific environmental or social sustainability policies. In literature see Szabó and Sørensen (2015), p. 316; Strampelli (2023), p. 829. It should be noted that an even stronger role is acknowledged to disclosure by Genovese (2022), p. 531, as interpreted in the light of Articles 9 and 41 of the Constitution and the Taxonomy Regulation, would bind corporate governance in a sustainable sense.

[29] By the way, further reconsideration seems on the agenda in the new mandate of the European Commission after the recent political elections, since it has adopted a package of proposals to simplify EU rules in particular in the fields of sustainable finance reporting, sustainability due diligence and EU Taxonomy. See European Commission, Proposal for a Directive of the European Parliament and of the Council amending Directives 2006/43/EC, 2013/34/EU, (EU) 2022/2464 and (EU) 2024/1760 as regards certain corporate sustainability reporting and due diligence requirements, COM(2025) 81 final.

[30] Its scope is set in Art. 2 of Directive EU 2024/1760. The recently approved text provides for considerably higher thresholds than those initially envisaged in the first drafts. Subsequent amendments have thus greatly weakened the scope of application of the Directive, which will be fully applied only in 2029 for a small number of companies. For more details see Addamo (2024), p. 1262–1264; Baltrunaite et al. (2024), para. 1–2. However, as regards the dates of application of the Directives, the European Commission has recently proposed postponing the entry into application of the CSDDD and of certain provisions of the CSRD. See European Commission, Proposal for a Directive of the European Parliament and of the Council amending Directives (EU) 2022/2464 and (EU) 2024/1760 as regards the dates from which Member States are to apply certain corporate sustainability reporting and due diligence requirements, COM(2025) 80 final.

adverse human rights and environmental impacts of their actions inside and outside Europe'.[31] For this aim, the Directive establishes obligations and consequent liabilities in relation to negative impacts on human rights and the environment.

Thus, firstly, it fixes 'rules on obligations for companies regarding actual and potential human rights adverse impacts and environmental adverse impacts, with respect to their own operations, the operations of their subsidiaries, and the operations carried out by their business partners in the chains of activities of those companies'.[32] Those obligations are summarised in the 'risk-based due diligence duty'. The latter requires that companies integrate due diligence into all their relevant policies and risk management systems and take appropriate measures to identify, assess, prevent and mitigate both potential and actual negative impacts on human rights and the environment within the activity of companies and their business partners.[33]

Secondly, the Directive provides for corporate liability for violations of such obligations. In particular, corporate sustainability due diligence duties will be enforced both through the administrative supervision of the competent authorities designated by Member States and the civil liability of companies, that will be held liable to compensate for damages resulting from an intentional or negligent failure to carry out due diligence.[34]

Furthermore, the Directive sets out an additional set of obligations for companies falling within its scope. Thus, companies will have not only to perform due diligence on business partners, to monitor and to assess the current and potential negative effects of their activities and those of their supply chain, but also to activate complaint procedures open to third parties, to prepare transition plans for climate change mitigation,[35] and, last but not least, to implement governance structures with stakeholder involvement procedures.[36]

---

[31] European Commission, webpage 'Corporate sustainability due diligence' (https://commission.europa.eu/business-economy-euro/doing-business-eu/sustainability-due-diligence-responsible-business/corporate-sustainability-due-diligence_en)

[32] See Art. 1(a), Directive (EU) 2024/1760.

[33] The emphasis on risk analysis is characteristic of the latest approved version of the Directive, which did not feature in the earlier proposals. Among the most recent comments on the Directive, from the national perspective, see Addamo (2024) 1265; Baltrunaite et al. (2024), para. 2; as well as Corgatelli (2024), p. 13–39.

[34] See Arts. 24–28 and 29, Directive (EU) 2024/1760. For further explanation and references see Addamo (2024), p. 1283–1286; Baltrunaite et al. (2024), para. 2.1–2.2; Corgatelli (2024), p. 39–46.

[35] See Art. 22, Directive (EU) 2024/1760.

[36] See Recital 65, as well as Arts. 7(2) and 13, Directive (EU) 2024/1760.

3 'Voluntary' Alignment with Sustainability Goals: Statutory Autonomy, Corporate Governance Codes and the Influence of Institutional Investors

Constraints on the sustainable (or environmentally sustainable) management of companies can, however, also come from sources that are not strictly legislative. Actually, in this matter a strong conditioning towards the voluntary adoption of a sustainable development model may come from the 'context' in which companies operate, which must then be taken into account for a deeper understanding of the phenomenon.[37]

In this sense, a fundamental role can be played by private and statutory autonomy itself. A first solution to make the pursuit of common-benefit purposes compulsory is the possibility of adopting, in the Italian regulatory panorama, a corporate model that is legislatively obliged to pursue (also) non-profit purposes, like the so-called benefit corporation.[38] However, apart from the adoption of corporate models that are already normatively hinged on purposes of collective benefit,[39] there is now a deep awareness of the plurality of instruments available to shareholders to align company management with ESG objectives. In addition to the possibility of binding management with statutory sustainability clauses[40] and codes of conduct,[41] the environmental and social policies of directors can, for example, be strongly conditioned by the remuneration policy practised by shareholders, where the variable part of the remuneration is linked to the achievement of sustainability objectives.[42]

Looking at further sources, including non-mandatory or soft law ones, significant attention to social and environmental dynamics emerges first and foremost

---

[37] The need to consider the reality of the functioning of companies as well as markets is emphasised by Montalenti (2024), p. 1191.

[38] Introduced into the Italian legal order by Law no. 208/2015, benefit corporations are defined in Art. 1(376), as those corporations that, in carrying out an economic activity, in addition to the purpose of dividing its profits, pursue one or more purposes of common benefit and operate in a responsible, sustainable and transparent manner towards people, communities, territories and the environment, cultural and social goods and activities, bodies and associations and other stakeholders. For a description of the model see *ex multis* Rescio (2022); Angelici (2017); Marasà (2017); Mosco (2018); as well as Butturini (2022), p. 1–33.

[39] A different phenomenon, although also well known in the Italian legal system, is that of the non-profit collective enterprise, carried out by so-called Social Enterprises or Third Sector Entities, within the limits established by Legislative Decrees no. 112/2017 and 117/2017 respectively. For a general overview of the phenomenon see Marcelli (2018), p. 123–154; Marasà (2023); Cetra (2019); as well as, in a broader perspective, Cetra (2003).

[40] They are expressly held to be legitimate by the Comitato interregionale dei Consigli Notarili delle Tre Venezie, in its Corporate Guidelines on ESG, available via https://www.notaitriveneto.it/dettaglio-massime-triveneto-300-esg-e-clausole-di-sostenibilita.html. See Ventoruzzo (2024).

[41] The practise of formalising the ethical standards that the company wants to pursue in corporate documents such as codes of ethics and codes of conduct, to ensure uniformity in the organisation and over time, is emphasised by Ferrarini (2023), p. 328.

[42] Ballerini and Sacchi (2023), p. 1468.

from corporate governance codes.[43] In the Italian context, the new Corporate Governance Code is prominent, since in its 2020 edition it introduced the concept of 'sustainable success', defining it as an objective that guides the action of the board of directors and that is substantiated by the creation of long-term value for the benefit of shareholders, taking into account the interests of other stakeholders relevant to the company.[44] The concept is then reiterated among its principles, affirming that the board of directors shall lead the company by pursuing its sustainable success.[45] Sustainable success is therefore assumed in this self-regulatory code as the primary goal of the management board, but it actually affects the entire corporate governance. In fact, the management remuneration policy must be oriented towards sustainable success.[46] Furthermore, the set of rules, procedures and organisational structures that constitute the internal control and risk management system must contribute to it.[47] The provisions of such self-regulatory code echo formulations already known in the international regulatory panorama.[48] They absorb the conception of sustainability as a 'game changer' in the conduct of business by boards of directors.[49]

In this complex regulatory universe, an important indirect pressure towards the adoption of a sustainable business model can finally come from institutional investors and the financial market, as can also be seen from the transparency regulation introduced by the EU with Regulation (EU) 2019/2088, so-called Sustainable Finance Disclosure Regulation ('SFDR'), in force since 10 March 2021 (together with the aforementioned Taxonomy Regulation). It establishes harmonised transparency rules on the integration of sustainability risks and the consideration of adverse sustainability effects in investment advice and portfolio management decision-making processes. The aim of this Regulation is to broaden and standardise the information provided to investors in relation to financial products with

[43] Rolli (2020), p. 57–69. On the level of integration of sustainability in Corporate Governance Codes among European Countries see the analysis carried out by Siri and Zhu (2021), p. 175.

[44] Italian Corporate Governance Committee, Corporate Governance Code, January 2020 (https://www.borsaitaliana.it/comitato-corporate-governance/codice/codice.htm) addressed to all companies listed on the Italian Stock Exchange 'Borsa Italiana'. For a general overview see Marchetti (2020), p. 272–273; Ginevra (2023), p. 1038.

[45] Art. 1, Principle I, Corporate Governance Code.

[46] Art. 5, Principle XV and Reccomendations 27(c), Corporate Governance Code.

[47] Art. 6, Principle XVIII, Corporate Governance Code.

[48] For a comparative analysis on how Corporate Codes address sustainability among European Countries see Siri and Zhu (2021), p. 201–205 and 221, where they finally notice 'that a growing number of codes tend to mention sustainability, CSR, social, and environmental issues, so signaling a growing interest towards the impact of environmental and social factors on business success in the long term'. The provisions of the Italian Corporate Governance Code are modelled, in particular, on those of the UK Corporate Governance Code. Similar normative provisions can be found in Art. 1833(2) of the French Civil Code, integrated by Law no. 019–486 of 22 May 2019 on the growth and transformation of companies, known as 'Loi PACTE', as well as in the Section 172(1) of the 2006 UK Companies Act, as highlighted by Ferrarini (2023), p. 329–330.

[49] Again Ferrarini (2023), p. 329.

environmental or social characteristics or which have a sustainable objective.[50] However, through a more penetrating disclosure of institutional investors' investment policies based on ESG factors, the aim is to influence the management of companies in the direction of sustainability.[51] European policies direct capital towards sustainable investments and can therefore be an 'element of persuasion' for companies to take a green turn and operate sustainably.[52]

In any case, and regardless of any disclosure or transparency obligations, institutional investors have so far been increasingly concerned about the sustainability profiles considered by investee or 'target' companies in their social management.[53] ESG issues have been increasingly taken into account in the investment policies of large institutional investors,[54] which, in order to maximise the value of their portfolios, have been concerned about environmental and social risks as systematic risks capable of affecting the financial stability of almost all the companies they finance.[55] Yet, although driven by financial reasons, the concern for the environmental and social impact of companies is capable of constraining, in this case directly, the operations of companies, requiring them to take environmental and social risks into account when developing their business policies and strategies.

4 Corporate Management and the New Paradigm of 'Sustainable Undertaking'

What we have seen so far highlights the plurality of 'theoretical concepts' and 'practical tools' through which sustainability can enter corporate governance.[56] Sustainability has penetrated European policies and national legal systems, imposing new constraints and obligations on companies to move towards an (environmentally) sustainable business model. Nevertheless, it still seems difficult to establish definitely and certainly whether, how and to what extent company directors should

[50] See Balp and Strampelli (2022), p. 878–880.

[51] Strampelli (2023), p. 828. See also Riolfo (2024), p. 59–61 and 67–68.

[52] Riolfo (2024), p. 67–68.

[53] Balp and Strampelli (2022), p. 878.

[54] Notorious is Larry Fink's 2020 letter to investors, where the CEO of Black Rock has recognized the defining impact of climate change on companies' long-term prospects and he has consequently announced the necessity to place sustainability at the centre of BlackRock investment approach. See Fink (2020).

[55] Giudici (2023), p. 827. The economic literature has been considering climate change as a financial risk since the 1980s, as illustrated by Bruno (2019), p. 688. Moreover, it should be noted that the impact of climate risks on the financial sector is also being addressed by the ECB, that decided to expand its work on climate change to face the effect of climate change and nature degradation on the economy and financial system, as well as on the ECB's own exposure to related risks. See European Central Bank (2024).

[56] Ferrarini (2023), p. 337.

consider environmental protection and social concerns when defining company strategies. In fact, reflections on sustainability in and of the business face multiple difficulties, arising from the stratification of national, European and international hard and soft law regulations; from the intersection of strictly legal profiles with economic and cultural considerations; and from the need to ensure the consistency of solutions with respect to the fundamental principles of the enterprise. Moreover, the issue is even more complex today, given that if up to now the European legislator has maintained a straight line towards the goal of green transition (albeit at a 'variable speed', we might say), recent developments in the international scenarios seem to open up doubts as to a possible *revirement.*[57] In such a context, it is then not surprising that there are ambiguous answers in the literature to the questions posed by sustainability, and indeed there are bitter contrasts between interpreters.

However, the sustainability legislation implemented so far seems to affect the management of companies and the content of directors' duties, without changing the purpose of the company. Directors are now called upon on several grounds to 'take into account' the environmental and social impact of their business activities. A definitive step in this direction was taken with the CSDD, which made immediately mandatory the sustainable management of the company, the binding nature of which had been excluded by the majority doctrine before the adoption of the Directive.[58]

However, this does not mean that the corporate purpose is coloured with social connotations.[59] The model that emerges from the multiple regulatory sources referred to (as well as the financial considerations that drive institutional investors) seems rather in line with the enlightened shareholder value theory. The ultimate purpose is and remains profit-making, but in the pursuit of profits the corporate management should find a limit in the need to consider the social and environmental impact of their strategies.[60] In the complex regulatory panorama outlined before, a sustainable business model seems to be emerging (at least with respect to the large joint-stock company), where companies retain their profit-making purpose and are still aimed at producing profits and remunerating the capital invested by shareholders, but in their business activities they must set up specific internal procedures—

---

[57] The need for simplification in the fields of sustainable finance reporting, sustainability due diligence and taxonomy is underlined by the European Commission itself in its latest Communication, 29 January 2025, A Competitiveness Compass for the EU, COM(2025) 30 final, p. 17–18. On the change of approach to ESG issues in the US see Stewart (2025); Wyderka and Egan (2025). A significant shift away from ESG is expected at the SEC as well, as stated by Breheny et al. (2025).

[58] See for all Libertini (2013), p. 80–83. Furthermore, although the distinguished author agrees with the thesis that ESG management criteria are only transposed into law as a principle and not as binding rules of conduct, he believes that the approval of the CSDD Directive may result in a timely duty to comply with these management criteria.

[59] The economic function of the enterprise is not changed, nor is it entrusted with tasks historically belonging to the state. See Tombari (2023), p. 135.

[60] The same duty is stated by Cerrato (2022), p. 109; as well as, more recently, by Cerrato and Sartoretti (2024), p. 1209, on the basis of the principle of solidarity under Article 2 of the Italian Constitution.

which we could define as environmental and social risk management—to ensure that management choices take into account the impacts generated by the activity on the environment and human rights.[61]

The European paradigm of the sustainable undertaking is therefore that of an undertaking that is not expected to abandon profit and pursue altruistic interests, but that is obliged to take into consideration the negative impacts of its activities on third parties. The paradigm has been summarised in Italian doctrine with the effective periphrasis 'from profit at any cost to dutiful consideration of the costs of profit'.[62] Therefore, on closer inspection, the new obligations do not alter the purpose but the proceedings of the functional action of the directors of the company.[63] This means that the obligations relating to ecological transition and respect for human rights draw limits to the directors' discretion as to how to realise the corporate purpose, while the ultimate purpose of their action remains unchanged.[64]

Furthermore, this view seems to be in line with the structure that the relationship between freedom of economic initiative and environmental protection has found in the new Art. 41 of the Italian Constitution. The norm now states that private economic initiative may not be carried out in conflict with social utility or in such a way as to damage health, the environment, security, freedom and human dignity and may be directed and coordinated for social and environmental purposes. The rule actually sets a limit in principle, which needs legislative implementation to become directly binding on the private individual. In this sense, however, it may find an elective field of application in general clauses.[65] But regardless of its 'mediated' or 'immediate' effectiveness, the rule establishes environmental protection as an explicit limit to economic initiative. The environment, as well as health, safety, freedom and human dignity, does not imply a functionalisation of the enterprise, but allows limits to be placed on the freedom of economic initiative.[66]

It would therefore seem that (at least as regards companies that are directly addressed by the regulatory provisions or soft law acts referred to, and therefore essentially medium-large companies) social management must be oriented (also) towards sustainability, but not in a finalistic sense, but rather in the *modus*

[61] The statement is made in Italian by Riolfo (2024), p. 86–87. Similarly, De Mari (2023), p. 877–881.

[62] Literally '*dal profitto ad ogni costo alla doverosa considerazione dei costi del profitto*', as affirmed by Riolfo (2024), p. 90. The Corporate Governance Code is also emblematic in this respect, with its new concept of 'sustainable success' as 'the creation of long-term value while taking into account the interests of other stakeholders relevant to society'.

[63] See expressly Genovese (2023b), p. 132.

[64] Addamo (2024), p. 1296.

[65] Libertini (2013), p. 73. However, see Genovese (2023b), p. 107; Cerrato (2022), p. 108–109, who postulate a direct application of the rule in relations between private individuals (*Drittwirkung*), albeit with different positions; as well as, more recently, Cerrato and Sartoretti (2024), p. 1208–1211.

[66] Bifulco (2022), p. 23; Zorzi Galgano (2023), p. 452. To the contrary, Pennasilico (2024), p. 79–80 for whom the new Arts. 9 and 41 of the Italian Constitution prelude a 'functionalisation of the enterprise', as a compulsory conformation of the undertaking's economic activity to the constitutional values enshrined therein.

operandi.[67] However, the step towards the generalisation of the duty to all companies does not seem so remote, given that the change that has taken place in the current regulatory framework and all the considerations made so far on the 'context' in which the regulatory constraints find their genesis and development seem to find expression in the principles of proper administration.

If, as demonstrated in doctrine, the principles of proper administration are aimed at aligning corporate management with the objective of the company's permanence in the context in which it operates, such a context clearly cannot be overlooked in the management of companies. It follows that the environmental impact of the company and, conversely, the impact that 'external' environmental factors (such as environmental risk, ecological transition and climate change) play on the company must be considered in management.[68]

This assertion can be supported by the economic considerations that have led large investors to turn to sustainability: if climate change is a risk factor for profitability and for the very survival of the company, it must be considered from the perspective of proper company management. At least in the 'outside-in' perspective, i.e. from the point of view of the financial impact that climate change and changes in the environment have on companies.[69]

However, the indication that comes from European sources, especially from the reporting perspective of the so-called dual materiality, requires a much broader horizon. In this sense, companies are called upon not only to consider the consequences that climatic and environmental factors have on their business activity, but also the impact that the latter generates on the surrounding environment ('inside-out' perspective).[70] This therefore leads to a rethinking of the interaction between business and the environment. When read as factors linked 'in a double thread', the

[67] See, even before the approval of the CSDD, Genovese (2023b), p. 144; Rolli (2021), p. 125. However, this intermediate conclusion is not unanimously shared in doctrine. To the contrary, see e.g. Boggio and Pinto (2024), p. 1242.

[68] Caprara (2021), p. 71. See also Genovese (2023b), p. 131, that arguing from the duty to establish adequate organisational structures also in function of the timely detection of the crisis (under Art. 2086 of the Italian Civil Code), on the one hand, and from the fact that the physical and transitional risks and ESG opportunities related to climate change are relevant as an exogenous factor (i.e. the context in which the economic initiative is deployed), on the other hand, states that because of the context, it is the same corporate legislation that requires directors to deal—in a managerial way—with certain profiles of environmental sustainability of the activity. That requires them to plan management with reference to the temporal horizon of the ecological transition, of the regulation related to it, and of climate change.

[69] The 'financial materiality' (outside-in perspective) concerns the financial effects that sustainability issues may have on the enterprise. In this sense, the sustainability issue is relevant if it generates risks and opportunities that have, or can have, a relevant influence on the development of the enterprise. See Verrascina and Pecoraio (2024), p. 31 and 35; Ponzio and Carlino (2024), p. 37–39.

[70] The 'impact materiality' (inside-out perspective) concerns the company's significant environmental, social and governance impacts on people or the environment, whether negative or positive, actual or potential, and whether in short, medium or long term. See again Verrascina and Pecoraio (2024), p. 31 and 35; Ponzio and Carlino (2024), p. 37–39.

survival of one is a *sine qua non* of the survival of the other and they must therefore be integrated into the management of companies in a long-term perspective.

To sum up, on the basis of both the review of the legislation carried out and the opinion that is becoming more and more consolidated in the literature, it seems possible to conclude that, in the creation of shareholder value (the ultimate profit purpose), companies can no longer disregard the local communities and groups (stakeholders) that gravitate around their activity, as well as their environmental impact.[71] Today, the perspective of sustainability is not entirely left to the discretion of directors.[72] Therefore, the failure or inadequate consideration of 'other' interests in management may result in a breach of fiduciary duties.[73]

However, even adhering to the idea of the existence of (also) environmental duties of directors, the parameters for assessing whether such duties have been breached remain to be clarified. We wonder what it means from the point of view of the directors to 'take into account' the social and environmental impact of the activity. In particular, we feel the need for a tool to assess whether the directors' decision is appropriate to the interests involved in the company's activity, in order to avoid: on the one hand, that the definition of over-general environmental duties disproportionately broadens the directors' discretion, making any strategic choice unquestionable[74]; and, on the other hand, that the vague protection of stakeholders' interests ends up allowing the judge to interfere in the composition of interests with the consequence of judicial 'over-power' in the resolution of conflicts between companies and stakeholders.[75] These risks are clearly revealed in some recent case law that have had considerable resonance in the doctrinal debate and that demonstrate the difficulties judges themselves experience in reviewing the decisions of directors in this matter.[76]

---

[71] About the possible relevance in corporate governance of citizens as stakeholders see Caprara (Chap. 3).

[72] Rolli (2021), p. 123.

[73] Tombari (2023), p. 140.

[74] It is the concern, for example, of Stabilini and Denozza (2008), para. 5, quoted by Ballerini and Sacchi (2023), p. 1466.

[75] See the opinion by Libertini, expressed in Perrone (2019), p. 602.

[76] The first case that comes to mind is of course the case ClientEarth v. Shell, decided by the High Court of Justice of London, 12 May 2023, as the first case of an action brought against the directors personally. In that case, Judge Tower denied permission to continue the derivative action brought by ClientEarth, finding it to be 'inconsistent with the well-established principle that it is for directors themselves to determine (acting in good faith) how best to promote the success of a company for the benefit of its members as a whole. (…) The weighing of all these considerations [as set out in s.172] is essentially a commercial decision, which the court is ill-equipped to take, except in a clear case'. The same principles were further confirmed following the oral hearing requested by ClientEarth, in which the permission to proceed with the filed action was definitively denied: see High Court of Justice of London, 24 July 2023, available via: https://www.judiciary.uk/judgments/clientearth-v-shell/. The difficulty of achieving a review with respect to the valuations made by the directors also emerges in Milieudefensie et al. v. Royal Dutch Shell Plc, first decided in The Hague District Court, 26 May 2021, ECLI:NL:GHDHA:2024:2100, and then reformed on appeal by The Hague Court of Appeal, 12 November 2024, ECLI:NL:RBDHA:2021:5339, available via: https://

5 The Principle of Proportionality in its General Relevance

Actually, the legal system already knows an effective tool for governing discretion in the exercise of so-called 'functionalised powers', i.e. powers designed towards a purpose (regardless of what that purpose is). It is enough to look just beyond the borders of the Commercial Law to realise how the problem of balancing interests in the exercise of discretionary powers has been thoroughly investigated, for example in public law, where it is addressed in particular by the principle of proportionality.[77]

The principle of proportionality (in its technical sense, associated with the particular three-phase scrutiny to be seen shortly after) has been shaped in EU law. It was first established in the case law of the EU Court of Justice as a general principle (derived from the German legal system) and then codified in 1992 with the Maastricht Treaty.[78] In its current version, Article 5(4) TEU states 'under the principle of proportionality, the content and form of Union action shall not exceed what is necessary to achieve the objectives of the Treaties'. The principle requires that the authorities may not impose, either by administrative or regulatory acts, obligations or restrictions on fundamental freedoms that are greater (disproportionate, precisely) than what is necessary to achieve the purpose pursued by the authority itself.

In the Italian legal system, the principle has received much attention in administrative law.[79] In this context, it imposes on the public administration the duty to weigh the multiple interests, public and private, involved in the exercise of its powers. The essential characteristic of this principle is to practise a balancing exercise between an interest or objective pursued through the adoption of a measure and the negative effects it entails.[80]

Trying therefore to identify what is proper to the meaning of proportionality, abstracting from the concrete applications and parameters that may come into

---

uitspraken.rechtspraak.nl/details?id=ECLI:NL:RBDHA:2021:5339. At first instance Shell (both directly and via its whole group) was ordered 'to limit or cause to be limited the aggregate annual volume of all CO2 emissions into the atmosphere (Scope 1, 2 and 3) due to the business operations and sold energy-carrying products of the Shell group to such an extent that this volume will have reduced by at least net 45% at end 2030, relative to 2019 levels'. However, the Court of Appeal quashed the previous judgement, because, 'however much Shell may be required to do its part in combating dangerous climate change, the available figures do not provide the court with sufficient support to oblige Shell to reduce its CO2 emissions by a certain percentage in 2030' (point 7.96). So, in this case, the Court shows a sort of self-restraint, denying the possibility for a Court to determine what specific reduction obligation can apply to a specific company.

[77] See *ex multis* Medda (2022), p. 77–78; Caringella (2021), p. 950; Scoca (2017), p. 209–210; Chieppa and Lopilato (2007), p. 293.

[78] See *ex multis* Van Den Brink et al. (2015), p. 186–187; Baruffi (2014), p. 25; Sauter (2013), p. 8–9; Galetta (2017), p. 153–154.

[79] Especially since the 1990s, when it began to be used in law and in the judicial scrutiny of the administrative judge. See Galetta (2017), p. 166.

[80] Tridimas (2006), p. 139.

consideration from time to time,[81] it can be said that it demands measures to be adopted to be calibrated with reference to the objective, so that they are not excessively restrictive with respect to the opposing right or interest. It introduces a limit to the intensity of (public) intervention, in that it requires that the exercise of (public, both legislative and administrative) power, affecting fundamental rights or private interests, contain its action within the boundaries of what is strictly necessary to pursue the objective of its action.[82] This essential core of proportionality is expressed by an effective formula developed in the European context, whereby 'the principle of proportionality prohibits the use of a steam hammer to crack a nut if a nutcracker would do it'.[83] Therefore, with respect to the public administration, it represents, first and foremost, a canon of action to which the administration must adhere in the exercise of public power, so as to ensure that the decision concretely taken is not disproportionate, i.e. excessive, with respect to the set of interests relevant to the decision to be taken.

In its 'technical' sense,[84] however, the principle is also associated with a particular criterion of scrutiny, the criterion of proportionality, which has been developed by European jurisprudence, in the wake of German jurisprudence. In its procedural moment, the principle is applied through an assessment that develops in three consecutive stages.[85] The first moment of the assessment concerns the so-called suitability of the measure (*Geeignetheit*), i.e. its capacity to permit the attainment of the aim, according to an *ex ante* perspective. The contested measure may be censured from the point of view of unsuitability, in particular if at the time of the decision it already appeared to be useless for the satisfaction of the interest targeted, in the light of the concrete circumstances.[86] The second step deals with the necessity test (*Erforderlichkeit*), according to which a certain act or measure can be said to be necessary when it enables the objective to be achieved with the least possible sacrifice of the right or interest affected by the exercise of power: when it is the 'least available means'. In this second test, a comparative assessment is introduced between the different options abstractly suitable for pursuing the aim. Such a comparison presupposes, firstly, that there may abstractly be a plurality of means suitable for achieving the goal. Further, that the several measures under evaluation may be equally effective in satisfying the objective: it requires opting for the least restric-

[81] In fact, it is only in its concrete application that one can identify the parameters to which the balancing act concretely refers, which can be the most varied, depending also on the sector in which the principle is referred to.

[82] This definition is usually used in doctrine to describe the principle in general terms. See Tridimas (2006), p. 140; Galetta (2019), p. 908.

[83] It is about Lord Diplock's famous aphorism, in UK House of Lords, 20 January 1983, as quoted by Emiliou (1996), p. 2; Van Den Brink, Den Ouden, Prechal, Widdershoven and Jans (2015), p. 197.

[84] Trimarchi Banfi (2016), p. 378.

[85] For a general overview see Jans (2000), p. 243–249; Van Den Brink, Den Ouden, Prechal, Widdershoven and Jans (2015), p. 189–191; Trimarchi Banfi (2016), p. 372–376; Galetta (2012), p. 390–393;

[86] Emiliou (1996), p. 26 and 191; Tridimas (2006), p. 144.

tive alternative, given the same result.[87] The third and final test is that of proportionality in the strict sense (*Verhältnismäßigkeit im engeren Sinne*), aimed at verifying that the measure, even if appropriate and necessary, is nevertheless not intolerable, since the costs or sacrifices involved are not excessive in relation to the benefit produced. In the light of this assessment, it is required that the more incisive the measure is with respect to the opposing interest, the greater must be the benefit obtained.[88]

These three criteria are traditionally described by the literature in a procedural sequence, according to a somehow 'scholastic' view[89] but certainly useful for reconstructing the prescriptive content of the principle. However, they are not always included in the judges' evaluations. On the contrary, deliberations usually stop at the second test, which is the true heart of the proportionality assessment.[90] In any case, the three tests are not only stages of review, but represent at the same time the substantive requirements that the regulatory or administrative measure must have in order to be legitimate from the perspective of proportionality.[91] Therefore, they contribute to defining ontologically the principle of proportionality.[92] This has a 'composite' nature, in which two components are combined, being at the same time a criterion of method to make proper decision and a criterion of scrutiny of the correctness of the decision itself.[93] Proportionality therefore requires a particular method in decision-making process, based on objective assessments, which at the same time represent the yardstick for evaluating correctness in court.

6 Proportionality as a Possible Criterion for Concretising and Reviewing Directors' Management Choices

The problems that sustainability raises in corporate governance seem to find a possible solution in the proportionality criterion, which could help to concretise the (sustainability) management obligations of directors, given the parallelism that can exist between public administration and corporate administration, particularly when placed in the context of sustainability. Indeed, the company can be described as an organisation functionally designed towards a result.[94] It is characterised by a func-

[87] Galetta (1998), p. 17 and 106; Sandulli (1998), p. 371; Jans (2000), p. 247; Schwarze (2006), p. 857.

[88] Galetta (1998), p. 19 and 111; Trimarchi Banfi (2016), p. 364; Schwarze (2003), p. 60–61.

[89] This is the well-known critique of the proportionality test by Cognetti (2011), p. 296–297.

[90] For an analysis of the different ways in which the proportionality test has been applied in case law see e.g. Sauter (2013).

[91] Tesauro (2012), p. 100.

[92] Lamberti (2017), p. 556.

[93] Ligugnana (2011), p. 447.

[94] Caprara (2021), p. 73.

tional autonomy to which corresponds a discretionary power to achieve a given aim.[95] Such an interpretation of the business activity and, by extension, of the activity of directors establishes the possibility of assessing the management decisions that impact on sustainability profiles according to the canons of proportionality in the technical sense. In fact, on closer inspection, if one agrees with the logical premise that the activity of the directors is a discretionary activity functional to a purpose, the duty to consider other interests in the management seems to result in a duty of proportionate management of the company. This means a management that, in pursuit of its own purpose, causes the least possible harm to opposing interests, such as the environmental and social interests of stakeholders.

However, this statement still appears too general to dispel fears of excessive discretionary power on the part of directors or, conversely, of vagueness in the content of the duties imposed upon them. Nevertheless, it can be effectively concretised in light of the aforementioned scrutiny in which the duty of proportionality is expressed. Interpreted along the lines of the three-phase test, this duty of proportionally sustainable management translates into precise canons of action, which, in the presence of decisions relevant to sustainability, call upon directors to select, among several possible options, the one that allows them to pursue the profitable purpose, safeguarding social and environmental interests as far as possible. In other words, when concretised through the criterion of proportionality, the 'elusive' concept of sustainable management of the company (i.e. the generic obligation to 'take into account' the impact of the activity) translates into a precise duty of: adequate and complete preliminary investigation, aimed at identifying the risks associated to the corporate activity and the multiple solutions that are concretely feasible to realise the kind of activity the corporation is intended to; assessing the consistency of such solutions with the corporate purpose, which is still lucrative; selecting the one that, given equal effectiveness, has the least invasive impact on the environment or society, without causing them intolerable damage.[96]

Such duties seem first and foremost consistent with the traditional notion of a company and with the duties that characterise the management function of directors. In fact, the lucrative purpose typical of the company contract is maintained, and the duties of acting in an informed manner and of proper management are declined with a view to sustainability. The CSDD is also heading in the same direction, calling for environmental and social risk to be first of all integrated into the company's policies and risk management system and then effectively addressed through appropriate measures.[97] The same proportionality assessment seems to be expressly reflected in the content of the sustainability report, which should specifically point out: the company's business model and strategy and how the model and strategy 'take account of the interests of the undertaking's stakeholders and of the impacts of the undertaking on sustainability matters'; the company's policies in

[95] *Id.*, p. 170.

[96] Galetta (2012), p. 408; Id. (2017), p. 168; Sandulli (1998), p. 379.

[97] See Addamo (2024), p. 1271.

relation to sustainability; its due diligence process; the 'actual or potential adverse impacts connected with the undertaking's own operations and with its value chain' as well as the actions taken to identify and monitor these impacts; any action taken to prevent or mitigate the actual or potential adverse impacts and the results of such an action.[98] The concretisation of the duty of sustainable management proposed here also corroborates the conclusion of the eminent doctrine that has clearly explained that sustainability does not impose 'entrepreneurial philanthropism'[99] but allows management decisions that have a negative impact on the environment to be considered legally questionable (with consequent liability of the company and its directors towards third parties) where the damage has occurred despite the fact that it was, on the basis of a prognostic assessment, technically and economically avoidable, without excessive sacrifice to the profitability of the business.[100] In this respect, an essential contribution towards responsible business management can be offered, on the one hand, by the solutions made possible by technological progress, which can make enterprise policies more efficient and sustainable[101]; as well as, on the other hand, by the circular economy itself, which can be a possible proportionate solution to combine sustainability and economic efficiency.

A similar duty has also been asserted by the doctrine on the different basis of the principle of solidarity, in terms of orienting actions according to the logic of proportionality, reasonableness and balancing between their own individual and selfish interest and that of those who, even in the future perspective, may be affected by the initiatives taken.[102] Enhancing the solidarity principle set out in Art. 2 of the Italian Constitution (filtered through Art. 41 and the general duties of fairness and good faith), this doctrine affirms the binding nature of ESG logic in the exercise of business activity, regardless of the existence of any specific rules. In this way, the social and environmental interests involved in the action of the company should find consideration in the management choices of the directors, not as a generic (and therefore unquestionable) ambition of an ethical governance of the company, but rather shaping the model of conduct to which the directors must adhere in making a decision.[103] The duty of solidarity would require them to weigh the relevant interests against the criteria of 'reasonableness and proportionality' as criteria for balancing the interest of the undertaking against other constitutionally protected values.[104]

---

[98] Art. 19-bis, Directive (EU) 2013/34 as amended by Directive (EU) 2022/2464. For an in-depth discussion of the CSRD and its contents—in addition to the relevant analysis here developed by Genovese (Chap. 2)—see Genovese (2023a), p. 88; Strampelli (2022), p. 153–158.

[99] Libertini (2023), p. 67.

[100] Genovese (2023b), p. 144, and moreover, in the context of the research framework at hand, Genovese (Chap. 2).

[101] On the relevance of considering available technology in environmental protection, see already Amirante (2012), p. 281, footnote 169.

[102] Literally translating Cerrato (2022), p. 109.

[103] Cerrato (2022), p. 111.

[104] Cerrato (2022), p. 110.

As mentioned above, proportionality is not only a criterion of method, which can define the correct way of exercising managerial power and govern the directors' discretion through objective decision-making parameters. At the same time, it can serve as a parameter for evaluating the correctness of that decision. Hence, the principle of proportionality, in view of its dual nature, may represent the instrument enabling courts to review the directors' discretionary act. A more precise definition of the content of the duty of sustainability (in light of the principle of proportionality) makes it clear that it is not a matter of assessing the appropriateness of the decision taken, but how it was taken and, specifically, whether it is necessary in light of the interests that can be identified in the transaction. Moreover, by anchoring itself to predetermined and justifiable parameters, the proportionality review makes the assessments of both the decision-maker and the judge objectively measurable, preventing the latter from substituting its own appreciation to the evaluation of the other.[105] By dividing the decision into its logical steps and translating it into an assessment based on a verifiable criterion (in particular the criterion of necessity), the proportionality review is then capable of establishing a managerial responsibility of the directors, removing from the sphere of incontestability decisions that are taken by the directors with a view to sustainability.[106]

The applicability of the proportionality test is also confirmed by the European legislator itself, which in the context of the new sustainability obligations imposes typical proportionality assessments on companies. See, for example, Article 10 CSDD, under which companies will be obliged to take 'appropriate measures (…) to prevent potential negative impacts' or 'to mitigate them sufficiently', in relation to the severity of the negative impact and the nature and complexity that the prevention measures require. Similarly, Article 11 CSDD will require appropriate measures to stop actual negative impacts, which are both proportionate to the severity of the negative impact and society's involvement in it. With respect to circular economy duties, see, for example, Art. 23 of the Eco-design Regulation, which instead requires the adoption of measures necessary to avoid the destruction of unsold consumer products. Thus, through European legislation, proportionality is imposing itself as a methodological criterion on private operators, who are expected to balance the costs and benefits of their actions by means of typical proportionality assessments.

[105] Trimarchi Banfi (2016), p. 379 and 390.

[106] Cerrato (2022), p. 111, albeit on the basis of the duty of solidarity.

7 Proportionality as a Tool Contributing to Human-Centred Development

We could now attempt to clarify how the duty of proportionality in the management of corporations for sustainability purposes can contribute to the transition to a human-centred development model. In fact, proportionality is usually invoked as an instrument that protects the private party (i.e., in this case, companies) from public interventions that are excessive for private interests. It would thus seem to respond to the opposite need to prevent sustainability obligations from being 'unsustainable' for companies.

Certainly, this profile is an ineliminable component of proportionality. However, in the light of what has been observed here, it serves at the same time as a means of strengthening the position of third parties, whose interests can and must finally be taken into account in corporate governance, but not in the sense of functionalising management activity in pursuit of other interests, which would insert unacceptable social purposes into the purpose of the company. It would rather limit the directors' discretion and bind them to the most balanced solution in the concrete case.

Recent European and national interventions aim to strengthen the protection of social and environmental interests and thus of society at large. They strengthen the human-centred perspective by balancing opposing instances in social action. The definition of a due criterion of proportionality contributes to the creation of a new economic paradigm that focuses economic development no longer on profit alone, but rather on the welfare of human communities in general, because it allows for a proper and verifiable balancing of the interests of stakeholders and society at large. In this sense, proportionality makes it possible to reconcile the corporate interest, as an interest ultimately directed towards business efficiency and profit maximisation, with the protection of the environment and stakeholders.

8 Conclusion

In our investigation, we moved from a research question. With a view to the environmentally sustainable management of companies, we wondered whether, in the current regulatory context, instruments could be found to govern the discretion of directors, and thus we hypothesised that the solution could be found in the principle of proportionality.

As a result of the investigation conducted here, proportionality has emerged as a possible criterion for weighing opposite interests in corporate management. It is implicitly referred to in the European rules that introduced the new paradigm of sustainable business and is also consistent with the typical features of business and corporate management. Among the three dimensions of which proportionality is composed in its technical sense of European derivation (suitability, necessity and proportionality in the strict sense), the necessity test is in particular the one that can provide the key to a reinterpretation of directors' management duties from the perspective of sustainability.

Filtered through the canon of proportionality, sustainability could become a concretely enforceable and verifiable managerial duty, while maintaining the profit-making purpose typical of companies. The environment and the consideration of the environmental and social impact of the activity thus find protection through procedural duties that render the assessments conducted by the directors objectively evaluable. This meets the need to contain managerial discretion and at the same time make it reviewable in the light of an objective parameter that does not result in arbitrariness on the part of the judge. In the light of the canon of proportionality, management decisions that, beyond any specific legal limits, have an unnecessary negative impact on the environment (for example, comparing them with alternative solutions or compensatory measures available and not excessively costly for the company) or that in any event generate intolerable externalities appear to be legally reviewable.

Allowing a deeper examination of discretionary decisions, proportionality could thus contribute to the shift towards a stronger 'human-centred' development model, where people could be entitled to a new right to 'proportionally sustainable' corporate management.

References

Addamo S (2024) Le novità del testo finale della Corporate Sustainability Due Diligence Directive: un cambio di passo per la politica di sostenibilità dell'UE? NLCC 47(5):1258–1297

Amirante D (2012) Profili di diritto costituzionale dell'ambiente. In: Dell'Anno P, Picozza E (eds) Trattato di diritto dell'ambiente, vol 1. Cedam, Padova, pp 233–283

Angelici C (2017) Società benefit. Rivista ODC 2

Ballerini G, Sacchi R (2023) Profili ESG e politiche di remunerazione. NLCC 46(6):1463–1485

Balp G, Strampelli G (2022) Institutional investor ESG engagement: the European experience. Eur Bus Organ Law Rev 23(4):869–904

Baltrunaite A, Canini R, Chiarelli F, Consigliere E, Coppotelli P, Fornasari F, Loizzo T, Mocetti S, Muraca C, Parrella R, Schimperna F, Sette E (2024) The corporate sustainability due diligence directive (CSDDD): an analysis of the potential economic and legal impacts. In: Questioni di Economia e Finanza (Occasional Papers). Banca d'Italia. (https://www.bancaditalia.it/pubblicazioni/qef/2024-0869/index.html?com. dotmarketing.htmlpage.language=1)

Barcellona E (2022a) La sustainable corporate governance nelle proposte di riforma del diritto europeo: a proposito dei limiti strutturali del c.d. stakeholderism Riv soc 67(1):1–52

Barcellona E (2022b) Shareholderism versus Stakeholderism: La società per azioni contemporanea dinanzi al "profitto". Giuffrè, Milano

Baruffi MC (2014) Art. 5 TUE. In: Pocar F, Baruffi MC (eds) Commentario breve ai Trattati dell'Unione Europea, 2nd edn. Padova, Cedam, pp 24–35

Bifulco R (2022) La legge costituzionale 1/2022: problemi e prospettive. Age 1:7–26. https://doi.org/10.1433/104828

Boggio L, Pinto M (2024) Sostenibilità e responsabilità degli amministratori. Giur it 5:1235–1252

Breheny BV, Fox R, Smith SE (2025) A significant shift away from ESG and toward crypto is expected at the SEC. In: Harvard Law School Forum on Corporate Governance. https://

corpgov.law.harvard.edu/2025/02/12/a-significant-shift-away-from-esg-and-toward-crypto-is-expected-at-the-sec/
Bruno S (2019) Climate Corporate Governance: Europe vs. USA? ECFR 16(6):687–723
Busch D, Ferrarini G, van den Hurk A (2021) The European Commission's sustainable finance action plan and other international initiatives. In: Busch D, Ferrarini G, Grünewald S (eds) Sustainable finance in Europe: corporate governance. Financial Stability and Financial Markets, Springer, Switzerland, pp 19–59
Butturini P (2022) Società benefit e diritto di recesso. Giappichelli, Torino
Caprara A (2021) I principi di corretta amministrazione: struttura, funzioni e rimedi. Giappichelli, Torino
Caringella F (2021) Manuale di Diritto Amministrativo: Parte Generale e Parte Speciale, 14th edn. Dike, Roma
Carroll AB (1999) Corporate social responsibility: evolution of a definitional construct. Bus Soc 38(3):268–295
Cerrato SA (2022) Appunti per una «via italiana» all'ESG: l'impresa «costituzionalmente solidale» (anche alla luce dei «nuovi» artt. 9 e 41, comma 3, Cost.). Age 1:63–114. https://doi.org/10.1433/104830
Cerrato SA, Sartoretti C (2024) Fattori ESG: profili costituzionali e riflessi applicativi diretti. Giur it 5:1201–1211
Cetra A (2019) Enti del terzo settore e attività di impresa. RDS 4:671–690
Cetra A (2003) L'impresa collettiva non societaria. Giappichelli, Torino
Chieppa R, Lopilato V (2007) Studi di diritto amministrativo. Giuffré, Milano
Cian M (2022) Principi dell'ordinamento giuridico-economico e sviluppo sostenibile in Italia e Austria. NLCC 45(1):100–111
Cognetti S (2011) Principio di proporzionalità: Profili di teoria generale e di analisi sistematica. Giappichelli, Torino
Corgatelli M (2024) The corporate sustainability due diligence directive: outstanding issues. https://ssrn.com/abstract=4887184
Costi R (2023) Sostenibilità e scopo della società. Banca, impresa e società 3:503–508. https://doi.org/10.1435/109108
Daccò A (2022) Spunti di riflessione su capitalismo sostenibile e strumenti a disposizione. Banca, borsa e tit cred 75(3):372–393
Denozza F (2023) Sostenibilità e corporate governance: dagli investitori agli stakeholders. Riv soc 68(2–3):301–316
De Mari M (2023) L'impresa sostenibile (non benefit). In: Caterino D (ed) Scritti in onore di Sabino Fortunato. Cacucci, Bari, pp 861–889
Di Cataldo V, Arcidiacono D (2021) Decisioni organizzative, dimensioni dell'impresa e business judgment rule. Giur comm 48(1):I/69-99
Di Majo FM (2024) The EU regulatory and standard setting action on corporate sustainability reporting and the environmental taxonomy: fighting against greenwashing practices with a global reach. Riv comm internaz 1:207–251
Emiliou N (1996) The principle of proportionality in European law: a comparative study. Kluwer, London
European Central Bank (2024) Climate and nature plan 2024–2025. https://www.ecb.europa.eu/ecb/climate/our-climate-and-nature-plan/shared/pdf/ecb.climate_nature_plan_2024-2025.en.pdf
Ferrarini G (2023) Lo scopo delle società tra valore dell'impresa e valore sociale. Riv soc 68(2–3):317–337
Fink L (2020) A fundamental reshaping of finance. In: Harvard Law School Forum on Corporate Governance. https://corpgov.law.harvard.edu/2020/01/16/a-fundamental-reshaping-of-finance/
Galetta DU (1998) Principio di proporzionalità e sindacato giurisdizionale nel diritto amministrativo. Giuffré, Milano

Galetta DU (2012) Il principio di proporzionalità. In: Renna M, Saitta F (eds) Studi sui principi del diritto amministrativo. Giuffrè, Milano, pp 389–412
Galetta DU (2017) Il principio di proporzionalità. In: Sandulli A (ed) Codice dell'azione amministrativa, 2nd edn. Giuffré, Milano, pp 151–173
Galetta DU (2019) Il principio di proporzionalità fra diritto nazionale e diritto europeo (e con uno sguardo anche al di là dei confini dell'Unione Europea). Riv it dir pubbl com 29(6):903–927
Genovese A (2022) Bilanci di sostenibilità, tassonomia UE delle attività economiche ecosostenibili e governo societario. Rivista ODC 2:497–560
Genovese A (2023a) L'armonizzazione del reporting di sostenibilità delle imprese azionarie europee dopo la CSRD. Contr e impr 39(1):88–111
Genovese A (2023b) La gestione ecosostenibile dell'impresa azionaria: fra regole e contesto. Il Mulino, Bologna
Ginevra E (2023) Il Codice di Corporate Governance: introduzione e Definizioni (con un approfondimento sul "Successo sostenibile"). Riv soc 68(5–6):1017–1051
Giudici P (2023) Sistematic stewardship, common ownership: I grandi gestori di patrimoni e "l'internalizzazione delle esternalità". Rivista ODC 3:822–835
Gortsos CV (2025) Sustainable finance under EU law. In: Alexander K, Gargantini M, Siri M (eds) The Cambridge handbook of EU sustainable finance. Cambridge University Press, Cambridge, pp 552–572
Jans JH (2000) Proportionality Revisited. LIEI 27(3):239–265
Lamberti L (2017) Attività amministrativa e principio di proporzionalità. In: Perlingieri P, Fachechi A (eds) Ragionevolezza e proporzionalità nel diritto contemporaneo, vol 1. ESI, Napoli, pp 535–561
Latapí Agudelo MA, Jóhannsdóttir L, Davídsdóttir B (2019) A literature review of the history and evolution of corporate social responsibility. Int J Corp Soc Responsib 4:1. https://doi.org/10.1186/s40991-018-0039-y
Libertini M (2013) Economia sociale di mercato e responsabilità sociale dell'impresa. Rivista ODC 3
Ligugnana G (2011) Principio di proporzionalità e integrazione tra ordinamenti: Il caso inglese e italiano. Riv it dir pubbl com 2:447–481
Luciano AM (2018) Il direttore generale di s.p.a. tra diritto societario comune e diritto societario delle banche. Riv dir civ 64(6):1492–1521
Marasà G (2017) Scopo di lucro e scopo e scopo di beneficio comune nelle società benefit. Rivista ODC 2
Marasà G (2023) Gli enti del Terzo Settore: attività e scopi. Riv dir civ 69(6):1168–1174
Marcelli VM (2018) L'ente del terzo settore e l'esercizio di attività d'impresa. In: Fici A (ed) La riforma del terzo settore e dell'impresa sociale. Una introduzione, Editoriale Scientifica, Napoli, pp 123–154
Marchetti P (2020) Il nuovo Codice di Autodisciplina delle società quotate. Riv soc 65(1):268–301
Medda R (2022) Il principio di proporzionalità. In: De Donno M, Gardini G, Magri M (eds) Il diritto amministrativo nella giurisprudenza, 2nd edn. Maggioli, Rimini, pp 77–83
Meruzzi G (2016) L'adeguatezza degli assetti. In: Irrera M (ed) Assetti adeguati e modelli organizzativi nella corporate governance delle società di capitali. Zanichelli, Bologna, pp 41–79
Montalenti P (2004) Il conflitto di interessi nella riforma del diritto societario. Riv dir civ 50(2):243–255
Montalenti P (2018) L'interesse sociale: una sintesi Riv soc 63(2–3):303–319
Montalenti P (2024) Impresa, sostenibilità e fattori ESG: profili generali. Giur it 5:1190–1201
Mosco GD (2018) Scopo e oggetto nell'impresa sociale e nella società benefit. Age 1:81–94. https://doi.org/10.1433/90943
Pennasilico M (2024) Ambiente e iniziativa economica: quale bilanciamento? NLCC 47(1):48–90
Perrone A (ed) (2019) Lo statement della Business Roundtable sugli scopi della società: Un dialogo a più voci. Rivista ODC 3:589–614

Pollman E (2021) Corporate social responsibility, ESG, and compliance. In: van Rooij B, Sokol DD (eds) The Cambridge handbook of compliance. Cambridge University Press, Cambridge, pp 662–672. https://doi.org/10.1017/9781108759458.045
Ponzio A, Carlino A (2024) I cross cutting standard degli ESRS: principi e requisiti generali di informativa. Bilancio e revisione 1:35–45
Rescio CA (2022) L'oggetto della società benefit. Riv dir civ 68(3):462–477
Riolfo G (2024) L'impresa "sostenibile": La rilevanza esterna degli obblighi e delle responsabilità degli amministratori. Wolters Kluwer, Milano
Rolli R (2021) L'impatto dei fattori ESG sull'impresa: Modelli di governance e nuove responsabilità. Il Mulino, Bologna
Sandulli A (1998) La proporzionalità dell'azione amministrativa. Cedam, Padova
Sauter W (2013) Proportionality in EU law: a balancing act? TILEC discussion paper Nr. 2013-003. https://ssrn.com/abstract=2208467
Schwarze J (2003) The principle of proportionality and the principle of impartiality in European administrative law. Riv Trim Dir Pubbl 1:53–75
Schwarze J (2006) European administrative law, 2nd edn. Sweet & Maxwell, London
Scoca FG (ed) (2017) Diritto amministrativo, 5th edn. Giappichelli, Torino
Siri M, Zhu S (2021) Integrating sustainability in EU corporate governance codes in sustainable finance in Europe. In: Busch D, Ferrarini G, Grünewald S (eds) Sustainable finance in Europe: corporate governance. Financial Stability and Financial Markets, Springer, Switzerland, pp 175–224
Stabilini A, Denozza F (2008) CSR and Corporate Law: The Case for Preferring Procedural Rules http://papers.ssrn.com/sol3/papers.cfm?abstract_id=1117576
Stanzione D (2022) Scopo e oggetto dell'impresa societaria sostenibile. Giur comm 49(6):I/1023-1051
Stella Richter M Jr (2021) Long-termism. Riv soc 66(1):16–52
Strampelli G (2022) L'informazione non finanziaria tra sostenibilità e profitto. Age 1:145–164. https://doi.org/10.1433/104833
Strampelli G (2023) ESG, disclosure di sostenibilità e stewardship degli investitori istituzionali. Riv soc 68(4):828–846
Stewart L (2025) Voting on ESG: a gap becomes a gulf. In: Harvard Law School Forum on Corporate Governance. https://corpgov.law.harvard.edu/2025/02/12/voting-on-esg-a-gap-becomes-a-gulf/
Szabó DG, Sørensen KE (2015) New Eu directive on the disclosure of non-financial information (CSR). Eur Comp Fin Law Rev 12(3):307–340
Tesauro G (2012) Diritto dell'Unione europea, 7th edn. Cedam, Padova
Tombari U (2021) Corporate purpose e diritto societario: dalla "supremazia degli interessi dei soci" alla libertà di scelta dello scopo sociale. Riv soc 66(1):1–15
Tombari U (2023) Lo "scopo della società": significati e problemi di una categoria giuridica. Riv soc 68(2–3):338–351
Tridimas T (2006) The general principles of EU law, 2nd edn. Oxford University Press, New York
Trimarchi Banfi F (2016) Canone di proporzione e test di proporzionalità nel diritto amministrativo. Dir proc amm 1:361–400
Van Den Brink JE, Den Ouden W, Prechal S, Widdershoven RJGM, Jans JH (2015) General principles of law. In: Jans JH, Prechal S, Widdershoven RJGM (eds) Europeanisation of public law, 2nd edn. Europa Law Publishing, Groningen, pp 137–269
Ventoruzzo M (2024) Osservazioni sulle conseguenze applicative dell'adozione di clausole statutarie (e di autodisciplina) sul "successo sostenibile". Riv soc 69(1):129–152
Verrascina L, Pecoraio F (2024) Gli standard trasversali ESRS 1 e ESRS 2: le fondamenta del bilancio di sostenibilità CSRD. Bilancio e revisione 3:29–45
Wyderka A, Egan W (2025) The evolving anti-DEI and anti-ESG landscape: implications for the public sector. In: Harvard Law School Forum

on Corporate Governance. https://corpgov.law.harvard.edu/2025/02/14/the-evolving-anti-dei-and-anti-esg-landscape-implications-for-the-public-sector/
Zaniboni G, Caristia S (2024) Corporate Sustainability Reporting Directive: punto della situazione e temi aperti. Bilancio e revisione 2:29–37
Zorzi Galgano N (2023) Iniziativa economica privata e pluralità degli interessi costituzionalmente tutelati: l'ambiente e gli animali. Contr e impr 39(2):442–469

Companies Regenerated with Workers' Buyout (WBO): A Human-Centric Tool for a Sustainable Circular Economy in Corporate Insolvency

Federica Pasquariello

Abstract Workers' buy-outs (hereafter: WBO) achieve the recovery of a company in crisis or insolvency through the involvement of workers who take over and continue its activity, resulting in a real 'regeneration'. This strategy is fully in line with the debate on Corporate Social Responsibility and the ESG profiles of sustainability, and it becomes even more relevant in the current paradigm shift towards circular economy. In particular, WBO succeed in crossing the two main lines of development of modern (European) business crisis law: the demand for social and economic sustainability, on the one hand, and the incentive to preserve business continuity, on the other hand. Furthermore, the new attitude of cooperative enterprises to play a crucial role in the social and economic development of a territory is also improved, also through the support of employment and the regeneration of distressed enterprises.

Moreover, it is also a matter of carrying out the idea of placing the rights of the individual as such at the center of regulatory policy options, with regard to the law of the enterprise and the enterprise in crisis, in a human-centred logic that could be at risk of being diluted in the purely capitalist and profit-oriented perspective. The rights of the individual that come into consideration are not only the right to work and to work in dignity, but also to the full expression of one's personality.

In this framework, the analysis of the WBO proceeds through a brief overview of three different WBO dynamics: respectively the so-called conflictual one, the negotiated one and the one based on Employee Stock Ownership Plans; finally, a focus on the Italian legislation is provided as a relevant case study.

F. Pasquariello (✉)
Università degli studi di Verona, Verona, Italy
e-mail: federica.pasquariello@univr.it

B. Calabrese (ed.), *Legal Perspectives for a Sustainable Circular Economy*, European Union and its Neighbours in a Globalized World 30,
https://doi.org/10.1007/978-3-032-07795-0_6

1 Introduction to the Topic and its Relevance for the New Paradigm of Sustainable Circular Economy

Workers' buyout (hereafter: WBO) operations achieve the recovery of a company in crisis or insolvency through the involvement of workers who take over and carry on the business, reaching a real 'regeneration'[1] or 'self-preservation'[2] of businesses.

This strategy not only serves a reorganization objective, but also succeeds in capitalizing—instead of losing—the professional skills already acquired by employees and allows the salvation of the very function of labour in the enterprise and in the economy, with workers not only and not so much as creditors, but above all as the stakeholders most deserving the legislator's attention.[3]

WBO can embody the value of a tool for the best reallocation of the enterprise on the market, avoiding atomistic liquidation and enhancing the interests of others (first and foremost the workers) in the pursuit and protection of the best satisfaction of creditors. In this sense, WBO is able to express a value of social responsibility and sustainability.[4]

First of all, this approach is fully in line with the debate on Corporate Social Responsibility and ESG profiles of sustainability[5]. Indeed, the salvation of the workforce can be a solid guarantee for long-term sustainability.[6]

---

[1] In the Argentinian tradition (characterized, moreover, by peculiar cases of expropriation and occupation of factories, as it will be seen here afterwards), the '*Empresa Recuperada por sus trabajadores* (ERT)' came out in the years 2001–2002: see Marchetti (2013); Pacchi (2021).

[2] Di Cecco (2016), p. 633: about this topic the Author mentions Italian Law no. 416/1981 on the acquisition of newspapers by cooperatives settled by journalists. See also Bassi (1982); Lungarella and Vella (2022); Niccolini (1983).

[3] Therefore see Cavazzuti (2004), 229, highlighting the role of solidarity not only as an active subject in the physiological moments of the enterprise's life, but also as a value to which resort in case of crisis. See Barcellona (2022), 2.

[4] See World Commission on Environment and Development (so-called Brundtland's Report 'Our Common Future'), 1987, para. 27 (http://www.un-documents.net/our-common-future.pdf), which defines 'sustainable development' as that kind of development capable 'to ensure that it meets the needs of the present without compromising the ability of future generations to meet their own needs": from the perspective here analyzed, this means that it should be about meeting the needs of the present (overcoming the crisis) without compromising the possibilities of a 'future' (of a tomorrow) of the company itself, all stakeholders and the territory. See Drexhage and Murphy (2010).

[5] In EU regulatory framework, see Directive (EU) 2019/2121 on cross-border transformations, mergers and divisions, which regulates the involvement of employees in the process, so as to—Recital 32—contribute 'to the assumption of a sustainable and long-term approach by part of the companies in the entire market': here, the rights of employees to information on the project and the possibility of submitting comments are also regulated. In addition, there is Directive (EU) 2022/2464 on Corporate Sustainability Reporting Directive (so called CSRD Directive), which concerns workers both as the object of information on working and health conditions and as subjects to be consulted in order to find useful information to measure the impact of business activity on work and the environment. Here EU law confirms its commitment to the creation of a framework that aims to increase corporate responsibility on sensitive sustainability issues and to spread common reporting standards. This implies that Italian companies—as all other national companies in EU Member States—will soon face a new challenge toward sustainable economic development, as analyzed more in depth by Genovese (Chap. 2).

[6] See Denozza (2020), p. 38; D'Attorre (2021b); Genco et al. (2020); Giovannini (2018); Vella (2013).

Actually, WBO represent an employment alternative, safeguard the know-how acquired and guarantee the continuation of the activity and the maximization of the company's assets. Many times, then, workers safeguard a typical production, which would otherwise be lost, or they ensure the permanence in a geographical area of a company that traditionally belongs to a certain territory, thus allowing the preservation—not only to the benefit of the workers themselves but also of the territory and the community—of a company otherwise destined to disappear.

Thus, WBO is deeply interconnected with the theme of enhancing the recovery of the viable business, which in modern business crisis law is placed alongside the protection of credit in the hierarchy of values pursued by the legal system.[7] It should also be considered, on the other hand, that empirical evidence shows that companies, although restructured or likely to be restructured, may still be unattractive to third party investors, be they financial or industrial.[8]

Secondly, it is also a matter of achieving the goal to place the rights of the individual as such back at the center of normative choices: this is all the more relevant in the field of company law and of the company in crisis,[9] following a human-centric

---

[7] See Buhmann (2017); Linn (2019), p. 212; Pacchi (2022), p. 5; Pacchi (2019), p. 1259.

[8] In 2021 Report "The Politics to Come", Fondazione Giangiacomo Feltrinelli (https://fondazione-feltrinelli.it/app/uploads/2021/12/Rapporto_Politicstocome-1.pdf), it is emphasized that a process of transition to a market economy characterized by processes of economic democratization is already underway. It is capable of overcoming old divisions and patterns, revitalizing economic relations linked to territories and local communities. In this context, WBOs are identified as vehicles capable of pursuing these social-economic objectives without hindering private enterprise. Economic support for WBO, it is argued in the above-mentioned Report, represents a type of public intervention detached from welfare logics, capable of being in tune with the entrepreneurial ecosystem.

[9] See Lowitzsch et al. (2014): this Study provides an overview of the development of employee financial participation, in particular employee share ownership, across the EU-28. Against the background of the policy development of the past 30 years, it highlights the growth of financial participation of employees over last decade using the most recent 2013 European Company Survey data which also show employee financial participation's potential positive impact on employment and productivity. The study analyses a range of policy options in depth and makes recommendations to the Commission in the form of a five-point plan. Most importantly, it proposes the establishment of a Virtual Centre for employee financial participation including an effective tax rate calculator in the short term, the development of a code of conduct in the mid-term, and an optional 'Common European Regime on Employee Financial Participation' in the long term. Overcoming the barriers especially to cross-border plans, is particularly important in view of the potential described in this Study for EU companies to implement such schemes and benefit from their impact. See Alaimo (1998); Baglioni (1995); Caragnano (2013); Demartini and Monni (2017); Fondazione Unipolis (2007); Pedrazzoli (2015), p. 6; Pendleton (2000); Russo (2003). It is worth mentioning the most recent Italian law no. 76 of 26 May 2025, which, according to art. 46 of the Constitution, regulates forms of information and participation of workers in companies, to encourage the involvement and collaboration of workers in the governance of the company and protect the rights of employees.

logic that could risk remaining diluted in the purely capitalist and profit-oriented perspective.[10] In this sense, the rights of the individual that come into consideration are not only the right to work and to have dignity in work, but also to the fulfillment and expression of one's personality.[11]

Indeed, evidence shows that WBO have tended to emerge in labour-intensive sectors with a prevalence of high-skilled workers as opposed to capital-intensive sectors with a low-skilled workforce. Furthermore, in WBO workers usually come from long-standing work experiences, they are territorially and socially integrated, with a low propensity to mobility and strong ties to existing social networks. The same social ties within the company of origin can foster internal solidarity processes in the workplace and be a stimulus for the creation of the 'newco' that implements the WBO process.12

Such a debate also takes place within the framework of the revival of the aptitude of cooperative enterprises to play a crucial role in the social and economic development of an area, including by supporting employment and the regeneration of (failing) enterprises, starting from the European[13] and international[14] regulatory framework. This is all the more true in the national system chosen here as a case study, Italy, where the link between cooperatives and WBO is well-established.

In particular, with regard to the Italian experience and the detailed regulations that will be analyzed later, it should be considered that the instrument used for the WBO operation—the cooperative company—enhances a spirit of 'intergenerational mutuality',[15] if one considers the relevant principles about non-distribution of profits, reserves and liquidation surpluses, to the extent that they are allocated to mutual funds.[16] WBOs, and with them cooperative structures, are deeply-rooted in the territory in which they operate. Such roots preserves from the risk of economic 'desertification' of rural areas or, in any case, areas distant from large production centers, and limits inter-territorial mobility while preserving continuity.

---

[10] See also UN Guiding Principles on Business and Human Rights, 2011 (https://www.ohchr.org/sites/default/files/documents/publications/guidingprinciplesbusinesshr_en.pdf). More broadly see Marzulli (Chap. 1).

[11] Tambasco (2020): 'Democratizing work', an initiative involving over 5500 scientists, including Thomas Piketty, Saskia Sassen, Nadia Urbinati and James Galbraith, called on governments to take advantage of the Covid-19 crisis to democratize labour.

[12] Ex multis Vieta (2020), 162; Vieta and Depedri (2015).

[13] European Commission Action Plan, 9 December 2021, Building an economy that works for people: an action plan for the social economy, COM (2021) 778 final, para 3.1, highlighting the importance of promoting the social economy and—within such framework—cooperative societies, whose support 'can play a crucial role when cooperatives are set up in the context of worker buyouts with a view to preserving jobs and the continuation of a viable economic activity'.

[14] See UN General Resolution 76/135 (Cooperatives in social development) and most recently, UN Resolution, 18 April 2023.

[15] Piscitelli (2024); Vieta (2015a, b).

[16] See Art.11, Law no. 59/1992.

In this perspective, it is no coincidence that the cooperative companies have been supported by European institutions several times.[17] Recently, the European Parliament, speaking on the contribution of cooperatives in overcoming crisis, emphasises how their peculiar model 'helps to ensure that cooperatives take a long-term approach across generations and anchors them in the local economy, contributing to local sustainable development and ensuring that they do not delocalise, even when they internationalise'.[18]

After this introduction about the relevance of this topic within the new paradigm of a sustainable circular economy, this chapter deals with WBO with the following structure: Section 2 provides a general presentation of WBO in the framework of European and international legislation; then, the Italian system is chosen as a relevant case study, analyzing WBO in its operative profiles (Sect. 4), in its applicative tradition (Sect. 5), and in its normative references within the recently approved Italian Crisis and Insolvency Code (Sect. 6); finally, Section 7 concludes, highlighting opportunities and pitfalls of this model.

2 WBO in the Framework of European and International Legislation

It should be made clear from the outset that behind the notion of 'WBO' hides in truth a multifaceted world, characterized by operations that in various ways result in the acquisition of ownership of the company (or one of its branches) by the

[17] Of all these actions, mention should be made of the Communication from the Commission, 23 February 2004, on the promotion of cooperative societies, COM /2004) 18 final, which reaffirmed the 'increasingly important and positive role of cooperatives as vehicles for the implementation of many Community objectives in fields like employment policy, social integration, regional and rural development, agriculture, etc'. The Opinion of the European Economic and Social Committee (EESC) on 'Cooperatives and Restructuring', 2012/C 191/05 had the opportunity to underline the potential interest of workers in the survival of their enterprises also outside crisis contexts, inviting Member States to develop policies and rules outlining 'for business transfers to employees based on best practices to avoid closure. As for example [...] Legge Marcora in Italy' (para. 3.5). The EESC, in the aforementioned document, also stresses the superior resilience of cooperatives 'in weathering the crisis than conventional enterprises' (para. 4.5), also in relation to the pre-eminence of the remuneration of production factors represented by human capital as well as investments, sacrificing, if necessary, the remuneration of capital. See Bernardi and Monni (2016).

[18] European Parliament, 2 July 2013, Resolution on the contribution of cooperatives to overcoming the crisis (2016/C 075/05); to this end, the very same Resolution promotes support for worker cooperatives and WBO, providing for specific EU budget lines to be allocated to appropriate financial instruments and for the creation (with the participation of the European Investment Bank, social partners and stakeholders of the cooperative movement) of an European mechanism to promote the development of cooperatives and, in particular, the conversion of enterprises into cooperatives also, for example, through the instrument of mutual funds.

employees who work there. However, WBO operations are here considered with a focus on such common final result, in terms of pursuing the double objective to rescue the failing company and to solve business succession issues.

Before moving to the analysis of the WBO discipline, using Italy as a case study, is interesting to offer a quick review of different international experiences: Argentina, United States and the EU. This outlines three different dynamics of WBO on the comparative level: respectively, 'conflictual', 'institutional' and 'negotiated'.

The first dynamic, of a 'conflictual' nature,[19] has found wide diffusion in Latin America, in the form of the '*Empresa Recuperada por sus Trabajadores*', developed in Argentina following the economic crisis of 2001. In such a situation of open conflict between entrepreneurs, local authorities and workers, many workers occupied their factories *sine titulo* and then set up workers' cooperative societies aimed at preserving the production complex. This led to the reform that radically innovated the regulatory Argentinian system of the previous insolvency law.[20]

The second dynamic, more 'institutional', refers to the WBO experience in the United States. In this context, WBOs are carried out through Employee Stock Ownership Plans (ESOPs),[21] institutions of a benefit nature officially recognized only with the enactment in 1974 of the Employee Retirement Income Security Act (ERISA). In particular, the company target of the WBO, so-called Sponsoring Company or Sponsoring Employer, contributes new shares or money, in an amount usually related to profits, to a trust—Employee Share Ownership Trust—set up for this purpose and which has independent legal personality. The trust then uses the contributions to buy shares in the Sponsoring Company and administer them on behalf of the employees.[22] The trust can also obtain outside loans from banks or financial intermediaries to buy newly issued or already outstanding shares in the Sponsoring Company, which agrees to stand as guarantor of the loan and

[19] See Pagani (2021), p. 135; Pagani (2020).

[20] See Argentinian Law no. 26684/2011. About that see Dasso (2011); Howarts (2017); Pacchi (2021), p. 10; Semenzin (2019); Sermasi (2012).

[21] ESOPs are also known in the British tradition as approved plans (introduced by the annual Finance Act) and plans not approved by the Inland Revenue: see Pagani (2021), p. 136.

[22] They are only made available to employees upon termination of employment (through resignation, dismissal, reaching retirement age), at which time they can sell them in the same way as other shareholders. ESOPs may then diversify their investments, but are required by a specific legal obligation to invest 'primarily' in shares of the sponsoring company: at least 51% of the fund's resources must therefore be invested in shares of the Sponsoring Company. See Blackiston et al. (1989); Hansmann (1990).

periodically pay sums (usually related to profits) to the trust to repay it (so-called Leveraged ESOP).[23]

Thus, the Leveraged ESOP model has played a key role in employee buyouts in the United States, allowing control of the failing company to pass into the hands of workers.[24]

The third dynamic, referred to as 'negotiated' WBO, is typical of the European context. It results from a process of confrontation between authorities, workers and owners of the company, very often with supportive legislation. It is a widespread experience, especially in those continental jurisdictions where cooperative societies are more established and legislation in favour of financing the take-over operation is enacted.

This is the case in Spain, where the unemployed worker is allowed to apply for a lump sum payment of 3 years' unemployment benefit (so-called "*pago único*") and to use such money for the realization of WBO through a cooperative body.[25]

Moreover, in France, workers have the right to be informed in the event of the transfer of a company or of its branches and provided the possibility of setting up 'transitional cooperative societies' ('*scop d'amorcage*'), which overcome the obligation to hold from the outset at least 51% of the share capital imposed on workers by the rules governing *société coopérative ouvrière de production*, allowing them to acquire the majority of the company's shareholdings over a 7-year period.[26] During this period, workers still have the majority of voting rights, thanks to the presence of investor members who subscribe to capital shares without voting rights and with the commitment to sell them to workers after the 7 years have elapsed.[27]

Overall, different instances in corporate law are emerging far from what has been called the 'idolatry' of shareholder value, with the recovery and the involvement of the company's stakeholders as a pillar of long-term sustainability. In this perspective, then, it is evident that employees play a key role, also in the form of worker participation in the company's ownership structure. The spread of WBO operations demonstrates the diffusion of related strategies of corporate recovery.[28]

---

[23] See Caragnano and Caruso (2010). Only once the loan has been repaid, the shares are allocated free of charge to employees in individual accounts and the dividends can be used to pay off the debt

[24] Through leverage, employees are able to acquire the shares necessary to hold the majority stake in the company. See Mishkind and Khorey (1985)

[25] For any reference to spanish regulatory framework see Vieta (2015a), 79.

[26] See French Law no. 85/2014. See Di Stefano (2018)

[27] See Pagani (2020), p. 8.

[28] See Lungarella and Vella (2022).

In fact, the rationale of the WBO is well consistent with the increasing awareness of so-called stakeholderism emerging from EU action in this field, starting with the 2001 Green Paper,[29] through the 2011 Green Paper,[30] the 2012 Action Plan on Company Law,[31] the 2014 EU Commission Communication[32] till Directive (EU)

[29] European Commission Green Paper, 18 July 2001, Promoting a European framework for Corporate Social Responsibility, COM (2001) 366 final, paras. 36–38 (within sect. 2.1.3 entitled 'Adaptation to change'): 36. Restructuring in a socially responsible manner means to balance and take into consideration the interests and concerns of all those who are affected by the changes and decisions. In practice the process is often as important as the substance to the success of restructuring. In particular this involves seeking the participation and involvement of those affected through open information and consultation. Furthermore, restructuring needs to be well prepared by identifying major risks, calculating all the costs, both direct and indirect, associated with alternative strategies and policies, and evaluating all of the alternatives which would reduce the need for redundancies. 37. Experience of the major restructuring operations carried out in Europe in the steel, coal and shipbuilding industries has shown that successful restructuring can be better achieved through joint efforts involving the public authorities, companies and employees' representatives. This process should seek to safeguard employees' rights and enable them to undergo vocational retraining where necessary, to modernise production tools and processes in order to develop on-site activities, to mobilise public and private financing and to establish procedures for information, dialogue, cooperation and partnership. Companies should take up their share of responsibility to ensure the employability of their staff. 38. By engaging in local development and active labour market strategies through involvement in local employment and/or social inclusion partnerships, companies can lessen the social and local impact of large scale restructuring'.

[30] European Commission Green Paper, 5 April 2011, The EU corporate governance framework, COM (2011) 164 final, para. 2.8: 'Employees' interest in the long-term sustainability of the company for which they work is an element that a corporate governance framework should take into account. Employees' involvement in the affairs of a company may take the form of information, consultation and participation in the board. But it can also relate to forms of financial involvement, particularly to employees becoming shareholders. Employee share ownership has a long tradition in some European countries [Communication on the framework for promoting employee financial participation—COM (2002) 364 -, The PEPPER IV Report: Benchmarking of Employee Participation in Profits and Enterprise Results in the Member and Candidate Countries of the European Union, 2008]. Such schemes are mainly considered as means to increase the commitment and motivation of workers, raise productivity and reduce social tension. But employee share ownership also involves risks from lack of diversification: if the company fails, employee shareholders may lose both their job and their savings. However, employees as investors could play an important role to increase the proportion of long-term-oriented shareholders'.

[31] Communication from the European Commission, 12 December 2012, Action Plan: European company law and corporate governance—a modern legal framework for more engaged shareholders and sustainable companies, COM (2012) 740 final, (in particular, para. 4.5 entitled 'Promoting and improving awareness of the European Company (SE) and the European Cooperative (SCE) Statutes'

[32] Communication from the European Commission, 22 January 2014, For a European Industrial Renaissance, COM (2014) 14 final.

2017/828.[33] Furthermore, confirmation can be found at the international level, as in the UN Guidelines[34] and the OECD Principles.[35]

In particular, it has been said that the EU legislator abandoned the exclusive and all-encompassing consideration of the interest of creditors in business crisis.[36] Very significant in this regard is Directive (EU) 2019/1023 (so-called 'Insolvency Directive') where it is expressly highlighted the relevance of stakeholders involvement and protection.[37] Furthermore, the EU legislator stresses also in the Recitals

[33] Directive (EU) 2017/828, regarding the encouragement of long-term shareholder engagement (Recital 14: 'Effective and sustainable shareholder engagement is one of the cornerstones of the corporate governance model of listed companies, which depends on checks and balances between the different organs and different stakeholders. Greater involvement of shareholders in corporate governance is one of the levers that can help improve the financial and non-financial performance of companies, including as regards environmental, social and governance factors, in particular as referred to in the Principles for Responsible Investment, supported by the United Nations. In addition, greater involvement of all stakeholders, in particular employees, in corporate governance is an important factor in ensuring a more long-term approach by listed companies that needs to be encouraged and taken into consideration').

[34] Agenda 2030 for Sustainable Development, signed by UN member countries on 25 September 2015: here are 17 goals, to be achieved by 2030, covering the three dimensions of economic, social and environmental sustainability, to end poverty, fight inequality and climate change (https://www.un.org/sustainabledevelopment/sustainable-development-goals). Actually, several implementation initiatives by EU institutions followed: e.g., European Commission, 8 March 2018, Action Plan: Financing Sustainable Growth, COM (2018) 97 final; European Commission, 11 December 2019, European Green Deal, COM (2019) 640 final; and also Directive (EU) 2022/2464 on Corporate Sustainability Reporting as mentioned above: on the latter see Genovese (Chap. 2).

[35] See G20/OECD Principles of Corporate Governance 2023 (https://www.oecd.org/en/publications/g20-oecd-principles-of-corporate-governance-2023_ed750b30-en.html), where specifically Sect. VI focuses on enterprises' 'Sustainability and resilience'.

[36] D'Attorre (2021a), p. 78.

[37] See textually Art. 13, Directive (EU) 2019/1023 (entitled 'Workers'): '1.Members States shall ensure that individual and collective workers' rights, under Union and national labour law, such as the following, are not affected by the preventive restructuring framework: (a) the right to collective bargaining and industrial action; and (b) the right to information and consultation in accordance with Directive 2002/14/EC and Directive 2009/38/EC, in particular: (i) information to employees' representatives about the recent and probable development of the undertaking's or the establishment's activities and economic situation, enabling them to communicate to the debtor concerns about the situation of the business and as regards the need to consider restructuring mechanisms; (ii) information to employees' representatives about any preventive restructuring procedure which could have an impact on employment, such as on the ability of workers to recover their wages and any future payments, including occupational pensions; (iii) information to and consultation of employees' representatives about restructuring plans before they are submitted for adoption in accordance with Article 9, or for confirmation by a judicial or administrative authority in accordance with Article 10; (c) the rights guaranteed by Directives 98/59/EC, 2001/23/EC and 2008/94/EC. 2.Where the restructuring plan includes measures leading to changes in the work organisation or in contractual relations with workers, those measures shall be approved by those workers, if national law or collective agreements provide for such approval in such cases'.

such importance of employee's involvement in case of restructuring operations,[38] as well as the relevance of workers' interests in terms of preventing losses of jobs and skills.[39]

In particular, WBO operations succeed in combining the two main lines of development of modern (European) business crisis law: the case for social and economic sustainability, on the one hand, and the incentive to preserve business continuity, on the other. These topics also integrates into the framework of the renewed aptitude of cooperative enterprises to play a crucial role in the social and economic development of a territory, including through the support of employment and the regeneration of (failing) enterprises.[40]

In this sense, with regard to the cooperative companies, emphasis is placed on the resilience of cooperatives "in weathering the crisis than conventional enterprises active in the same sectors and the same territories", and on the ability of social cooperatives to adopt a long-term approach to achieve economic and social sustainability for cooperative members, ready to sacrifice return on capital in order to maintain employment and investment.[41]

Along the same lines already was the action to encourage responsible corporate restructuring through worker participation and involvement.[42] In this sense, cooperatives are appreciated for their contribution to overcoming the crisis and, to this end, support of worker cooperatives and WBO was invoked by means of a specific

---

[38] Recital 10, Directive (EU) 2019/1023: 'Any restructuring operation, in particular one of major size which generates a significant impact, should be based on a dialogue with the stakeholders. That dialogue should cover the choice of the measures envisaged in relation to the objectives of the restructuring operation, as well as alternative options, and there should be appropriate involvement of employees' representatives as provided for in Union and national law'.

[39] Recital 2, Directive (EU) 2019/1023: "Restructuring should enable debtors in financial difficulties to continue business, in whole or in part, by changing the composition, conditions or structure of their assets and their liabilities or any other part of their capital structure — including by sales of assets or parts of the business or, where so provided under national law, the business as a whole — as well as by carrying out operational changes. Unless otherwise specifically provided for by national law, operational changes, such as the termination or amendment of contracts or the sale or other disposal of assets, should comply with the general requirements that are provided for under national law for such measures, in particular civil law and labour law rules. Any debt-to-equity swaps should also comply with safeguards provided for by national law. Preventive restructuring frameworks should, above all, enable debtors to restructure effectively at an early stage and to avoid insolvency, thus limiting the unnecessary liquidation of viable enterprises. Those frameworks should help to prevent job losses and the loss of know-how and skills, and maximise the total value to creditors — in comparison to what they would receive in the event of the liquidation of the enterprise's assets or in the event of the next-best-alternative scenario in the absence of a plan — as well as to owners and the economy as a whole".

[40] Notably in light of the EU regulatory framework: see again European Commission, DATA, EU Commission Action Plan 2021 Creating an economy that serves people: an action plan for the social economy, COM (2021) final.

[41] Opinion of the European Economic and Social Committee (EESC) on 'Cooperatives and Restructuring', 2012/C 191/05 (especially paras. 4.5 and 5.2).

[42] European Commission Green Paper, 18 July 2001, Promoting a European framework for Corporate Social Responsibility, COM (2001) 366 final.

EU budget line providing appropriate financial instruments, as well as the creation, with the participation of the European Investment Bank (EIB) and the social partners, and with stakeholders from the cooperative movement, of a European mechanism designed to promote the development of cooperatives and, in particular, business transfers under the cooperative form, also through, for example, the instrument of mutualisation funds[43].

3 WBO in the Italian System: A Case Study

Passing now to consider the Italian legal framework as a case study, it must be pointed out that it is fully agreed that both commercial law and bankruptcy law increasingly incorporate constitutional principles and values. In this regard, specific reference should be made to Arts. 9 and 41 (as recently reformed), as well as to Art. 45 of the Italian Constitution.[44] In this context, the core objective of protecting the healthy environment, land and production activities, including those resulting from cooperative monitoring, is stressed, with a view to protecting future generations.

The same trend emerges in the most recent reforms of business crisis law, following the transposition in Italy of the Insolvency Directive,[45] which merged into the Crisis and Insolvency Code (hereafter: 'CCI').[46]

In particular, the case for sustainability, declined in terms of mitigating the impact of the crisis on labour relations and in terms of preserving employment levels, emerges within several provisions of CCI. Although the goal of credit recovery remains central in the hierarchy of values protected by the Italian legislation, the preservation of jobs is affirmed right from the objectives of the Negotiated Crisis Settlement (art. 12 CCI), as well as in those of the arrangement with creditors in

---

[43] European Parliament, 2 July 2013, Resolution on the contribution of cooperatives to overcoming the crisis (2016/C 075/05), para. 25.

[44] Here the official translation by the Italian Senate (https://www.senato.it/documenti/repository/istituzione/costituzione_inglese.pdf): Art. 9 Cost.: 'The Republic promotes the development of culture and of scientific and technical research. It safeguards natural landscape and the historical and artistic heritage of the Nation'; Art. 41 Cost.: 'Private economic enterprise is free. It may not be carried out against the common good or in such a manner that could damage safety, liberty and human dignity. The law shall provide for appropriate programmes and controls so that public and private-sector economic activity may be oriented and co-ordinated for social purposes.'; Art. 45 Cost.: 'The Republic recognises the social function of co-operation of a mutually supportive, non-speculative nature. The law promotes and encourages co- operation through appropriate means and ensures its character and purposes through appropriate checks. The law safeguards and promotes the handicrafts'. On this economic constitutional profiles see Ambrosini (2024). More broadly on such constitutional dimension and its relevan innovation see Cozzi (Chap. 9).

[45] Directive (EU) 2019/1023.

[46] See Legislative Decree no. 14/2019, enacting the said Italian Crisis and Insolvency Code, then subject to various reform: especially, see Arts. 84–87 CCI. See Ambrosini (2022); Corno (2014); Nigro (2017), p. 201; Pacchi (2015), p. 537; Panzani (2019); Paulus and Damman (2021); Stanghellini (2017), p. 873; Wessels (2007), p. 253;

continuity (art. 84(2) CCI); it also influences the choices of the procedural business lease (art. 212 CCI), and the strategies of provisional business operation (art. 211 CCI).[47]

In this respect, WBO results in an active labour policy. It involves a combined complex of corporate and financial transactions aimed at the acquisition of a company (or part of a company) by its employees. Actually, the employees of the company in crisis can set up a cooperative that, within the mutualistic purpose of providing work for its members, takes over the company. In this way, it exploits both the coincidence between entrepreneurship and work that is typical of the world of cooperation, and the appropriate financial channels as an alternative to traditional banking.

As to the specific regulation, WBO started to spread in Italy as early as the 1980s, following the first positive experiences in the United States. In Italy, the WBO developed mainly through the establishment of 'production and work cooperatives', thanks also to the support of trade associations and favorable legislation. The first regulatory recognition of the WBO in Italy came with the so-called 'Marcora Law' (Law no. 49/1985), which regulated cooperative funds for development and promotion, and entitled the pre-emption for the purchase of firms in crisis in favour of cooperatives settled by employees. Subsequently, Law no. 223/1991 allowed employees of companies in crisis to apply for an advance payment on their job-mobility allowance to set up a cooperative. Eventually, with Law Decree no. 145/2013, a new aid scheme was introduced to support the creation of cooperatives formed by workers from companies in crisis, strengthening the right of first refusal to rent or purchase companies in difficulty. In summary, the WBO in Italy developed thanks to a regulatory framework that promoted the establishment of production and work cooperatives, offering facilitation and funding to support workers in the management of companies in crisis.

More in detail, the abovementioned Marcora Law was indeed the first regulation of WBO in Italy,[48] but later it was the subject of infringement proceedings by the EU[49] in terms of State aid. In particular, the objection concerned the provision of disbursements, through a special fund, of non-repayable public contributions for the benefit of production and work cooperatives.[50]

Following this proceeding, the contested piece of legislation was replaced by the so-called 'Marcora II Law' (Law no. 57/2001), which provided for the elimination

[47] See following Sect. 6.

[48] See Biagi (1985), p. 289; Dandolo (2006), p. 263; Orlando (2017), p. 661; Pandolfo et al. (1986), p. 490; Picozza (1986), p. 31; Verrucoli (1985), p. 167; Vieta et al. (2017); Vigiani (1992), p. 20.

[49] See Commission notice pursuant to Article 93 (2) of the EC Treaty to other Member States and interested parties concerning the refinancing and modification of the measures to assist cooperative enterprises provided for in Italian Law 47/85 (the Marcora Law), 97/C 309/03.

[50] Such cooperative companies, based on the principles of mutuality and registered in a special register, were formed by workers admitted to the extraordinary redundancy fund, or employees of companies subject to bankruptcy proceedings; the contributions were disbursed through financial companies at least 80% owned by production and work cooperatives.

of the mechanism of non-repayable public contributions. At the same time, it was added that the Ministry of Productive Activities could use the resources of the special fund to participate in the share capital of finance companies. It was also established that the aforementioned finance companies could take temporary minority shareholdings in cooperatives, to an extent less than risk capital, with priority given to those formed by workers from companies in crisis, as well as to grant the cooperatives themselves financing and financial facilities for the implementation of business projects. Furthermore, the financing of a WBO by the State was restricted within the limit of 1:1 ratio, and such financing must be repaid by the employees within a period of 7/10 years. Besides, it is allowed for the WBO to have a financing member as a member of the cooperative for the entire duration of the investment. The financing member can be a legal entity, a cooperative, or any other entity with 'financial interests', rather than mutual interests. A financing member's voting share at the meeting may not exceed one-third of the total.[51]

In terms of implementing regulations, it was further clarified that the Ministry's participation in the share capital of finance companies must be provided through subscription of financing member shares issued by them; as for the duration of the participation of finance companies in rescue cooperatives, it was set at a maximum of 10 years from recruitment.[52]

In order to foster economic development and the growth of employment levels in the country, it was then introduced a special aid scheme aimed at promoting the establishment and development of small and medium-sized cooperative companies.[53] Such regulation was then followed by the provision of another aid scheme (the so-called 'New Marcora'), also aimed at promoting the birth and development of small and medium-sized cooperatives through the granting of subsidized financing for the establishment in the national territory of cooperatives made up predominantly of workers from companies in crisis, social cooperatives or those managing companies confiscated from organized crime, as well as for the birth, development or restructuring of cooperatives in Southern Italy.[54]

The Government also intervened with 'measures to favor the resolution of business crises and defend employment', within which it instituted preemption for business leasing or sale of companies or branches of companies in crisis.[55]

More recently, public resources were expanded with an additional allocation of 15 million euros intended to support these initiatives[56]: this new aid scheme aims at strengthening these operations, and provided—among other things—for the disbursement of subsidized financing for the establishment of new companies, includ-

[51] Art. 17(5), Law no. 57/2001.

[52] Ministerial Decree, 4 April 2001.

[53] Ministerial Decree, 4 December 2014, pursuant to the provisions of Art. 1(845), Law no. 296/2006.

[54] Directorial Decree, 16 April 2015.

[55] Law Decree no. 145/2013 (converted into Law no. 9/2014), so-called 'Destination Italy' Decree.

[56] Art. 39(5-bis), Law Decree no. 34/2020 (converted with amendments into Law no. 77/2020), so-called 'Relaunch' Decree.

ing in the form of cooperative companies, by workers from companies in crisis or from companies in crisis.

Finally, recent implementing regulations gave 'new life' to the additional promotional intervention synthetically identified above as the 'New Marcora' to support the establishment, development and consolidation of cooperative companies with the aim of fostering economic development and the growth of employment levels in the country.[57]

Actually, a revitalization of the original Marcora Law was brought about years before by Law no. 59/1992, which provided for new regulations of cooperative companies in general: here it was regulated the subsidizing member as a full member of the cooperative (inspired precisely by the model introduced by the original Marcora Law) and the cooperative participation shareholder.

Two funds were provided for WBO operations, in order to promote and secure employment levels and to encourage the conversion of companies into cooperatives, especially in times of crisis: (a) Foncooper, a revolving fund consisting of low-interest loans (controlled by Banca Nazionale del Lavoro), and (b) the 'Special Fund for Safeguarding Employment Levels' (hereinafter: the 'Special Fund') for the development of new cooperatives.[58]

In this framework, Cooperazione Finanza Impresa (CFI) was then established as early as 1986.[59] CFI is the main and historical institutional investor for the support and financing of WBO in Italy. In particular, CFI has been entrusted with the management of the Special Fund, and to date is the only financial cooperative for the management of the interventions provided by the Marcora Law. At the same time, *Lega Nazionale delle Cooperative e Mutue* (Legacoop), *Confederazione delle Cooperative Italiane* (Confcooperative) and other federations have made available equity or debt financing mainly through the cooperative movement's mutual funds,[60]

---

[57] Ministerial Decree 4 January 2021, together with the subsequent Ministerial Decree 31 March 2021.

[58] For any reference to such a regulatory framework see Pagani (2020).

[59] Shared and supervised by the Ministry of Enterprise and Made in Italy, its aim is to promote the birth and development of production and work and social cooperative enterprises. In addition to the Ministry of Enterprise and Made in Italy, CFI's capital includes Invitalia, the mutual funds of AGCI, Confcooperative, Legacoop and 393 cooperative enterprises. It adheres to the 3 main Cooperative Associations and Cecop-Cicopa (European Confederation of Cooperatives and Worker-Owned Enterprises). It collaborates with Cooperfidi Italia and, in the European context, with Soficatra, a financial company for the social economy. With the aim of safeguarding and increasing employment, CFI, in its role as an institutional investor, participates in the share capital of companies, finances long-term investment plans and assists workers in the elaboration of the business plan and the start-up of the new company. Throughout the duration of the participation, it monitors the company's economic/financial situation and performance to prevent potential risk situations. In these decades of activity, while intervening in critical situations, CFI has demonstrated in practice that it is a useful instrument of active labour policy and promotion of new entrepreneurship. The activities carried out by CFI not only had an important return in terms of employment, but thanks to the revenue from taxes and social security contributions paid and the cessation of the use of social safety nets, it ensured a significant economic return for the State. From its inception to 31 December 2022, CFI has supported 586 cooperatives, saving and creating over 27,205 jobs (source: CFI: www.cfi.it)

[60] Fici (2013).

but also technical assistance and access to know-how, often in synergy with CFI and other organizations.

4 WBO in Italy and its Operative Profiles

Turning now to summarize such a complex regulatory framework, it can be affirmed that, in concrete terms, WBO in Italy involves the implementation of an indirect continuity restructuring operation, whereby employees who manifest entrepreneurial vocation take over, through these steps:

(a) the employees of the company in bankruptcy proceedings manage to take over the company or part of it;
(b) with this aim, they set up a cooperative, which is financed by the advance payment of the wage allowances provided for by the law;
(c) institutional investors may participate as financing members;
(d) the cooperative may request, on the basis of a sustainable business plan, the intervention of bank credit;
(e) the cooperative acquires a branch or the entire company.

Step a) presumes a positive entrepreneurial vocation on the part of the workers, who must find the reasons and interest in converting their position as employees into that of partners. Statistically, more middle-aged (difficult to re-employ and interested in reaching retirement age) and better educated workers are involved; on the other hand, there are no significant gender-related indicators.[61] Obviously, the economic feasibility of the operation must be verified.

Step b) is improved by the capitalization of the NASpi.[62] The incentive for self-entrepreneurship (the "NASpi advance") is regulated by Art. 8, Legislative Decree no. 22/2015 which envisages the option for the employee entitled to NASpi pay-

---

[61] Legacoop (2020).

[62] NASpi stay for '*Nuova Assicurazione Sociale per l'impiego*' (New Social Insurance for Employment), as part of the instruments introduced by the relevant Labour Market Reform (also known as 'Jobs Act', by means of Legislative Decree no. 22/2014, as modified by Art. 1(221)(222) Law no. 234/2021), replacing the previous instruments of Aspi and Mini-Aspi. As regards the NASpi, INPS Circ. no. 21 of 10 February 2023 specified that the employee, in the case of judicial liquidation, must submit the application within the time limit of 68 days starting from the date on which the employee tenders his resignation and not from the date of termination of employment (date of opening of the judicial liquidation) and in the case of termination of employment due to withdrawal by insolvency administrator, from the date on which the employee came to the knowledge of the insolvency adminsitrator's communication or for termination by law, from the date on which the relationship is understood to be legally terminated. As specified by INPS and as is known, the unemployment benefit starts from the eighth day following the date of either resignation, termination by the insolvency administrator, termination by law of employment relationship, if the application is submitted before the eighth day; conversely, it starts from the first day following the date of submission of the application, if the application is submitted after the eighth day. See Bellè and Russo (2023), p. 1601.

ment to request the advance payment of the total amount of the treatment he or she is entitled **to.** By that way, they are enabled to capitalize the job-mobility allowance without going through the dismissal and the consequent placing in mobility. NASpi can be used for subscribing to a capital share of a cooperative in which the mutual relationship has as its object the performance of work activities by the member. This allows an employee who is entitled to NASpi treatment to obtain its payment in advance (net of any amount already disbursed) and in one lump sum upon the occurrence of certain conditions, including the subscription of a share capital of a production and work cooperative with which the beneficiary establishes the mutualistic employement relationship. The incentive is intended directly for the worker who, therefore, upon receipt of his/her own amount must contribute it in full, as a share capital subscription, to the production and work cooperative with which he or she establishes a subordinate or self-employed employment or collaboration relationship pursuant to Law no. 142/2001. In this regard, it is required that the contributing partner remain with the company for as many months as the number of NASpi months he or she contributed; this is generally about 24 months on average. In the event of an early exit, the remaining NASpi amount reverts to the National Institute for Social Welfare (INPS).

Step c): the finance companies, created by the Marcora Law, take participation in cooperative companies 'with priority for those formed by workers from companies in crisis'. This is the point that encourages WBO and, as can easily be seen, it originates in the world of cooperation and is ultimately intended to stimulate the birth of work cooperatives, with a special focus on those in the WBO field. The result is that the WBO cooperative can also rely on the support of a financing member for the entire duration of the investment. This also allows the financier to participate in the decision-making process and management of the financed cooperatives.

Finally, save the possibility of bank credit under step d), there is the real acquisition: step e). In this regard, it is provided the right of first refusal for the lease or purchase of the business or a branch thereof in favor of cooperatives formed by employees of an enterprise subject to bankruptcy, composition with creditors, extraordinary administration or compulsory administrative liquidation.[63] Thus, the rule introduced a legal pre-emption in favor of rescue cooperatives, on equal terms and conditions with other competing parties, in the lease or purchase of companies admitted to bankruptcy proceedings.[64] Therefore, it is believed that the legal right of pre-emption finds a better explanation when read also in light of the constitutional favor for cooperation (Art. 45 of the Italian Constitution) and, above all, for work-

---

[63] According to Art. 11(2) and (3), Law Decree no. 145/2013 (converted into Law no. 9/2014).

[64] In a critical sense see Di Cecco (2016), p. 640: what is relevant for the purpose of safeguarding the continuation of the business is simply the fact that the business is rented and, in the event of a plurality of offers, that it is rented to whoever best ensures such continuation If, in fact, workers are recognized as always having the right to be preferred to anyone else (albeit on equal terms) in the leasing or sale of companies in crisis, the main effect is to risk significantly depressing the interest in participating in competitive procedures for the selection of the tenant or buyer. See Lamanna (2017).

ers' participation and cooperation in the capital and management of enterprises (Arts. 46 and 47 of the Italian Constitution). Article 11, paragraph 2, of Decree Law No. 145 of 2013, in its version in force today, establishes the right of pre-emption in favor of cooperatives formed by employees of the enterprise subject to judicial liquidation, composition with creditors, extraordinary administration or compulsory administrative liquidation, in the event that, within the framework of these procedures, the lease or sale of companies, business branches or complexes of assets and contracts is reached pre-emption to the coop. in the sale of the company or its branches and recognition to the coop of the right to raise in the competitive sales that take place.[65]

The abovementioned fund of Cooperative enters as a member, bringing in a non-repayable grant. The competent Ministry (of Enterprise and Made in Italy) is entrusted with the task to support the development of small and medium-sized enterprises in the form of cooperative company, including social, production and work, in order to safeguard employment.[66] The objective is pursued through participation in specially established finance companies (so-called 'Marcora Companies'), which in turn take minority stakes in cooperatives, including those formed by workers from companies in crisis, where each worker member takes a stake worth at least euro 4000 (reduced to euro 1000 for social cooperatives) to be paid for 50% within 30 days of the intervention and for the remaining 50% within 2 years. However, the participation by Marcora Companies is temporary and must be dismissed within the maximum period of 10 years.

5 WBO in Italy and its Applicative Tradition

In Italy, a first example of WBO can be traced back to 1874, when the owner of a crockery and majolica factory donated the business to workers who turned it into the Cooperativa Ceramica d'Imola, thus becoming Italy's oldest production and work cooperative.[67]

Then, many cases followed and some of them is worth mentioning: Coop. Fonderia Dante Ferroli 2017, which on July 2017 started with 62 workers, while in 2023 the factory had 150 workers. The equity was provided in the form of approximately 980 k Euro NASpi; 525 k Euro Coopfond; 500 k Euro; in addition to the contribution of bank loans[68].

---

[65] This is textually provided for in the case of disposals made in the context of Judicial Liquidation and composition with creditors, while it remains doubtful whether the preemption also operates in the case of "Composizione Negoziata della Crisi" with indirect continuity and sale of the company ex art. 22 paragraph 1, lett d) c.c.i. and in the "Concordato Minore" (art. 74 c.c.i.).

[66] According to Art. 17, Law no. 57/2001 (Marcora II Law). See Cataudella (2016), p. 437.

[67] See Pacchi (2021), p. 12.

[68] LegaCoop (2020).

More recently, the case examined by Tribunal of Milan[69] is interesting, because shows admission of competing bids under a procedure of composition with creditors, and at the outcome ordered the execution of a WBO.

The Tribunal of Forlì recently examined a composition plan jointly proposed by two companies: it was based on the extraordinary reverse merger by incorporation of the parent company into the subsidiary, and the continuation of the business activity indirectly by means of a business lease under a contract signed in May 2021 with a new cooperative formed by 16 former employees in a WBO and subsequent sale of the same company during the procedure.[70]

According to a recent business report,[71] in Italy WBO operations, as far as production sectors are concerned, emerges to a greater extent in industry, in which most of WBO are concentrated (60%), followed by services (35%) and agriculture (5%). Therefore, this model is preferred by small and medium-sized enterprises and, more specifically, those belonging to the manufacturing sector (to which in fact 79.6% of WBO can be traced), with prevalence of the phenomenon in the textile, mechanical and woodworking industries. As for the geographical location of WBO, they are found to be prevalent in the Central and Northeastern Regions of the country.

According to a resolution of the Italian Parliament,[72] WBO has ensured a positive public finance balance: actually, the resources that the Ministry of Economic Development has allocated to the participation in CFI in the years 2007–2015 amount to 84 million euros and have generated an economic return for the Italian State estimated at 576 million euros, equal to 6.8 times the capital employed, net of taxes paid by workers and companies and less recourse to social shock absorbers.[73]

According to CFI data, in Italy in the period 2011–2021, the same CFI approved 146 interventions in support of 88 WBO projects that develop a production value of more than EUR 365 million and employ 2286 people.[74]

The benefit that these operations generates for the system is notable: a redundant, worker costs 30 to 40 thousand euros in social security cushions, money out of pocket. Through the WBO, contributions are transformed into capital and the regenerated company continues to make social security contributions. Moreover, WBO is characterized by reduced leverage since in most cases the target company's problem is excessive debt levels. Leverage can be avoided through the intervention of specialized intermediaries, including a range of institutional investors and lenders who bring in the necessary financial resources.

[69] Trib. Milano, October 3, 2019, www.tribunale.milano.it. See also Gruppo editoriale Zanardi case, Padova 2013 (source: CFI: www.cfi.it)

[70] Trib. Forlì, 23 ottobre 2023 (accessible in the database *OneLegale—Leggi d'Italia*).

[71] Legacoop (2020).

[72] Resolution approved on 29 March 2017 by the Joint Committees X (Productive Activities, Trade and Tourism) and XI (Public and Private Labor) of the Italian Parliament.

[73] Pagani (2020), p. 24.

[74] https://www.cfi.it/workers-buyout.php

6 WBO within the Italian Crisis and Insolvency Code ('CCI')

The Italian Crisis and Insolvency Code (as mentioned, 'CCI') does not expressly deal with WBO, except by means of a reference contained in Art. 191 CCI (Effects of business transfers on labor relations), which declares applicable to business transfers both Art. 47 Law no. 428/1990 and Art. 11 Law Decree no. 145/2013 (converted in Law no. 9/2014) and other relevant provisions in force. Corrective reform to CCI then reworded Art. 191 itself and extended the pre-emption under the just mentioned Art. 11 Law Decree no. 145/2013 to all the instruments for the regulation of crisis and insolvency,.[75] The corrective intervention was aimed at standardizing the expressions used in the normative body of the Code, with the more precise terminological reference to the instruments of crisis and insolvency regulation or judicial or controlled liquidation.

Nonetheless, other norms of the CCI would require further consideration in order to verify their coordination with the WBO.[76]

With no claim to be exhaustive, they can just be reported here as follows:

- the discipline on the effects of the judicial liquidation on labor relations (Art. 189 CCI): the law provides for a time limit of suspension of employment relationships, not less than 4 months, starting from the date of opening of the judicial liquidation. At the end of the same, the employment relationships, still in existence, are terminated *ex officio* with effect from the date of declaration of compulsory winding up judicial liquidation, without prejudice to the provisions of the collective dismissal as regulated. This regulation also provides for the possibility of requesting the extension of such term, which the judge may order for a maximum period of 8 months (maximum period of 12 months in total), to be filed by the insolvency administrator or the competent Labour Inspectorate,[77] or also by individual employees with certain limitations, in the presence of subsisting possibilities of resumption or transfer to third parties of the company. This provision is also functional to encourage the possible exercise of the right of pre-emption according to Art. 191 CCI, in relation to cooperatives established by the employees of the enterprise under judicial liquidation (i.e. WBO)[78];

[75] After the modification by Legislative Decree no. 136/2024 (so-called 'Corrective-ter'), Art. 191 CCI now provides that, to the transfer of business arranged within the instruments for the regulation of crisis and insolvency or judicial or controlled liquidation, Art. 47 of Law no. 428/1990, Art. 11 Law Decree no 145/2013 (converted into Law no. 9/2014) and other relevant provisions in force shall apply, subject to the relevant conditions.

[76] See Aprile (2022); Pacchi (2021), p. 10; De Martini and Monni (2017); Patti (2022), p. 1338; Pizzolato (2024).

[77] Namely, the Labour Inspectorate where the liquidation was opened, which has to be informed in advance pursuant to the same Art. 189 CCI.

[78] Bellomo and Rocchi (2023).

- the regulation of continuation of the business during judicial liquidation (Art. 211 CCI) or business lease (Art. 212 CCI), which shows a link between going concern and the maintenance of the employment relationship. In particular, art. 211 CCI allows continuation of the business, with undoubted job-preservation effects. Equally, Art. 212(2) CCI provides that the choice of the tenant shall be made by the insolvency administrator pursuant to Art. 216 CCI, on the basis of an estimate, ensuring, by means of appropriate forms of publicity, the maximum information and participation of the interested parties. The choice of the tenant must take into account not only the amount of the rent offered, but also the guarantees provided and the reliability of the business continuation plan, having regard to the preservation of employment levels;
- the regulation of the arrangement in the judicial liquidation (Art. 240 CCI), which ideally would be a ground of choice for the WBO, given that the operation may have been facilitated by a phase of provisional exercise (or endoprocedural lease) of the company or its branches, so as to maintain continuity. Consideration should be given to the possibility for workers to have early access to information essential for preparing a proposal for an arrangement. Although these favorable contextual conditions may exist, they pertain to a phase of the crisis that is already advanced, a period during which workers often suffer instability and hardly receive clear communications from top management: all situations that discourage workers, wear down internal relations and turn those favorable contextual conditions into a merely theoretical opportunity[79];
- the regulation of competing proposals in the arrangement with creditors (Art. 90 CCI), considering that they could come from the employees of the company during a procedure of composition with creditors. Actually, the very same employees qualify also as creditors of the cooperative they established, having endowed it with their credits. In addition, they could proceed directly with the proposal if they represent at least 5% of the credits.[80] However, in the context of the approval of such proposals by the creditors, it should also be pointed out that, according to Art. 109(5) CCI, there is an exclusion of the voting rights of employees, which are privileged under Art. 2751-bis Italian Civil Code, if paid in full in cash at 30 days;
- the regulation on competing bids in the arrangement with creditors (Art. 91 CCI), which must be coordinated with the right of pre-emption enjoyed by workers' cooperatives (as already mentioned), also in order to assess at what point in time pre-emption can be exercised. Whatever the position of the cooperative (original bidder already identified under Art. 91(1) CCI, or subsequent bidder), it can certainly exercise its right of pre-emption following the competitive procedure arranged under art. 91(3) CCI, which, precisely, presupposes the prior acquisition of expressions of interest. Moreover, it is reasonable to argue that the

[79] Pacchi (2021).

[80] The original percentage of 10% was lowered to 5% in the so-called Corrective-ter Decree, recently reforming the said Art. 90 CCI in September 2024.

cooperative (other than the bidder pursuant to art. 91(1) CCI), at the outcome of the publicity ordered by the Tribunal to acquire competing bids, could not already make explicit any expression of interest (from which, therefore, the subsequent competitive procedure would be triggered). The immediate application of Art. 11(2) Law Decree Law no. 145/2001 could be rather requested. Such a regulation, as known, simply provides for the right of pre-emption in the case of the lease or sale of companies or branches thereof (without subordinating the exercise of the same to the carrying out of any competitive procedure). In such case, with no further expressions of interest (a condition that would not result in the initiation of competitive procedures under art. 91(3) CCI), the judge should order the immediate application of the right of pre-emption in favor of the cooperative;
- the rules on cross restructuring in the arrangement with creditors in continuity (art. 112 CCI), which also applies to competing proposals, which, therefore, can be approved according to this principle when the proposal does not reach the majorities provided for in Art. 109(5) CCI. The corrective reform clarified that, in the case of a competing proposal, the debtor's consent is required for the approval only if the proponent is a small and medium-sized enterprise according to the EU parameters defining SMEs.[81] As a matter of principle, in WBO operations such a consent will always be necessary, given that CFI can only support its interventions in favor of SMEs according to EU regulations, as recalled by the relevant domestic law[82];
- the going concern objectives envisaged both in the context of the arrangement with creditors as a going concern (art. 84 CCI) and in the context of the procedure of negotiated crisis settlement (art. 12 CCI) include, in addition to the primary purpose of ensuring the recovery of creditors, also the further purpose of preserving jobs, to the extent possible. Thus, as it was said before, the target of maintaining employment levels formally enters the hierarchy of values protected in the management of business crises, with a marked focus on the objectives of sustainability in a human-centric logic.[83]

7 Final Remarks

Beyond the relevant opportunities provided by WBO as here highlighted, Italian practice teaches us nevertheless that WBO are not always successful. In some cases, the difficulties of the recovered company are transferred to the cooperative, making in fact not possible any recovery, consolidation and future development. It is therefore necessary for the operation to be carefully planned, assessing the concrete

[81] In addition to what already mentioned in Sect. 1, see more broadly Marzulli (Chap. 1).

[82] EU size limits are precisely referred to in Art. 112(2) CCI, which, in turn, refers to the last sentence in Art. 85(3) CCI, as amended by the Corrective-ter Decree.

[83] See the Explanatory Report to the amendment made to Art. 112(2)(a) CCI accompanying the Corrective-ter Decree.

feasibility of the project and trying to reconcile the interests and expectations of all those involved.

In other words, the risk is that the criticality present in the target company will be reproduced in the cooperative, leading to the failure of the initiative; preparatory phase is, therefore, fundamental in order to set up a project that has a chance of success. It should be articulated in a sustainable business plan and in a financial plan adequate to the initial needs and the cooperative's return possibilities. Moreover, the operation is triggered by a company crisis and it is not always possible to identify or eliminate all the factors that led to it; it is necessary to work on this aspect in order to give a signal of discontinuity with the past.

Another critical issue lies in the fact that the procedure for requesting an advance payment on NASpI, which—as explained above—is essential for the initial entry into equity by workers, takes time, leading to liquidity problems.

On the other hand, it should be considered that WBO requires many more technical aspects: specific training in professional skills, policies that facilitate employee initiatives for participation in the capital and profits of their enterprises, and adequate support for the structural funds already in place. The assessment of the sustainability of the WBO operation is critical. WBO impose a careful examination of the real possibilities for regeneration of the enterprise moving from current, operational and market conditions. That analysis on the company and the enterprise that must guide the professional in the selection of the instrument to resolve the crisis becomes, and in this case all the more so, indispensable and preparatory to any hypothesis of a WBO plan.

At the same time, however, the reorganization of the business will generally be necessary, because, due to the size of the possible investment, it is required to either downsize the business to one or more branches or to redesign the production structure making it harmonious with the financial capacity. Downsizing also often invests jobs, both because the turnaround of the business often requires downsizing employment and because of the financial commitment required.

That's why, in this sense, one can speak of a regenerated enterprise, because preservation passes through reconfiguration/restructuring that can be compared to a 'new birth'.[84]

References

Alaimo A (1998) La partecipazione azionaria dei lavoratori. Retribuzione, rischio e controllo. Giuffrè, Milano

Ambrosini S (2024) L'impresa nella Costituzione. Zanichelli, Bologna

Ambrosini S (2022) I "principi generali" nel Codice della crisi. In: Ambrosini S (ed) Crisi e insolvenza nel nuovo Codice. Zanichelli, Bologna

Aprile F (2022) Note sparse in tema di interesse dei creditori e tutela dei posti di lavoro nel concordato preventivo in continuità. Diritto della crisi 28(7):2022

[84] See De Micheli et al. (2017); Padoa Schioppa (2009).

Baglioni G (1995) Democrazia impossibile? I modelli collaborativi nell'impresa: il difficile camino della partecipazione tra democrazia ed efficienza. Il Mulino, Bologna
Barcellona E (2022) La sustainable corporate governance nelle proposte di riforma del diritto europeo: a proposito dei limiti strutturali del c.d. stakeholderism. RDS 1:1–52
Bassi A (1982) Le cooperative nella legge sull'editoria. Riv not 3:223–234
Bellè R, Russo O (2023) Lavoro e procedure concorsuali. Fallimento 8-9:1162–1166
Bellomo S, Rocchi L (2023) La sorte dei rapporti di lavoro subordinato ed autonomo nella liquidazione giudiziale. In: Alvino I, Imberti L, Romei R (eds) La gestione dei rapporti di lavoro nelle crisi di impresa. Giuffrè, Milano, pp 265–288
Bernardi A, Monni S (2016) The co-operative firm. Keywords. Tre-Press, Roma
Biagi M (1985) Cooperative e relazioni industriali della crisi; prime note alla legge 27 febbraio 1985, n. 49. Riv it dir lav (3): I/287–306
Blackiston HC, Rappaport LE, Pasini LA (1989) ESOPs: what they are and how they work. The Business Lawyer 45(1):85–143
Buhmann K (2017) Power, procedure, participation and legitimacy in global sustainability norms: a theory of collaborative regulation. Routledge, London-New York
Cataudella MC (2016) Workers buyout e soci lavoratori di cooperativa. In: Zilio Grandi G, Biasi M (eds) Commentario breve alla riforma jobs act. WKI, Padova, pp 437–450
Caragnano R (2013) Il Codice della partecipazione. Contributo allo studio della partecipazione dei lavoratori, Giuffrè, Milano
Caragnano R, Caruso G (2010) L'ESOP, uno strumento per l'impresa minore. Dossier Adapt 1:3
Cavazzuti F (2004) Il socio lavoratore fra disciplina speciale e codice civile. Giur comm 31(2):I/229-239
Corno G (2014) Un altro (significativo) passo avanti a livello comunitario verso l'armonizzazione di alcuni aspetti della normativa in materia di crisi d'impresa. La Raccomandazione della Commissione Europea 12 marzo 2014 e il possibile impatto sulla normativa italiana. Il Fallimentarista 20(6):2014
Dandolo F (2006) Giovanni Marcora e la legge sulla partecipazione dei lavoratori nella gestione delle imprese in crisi (1981-1985). Storia economica 9(2–3, 263):–304
D'Attorre G (2021a) La responsabilità sociale dell'impresa insolvente. Riv dir civ 67(1):60–92
D'Attorre G (2021b) Sostenibilità e responsabilità sociale nella crisi d'impresa. Diritto della crisi, 13.4.2021
Dasso A (2011) La inmortalidad de la empresa por la via de la cooperativa de trabajadores. Revista Societaria y Concursal 284:31
Demartini P, Monni S (2017) Workers' buyout corporate governance e sistemi di controllo. TrE-Press, Roma
De Micheli P, Imbruglia S, Misiani A (2017) Se chiudi ti compro. Le imprese rigenerate dai lavoratori. Guerini e Associati, Firenze
Denozza F (2020) Rendere lo sviluppo sostenibile e democratico. In: Caterino D, Ingravallo I (eds) L'impresa sostenibile. Euriconv, Lecce, pp 27–42
Di Cecco G (2016) Il diritto di "prelazione" previsto dalla disciplina italiana del workers' buyout a favore delle cooperative costituite dai lavoratori delle imprese in crisi. Fallimento 6:633–648
Di Stefano C (2018) The business transfer through the cooperative model. A comparative analysis Italy-France. Journal of Entrapeneurial and Organizational Diversity 7(2):62–86. (www.euricse.eu)
Drexhage J, Murphy D (2010) Sustainable development: from Brundtland to Rio 2012: background paper prepared for consideration by high level panel on sustainability at its first meeting, 19 September 2010. United Nations, New York
Fondazione Unipolis (2007) La partecipazione dei lavoratori nelle imprese. Il Mulino, Bologna
Genco R, Morara PL, Vella F (2020) Lavoratori che si ricomprano l'azienda, modello per la crisi. La voce 23(7):2020
Giovannini E (2018) L'utopia sostenibile. Laterza, Bari

Hansmann H (1990) When does worker ownership work? ESOPs, law firms, codetermination and economic democracy. Yale Law Journal 99(8):1749–1816

Howarts M (2017) Worker co-operatives and the phenomenon of Empresas Recuperadas in Argentina: an analysis of their potential for replication, Manchester

Lamanna F (2017) La prelazione a favore delle cooperative di ex dipendenti. Il Fallimentarista 9(6):2017

Legacoop (2020) Nota 8–Le imprese recuperate in Italia, marzo 2020 (http://areastudi.legacoop.coop/note-brevi-2/)

Linn T (2019) Insolvency proceedings from a sustainability perspective. International Insolvency Revue 28(2):210–232

Lowitzsch J, Hashani A, Lemmens D, Schneider S et al. (2014) The promotion of employee share ownership and participation. European Commission: Directorate-General for the Internal Market and Services, The promotion of employee ownership and participation—Executive summary, European Commission. https://data.europa.eu/doi/10.2780/15951

Lungarella R, Vella F (2022) Le nuove vie per la partecipazione dei lavoratori. La voce 22(2):2022

Marchetti A (2013) Fabbriche aperte. L'esperienza delle imprese recuperate dai lavoratori in Argentina, Il Mulino, Bologna

Mishkind S, Khorey DE (1985) Employee stock ownership plans: fables and facts. Employee Relat Law J 11(1):89–105

Niccolini G (1983) Le cooperative giornalistiche. In: Vassalli F, Visentini G (eds) Legislazione economica. Rassegne e problemi, VI. Giuffré, Milano, p 559

Nigro A (2017) La proposta di direttiva comunitaria in materia di disciplina della crisi delle imprese. Riv dir comm 115(2):II/201-221

Orlando G (2017) Le imprese recuperate in Italia. Teoria, storia e primi materiali empirici. Rassegna italiana di sociologia 3:661–678. https://doi.org/10.1423/88032

Pacchi S (2022) La gestione sostenibile della crisi d'impresa. Quaderni di Ristrutturazioni aziendali 4:5–27

Pacchi S (2021) Una possibile alternativa per la continuità indiretta: l'acquisto dell'azienda da parte dei lavoratori. Ristrutturazioni aziendali 30(6):2021

Pacchi S (2019) La ristrutturazione dell'impresa come strumento per la continuità nella Direttiva del Parlamento europeo e del Consiglio 2019/1023. Dir fall 6:I/1259-1294

Pacchi S (2015) La Raccomandazione della Commissione UE su un nuovo approccio all'insolvenza anche alla luce di una prima lettura del Regolamento UE 848/2015. Giust Civ 3:537–568

Padoa Schioppa T (2009) La veduta corta. Il Mulino, Bologna

Pagani E (2020) Il WBO quale possibile strumento di risoluzione della crisi della piccola e media impresa italiana. Il caso 1(10):2020

Pagani E (2021) La partecipazione finanziaria dei lavoratori tra diritto interno e diritto europeo. Giuffré, Milano

Pandolfo A, Rispoli Farina M, Santoro V (1986) Commentario alla legge 27 febbraio 1985, n. 49. NLCC 7: 490

Panzani L (2019) Il preventive restructuring framework nella direttiva 2019/1023 del 20 giugno 2019 ed il codice della crisi. Assonanze e dissonanze. Il caso, 14.10.2019

Patti A (2022) Tutela dei diritti dei lavoratori, salvaguardia dell'impresa e CCII. Fallimento 11:1337–1348

Paulus CG, Damman R (2021) European preventive restructuring: directive (EU) 2019/1023. Beck Hart Nomos, Oxford

Pedrazzoli M (2015) La partecipazione dei lavoratori. Un tema di natura costituzionale e politica. In: Zoli C (ed) Lavoro e impresa: la partecipazione dei lavoratori e le sue forme nel diritto italiano e comparato. Giappichelli, Torino, pp 1–14

Pendleton A (2000) Employee ownership, participation and governance: a study of ESOPs in the UK. Routledge, London

Picozza C (1986) La "Marcora" come job creation? Politica ed economia 11:31–32

Pizzolato M (2024) Le operazioni di "workers buy out" ed il CCII tra coordinamento normativo e opportunità operative. Diritto della crisi 25(11):2024
Russo R (2003) La partecipazione azionaria dei dipendenti: valutazioni comparative. In: Izar AV (ed) La partecipazione azionaria dei dipendenti. Giappichelli, Torino
Semenzin M (2019) Riprendiamoci il lavoro. Imprese recuperate e autogestite tra Argentina e Italia. Ombre Corte, Verona
Sermasi J (2012) Imprese recuperate in Argentina: pratiche collettive di reazione alla disoccupazione, 20 maggio 2012 (www.euronomade.info)
Stanghellini L (2017) La proposta di Direttiva UE in materia di insolvenza. Fallimento 8-9:873–879
Tambasco D (2020) Democratizzare il lavoro: tre proposte a 50 anni dallo Statuto dei Lavoratori. MicroMega 20(05):2020. http://temi.repubblica.it/micromega-online/democratizzare-il-lavoro-tre-proposte-a-50-anni-dallo-statuto-dei-lavoratori/
Vella F (2013) L'impresa e il lavoro: vecchi e nuovi paradigmi della partecipazione. Giur comm 40(6):1120–1152
Verrucoli P (1985) Prime osservazioni sulla legge 27 febbraio 1985, n. 49 (proposta Marcora e "Foncooper"). Riv coop (22): 167-...
Vieta M, Depedri S, Carrano A (2017) The Italian road to recuperating enterprises and the Legge Marcora framework's: Italy's worker buyouts in times of crisis, Euricse Research Report n. 15
Vieta M (2015a) The Italian road to creating worker cooperatives from worker buyouts: Italy's worker-recuperated enterprises and the Legge Marcora framework, Euricse Working Paper n. 78
Vieta M (2015b) Workers buyout. In: Bernardi A, Monni S (eds) Impresa cooperativa: Parole chiave. Il Mulino, Roma
Vieta M (2020) Saving job and businesses in times of crisis. In: Roelants B, Eum H, Esim S, Novkovic S, Katajamäki W (eds) Cooperative and the world of work. Routledge, Abingdon, pp 164–187
Vieta M, Depedri S (2015) Le imprese recuperate in Italia, EURICSE–European Research Institute on Cooperative and Social Enterprises
Vigiani F (1992) La riforma della "Marcora": una proposta. Riv coop 20
Wessels B (2007) Europe deserves a new approach to insolvency proceedings. European Company law 4(6):253–258

Right to Repair Between Intellectual Property and Servitization

Bernardo Calabrese

Abstract In the paradigm shift towards circular economy, the so-called right to repair ('R2R') is pivotal for promoting sustainable development within an innovative productive system. This proves true looking at the legislative agenda all over the world: in the European Union, such reform program gained momentum more recently, especially with Directive (EU) 2024/1799.

At a closer look, however, this Directive seems to disregard the issues of intellectual property and servitization, which represent relevant obstacles for R2R in law and in fact.

This paper criticizes such an approach, considering how the EU legislator seems to (green)wash its hands under both perspectives. Therefore, an evolutive interpretation of the Directive is here proposed in order ensure effectivity to R2R.

On one side, against an excessive reverence to intellectual property, it is maintained that the pursuit of public interest underlying repair could well entail a 'due prejudice' to private business rights, limiting their prevalence to abuse cases.

On the other side, against biased presumption that servitization is always beneficial for a sustainable circular economy, it is maintained that the consumer shall instead enjoy the right to freely turn to an open competitive market for repair, in order to counteract the relevant foreclosure effects of this contract model.

1 Introduction

In the paradigm shift towards a circular economy, the Right to Repair ('R2R') is pivotal for promoting sustainable development within an innovative productive system. This proves true looking at the legislative agenda all over the world: while

B. Calabrese (✉)
Università degli studi di Verona, Verona, Italy
e-mail: bernardo.calabrese@univr.it

B. Calabrese (ed.), *Legal Perspectives for a Sustainable Circular Economy*, European Union and its Neighbours in a Globalized World 30,
https://doi.org/10.1007/978-3-032-07795-0_7

abroad there are already important examples[1], in the EU the reform program has gained momentum more recently[2].

Looking at the content of the EU reform, major problems arise that could be significant for R2R itself, even beyond the boundaries of Europe: actually, the issues of intellectual property rights ('IPR') and servitization or product-service system ('PSS') represent critical obstacles that could impair legally and factually R2R in its effectivity.

However, the tension between R2R and such obstacles seems overlooked in the reform: in fact, on one side, the EU legislator decided to introduce repair obligations for manufactures 'unless justified by' and 'without prejudice to' the protection of IPR; moreover, on the other side, repair obligations are primarily addressed to traditional sale contracts, assuming the manufacturers' reluctance to provide relevant services, without considering the ambivalent nature of PSS.

This paper criticizes such an approach, considering—with some provocative tone—how the EU legislator seems to (green)wash its hands under both perspectives. In particular, the paper develops the argumentation as follows: after a brief presentation in Sect. 2 of R2R within the framework of sustainable circular economy, Sect. 3 reports the obstacles to an effective R2R that derive respectively from IPR (3.1) and PSS (3.2); then, Sect. 4 focuses on the EU legislative agenda on R2R, analyzing its core element represented by Directive (EU) 2024/1799 (hereinafter also just the 'Directive'); Sect. 5 sets out the critical issues of such reform, under each of the considered perspectives of IPR (5.1) and PSS (5.2); accordingly, Sect. 6 illustrates possible corrective solutions, again respectively for IPR (6.1) and PSS (6.2); finally, Sect. 7 concludes.

2 The New Paradigm of Sustainable Circular Economy and the Right to Repair

The so-called circular economy—according to the common definition of 'an economy that is restorative and regenerative by design'[3]—represents the main conversion of the new paradigm of sustainability in terms of productive model, whose

[1] For an updated recap of the situation in the US see Calboli (2023), as well as Grinvald and Tur-Sinai (2024); even more recently, with a specific focus on the agricultural sector (where the famous case of John Deere tractors brought to light the controversial nature of repair for current technological products with relevant intellectual property rights), see Rimmer (2025). More in general, about the international agenda towards circular economy and sustainability beyond the EU policy action see Candelmo (Chap. 10).

[2] Actually, the EU reform here discussed has been approved in the time of writing, however confirming the text agreed by the European Parliament and the Council in the last rounds of negotiations, with relevant amendments to the original proposal: therefore, save where specified otherwise, all comments can be referred to the promulgated version of Directive (EU) 2024/1799, of 13 June 2024, on common rules promoting the repair of goods (OJEU, 10 July 2024, L).

[3] Ellen Macarthur Foundation (2015), p. 47.

significance is not limited to business concerns but is intended to reshape the world we live in.

From this perspective, economic growth is traditionally seen as bringing about greater entropy, with inevitable negative social and environmental repercussions, almost as if it were a necessary price to be paid for achieving progress. However, the novelty of circular economy lies precisely in its discontinuity with previous models, internalizing sustainability as its cardinal principle.

This new paradigm of an economy that is circular and thus sustainable represents a real challenge for the system, and it would be wrong to consider it in a reductive way as a mere return to traditional—albeit valid and wise—good practices of reusing and saving from a pre-industrial era: in fact, the challenge is to reconcile an advanced and innovative economy, such as that of today's global and digital market, with principles of socio-environmental sustainability, so that the level of collective wellbeing achieved becomes the basis for further flourishing, to the benefit of all. Such a radical change would have a major impact on current production and consumption patterns, which in turn is meant to revolutionize not only the economy but also society as a whole[4].

This is the context where R2R is framed, which by the way has now risen to the status of a truly global movement[5]. In opposition to the exasperation of an economic model that pushes to consume more and more, in a swirling and endless chase towards productive novelties (whether real or narrated), R2R responds to the need to preserve the utility of existing goods, in some ways 'reclaiming' control over one's possessions and, by extension, one's autonomy[6]. This is enough to understand how R2R fits perfectly into the discourse on circular economy, epitomizing the disavowal of the linear 'make-take-dispose' model in favor of practices aimed at saving the value inherent in circulating goods and putting it back into the production cycle[7].

As much as repair is a historical need, perhaps as old as human manufacturing, the existing legal system does not provide a specific discipline. Usually, repair is concerned when regulating products defect in terms of conformity and related warranty on the manufacturer, but this perspective is closely related more to purchase contracts than to the possession of the good apart from the relevant commercial transaction[8]. What is lacking, therefore, is a true statute for R2R, which goes beyond

---

[4] For a brief manifesto see Stahel (2016); for a recent empirical study in the field see Fedele and Hysa (2024).

[5] As demonstrated by the attention in general media: 'Fix, or Toss? The 'Right to Repair' Movement Gains Ground', New York Times, 23 October 2020 (https://www.nytimes.com/2020/10/23/climate/right-to-repair.html); in parallel, stakeholders associations are growing almost all over the world: for example, in the geographic context of the legislation here analyzed, see 'Right to Repair Europe', a coalition representing over 100 organizations from 21 European Countries (https://repair.eu/about/); for a general framework see Ozturkcan (2023).

[6] Express reference is to the pivotal work of Perzanowski (2022).

[7] As a confirm from a technical perspective, see for example Jonas et al. (2023).

[8] For an analysis of direct contractual remedies (and their limits) see Terryn (2019).

the simplistic consideration of this need as something to be dealt with on a 'do-it-yourself' basis.

From this point of view, technological progress has made such an approach to R2R totally anti-historical. There is too much technical (especially IT) complexity in the products we have access to, even for everyday needs. It is therefore crucial to contextualize R2R in its market dimension, that is, as an economic sector of services (assistance) and goods (tools and spare parts) that consumers must rely on, in order to effectively achieve a practical result otherwise beyond their reach. Without this commercial dimension, one cannot appreciate the extent of repair in its various individual and systemic implications. At the same time, without considering the market, one cannot understand the problems that currently impair repair, in terms of obstacles to its effective realization.

3 Obstacles to an Effective Right to Repair

It is precisely the market dimension of repair that may explain the existence of obstacles to R2R, arising from the conflict between the economic actors involved: manufacturers, on the one hand, and repairers, on the other hand.

Manufacturers aim to internalize repair, both to cash in on the associated economic value (often far from negligible, compared to the product's price alone) and to seize strategic control of their supply (so as to manage the 'generational' replacement of products, according to the classic pattern of planned obsolescence)[9].

In contrast, repairers are independent operators that intervene downstream of the product sale, and that base their business on the competitive supply of repair services directly to customers, trying to take advantage of economic opportunities that, deliberately or naturally, manufacturers leave behind[10].

In this framework, consumers stand primarily alongside repairers, to whom they can—and, as mentioned, to some extent must—turn to implement their personal choice of repair. Beyond that, the role of consumers is, in truth, more ambiguous[11]: while repairers certainly live on the demand of consumers, at the same time consumers themselves often fuel the continuous renewal policies of manufacturers, favoring replacement over repair of the broken product, as evidence of how deeply the consumerist model pervades our social habits[12].

In any case, this situation illustrates well the conflict that characterizes the repair market, with manufacturers attempting to tackle any 'hostile' initiative to their

[9] In general, see Slade (2007); from the legal perspective at hand, see Malinauskaite and Erdem (2021), as well as more recently Philippe (2024) and Pihlajarinne (2024).

[10] For a practical study see van der Velden et al. (2024).

[11] More broadly on this in the EU context see Deana (Chap. 7).

[12] For a confirm, in the context of a wider analysis on the relevance of 'cultural' barriers to circular economy, see Kirchherr et al. (2018). More in general, for a sociological perspective about the reigning economic model see Marzulli (Chap. 1).

economic interests. Actually, the opposition is so strong that it entails not only typical restrictions against repairers, like for any other threatening competitor, but a more comprehensive constraint to repair as an objective result itself: namely, the aim is to avoid relevant economic losses deriving both directly and indirectly from independent repair, with the consequent effect of impairing the respective substantive need of personal users.

In this sense, manufacturers have historically deployed various strategies to limit the possibilities of independent product repair, along (and often across) the uncertain boundary between legitimate claims and abusive practices. Such strategies are based on different obstacles of technical, legal and factual nature[13]. For the purposes of this analysis, two in particular will be explored: intellectual property rights and servitization.

3.1 *Obstacles: Intellectual Property*

In the first place, intellectualy property rights (again 'IPR') could hinder repair in many ways. As vastly denounced by scholars all over the world[14], almost each and every IPR can conflict with initiatives for repair by independent operators and personal users. Since the issue in question is already well-known, just a brief summary is provided here.

Patents for invention are the most classic case. In a certain way, it could be said that patents are so immediately in contrast with repair that they are not so puzzling or, better, that the issue revolves around a quite simple point: it should be verified to what extent repair does represent the reconstruction of the protected invention itself, which as such falls within the legitimate monopoly of the rightholder[15]. If this verification is inevitably less simple and depends on a case-by-case assessment, the increasing presence of patented components in technological products makes the situation more intricate and, therefore, more uncertain for repair activities[16].

Exclusive rights on design—to be intended as the aesthetic appearance of products[17]—could seem less significant, being separated from the technical dimension. Furthermore, the legal regime seems well aware of this distinction, avoiding that

[13] Epitomized by the practice of serialization and parts pairing, specifically denounced as an obstacle to repair to be tackled by the reform in Opinion of the European Economic and Social Committee (2023/C 293/11), para. 4.3.3; for a general overview of such practical barriers see Svensson-Hoglund et al. (2021).

[14] In addition to Perzanowski (2022), p. 105, see from different international perspectives, just as examples, Grinvald and Tur-Sinai (2019); Pihlajarinne (2021); Arora (2021); Rosborough (2022a); Rimmer (2022); Reynolds (2023); Quan and Zhang (2023); Montagnani (2023); Wiseman (2024); Calboli (2024).

[15] In these terms the historical case in the US, *Aro Mfg. Co. v. Convertible Top Replacement Co.*, 365 U.S. 336 (1961).

[16] On the point, with a focus on relevant case-law, see Mohri (2010).

[17] In EU law, product design is mainly protected with exclusive rights based on registration as a unitary title under Regulation (EC) 2002/6, as recently reformed by Regulation (EU) 2024/2822;

design rights could extend to relevant technical features of products[18]. However, design rights enter into question every time the restoration of the product involves also its appearance: all the more so considering that such exclusive rights can protect both the product as a whole and its individual components, with consequent impact on spare parts[19]. In this sense, repair by its very nature tends to conflict with design rights[20].

Trademarks could appear even less problematic, being essentially related to matters of commercial origin. However, the recognized extension of trademark functions also to brand image protection, together with the pervasive material affixing of the sign on products, entails a broad possibility of control against repair. This proves true especially for spare parts, which are always more frequently 'marked' with names and logos[21]. The same is also true for products as such, if the repaired product is then put again on the market, because this independent activity could interfere

and in parallel with national titles originally harmonized by Directive (EC) 1998/71, now equally recast by Directive (EU) 2024/2823.

[18] Including so-called 'must-fit' parts, as stated by Art. 8(2) Regulation (EC) 2002/6 and Art. 7(2) Directive (EC) 1998/71; see Schovsbo and Dinwoodie (2018); in a comparative perspective see Janis (2021).

[19] Design protection can extend also to component part of complex products, as long as such parts fulfills individually the requirements of novelty and individual character, plus remaining visible under normal use; on such conditions see CJEU, 16 February 2023, Case C-472/21, *Monz v. Büchel*, ECLI:EU:C:2023:105; in general on this conflict see Firth (2009); all this without mentioning the thorny issue of overlap with trademark rights: more broadly on this point see Tischner (2021).

[20] In fact, so-called 'must-match' parts were regulated by virtue of a controversial transitional provision in favour of free replicability for repair under Art. 110 Regulation (EC) 2002/6, save some difference at the national level as admitted by Art. 14 Directive (EC) 1998/71: for the practical application of this exemption see CJEU, 20 December 2017, Joined Cases C-397/16 and C-435/16, *Acacia v. Audi*, ECLI:EU:C:2017:992; however, the so-called 'repair clause' has now been definitely established by the recent reform in Art. 20a Regulation (EC) 2002/6 and Art. 19 Directive (EU) 2024/2823, as a denial of protection for rightholders against 'component part of a complex product upon whose appearance the design of the component part is dependent, and which is used [...] for the sole purpose of the repair of that complex product so as to restore its original appearance', subject to certain diligence obligations by third-party manufacturers and sellers to 'duly inform consumers, through a clear and visible indication on the product or in another appropriate form, about the commercial origin, and the identity of the manufacturer, of the product to be used for the purpose of the repair of the complex product, so that they can make an informed choice between competing products that can be used for the repair', without resulting in the 'guarantee that the component parts they make or sell are ultimately used by end users for the sole purpose of repair so as to restore the original appearance of the complex product'.

[21] In EU see recently CJEU, 25 January 2024, Case C-334/22, *Audi v. GQ*, ECLI:EU:C:2024:76; for the background of this case see Tischner and Stasiuk (2023); another recent famous case coming from 'continental' Europe is Norwegian Supreme Court, 2 June 2020, *Henrik Huseby v Apple*, HR-2020-1142-A (available in English at https://www.domstol.no/globalassets/upload/hret/decisions-in-english-translation/hr-2020-1142-a.pdf), commented by Rognstad (2021).

with the rightholder's prerogatives in authorizing the manipulation and reselling of the 'marked' product[22].

Copyright epitomizes the new kind of obstacles that IPR poses to repair in the contemporary world. This is not so much for the question of the (cumulative) protection of aesthetic appearance as a work of art[23], but instead for digital copyright, since it covers software that, as known, characterizes almost every product in today's Internet-of-Things ('IoT') era[24]. Thus, if there is an unavoidable need to intervene on software to perform repair, copyright becomes an effective barrier in practice[25], particularly considering the additional layer posed by technological protection measures[26].

Copyright is also relevant to instruction manuals, and this broadens the field to include in the discourse other forms of protection that may cover 'instrumental' aspects, such as technical information and data, which are increasingly important for repair[27]. From this point of view, trade secrets and further means of *de facto* exclusivity may entail all but negligible impeding effects[28].

To sum up, it is important to stress that all these possible conflicts constitute a significant obstacle mainly because it lacks a specific discipline that regulates repair in the presence of IPR: it follows that exclusive rights can therefore be—more or less legitimately, but promptly—opposed by the manufacturer against repair,

---

[22] See more specifically Kur (2021); Senftleben (2024); Geiregat (2024); and also please concede the reference to Calabrese (2025); for a similar analysis under the US system see Cahoy (2023).

[23] Although this issue should not be underestimated, especially in the context of recent EU expansive trends: see CJEU, 12 September 2019, Case C-683/17, *Cofemel v. G-Star Raw*, ECLI:EU:C:2019:721, followed by CJEU, 11 June 2020, Case C-833/18, *Brompton Bicycle v. Get2Get*, ECLI:EU:C:2020:461; the principle of cumulative protection has been codified in the recent design reform by Art. 96(2), Regulation (EC) 6/2002 (as amended by Regulation (EU) 2024/2822), and in parallel Art. 23, Directive (EU) 2024/2823; on this problematic overlap see generally Fabbio (2018) and more recently Ricketson and Suthersanen (2023); for a specific focus on EU case law see Kur (2020) as well as Levin (2021); for a further critical review see Musso (2024).

[24] Among many, see recently Noto La Diega (2023), p. 275; for practical confirmation, involving the (denied) registration of 'FOOTWARE' as a trademark for 'electronic devices and computer software that allow users to remotely interact with other smart devices for monitoring and controlling automated systems' and similar classes, see GCEU, 12 June 2024, Case T-130/23, *Nike Innovation v. EUIPO*, ECLI:EU:T:2024:373.

[25] Specifically from EU law perspective see Widła (2023).

[26] In this sense, referring comparatively also to the exemption to prohibition on circumvention of copyright protection systems for access control technologies by US Copyright Office (Library of Congress 37 CFR 201, Docket No 2020–11), see Rosborough (2020), and even more broadly see Derclaye (2009).

[27] In addition see Rosborough (2022b).

[28] This is true also in terms of how consumers perceive the existence of obstacles to repair, as illustrated by Perzanowski (2021); generally on this topic of '*de facto*' powers with respect to IPR see Ricolfi (2022).

notwithstanding the principle of exhaustion[29]. The result is that the system is far from favorable to R2R, all the more so when one considers the high level of protection that characterizes IPR enforcement at the international level[30].

3.2 Obstacles: Servitization

A further problem is hiding in the mesh of the system, which could paradoxically impair the effectiveness of R2R even more strongly. Namely, the personal choice to repair could be deprived of its substance through manufacturers' strategy of changing consumers' habits, offering PSS (as said 'product-service-system', tantamount to 'product-as-a-service' or 'servitization') instead of classic ownership[31].

Apparently, one might think that this kind of offer is not problematic in itself, following normal market dynamics, if not even improving sustainability of traditional industrial models[32].

However, assessing the impact of PSS is more complicated: in fact, such a model allows manufacturers to internalize the management of product lifespan, including the provision of repair services, so that this deferral of control over personal goods entails several risks for R2R[33].

The first and most obvious risk is to surreptitiously encourage product obsolescence. This is because of the convergence between the producer's business advantage and the consumer's longing for innovation (promptly supported by the productive system itself), which, however, sacrifices all the collective benefits of repair[34].

Further risks relate to the anticompetitive consequences of PSS, which take the form of both consumer lock-in and competitor lock-out effects. This is explained by the joint functioning of contractual constraints and customer loyalty, which causes an exclusionary mechanism for independent repairers. As an example, it is enough

---

[29] For a specific analysis in this perspective, struggling with the existing limits of exhaustion, for example about patent law, see Heath (2014), as well as Liu (2014); along this line, pushing for an evolutive interpretation of exhaustion, see Calboli (2024); similarly, with specific regard to trademarks, see Geiregat (2024) and also by analogy please concede again the reference to Calabrese (2025); more broadly on such fundamental principle applied to repair see Ghosh (2022).

[30] For a critical review of the overall IP system see Ghidini (2018); for a specific collection of cases and comments in this sense see Bonadio and O'Connell (2022).

[31] For this equivalence in terminology see Annarelli et al. (2016); for a classic definition of PSS, expressing its environmentally-friendly character, see Mont (2002); however, highlighting a shift of focus from environmental to economic aspects of PSS, see Haase et al. (2017).

[32] The critical remarks here moved about repair do not imply a total denial of potential positive aspects of PSS in the broader perspective of sustainability: in this sense see De Franceschi (2023), who actually confirms the ambivalence of PSS in terms of potential benefits and risks.

[33] For an effective presentation of detrimental effects for repair related to PSS see Perzanwoski (2022), p. 243.

[34] For this combined attitude less favourable for repair see Mak and Terryn (2020).

to recall the case of ancillary repair services offered ostensibly free of charge, but whose price is actually incorporated in the general fee for PSS: this implies that, in truth, consumers have already paid for repair from the outset, with a consequent disincentive to turn to independent repairers[35].

It is important to note how this situation of 'relativized' dependence represents an anticompetitive leverage for manufacturers, which are attracted by the possibility of enclosing their commercial system so as to insulate it from the competitive pressure of independent repairers[36]. What is more, PSS allows manufacturers to protect from users themselves and their countervailing power arising from private property, also considering the conceivable convergence of the industry towards these much-preferred formulas of totalized control over consumption dynamics[37].

To sum up, the problem of PSS revolves around a basic conflict of interest that concerns the manufacturer, because the best repair of its products is usually less convenient for its own business. The result is the tendency to employ such a contractual model as a tying mechanism, making it more difficult for consumers to exercise their autonomy about repair outside the manufacturer's network and preferences.

In essence, it can be said that PSS entails a risk of 'legal rebound effect': as, in economic terms, systems based on 'using' instead of 'owning' have been seen to often cause a paradoxical rebound, pushing people to consume more (and worse), PSS also affects repair despite the contractual provision of relevant services, which paradoxically push back market alternatives and user freedom to the detriment of R2R[38].

4 The EU Legislative Agenda and the New Directive on Right to Repair

From (legal) theory to reality, the EU has fully embraced the paradigm of sustainable circular economy as a necessary step for its future, according to an ambitious political program of structural reforms.

Without going into the merits of an obviously more complex discourse, the rather 'rose-tinted' tones of the EU programmatic statements cannot hide the perplexity about the actual salvific capacity of this new model, first of all because it should at least be shared on a global scale. However, even if it were not decisive, it is equally true that the beneficial impact of circular economy might be significant, and that,

[35] On these economic profiles of PSS see Hojnik (2016); for an updated reflection see also Hojnik (2023).

[36] About this disincentive for manufacturers to open up repair in case of PSS, even against sustainability concerns, see expressly Hernandez et al. (2020).

[37] More broadly on this topic Perzanowski and Schultz (2016).

[38] This idea of possible 'rebound effects' of PSS not only in economic but also in regulatory terms can be found in Hojnik (2016), p. 10–11.

aside from any doubts about its effectiveness, its approach remains appreciable in promoting practices of economic 'common sense'.

Therefore, any mistrust of this kind does not legitimize discrediting this policy action *per se*, which, on the contrary—given the urgency of the situation and the meritorious goal of attempting to remedy it—must necessarily be taken seriously, not least because it is a paradigm shift that seems here to stay. That is why the EU policy agenda for circular economy remains absolutely relevant, not only (obviously) for European citizens, but also for other countries, which could look at this initiative in order to gain useful experiences for their own regulatory purposes, as well as for the international action at the global level.

Moving into the details of the legislative agenda, the EU has envisioned reforms that address many profiles of sustainable circular economy, as stated in the relevant policy manifesto[39].

In particular, with regard to product repairability, a distinction should be made between pre-sale and after-sale measures.

In the pre-sale context, the major instrument is the equally recent Regulation (EU) 2024/1781 on ecodesign requirements for sustainable products, which includes specific action for improving product repairability[40]. This reform also supports the establishment of a harmonized repairability score[41], which comes in addition to relevant informative requirements of products at the point of sale, as disciplined by Directive (EU) 2024/825[42]. In this latter normative frame, mention should also be made of the relevant provisions that regulate the fairness of commercial practices in terms of sustainability labels and environmental claims, to counter the increasing phenomenon of greenwashing in market communication[43].

In the after-sale context, there are also several norms that concern R2R, such as the regime for requesting repair as a legal remedy for defective products under

[39] With specific regard to circular economy see Communication from the Commission, 'Closing the loop—An EU action plan for the Circular Economy', COM(2015) 614 final, followed by Communication from the Commission, 'A new Circular Economy Action Plan–For a cleaner and more competitive Europe', COM(2020) 98 final; in parallel, on the side of consumers, see Communication from the Commission, 'New Consumer Agenda–Strengthening consumer resilience for sustainable recovery', COM/2020/696 final; more in general for the paradigm transition of EU towards sustainability see Communication from the Commission, 'The European Green Deal', COM(2019) 640 final; for a comparison with other policy initiatives at the international level see again Candelmo (Chap. 10).

[40] Art. 5(1)(e), Regulation (EU) 2024/1781, and also—as an indirect confirm of the risk mentioned above about leaving the management of product life-cycle only in the hands of manufacturers—Art. 5(2) in terms of assuring repairability against practices of planned obsolenscence: on this, see more specifically Deana (Chap. 7).

[41] Art. 7(2)(b)(i), Regulation (EU) 2024/1781.

[42] Art. 2, Directive (EU) 2024/825.

[43] Art. 1, Directive (EU) 2024/825; on the relevant implications for intellectual property, see Spedicato (2024).

Directive (EU) 2019/771[44], as well as the exemption for independent repairers under Dircctive (EU) 2024/2853 on liability for defective products[45]. But most importantly, there is the main reform for the issue at hand, namely Directive (EU) 2024/1799 on common rules promoting the repair of goods, which has been publicly presented as the introduction of a EU-wide R2R[46]. This is why the analysis will focus on this new piece of legislation[47].

In principle, it is undoubtedly an important decision to act in favour of R2R at the EU level with strong harmonization, in order to avoid national fragmentation and, therefore, ineffectiveness within the single market[48]. In this sense, also the outward approach seems correct, looking beyond the European borders through the involvement of the relevant 'authorised representative, importer and distributor' as local business gatekeepers for extra-territorial producers[49]. Even more important is the express recognition that the objectives of the reform are directly related to circular economy and sustainability, so as to create solid foundations for the new provisions[50].

Beyond the political statements, however, there is the normative content: and here certain critical points come to attention.

---

[44] Art. 14, Directive (EU) 2019/771, together with Recital 48 highlighting the connection of such provision with the new paradigm of sustainable circular economy.

[45] Art. 11(1)(g), Directive (EU) 2024/2853, again to be read in conjunction with Recital 39 that underlines the connection with sustainable circular economy.

[46] About the recent Directive (EU) 2024/1799 on common rules for promoting the repair of goods, see the relevant press release by European Commission, 2 February 2024, 'Commission welcomes political agreement on new consumer rights for easy and attractive repairs', IP/24/608 (https://ec.europa.eu/commission/presscorner/detail/en/ip_24_608).

[47] This does not mean that R2R is confined to this single piece of legislation: it is just to stress the pivotal role of the new Directive (EU) 2024/1799, without disregarding other complementary initiatives that can be very important for product repairability and circularity, also from a less legal and more technical perspective, like the standardization of a common USB-C charger for every mobile devices in EU as recently mandated by Directive (EU) 2022/2380.

[48] See Art. 3, Directive (EU) 2024/1799 (together with Recital 2 and 46 of the same legal text).

[49] See Arts. 5(3) and 6, Directive (EU) 2024/1799.

[50] See expressly Recitals 1, 40, 41 Directive (EU) 2024/1799, and even more clearly Recital 5, which states that 'this Directive thus pursues the objectives, in the context of the European Green Deal, of promoting a more sustainable consumption, a circular economy and the green transition'.

5 Critical Issues of the Approved EU Reform

The new EU Directive regulating a right to repair—or, more correctly, an 'obligation' to repair, as it will be explained immediately—has been finally approved, after relevant discussion and amendments[51]. In brief, the Directive provides different measures to promote repair in a market environment.

On one side, there are mandatory informative actions, also in terms of standard forms and public platforms, in order to give to consumers the necessary means to evaluate and eventually compare the possible options for repairing the product[52].

On the other side, the Directive imposes on manufacturers a new general obligation to repair, which represents the real core of the reform[53].

In particular, this obligation consists not only of the active duty to repair the product upon consumer's request (save technical impossibility)[54], but also of the condition to perform repair in a reasonable time and for a reasonable price, if not even free of charge[55]. In addition, a reasonable price is also mandated for spare parts and tools made accessible by manufacturers, without actually indicating how to calculate its amount but specifying that it 'shall not deter repair'[56]. Finally, such obligation is integrated by a correspondent prohibition on the same manufacturers to oppose legal or factual restraints to repair, in terms of 'contractual clauses, hardware or software techniques', also against the use of 'original or second-hand spare parts, compatible spare parts and spare parts issued from 3D-printing' by independent repairers[57]. In this sense, the freedom for consumers to seek repair services from competitors is expressly safeguarded[58], together with the non-derogability by contract of all the abovementioned measures to their benefit[59].

The analysis here does not go on to comment on all the innovations of the Directive, which do introduce interesting aspects, such as the categorization of

[51] For the original proposal see EU Commission, Proposal for a Directive COM(2023) 155 final; the relevant preparatory works of procedure 2023/0083 (COD) can be found on the EU official website https://eur-lex.europa.eu/legal-content/EN/HIS/?uri=CELEX:52023PC0155.

[52] See, respectively, Arts. 4 and 7, Directive (EU) 2024/1799.

[53] See, Art. 5, Directive (EU) 2024/1799, indexed as 'Obligation to repair'.

[54] See Art. 5(1), Directive (EU) 2024/1799, together with Recital 24, where it is explained that 'a manufacturer should be exempted from the obligation to repair where repair is factually or legally impossible. Therefore, the manufacturer should not be able to refuse repair for purely economic reasons, such as the cost of spare parts, or for the sole reason that a previous repair has been performed by other repairers or, where applicable, by the consumer'.

[55] See Art. 5(2), Directive (EU) 2024/1799, which adds that 'in cases where the repair is impossible, the manufacturer may offer the consumer a refurbished good'.

[56] See expressly Art. 5(4), Directive (EU) 2024/1799.

[57] See Art. 5(6), Directive (EU) 2024/1799, to which the following Art. 5(7) adds that 'manufacturers shall not refuse to repair goods covered by Union legal acts listed in Annex II for the sole reason that a previous repair has been performed by other repairers or by other persons'.

[58] See Art. 5(8), Directive (EU) 2024/1799.

[59] See Art. 14, Directive (EU) 2024/1799.

misleading repair information as unfair commercial practice[60] or the institutional provision of effective penalties[61]. Likewise, the comment will not cover all the critical aspects of the reform, whether more technical, such as the online platform system[62], or more general, such as the limited scope of the goods actually encompassed[63].

In fact, the present analysis will focus on those two specific aspects of IPR and PSS already anticipated as widely-recognized barriers to R2R. This is not so much because they deserve more attention than others in the abstract, but because they turn out to be almost totally overlooked by the EU legislator, who from this point of view seems to have been (green)washing its hands.

5.1 Critical Issues: Intellectual Property

As said, it is well known that R2R clashes with IPR that insist on various aspects of the product. From this point of view, it is true that the Directive takes expressly into account intellectual property: this can be considered, at first glance, an appropriate improvement with respect to the original proposal that did not even mention it[64].

However, the norm is too ambiguous to say that the issue of IPR has been duly tackled by the EU legislator, and even more that it provides a discipline capable of resolving the conflict caused by such exclusive rights with R2R.

In fact, the Directive juxtaposes repair obligations with possible counter-interests by manufacturers based on IPR. In particular, the opposition of legal and technical barriers to repair is prohibited 'unless justified by legitimate and objective factors including the protection of intellectual property rights'; equally, the ban on manufacturers' impediment against non-original spare parts is confined only to 'when those spare parts are in conformity with requirements under Union or national law such as requirements on product safety or in compliance with intellectual property';

[60] See Recital 19, Directive (EU) 2024/1799, where it is affirmed that 'traders' practices that induce consumers to think that their goods cannot be repaired due to previous repair or inspection by an independent repairer, non-professional repairer or end-users, or false claims that such repair or inspection generates risks related to safety, thereby misleading consumers, could, where applicable, constitute unfair commercial practices'.

[61] See Art. 15, Directive (EU) 2024/1799.

[62] The EU platform, appreciable as a matter of principle, leaves some doubt about its practical organization: in this sense, see the joint statement of Estonia and Latvia, who abstained from approval (Council, 27 May 2024, ST 9378 2024 ADD 1); in fact, some intricacy between European and national levels for such online platform emerges from Recital 27, Directive (EU) 2024/1799.

[63] More precisely, the scope of such repair obligations is limited only to the categories of products listed in Annex II, following the rationale of matching repairability requirements imposed elsewhere in EU law, especially connecting to the new ecodesign Regulation (EU) 2024/1781: see Art. 1(3), Directive (EU) 2024/1799.

[64] Just check the very same wording of Commission, Proposal for a Directive COM(2023) 155 final; in fact, during preparatory works this gap was highlighted by Opinion of the European Committee of the Regions—Consumers' protection package, (C/2023/1330), para. 23.

eventually, the entire norm on repair obligations is circumscribed in being 'without prejudice to Union and national law providing for the protection of intellectual property rights'[65].

The (in)famous 'without prejudice' formula inevitably raises some concerns. One could say that the situation is not as problematic as it seems, by virtue of the combined reading with Regulation (EU) 2024/1781 on ecodesign requirements, which the Directive expressly recalls: in fact, that Regulation imposes an obligation to producers to provide access to spare parts, repair and maintenance information and any repair related software tools, firmware or similar auxiliary means; moreover, the same Directive reinforces such beneficial effects, adding that access to spare parts and tools should be made available at reasonable price that does not deter repair[66].

However, this is exactly where the problem stays with the chosen 'without prejudice' formula. Namely, any repair obligation promoted directly or indirectly by the legal text becomes weakened, or even deprived of its useful content, if it cannot implicate a relevant compression of exclusive rights. In other words, this normative construction is problematic because it tends to subordinate R2R to IPR—and apparently to each type of IPR[67]—in every conflict situation.

Certainly, the relationship between IPR and competing interests, in terms of related 'prejudice' and possible justifications, is far more complex. In this case, looking at the Directive, there is a feeling that the EU legislator wanted to support R2R, encouraging a general procompetitive approach to the repair market, instead of putting IPR at the center as with the dangerous rhetoric of fundamental rights[68].

---

[65] See literally Art. 5(6), Directive (EU) 2024/1799.

[66] In this sense, see Recital 18, Directive (EU) 2024/1799, where it is specified that 'under the requirements laid down in delegated acts adopted pursuant to Regulation (EU) 2024/1781 or implementing measures adopted pursuant to Directive 2009/125/EC of the European Parliament and of the Council, manufacturers are to provide access to spare parts, repair and maintenance information or any repair related software tools, firmware or similar auxiliary means. Those requirements ensure the technical feasibility of repair, not only by the manufacturer, but also by other repairers. As a consequence, the repairers and, where applicable, consumers will have access to spare parts and repair-related information and tools in accordance with Union legal acts and consumers will have a wider choice of repairers or, where applicable, the possibility to repair by themselves. Spare parts should be made available at least for the time period set out in Union legal acts. Manufacturers that make spare parts and tools available for goods covered by legal acts listed in Annex II to this Directive, whether because of corresponding legal obligations under Union law or voluntarily, should charge a reasonable price that does not deter access to such spare parts and tools, thereby preventing repair'.

[67] See again Recital 18, Directive (EU) 2024/1799, which, notwithstanding the declamatory conclusion that 'this should encourage competition and benefit consumers with better services and lower repair prices', recalls expressly Directive (EC) 2004/48 on the enforcement of intellectual property rights that in turn, at its Art. 1, refers to all kind of intellectual property rights, including 'industrial property rights', as further confirmed by Communication from the Commission, 'Guidance on certain aspects of Directive 2004/48/EC of the European Parliament and of the Council on the enforcement of intellectual property rights', COM(2017) 708 final, para. V.1.

[68] See Recital 47, Directive (EU) 2024/1799, where intellectual property is not actually mentioned as a fundamental right protected under Art. 17(2), EU Charter of Fundamental Rights, while it is

Such a feeling, however, clashes with the stark normative reality. Leveraging on the strict rule of the Directive, it would be immediate for manufacturers to invoke IPR as a valid justification against R2R[69].

The situation gets exacerbated considering that EU intellectual property law, as it stands, is not so friendly towards R2R. While it is true that further reforms proceed in this direction, such as the definitive enactment of the repair clause for design rights[70], it is equally true that, conversely, in the absence of specific modifications, the system shows little flexibility in favour of this principle[71].

In order to show how it is not so straightforward to reconstruct within the current system an effective R2R 'without prejudice' to IPR, it is enough to mention copyright[72]. In this matter, at EU level reigns an approach of 'exceptionalism' that makes any pro-competitive or even pro-user interpretation difficult[73]. As is well known, copyright is far from secondary to IoT products, which may have software problems whose repairability is strongly limited by the relevant exclusive protection[74]. This demonstrates how critical the reform is, because the rule that ostensibly prohibits 'software techniques' that impede R2R also subordinates such a prohibition to the legitimate justification of IPR, with the paradoxical result of emptying the very

specifically recognized that the Directive—in addition that 'it contributes to an improvement of the quality of the environment in accordance with Article 37 of the Charter by promoting sustainable consumption of goods and thereby reducing negative environmental impacts from premature disposal of viable goods'—also 'ensures respect for the freedom to conduct a business in accordance with Article 16 of the Charter by safeguarding contractual freedom and encouraging the development of repair services in the internal market'.

[69] In fact, Art. 5(6), Directive (EU) 2024/1799 in its overall reading entails a 'three-time' denial of R2R in favor of IPR (almost of evangelic echo).

[70] See recently Art. 20a, Regulation (EC) 6/2002 (as amended by Regulation (EU) 2024/2822), and in parallel Art. 19, Directive (EU) 2024/2823.

[71] See again very recently CJEU, 25 January 2024, Case C-334/22, *Audi v. GQ*, ECLI:EU:C:2024:76, where it is affirmed that 'it should be pointed out, as the referring court did, that a so-called 'repair' clause, such as that existing in design law under Article 110 of Regulation No 6/2002, was not provided for by the EU legislature in Regulation 2017/1001. Furthermore, the Court has already clarified the scope of Article 110 of Regulation No 6/2002, in that it imposes certain limitations only on protection conferred on designs and applies without prejudice to the provisions of EU law relating to trade marks. That provision therefore contains no derogation from EU trade mark law' (paras. 26–27); this need for a broader approach to R2R with regard to all IPR (and even beyond) is to some extent testified, in the context of preparatory works of the same Directive here analyzed, by the Opinion of the European Economic and Social Committee (2023/C 293/11), para. 1.6, where 'the EESC calls on the Commission to assess the possibility of supporting data sharing for spare parts and product repairability, as part of the ongoing modernisation of the intellectual property framework'.

[72] By the way, even the recent reform of EU design rights does not mention copyright within the new repair clause, although it maintains a direct recognition of the principle of cumulative protection: see Art. 96(2), Regulation (EC) 6/2002 (as amended by Regulation (EU) 2024/2822), and in parallel Art. 23, Directive (EU) 2024/2823.

[73] Literally for this expression see Margoni and Kretschmer (2022); more broadly in this perspective see Sganga (2024).

[74] For a discussion of such cases within the EU system see Widła (2023).

same obligation just affirmed. This ends up in a sort of fallacious (and ironical) argumentative 'circularity'.

But even apart from deeper questions about the balancing of intellectual property, the problematic nature of this legal formula emerges in all its concreteness looking at the burden of proof it entails, which is totally in favour of manufacturers. In fact, by relying on the reading that IPR are presumed to be a viable justification by the Directive, which in turn is based on the general presumption of validity and protection of IPR by the legal order, manufacturers are in the position to discharge themselves and turn everything over to independent repairers and consumers, who must subsequently demonstrate to the contrary that such business justification is not 'legitimate and objective'[75]. This issue of burden of proof alone, which adds obstacles to R2R instead of removing them, is sufficient to illustrate the critical implications of the reform.

5.2 *Critical Issues: Servitization*

With regard to the second issue considered here, the Directive does not mention PSS at all. Even more critically, it does not seem to have duly taken into account PSS in the regulation of R2R. The problem in this regard becomes twofold.

Firstly, PSS may be claimed to fall out of the scope of the Directive on R2R, and consequently of the relevant obligations to repair. Actually, Directive (EU) 2024/1799 is structured with express reference to Directive (EU) 2019/771 on certain aspects concerning contracts for the sale of goods, as it can be appreciated in terms of objectives[76], definitions[77] and also amendments[78]. However, this other piece of legislation—Directive (EU) 2019/771—does not cover hybrid forms of supply between goods and services like PSS, being referred just to traditional sales based on the transfer of ownership[79]. Therefore, the risk is that manufacturers providing PSS could try to use this argument in order to avoid such new repair obligations.

[75] See again Art. 5(6), Directive (EU) 2024/1799, where IPR are mentioned in an exemplifying tone that could be easily read as a direct confirmation of their nature of 'legitimate and objective factor' by default; moreover, it should be remembered that IPR enjoy a general presumption of validity that tends to be supported by the system at the enforcement level, as shown by CJEU, 28 April 2022, Case C-44/21, *Phoenix Contact v. Harting*, ECLI:EU:C:2022:309.

[76] See Art. 1(2), Directive (EU) 2024/1799.

[77] See Art. 2(1), Directive (EU) 2024/1799, especially for the direct recall of Directive (EU) 2019/771 for the relevant definitions of 'consumer' (no. 1), 'seller' (no. 4) and 'goods' (no. 9).

[78] See Art. 16, Directive (EU) 2024/1799.

[79] In particular, see Art. 1(2), Directive (EU) 2019/771, where the definition of 'sales contract' (no. 1) as 'any contract under which the seller transfers or undertakes to transfer ownership of goods to a consumer, and the consumer pays or undertakes to pay the price thereof'; even more explicitly see Recital 17 of the same Directive (EU) 2019/771, which states that 'for the purpose of legal clarity this Directive should lay down a definition of a sales contract and also clearly define its scope. The scope of this Directive should also cover contracts for goods that are yet to be produced

Secondly, and as said more critically, PSS could escape repair obligations on the grounds of the same norms within the Directive on R2R. Although the described obligations on manufacturers under Art. 5(6) include also a ban on contractual clauses impeding repair (always save 'legitimative and objective factors'), the Directive addresses more thoroughly the contractual aspects in a specific rule about clauses derogating from repair obligations: and, apparently, Art. 14(1) seems quite incisive in stating that manufacturers cannot exclude or affect by contract the protection so granted to consumers[80]. However, this anti-derogation rule goes together with an exception under Art. 14(2) that expressly admits a certain deviation, in terms of 'contractual arrangements that go beyond the protections provided for in this Directive'[81].

In principle, one can only look favourably at rules that raise the level of R2R protection in more consumer-friendly terms, but the problem is that with PSS the situation is not so straightforward. In fact, the tricky aspect is that a PSS model could easily be 'sold' by manufacturers as an ameliorative solution to the benefit of consumers, because it already includes the provision of official repair services, without the need to resort to the repair obligations imposed by law. But this would completely disregard all the issues that PSS poses to R2R on a wider scale, especially in its necessary competitive market dimension, which is instead affected by those lock-in and lock-out effects that preclude a real space for independent repair.

This misalignment derives from the peculiar approach taken by the EU legislator, who seems concerned only with the inaction of manufacturers about R2R: that is, when manufacturers refuse to provide repair in reasonable terms[82], relying on

or manufactured, including under the consumer's specifications. Furthermore, an installation of the goods could fall within the scope of this Directive if the installation forms part of the sales contract and has to be carried out by the seller or under the seller's responsibility. Where a contract includes elements of both sales of goods and provision of services, it should be left to national law to determine whether the whole contract can be classified as a sales contract within the meaning of this Directive'.

[80] See Art. 14(1), Directive (EU) 2024/1799, which states that 'unless otherwise provided for in this Directive, any contractual agreement which, to the detriment of the consumer, excludes the application of national measures transposing this Directive, derogates from them, or varies their effect, shall not be binding on the consumer'.

[81] See however Art. 14(2), Directive (EU) 2024/1799, which adds that 'this Directive shall not prevent the repairer from offering to the consumer contractual arrangements that go beyond the protections provided for in this Directive'.

[82] See Recital 16, Directive (EU) 2024/1799, where it can be read that 'the price should be reasonable, meaning it should be set in such a way that consumers are not intentionally deterred from benefitting from the manufacturers' obligation to repair. The price for and the conditions of repair should be agreed in a contract between the consumer and the manufacturer and the consumer should remain free to decide whether that price and those conditions are acceptable. The need for such a contract and the competitive pressure from other repairers should encourage manufacturers who are obliged to repair to keep the price acceptable for the consumer'.

technical constraints[83] or making excuses of economic convenience[84]. However, the problem with PSS is exactly the opposite: i.e. that manufacturers become pro-active with the aim of internalizing repair services, so as to gain total control over consumers' goods and their life-cycle management.

The abovementioned perplexity is far from unfounded considering that today manufacturers tend to emphasize more and more the (real or alleged) sustainability aspects of their industrial production, which, as is well known, brings with it a very high risk of greenwashing[85]. Not only that, but the problem is also more challenging because the EU legislator is keeping the door open to such arguments, announcing its interest in PSS for some (other) profiles of circular economy, in the wake of a new paradigm intended to prevail over ancient market schemes[86].

The result is that, from this second perspective, the situation seems even worse: instead of claiming to be out of the applicative scope of the Directive, manufacturers can claim either under Art. 5(6) that PSS is a legitimate objective factor to contractually restrict repair, or even more directly under Art. 14(2) that, acting as 'repairers', their contractual offer is 'beyond' any regulatory need, because PSS can be presumed as more advantageous for R2R and so *per se* compatible with the obligations imposed by the Directive.

It goes without saying that this result cannot be accepted, being too apodictic if not simplistic, against a more controversial economic literature[87]. In fact, it is manifest the risk of conflict of interest, which should impede the law to rely just on

---

[83] See the contextual reading of Art. 5(6) on the ban of hardware and software techniques by Recital 18, Directive (EU) 2024/1799.

[84] See respectively Recital 24, Directive (EU) 2024/1799, where it is specified that 'manufacturer should not be able to refuse repair for purely economic reasons, such as the cost of spare parts, or for the sole reason that a previous repair has been performed by other repairers or, where applicable, by the consumer'.

[85] The new Directive (EU) 2024/825 sounds as a direct confirmation of this very fact, as it can be appreciated (leaving aside the specific provisions about repair) in reading its Recital 1, which declares its policy objectives as follows: 'in order to contribute to the proper functioning of the internal market, based on a high level of consumer protection and environmental protection, and to make progress in the green transition, it is essential that consumers can make informed purchasing decisions and thus contribute to more sustainable consumption patterns. That implies that traders have a responsibility to provide clear, relevant and reliable information. Therefore, specific rules should be introduced in Union consumer law to tackle unfair commercial practices that mislead consumers and prevent them from making sustainable consumption choices, such as practices associated with the early obsolescence of goods, misleading environmental claims ('greenwashing'), misleading information about the social characteristics of products or traders' businesses, or non-transparent and non-credible sustainability labels'.

[86] See Communication from the Commission, 'Closing the loop—An EU action plan for the Circular Economy', COM(2015) 614 final, para. 2, as well as Communication from the Commission, 'A new Circular Economy Action Plan—For a cleaner and more competitive Europe', COM(2020) 98 final, para. 2.1 (although PSS are welcomed for matters of consumption patterns not directly related to the issue of repair, which remains instead strongly supported in general terms).

[87] About the effective contribution to sustainability, stating expressly that 'PSS is not a panacea', see Tukker (2015), p. 76; on equivalent positions see Laumann Kjaer et al. (2018).

unilateral assertions of greater sustainability by manufacturers. This is why the silence of the Directive with regard to PSS does not represent an adequate response for R2R.

6 'Repairing' a Defective Reform? Possible Corrective Interpretation

Expectations towards the reform that declared to introduce a right to repair in EU were inevitably high. Not least because it set out to intervene in accordance with that approach advocated by many, including in the field of intellectual property law, through the imposition of rules that would guarantee such individual prerogatives of public interest in a 'horizontal' way, i.e. across different exclusive rights as well as contractual and technical restrictions[88].

However, it cannot be said that the reform has lived up to expectations. In the face of such an ambiguous—if not frustrating—normative wording, for the reasons explained above, the EU legislature has not offered effective solutions to the issues of IPR and PSS, nor it does certainly appear to have facilitated the interpreter in establishing R2R against current obstacles[89].

Therefore, although it appears uphill, the only way forward seems to be an evolutionary interpretation of the Directive according to the paradigm shift towards a sustainable circular economy, considering how repair represents a fundamental building block of this new systemic model[90].

In this regard, it should not be forgotten that the Directive itself expressly recalls these policy objectives[91], which now rest on real 'constitutional' grounds that can support this evolutionary reading[92]. There is thus a substantial basis for trying to put

---

[88] It was the same EU legislator that announced the right to repair as one of 'new horizontal material rights for consumers' of its policy agenda (see Communication from the Commission, 'A new Circular Economy Action Plan—For a cleaner and more competitive Europe', COM(2020) 98 final, para. 2.2); in favor of this approach for reforming intellectual property law, see for example Senftleben (2021); for a further horizontal reading of exceptions and limitations as expression of general principles aimed at rebalancing intellectual property see Musso (2012); for a broader discourse in this perspective see Ghidini (2014).

[89] In this sense, following the exhortation to denounce the relevant 'bad' rules as proclaimed by Di Cataldo (2015).

[90] Some advancement in this direction can be appreciated in recent case-law: see CJEU, 27 October 2022, Case C-197/21, *Soda-Club v. MySoda*, ECLI:EU:C:2022:834; in favour of an 'internal' integration of environmental consideration in IP law by means of interpretation see Izyumenko (2024); furthermore in this sense see Calboli (2024) and also Pihlajarinne and Ballardini (2020).

[91] See again Recital 5, Directive (EU) 2024/1799.

[92] See Art. 3(2) TUE, with express reference to 'sustainable development'; at the national level, constitutional reforms are moving in the same direction of inserting social and environmental principles as fundamental values, such as Arts. 8 and 41 of the Italian Constitution. On such constitutional aspects see Cozzi (Chap. 9).

forward corrective proposals, in order to 'repair' on the interpretative level a reform that would otherwise be 'defective' from the outset.

6.1 *Corrective Interpretation: Intellectual Property*

As seen above, the Directive deals with the issue of IPR according to a 'carve-out' formula, following a quite usual tendency in this field[93]. However, a common approach is getting momentum towards such provisions, in order to better frame their meaning beyond the plain black letter and make them consistent with the public interest that underlies the relevant obligations on business operators[94].

The interpretation proposed here shares this approach. This is because, looking more deeply into the reform, it can be appreciated that R2R represents the real policy objective. Not only the same norm which mentions IPR is titled 'Obligation to repair'[95], but the overall structure of the Directive is centered around the core principle of 'strengthening' repair, 'with a view to contributing to the proper functioning of the internal market, while providing for a high level of consumer and environmental protection'[96]. And this policy objective is translated not just into promotional and informative measures, but also into mandatory obligations to be enacted even against manufacturers' will[97]. Moreover, the Directive takes into account the position of independent repairers, confirming the idea of repair as an 'open' competitive market that goes beyond the 'close' relationship between manufacturer and consumer[98].

But then, if R2R is the real policy objective that pursues the public interest in light of the paradigm shift towards a sustainable circular economy, it cannot be other than the overriding principle in balancing rules and limitations[99]. In other words, it is IPR that should truly be considered an exception to R2R. This means that any literal and too decontextualized reading of the provision at issue would only apparently be more accurate, while it would be actually inconsistent, turning the

[93] As a quite recent and emblematic example see—in the so-called 'AI Act'—Art. 53(1)(b), Regulation (EU) 2024/1689.

[94] With regard to the equivalent 'without prejudice' provision of Art. 3(9), Directive (EU) 2019/770, see Geiregat (2022).

[95] See again Art. 5, Directive (EU) 2024/1799.

[96] See literally Art. 1(1), Directive (EU) 2024/1799.

[97] Compare just Arts. 5 and 6, Directive (EU) 2024/1799.

[98] As it is implied by the direct reference to the use of spare parts by 'independent repairers' under Art. 5(6), and even more broadly by the principle that 'consumers may seek repair from any repairer of their choice' under Art. 5(8), as well as in terms of policy objectives in Recital 2 of the same Directive (EU) 2024/1799, declaring that the new rules on R2R are intended 'in particular to facilitate cross-border provision of services and competition among repairers of goods purchased by consumers in the internal market'.

[99] Expressly in this sense of the right to repair as a 'positive user's right' see Rosborough et al. (2023).

balance upside down: that is, IPR shall be construed restrictively, in order to maintain the 'useful effect' of the public objective so established[100].

Having said that, an evolutive interpretation of the norm regulating the relationship between R2R and IPR seems compatible with the normative text. As reported above, the Directive provides three different rules in this sense: contractual and technical restrictions to R2R are prohibited, 'unless justified' by IPR; spare parts for R2R shall be available, when 'in compliance' with IPR; all such obligations in favor of R2R shall be 'without prejudice' to IPR[101].

Starting from the last, this provision appears less meaningful, being a safeguard clause so generic that it can be considered a boilerplate. Conversely, it gains significance by reason of the very same premise maintained here: since R2R is the overriding principle that can actually prejudice IPR, and admitting that IPR have a broader scope which is not limited to repair, there comes the need to preserve IPR in general. Therefore, this rule serves the purpose of circumscribing the prevalence of R2R over only such exclusive claims that affect relevantly the objective of repair, without intending to question—or indeed 'without prejudice' to—the remaining validity of IPR.

Coming to the second rule, the issue of spare parts appears thorny, because of the criteria of direct compliance with IPR. However, the provision expressly refers to independent repairers and compatible spare parts, therefore recognizing the lawfulness of such 'non-original' supply of products and services as a matter of principle. Then, this rule also confirms the primacy of R2R, with IPR to be applied restrictively only in cases when the interference with exclusive rights is not necessary and proportionate for repair[102].

This leads to the first and most weighty rule of the Directive, the one that generally tackles business obstacles to R2R, but exempting the relevant contractual and technical restrictions when justified by IPR. In fact, the same evolutionary interpretation applies also in this case. Namely, once it turns out that R2R is the prevailing principle that can justify some proportionate prejudice to IPR, it is logical to conclude in reverse that IPR cannot always be valid justifications in opposition to R2R. This interpretation is somehow supported by the normative wording, which specifies that R2R can be limited only by 'legitimate and objective factors', meaning that not any 'subjective' claim, even when legitimate, can be invoked to the contrary. This objectivity shall then be valorized in construing correctly the admissible justifications against R2R, among which IPR are included by the legislator:

---

[100] As already advocated especially in the field of copyright law by Borghi (2021), Rosati (2023) p. 218, Geiger and Jütte (2024), and in more systemic terms by Dusollier (2022).

[101] See in detail Art. 5(6), Directive (EU) 2024/1799.

[102] The final establishment of a 'repair clause' in EU design law comes as a confirmation of this view, excluding from protection the relevant uses for restoring product appearance subject to due diligence obligations in terms of consumer information: see again Art. 20a, Regulation (EC) 6/2002 (as amended by Regulation (EU) 2024/2822), and in parallel Art. 19, Directive (EU) 2024/2823.

consequently, this criterion entails a specific (and indeed restrictive) selection of relevant conflicts.

The idea is that, although IPR are expressly mentioned by the legislator, it should always be checked their 'legitimate and objective' nature as a justification in the specific case, which is tantamount to deny a general primacy presumption of IPR against repair. In particular, it is here argued that the relevance of IPR should be confined to cases of R2R 'abuse', that is when repair conceals competitive misconduct or fraudulent intent, so that the compression of IPR cannot be tolerated[103]. Otherwise, in cases of 'normal' conflict between IPR and R2R, the latter principle should generally prevail, because the Directive should be interpreted consistently with its paradigmatic goals in favor of prioritizing consumer freedom and competitive openness that substantiate the market dimension of R2R[104].

This means also that an abusive violation of IPR, still possible, would specifically have to be claimed and demonstrated by the rightholder, in line with the said exceptional nature of IPR in this conflict scenario. Such an interpretation would then be more balanced in procedural terms, reallocating aptly on manufacturers the burden of proof against any risk of shifting on individual consumers and independent repairers, all to the benefit of the collective interest in R2R[105].

It is easy to imagine that such a position would be censured as too farfetched with respect to the existing IPR system. For example, because of its contrast with the 'three-steps' test established by TRIPS Agreement at the international level[106]. However, apart from the large number of critics that this model has attracted, there are two considerations that appear decisive. In policy terms, if any evolutive interpretation of the Directive were rejected, the result of the rigid application of such a norm would inevitably be a manifest contradiction, bringing to a new regulation for

[103] Like for possible cases of trade secrets misappropriation, on condition that the relevant information is actually eligible for protection, so going beyond the mere technical features related to repair activity, as correctly noted by Grinvald and Tur-Sinai (2019) p. 121.

[104] In this sense, further support can be found in the historical approach towards IPR in the framework of the EU single market: according to such an approach, the enforceability of IPR is not contested in terms of their 'existence', but it could well be subject to scrutiny in terms of their 'exercise' (starting from the historical decision by CJEU, 13 July 1966, Joined Cases 56 and 58–64, *Établissements Consten and Grundig-Verkaufs v Commission*, ECLI:EU:C:1966:41); leaving aside all the peculiar (and critical) contingencies of this judicial interpretation, for a reflection on its key role for resolving the tension between the construction of an integrated single market and the obstacle to it represented by IPR, thus paving the way for the normative harmonization by the EU legislature, see Pila (2013); therefore, it seems possible to derive from this approach—at least as a matter of principle—that IPR, although recognized as fully valid, cannot be considered as always predominant in the conflict with systemic market interests and freedoms within the very same EU legal order.

[105] As it is specifically established in Australia: about this interesting legal model, including the relevant case-law, see Wiseman and Kariyawasam (2020).

[106] See respectively for copyright, trademarks, designs and patents, Arts. 13, 17, 26(2), 30, TRIPS; for an overall presentation see Christie and Wright (2014).

R2R even more restrictive than the current (over)protective TRIPS standard[107]. But also in strict legal terms, this reading of the Directive seems compatible with the well-known threefold clause: not only because repair can arguably qualify as a 'certain special case' that does not affect the 'normal exploitation' of IPR, leaving untouched the primary market of the product; but mostly because the proposed interpretation would follow the very same idea that IPR should be protected against 'unreasonable' prejudice (as indeed abuses of R2R), implying conversely that reasonable prejudices to IPR can be tolerated, especially 'taking account of legitimate interest of third parties'[108]. And, in this sense, there is no doubt that R2R constitutes a legitimate interest of third parties, if not society as a whole, as dictated by the new paradigm of a sustainable circular economy[109].

Admittedly, this does not mean that the interpretation proposed here can solve all the problems that arise in practice when IPR and R2R clash. However, it does mean establishing a suitable starting point for setting up an effective and balanced discipline of this conflict, upon which intellectual property law can then build solutions in order to fit R2R within existing IPR regimes[110]. In other words, this interpretation may not be the salvation from all problems, yet it is indispensable to save R2R itself, in order to prevent this principle from succumbing to IPR in a flat reading of the Directive that would leave no real leeway for repair in the EU legal order.

As further support, in this way it can be enacted what was declared by the same EU policy agenda, according to which IPR represent a key element for the strategic future of the system in times of changing, advocating—in the words of the EU Commission—for a renewed balancing between exclusivity and openness in front of such a 'unique window of opportunity to modernize our approach to protecting our intangible assets'[111]. From this perspective, the solution here proposed in favour of R2R may have various shortcomings, but surely not the lack of reinterpretation of the traditional IPR system in such an innovative fashion, so as to make the market more capable of serving the collective interest of society[112].

After all, it is important to remember that intellectual property does not live in the empyrean, but is a concrete entity that affects everyday actions: and if R2R is to

---

[107] For such critical positions, it is enough to mention the interpretative manifesto promoted by Geiger et al. (2008).

[108] For this kind of alternative and more proportional approach see, among many, Geiger et al. (2015).

[109] By the way, also Art. 7 TRIPS Agreement can be said to encompass relevant systemic values, considering its objective to protect and enforce IPR 'in a manner conducive to social and economic welfare, and to a balance of rights and obligations'; for a wider interpretation in this sense see Yu (2009).

[110] For example, extending the threshold of repair vis-à-vis remake in the context of patent law, as recently argued by Heath (2024).

[111] See Communication from the Commission, 'Making the most of the EU's innovative potential—An intellectual property action plan to support the EU's recovery and resilience', COM(2020) 760 final.

[112] For a similar propositional approach about IP law and the challenges of artificial intelligence in the new framework of sustainability see Jütte (2023).

be fostered in the new economic reality, it is a necessary and inevitable step to reconfigure the actual scope of IPR, even if this may entail a relevant 'prejudice'—yet 'reasonable'—with respect to those ideal expectations[113].

6.2 *Corrective Interpretation: Servitization*

With regard to PSS, the main problem posed by the Directive is that it does not take a real position, with the risk of leaving R2R—which, it should be reiterated, represents the public interest in the new paradigm of a sustainable circular economy—at the mercy of the conflict of interest that characterizes such contractual model.

But then, as with any conflict of interest, an institutional approach of 'scepticism' should be invoked towards a situation that remits the management of the risk itself to the counter-interested party[114]: which means, in this case, the inadmissibility of a normative reading that leaves the issue of R2R in PSS merely to business judgement and its narrative[115]. In other words, R2R requires regulatory 'caution' against any risk of regulatory 'capture' that would result from the choice to rely entirely on the private conscientiousness of manufacturers[116], which generally take advantage of any market foreclosure about repair[117]. It is evident that this conflict of interest would call into question the very same credibility of such public policy.

Certainly, this does not mean that PSS should be prohibited outright, but it highlights the need for an effective solution that allows R2R to be safeguarded even within this contractual framework, guaranteeing the necessary freedom of operation for consumers and independent repairers. This contractual 'neutrality' of R2R seems preferable in light of a reality that tends to overcome the dichotomy between goods and services, both in economic and legal terms[118].

---

[113] For such a concrete approach to IPR, see Tamura (2024).

[114] In a sort of paraphrasing of the relevant notion of 'professional scepticism' required to statutory auditors of annual accounts, in terms of 'an attitude that includes a questioning mind, being alert to conditions which may indicate possible misstatement due to error or fraud, and a critical assessment of audit evidence' (Art. 1(13), Directive (EU) 2014/56).

[115] As a (sad) matter of fact, evidence that negates the validity of closed 'proprietary' firm recycling system is already emerging: see Liu (2014), p. 337–338.

[116] As anticipated to a certain extent, the phenomenon of greenwashing epitomizes the issue of market unreliability, when leaving matters of general interests merely to business storytelling: on the relevance of the new Directive (EU) 2024/825 in this field within the European framework see Deana (Chap. 7) and also from a wider perspective see De Vido (Chap. 12); along the same line it could be read the EU normative intervention on corporate sustainability reporting, about which see more extensively Genovese (Chap. 2).

[117] It should be noted that regulatory capture goes well beyond direct collusion, deriving also from the widespread production of biased information for regulatory and policy use: see Agrell and Gautier (2012).

[118] In this sense see Peng (2020).

A proper remedy should then be sought at the interpretative level. Going back to the Directive, which is after all the new legislation specifically aimed at implementing R2R in the EU, a few considerations can be made to move in this direction.

Regarding the first argument that PSS would be outside the scope of the Directive, such objection can be rebutted quite easily by looking at the Directive itself, which expressly states the intention to impose repair obligations in addition to the legal liability provided by Directive (UE) 2019/771 for sale contracts[119]. This means that the safeguard of R2R may well go beyond the applicative perimeter of traditional sale contracts, notwithstanding the normative links to that other Directive, so to cover also non-traditional contractual models like PSS. On closer inspection, this idea seemed already in the mind of the EU legislator, given the reference to 'manufacturers' and not 'sellers' in the specific provision about repair obligations, thus freeing it from the strict contractual definition[120].

Moreover, with regard to the second and most problematic argument that PSS would be exempted from repair obligations because it is more favorable to consumers, a combined reading of the relevant provisions of the Directive can open up a different construction.

Starting from the pivotal norm tackling the restrictive practices by manufacturers, this provision reveals a deeper content that amounts to the affirmation of an all-encompassing obligation to repair, not only positive-active ('do the repair'), but also negative-passive ('allow the repair'), as a right enforceable against the manufacturer itself and its contractual will[121].

This supports a parallel interpretation of the rule governing the mandatory nature of R2R. In particular, as mentioned, the Directive enables manufacturers to derogate from their obligations to repair when the conditions included in the contract go beyond the legal protection provided by the reform. However, the legal text speaks in terms of 'offering' such contractual arrangements, which implies that no binding effect is intended, suggesting that consumer freedom should remain the basis[122].

From this normative framework, it emerges that R2R is a guaranteed minimum objective that the Directive wants to secure in general, so that it can only be improved more favourably for the consumer, but not varied in detrimental terms. At the same time, this fundamental guarantee must be appreciated according to the aforementioned dual nature of R2R, in both an active and passive sense[123].

---

[119] See Art. 1(2), Directive (EU) 2024/1799.

[120] See Art. 5, Directive (EU) 2024/1799.

[121] For a direct confirmation, see again Art. 5(8), Directive (EU) 2024/1799, which affirms—almost in terms of general principle—that 'without prejudice to the obligation to repair under this Article, consumers may seek repair from any repairer of their choice'.

[122] See literally Art. 14(2), Directive (EU) 2024/1799.

[123] In support of this reading, it should be underlined that Art. 5(6), Directive (EU) 2024/1799, dealing with the prohibition of manufacturers' practices against repair, speaks expressly of 'contractual clauses', that should therefore be appreciated also in the complementary perspective of limiting contractual freedom under Art. 14 of the same Directive; in this sense, the following argument about the inadmissibility of such restrictions to repair freedom applies *a fortiori* to the possible

In light of this reading, it can be affirmed that the Directive always imposes the consumer's right to turn to an independent repairer, even when the producer 'offers' special repair services: this is because, in the public interest perspective characterizing R2R, no solution that restricts such freedom of choice can be considered more favourable than the protection guaranteed by the Directive[124]. Therefore, this essential right could not be derogated by contract, including in the case of PSS, leaving aside the general validity of the agreements for the remaining part of such hybrid product-service supply.

Technically speaking, this hypothesis can be configured as a special contractual invalidity/ineffectiveness that can be invoked unilaterally by the interested party pursuing repair. In truth, solutions of this kind are far from unusual to the EU legal system and can be found (not by chance) both in consumer law[125] and antitrust law[126]. Apart from these more specific categorizations, it can be maintained more substantially—with a reconstruction that may then be conjugated according to the peculiarities of different jurisdictions—that such contractual restrictions to R2R, affecting an individual right which is functional for the benefit of a collective systemic interest, can be considered contrary to economic public order, and as such null

claim that PSS amounts to a 'legitimate and objective factor', being apparently based on mere subjective business expectations that cannot override the public interest of the system in R2R.

[124] As indirectly demonstrated by Art. 5(7), Directive (EU) 2024/1799, providing that 'manufacturers shall not refuse to repair goods [...] for the sole reason that a previous repair has been performed by other repairers or by other persons', as an evidence of the intended aim to safeguard a competitive market for repair and the revelant freedom for consumers.

[125] For example, as mandated for consumer protection against unfair commercial terms by Art. 6(1), Directive (EEC) 1993/13, providing that such terms shall 'not be binding on the consumer and that the contract shall continue to bind the parties upon those terms if it is capable of continuing in existence without the unfair terms'; in addition, case-law specified that the judge 'is required to assess of its own motion whether a contractual term [...] is unfair, compensating in this way for the imbalance which exists between the consumer and the seller or supplier' (CJEU, 14 June 2012, Case C-618/10, *Banco Español de Crédito SA v. Joaquín Calderón Camino*, ECLI:EU:C:2012:349); in this sense, it has to be remembered that the Directive (EU) 2024/1799 on R2R has its formal legal basis exactly in Art. 114 TFEU, related to 'the establishment and functioning of the internal market', including the specific objective of 'consumer protection' in terms of 'a high level of protection'; this is not to say that consumer protection law is sufficient to solve all problems of R2R, considering the need of a special and at the same time holistic approach to R2R, as confirmed by Artigot Golobardes (2024).

[126] Contractual restrictions to competition, in terms of agreements or concerted practices, are declared 'automatically void' under Art. 101(2) TFEU; in this sense, it should be remembered that under EU competition law the affected party can always invoke such invalidity, notwithstanding its consent to the contract (since CJEU, 20 September 2001, Case C-453/99, *Courage v. Crehan*, ECLI:EU:C:2001:465). By the way, competition law might be considered a helpful instrument in support of R2R, supplementing the lack of other normative solutions: for a comparative example regarding IPR, see Furuta and Heath (2023); however, competition law is not that solid to represent an effective remedy for R2R in all the relevant situations, as highlighted in an alternative reconstruction by Carrier (2022); for similar critics about antitrust law, including for PSS, see Perzanowski (2022), p. 173.

and void[127]. In this sense, the new paradigm shift towards a sustainable circular economy can readily offer the necessary constitutional grounds, as recalled above[128].

Admittedly, this is again an evolutionary interpretation with respect to the normative text: however, considering the outcome of the reform, this seems the only viable solution to make this Directive fit for purpose in ensuring an effective R2R also in the case of PSS. Moreover, this reconstruction would reinforce, if not encompass, the same arguments illustrated above about IPR, with the not negligible advantage of shaping a common approach in response to both these issues[129]. And this leads to some concluding remarks.

7 Conclusive Remarks

In conclusion, the interpretation proposed here tries to fix some troublesome aspects of the Directive as criticized above. However, this does not mean that the reform is to be rejected in its entirety, considering other interesting actions in support of R2R[130].

In a certain sense, it is exactly because the policy effort is appreciable that the legislative result can be said to be disappointing, especially in terms of missed opportunity. This is all the more so considering the major relevance for R2R of the two issues at hand, IPR and PSS: and that is why such a normative hesitation sounds as if the EU legislator has (green)washed its hands of them.

Nevertheless, where reforms hesitate, the only alternative is to push for a corrective interpretation that is 'paradigmatically' oriented towards a sustainable circular economy, and thus in favour of R2R, even struggling with the limits of the existing norms.

As to future reform, this EU attempt highlights the importance of a wider legal approach in terms of market regulation for R2R, indeed to be understood correctly:

[127] Like for contractual restrictions that go beyond the inherent limits of IPR, as recently ruled in the interesting Italian case by Court of Cassation, 9 April 2024, n. 9429, *M.A. v. SunWorld International*, published in IIC 56:204–214 (2025); for an equivalent reasoning see Grinvald and Tur-Sinai (2019), p. 103.

[128] See again Cozzi (Chap. 9); further along this line, for a rethinking of consumers prerogatives in terms of human rights at the international level see Dal Monico (Chap. 11).

[129] In this sense, stressing the importance of a contextual reading tackling both intellectual property claims and contractual restrictions against R2R, see Ghosh (2022), p. 1111.

[130] Apart from the informative and promotional measures already mentioned, a general observation can explain this view: on one side, it is true that the scope of application of the Directive is quite limited in terms of goods, but, on the other side, it is equally true that it already includes important products like mobile phones (Annex II, no. 8); from this point of view, it is understandable that the legislature decided to introduce such potentially impactful discipline in a graduated manner, considering also that the Commission is already vested with the delegated power to update the list of products subject to repairability requirements in light of regulatory developments (Art. 5(9), Directive 2024/1799).

not as a juxtaposition of fields where each specialized discipline—such as intellectual property—is not considered by the other, but as a moment of comparison and integration exceeding separated self-referential logic, according to the promoted 'human-centered' economic model[131].

Therefore, with a more constructive attitude, the just enacted Directive (EU) 2024/1799 should be considered not so much as the ultimate definition of R2R, but only as a first step, a sort of starting point for further more effective solutions, which should necessarily revolve around the fundamental core identified here[132]: that is, a right that every consumer shall enjoy to have the product repaired by freely turning to a competitive and open repair market, as such capable of counteracting the relevant foreclosure effects deriving from manufacturers' claims of control by means of IPR and PSS[133].

Only in this way can R2R become real, in the EU as in every other legal order, and bring about the systemic benefits of a sustainable circular economy that are needed now more than ever.

References

Agrell PJ, Gautier A (2012) Rethinking regulatory capture. In: Harrington JE Jr, Katsoulacos Y (eds) Recent advances in the analysis of competition policy and regulation. Edward Elgar, Cheltenham, pp 286–302

Annarelli A, Battistella C, Nonino F (2016) Product service system: a conceptual framework from a systematic review. J Clean Prod 139:1011–1032. https://doi.org/10.1016/j.jclepro.2016.08.061

Arora H (2021) "Right to repair" Vis-à-Vis Indian trade mark law: a comparative analysis. J World Intell Prop 24:41–54. https://doi.org/10.1111/jwip.12183

[131] At the EU level, the human-centered approach is declared to be at the basis of the industrial transition inspired by this paradigm shift: see e.g. European Commission, 'Industry 5.0: A Transformative Vision for Europe', ESIR Policy Brief No. 3, 2022; in literature, confirming the need for such an approach, see Murray et al. (2017), as well as in terms of applicable model Clube and Tennant (2023); from a policy theory perspective, focused on R2R, see also Lloveras et al. (2025).

[132] In this sense, given the specific formulation of the Directive, the room for manoeuvre by Member States is not really relevant, therefore significant changes are not expected at the stage of transposition (to be completed within 31 July 2026: Art. 22 Directive (EU) 2024/1799). In the meantime, critical observations are already arising: see e.g. López-Bermúdez and Vence (2025).

[133] This fundamental reconstruction of R2R as implying an open competitive market is confirmed by the recent reform of EU design law, where the final enactment of the relevant 'repair clause' is expressly reconnected to the 'liberalisation of the spare parts aftermarket' (see Recital 35, Directive (EU) 2024/2823, and equally Recital 20, Regulation (EU) 2024/2822); moreover, this reform is presented in policy terms not only as 'at the core of a sustainable economy', but also as directly related to the 'establishment and functioning of the internal market' against legal uncertainties that 'distort competition and trade' (see Recital 33, Directive (EU) 2024/2823, also indirectly recalled by Recital 19, Regulation (EU) 2024/2822).

Artigot Golobardes M (2024) Revisiting European consumer protection through the lens of sustainable markets. In: Santos Silva M et al (eds) Routledge handbook of private law and sustainability. Routledge, London, pp 153–175
Bonadio E, O'Connell A (eds) (2022) Intellectual property excesses: exploring the boundaries of IP protection. Bloomsbury, London
Borghi M (2021) Exceptions as users' rights? In: Rosati E (ed) The Routledge handbook of EU copyright law. Edward Elgar, Cheltenham, pp 263–280
Cahoy DR (2023) Trademark's grip over sustainability. Univ Colorado L Rev 94:1043–1100
Calabrese B (2025) Trademark law and upcycling: tailoring 'old-fashioned' principles. In: Mezei P, Härkönen H (eds) The research handbook on upcycling and intellectual property. Cambridge University Press, Cambridge (forthcoming)
Calboli I (2023) The right to repair: recent developments in the USA. WIPO Magazine. https://www.wipo.int/wipo_magazine_digital/en/2023/article_0023.html
Calboli I (2024) Pushing a square pin into a round hole? Intellectual property challenges to a sustainable and circular economy, and what to do about it. IIC 55:237–248. https://doi.org/10.1007/s40319-024-01431-1
Carrier MA (2022) How the Federal Trade Commission can use section 5 to strengthen the right to repair. Berkeley Tech L J 37:1145–1196. https://doi.org/10.15779/Z38PN8XG5W
Christie AF, Wright R (2014) A comparative analysis of the three-step tests in international treaties. IIC 45:409–433. https://doi.org/10.1007/s40319-014-0202-2
Clube RKM, Tennant M (2023) What would a human-centred 'social' circular economy look like? Drawing from max-Neef's human-scale development proposal. J Clean Prod 383:135455. https://doi.org/10.1016/j.jclepro.2022.135455
De Franceschi A (2023) Ensuring circularity in service contracts. In: Keirsblick B et al (eds) Servitization and circular economy: economic and legal challenges. Intersentia, Cambridge, pp 167–180
Derclaye E (2009) Repair and recycle between IP rights, end user license agreements and encryption. In: Heath C, Kamperman Sanders A (eds) Spares, repairs and intellectual property rights. Wolters Kluwer, Alphen aan den Rijn, pp 21–56
Di Cataldo V (2015) The role of law, the role of reason and intellectual property: the passing of time and the sense of the rules. IIC 46:383–385. https://doi.org/10.1007/s40319-015-0342-z
Dusollier S (2022) Unlimiting limitations in intellectual property. In: Ghidini G, Falce V (eds) Reforming intellectual property. Edward Elgar, Cheltenham, pp 64–76
Ellen Macarthur Foundation (2015) Growth within: a circular economy vision for a competitive Europe. https://www.ellenmacarthurfoundation.org/growth-within-a-circular-economy-vision-for-a-competitive-europe
Fabbio P (2018) Copyright protection for design creations. In: Kur A, Levin M, Schovsbo J (eds) The EU design approach: a global appraisal. Edward Elgar, Cheltenham, pp 81–107
Fedele M, Hysa X (2024) Circular economy in Italian firms: present and future perspectives. Giappichelli, Torino
Firth A (2009) Repairs, interconnections, and consumer welfare in the field of design. In: Heath C, Kamperman Sanders A (eds) Spares, repairs and intellectual property rights. Wolters Kluwer, Alphen aan den Rijn, p. 2009, p 147–180;
Furuta A, Heath C (2023) The right to repair, refill and recycle by way of an anti-trust defence–comment on the Japanese decisions *Ricoh I, Ricoh II* and *brother*. GRUR Int 72:1053–1062. https://doi.org/10.1093/grurint/ikad088
Geiger C, Gervais D, Senftleben M (2015) Understanding the 'three-step test'. In: Gervais D (ed) International intellectual property: a handbook of contemporary research. Edward Elgar, Cheltenham, pp 167–189
Geiger C, Hilty RM, Griffiths J, Suthersanen U (2008) Declaration on a balanced interpretation of the "three-step test" in copyright law. IIC 39:707–713

Geiger C, Jütte BJ (2024) Copyright as an access right: concretizing positive obligations for rightholders to ensure the exercise of user rights. GRUR Int 73:1019–1035. https://doi.org/10.1093/grurint/ikae130

Geiregat S (2022) Copyright meets consumer data portability rights: inevitable friction between IP and the remedies in the digital content directive. GRUR Int 71:495–515. https://doi.org/10.1093/grurint/ikac042

Geiregat S (2024) Trading repaired and refurbished goods: how sustainable is EU exhaustion of trade marks? GRUR Int 73:287–298. https://doi.org/10.1093/grurint/ikad124

Ghidini G (2014) For a holistic and systemic approach to IP law. IIC 45:381–382. https://doi.org/10.1007/s40319-014-0205-z

Ghidini G (2018) Rethinking intellectual property: balancing conflicts of interest in the constitutional paradigm. Edward Elgar, Cheltenham

Ghosh S (2022) The continuing right to repair. Berkeley Tech L J 37:1097–1122

Grinvald L, Tur-Sinai O (2024) The right to repair in the United States. In: Rognstad O, Pihlajarinne T, Mähönen J (eds) Promoting sustainable innovation and the circular economy. Routledge, London, pp 133–155

Grinvald LC, Tur-Sinai O (2019) Intellectual property law and the right to repair. Fordham L Rev 88:63–128

Haase RP, Pigosso DCA, McAloone TC (2017) Product/service-system origins and trajectories: a systematic literature review of PSS definitions and their characteristics. Procedia CIRP 64:157–162. https://doi.org/10.1016/j.procir.2017.03.053

Heath C (2014) Exhaustion and patent rights. In: Okediji RL, Bagley MA (eds) Patent law in global perspective. Oxford University Press, Oxford, pp 419–484

Heath C (2024) A three-step test for determining patent infringement related to repair. IIC 55:762–773. https://doi.org/10.1007/s40319-024-01458-4

Hernandez RJ, Miranda C, Goñi J (2020) Empowering sustainable consumption by giving back to consumers the 'right to repair'. Sustainability 12:850. https://doi.org/10.3390/su12030850

Hojnik J (2016) The servitization of manufacturing: EU law implications and challenges. CMLR 53:1575–1623. https://doi.org/10.54648/cola2016143

Hojnik J (2023) Servitization, IoT and circular economy. Need for regulatory intervention at EU level? In: Keirsblick B et al (eds) Servitization and circular economy: economic and legal challenges. Intersentia, Cambridge, pp 33–68

Izyumenko E (2024) Intellectual property in the age of the environmental crisis: how trademarks and copyright challenge the human right to a healthy environment. IIC 55:864–900. https://doi.org/10.1007/s40319-024-01478-0

Janis MD (2021) Examining functionality. In: Brunn N, Dinwoodie GB, Levin M, Ohly A (eds) Transition and coherence in intellectual property law—essays in honour of Annette Kur. Cambridge University Press, Cambridge, pp 364–372

Jonas M, Nessel S, Tröger N (eds) (2023) Repair, do-it-yourself and circular rconomy: alternative practices for sustainable consumption. Springer VS, Wiesbaden

Jütte BJ (2023) What is sust[AI]nable intellectual property? IIC 54:1311–1315. https://doi.org/10.1007/s40319-023-01368-x

Kirchherr et al (2018) Barriers to the circular economy: evidence from the European Union (EU). Ecol Econ 150:264–272. https://doi.org/10.1016/j.ecolecon.2018.04.028

Kur A (2020) *Unité de l'art* is here to stay–*Cofemel* and its consequences. JIPLP 15:290–300. https://doi.org/10.1093/jiplp/jpaa035

Kur A (2021) 'As good as new'–Sale of repaired or refurbished goods: commendable practice or trade mark infringement? GRUR Int 70:228–236. https://doi.org/10.1093/grurint/ikaa187

Laumann Kjaer L et al (2018) Product/service-systems for a circular economy: the route to decoupling economic growth from resource consumption? J Ind Ecol 23:22–35. https://doi.org/10.1111/jiec.12747

Levin M (2021) The Cofemel revolution—originality, equality and neutrality. In: Rosati E (ed) The Routledge handbook of EU copyright law. Edward Elgar, Cheltenham, pp 82–100

Liu B (2014) Towards a patent exhaustion regime for sustainable development. Berkeley J Int'l L 32:330–386. https://doi.org/10.15779/Z38K94Z

Lloveras J, Pansera M, Smith A (2025) On 'the politics of repair beyond repair': radical democracy and the right to repair movement. J Bus Ethics 196:325–344. https://doi.org/10.1007/s10551-024-05705-z

López-Bermúdez F, Vence X (2025) A critical assessment of the European Directive proposal on the common rules promoting the repair of goods. Resources, Conservation & Recycling 212:107996. https://doi.org/10.1016/j.resconrec.2024.107996

Mak V, Terryn E (2020) Circular economy and consumer protection: the consumer as a citizen and the limits of empowerment through consumer law. J Consumer Policy 43:227–248. https://doi.org/10.1007/s10603-019-09435-y

Malinauskaite J, Erdem FB (2021) Planned obsolescence in the context of a holistic legal sphere and the circular economy. Oxford J Legal Stud 41:719–749. https://doi.org/10.1093/ojls/gqaa061

Margoni T, Kretschmer M (2022) A deeper look into the EU text and data mining exceptions: harmonisation, data ownership, and the future of technology. GRUR Int 71:685–701. https://doi.org/10.1093/grurint/ikac054

Mohri M (2010) Patents, repair and recycling from a comparative perspective. IIC 41:779–805

Mont OK (2002) Clarifying the concept of product-service system. J Clean Prod 10:237–245. https://doi.org/10.1016/S0959-6526(01)00039-7

Montagnani ML (2023) (digital) circular economy and IPRs: a story of challenges and opportunities. IIC 54:1009–1012. https://doi.org/10.1007/s40319-023-01359-y

Murray A, Skene K, Haynes K (2017) The circular economy: an interdisciplinary exploration of the concept and application in a global context. J Bus Ethics 140:369–380. https://doi.org/10.1007/s10551-015-2693-2

Musso A (2012) Grounds of protection: how far does the incentive paradigm carry? In: Ohly A (ed) Common principles of European intellectual property law. Mohr Siebeck, Tübingen, pp 33–98

Musso A (2024) *Lex generalis derogat speciali*: may works of applied art have no artistic relevance? In: Thouvenin F et al (eds) Kreation innovation märkte – Creation innovation markets. Festschrift Reto M. Hilty, Springer, Berlin, pp 107–120

Noto La Diega G (2023) Internet of things and the law–legal strategies for consumer-centric smart technologies. Routledge, London

Ozturkcan S (2023) The right-to-repair movement: sustainability and consumer rights. J Inf Tech Teach Cases 14. https://doi.org/10.1177/20438869231117

Peng S (2020) A new trade regime for the servitization of manufacturing: rethinking the goods-services dichotomy. J World Trade 54:669–726. https://doi.org/10.54648/trad2020030

Perzanowski A (2021) Consumer perceptions of the right to repair. Indiana L J:361-394

Perzanowski A (2022) The right to repair: reclaiming the things we own. Cambridge University Press, Cambridge

Perzanowski A, Schultz J (2016) The end of ownership–personal property in the digital economy. MIT Press, Cambridge

Philippe D (2024) The battle against planned obsolescence–legal remedies. In: Santos Silva M et al (eds) Routledge handbook of private law and sustainability. Routledge, London, pp 402–415

Pihlajarinne T (2021) Repairing and re-using from an exclusive rights perspective: towards sustainable lifespan as part of a new normal? In: Rognstad O, Ørstavik IB (eds) Intellectual property and sustainable markets. Edward Elgar, Cheltenham, pp 81–100

Pihlajarinne T (2024) Shifting normality–regulation of planned and premature obsolescence in Europe. In: Rognstad O, Pihlajarinne T, Mähönen J (eds) Promoting sustainable innovation and the circular economy. Routledge, London, pp 183–200

Pihlajarinne T, Ballardini RM (2020) Paving the way for the environment: channelling 'strong' sustainability into the European IP system. EIPR 42:239–250

Pila J (2013) Intellectual property as a case study in Europeanization: methodological themes and context. In: Ohly A, Pila J (eds) The Europeanization of intellectual property law. Oxford University Press, Oxford, pp 3–24

Quan Y, Zhang X (2023) Outlook on the right to repair: how will it find its way into China's copyright law? JIPLP 18:382–385. https://doi.org/10.1093/jiplp/jpad016
Reynolds GJ (2023) Of lock-breaking and stock taking: IP, climate change, and the right to repair in Canada. Canadian Bar Rev 101:31–60
Ricketson S, Suthersanen U (2023) The design/copyright overlap: is there a resolution? In: Wilkof N, Basheer S, Calboli I (eds) Overlapping intellectual property rights. Oxford University Press, Oxford, pp 213–260
Ricolfi M (2022) Regulating de facto powers: shifting the focus. In: Ghidini G, Falce V (eds) Reforming intellectual property. Edward Elgar, Cheltenham, pp 174–182
Rimmer M (2022) Shane Rattenbury, the productivity commission, and the right to repair: intellectual property, consumer rights, and sustainable development in Australia. Berkeley Tech L J 37:989–1056. https://doi.org/10.15779/Z38PR7MV7X
Rimmer M (2025) Tractor rage: intellectual property, agriculture, competition policy, and the right to repair. IIC 56:115–152. https://doi.org/10.1007/s40319-024-01538-5
Rognstad O (2021) Revisiting the concept of 'trade mark piracy' in light of sustainable development goals: a discussion of the Norwegian 'apple case'. In: Rognstad O, Ørstavik IB (eds) Intellectual property and sustainable markets. Edward Elgar, Cheltenham, pp 101–114
Rosborough AD (2020) Unscrewing the future: the right to repair and the circumvention of software TPMs in the EU. JIPITEC 11:26–48
Rosati E (2023) Copyright and the Court of Justice of the European Union. Oxford University Press, Oxford
Rosborough AD (2022a) Toward a Canadian right to repair: opportunities and challenges. Berkeley Tech L J 37:1197–1226. https://doi.org/10.15779/Z38S756M3M
Rosborough AD (2022b) Zen and the art of repair manuals: enabling a participatory right to repair through an autonomous concept of EU copyright law. JIPITEC 13:113–131
Rosborough AD, Wiseman L, Pihlajarinne T (2023) Achieving a (copy)right to repair for the EU'S green economy. JIPLP 18:344–352. https://doi.org/10.1093/jiplp/jpad034
Schovsbo J, Dinwoodie GB (2018) Design protection for products that are "dictated by function". In: Kur A, Levin M, Schovsbo J (eds) The EU design approach: a global appraisal. Edward Elgar, Cheltenham, pp 142–171
Senftleben M (2021) Overprotection and protection overlaps in intellectual property law–the need for horizontal fair use defences. In: Kur A, Mizaras V (eds) The structure of intellectual property law: can one size fit all? Edward Elgar, Cheltenham, pp 136–181
Senftleben M (2024) Developing defences for fashion upcycling in EU trademark law. GRUR Int 73:99–110. https://doi.org/10.1093/grurint/ikad131
Sganga C (2024) The past, present and future of EU copyright flexibilities. IIC 55:5–36. https://doi.org/10.1007/s40319-023-01413-9
Slade G (2007) Made to break: technology and obsolescence in America. Harvard University Press, Cambridge
Spedicato G (2024) Deceptively green: how the EU's unfair commercial practices directive can support trademark law in combating corporate greenwashing. In: Thouvenin F et al (eds) Kreation innovation märkte - Creation innovation markets. Festschrift Reto M. Hilty, Springer, Berlin, pp 1065–1078
Stahel W (2016) The circular economy. Nature 531:435–438. https://doi.org/10.1038/531435a
Svensson-Hoglund S et al (2021) Barriers, enablers and market governance: a review of the policy landscape for repair of consumer electronics in the EU and the U.S. J Clean Prod 288:125488. https://doi.org/10.1016/j.jclepro.2020.125488
Tamura Y (2024) Intellectual property' as a metaphor: a recommendation for an understanding as 'governmental regulation of actions. GRUR Int 73:285–286. https://doi.org/10.1093/grurint/ikad120
Terryn E (2019) A right to repair? Towards sustainable remedies in consumer law. Eur Rev Private L 27:851–873. https://doi.org/10.54648/erpl2019044

Tischner (2021) Chopping off hydra's heads: spare parts in EU design and trade mark law. In: Brunn N, Dinwoodie GB, Levin M, Ohly A (eds) Transition and coherence in intellectual property law—essays in honour of Annette Kur. Cambridge University Press, Cambridge, pp 392–404

Tischner A, Stasiuk K (2023) Spare parts, repairs, trade marks and consumer understanding. IIC 54:26–60. https://doi.org/10.1007/s40319-022-01274-8

Tukker A (2015) Product services for a resource-efficient and circular economy–a review. J Clean Prod 97:76–91. https://doi.org/10.1016/j.jclepro.2013.11.049

van der Velden M, Maitre-Ekern E, Wanja DK (2024) The role of independent repair in a circular and regenerative economy. Circ Econ Sustain 4:2981–3006. https://doi.org/10.1007/s43615-023-00304-y

Widła B (2023) Circular economy versus copyright protection of computer programs in the EU: challenges and lessons from the CJEU'S judgment in *top system*. JIPLP 18:353–359. https://doi.org/10.1093/jiplp/jpad021:353

Wiseman L (2024) The right to repair in Australia. In: Rognstad O, Pihlajarinne T, Mähönen J (eds) Promoting sustainable innovation and the circular economy. Routledge, London, pp 156–183

Wiseman L, Kariyawasam K (2020) Revisiting the repair defence in the 'designs act' (2003) in light of the right to repair movement and the circular economy. Australian Intell Prop J 31:133–146

Yu PK (2009) The objectives and principles of the TRIPS agreement. Houston L Rev 46:979–1046

Reshaping Consumer Powers and Responsibilities in the European Union's Transition to a Sustainable Circular Economy

Francesco Deana

Abstract The chapter examines the consequences of the EU's paradigm shift towards a Sustainable Circular Economy (SCE) on the relationship between consumers and businesses in the context of the EU Single Market. First, this study argues that the EU is recalibrating consumer protection rules to empower consumers to make (even more) informed and sustainable decisions, aligned with the EU's climate and environmental objectives. However, it is emphasized that information alone is insufficient to enable consumers to make sustainable choices, especially considering issues such as information overload and insufficient literacy on complex environmental data. Therefore, the chapter further explores the crucial role of consumer education, which is necessary for ensuring that consumers can understand and apply sustainability-related information in their decision-making. The chapter then introduces new consumer rights within the SCE, specifically the right to product longevity and the right to product repairability. Brand new EU laws ensures that goods are designed to last longer, reducing the need for frequent replacements and minimizing waste. Similarly, they address planned obsolescence by requiring manufacturers to provide consumers with access to repair tools, parts, and information, allowing products to be maintained and used for a longer period. Ultimately, this study proposes an integrated vision of how EU reforms can facilitate a transition toward a more sustainable, equitable, and responsible economic model. However, it also argues that the effectiveness of such transition can be undermined by critical gaps—namely, the absence of a legal framework for returning non-sustainable products and the inherent tension between expansive consumer rights and their environmental impact.

F. Deana (✉)
Università degli Studi di Udine, Udine, Italy
e-mail: francesco.deana@uniud.it

B. Calabrese (ed.), *Legal Perspectives for a Sustainable Circular Economy*, European Union and its Neighbours in a Globalized World 30,
https://doi.org/10.1007/978-3-032-07795-0_8

1 Introduction

Redefining consumer powers and business obligations within the framework of the EU Single Market, in light of a human-centred circular economy, represents a crucial legal and conceptual challenge for the European Union.

Traditionally, EU consumer law had both the goals to empower consumers giving them the rights and information necessary to act in their own interests, and to compensate consumers' vulnerability and commercial weakness where those prevent consumers from protecting their rights, interests and safety. Evolving consumption and production dynamics, combined with the increasing importance of sustainability and environmental concerns, necessitate a profound transformation of the regulatory framework. The evolution of the regulatory framework for the Single Market must notably align with the EU's ambitions outlined in the European Green Deal,[1] the Circular Economy Action Plan[2] and the New Consumer Agenda,[3] which presents an updated vision of EU consumer policy with the aim of strengthening consumer resilience for a sustainable recovery.

These policy initiatives aim to transform the European economy by encouraging sustainable production and consumption models and promoting circularity.

One of the key aspects of this transformation concerns the obligation for businesses to provide detailed and verifiable information regarding the environmental performance of their products (Sect. 2). Missing or unclear information for consumers on the environmental performance of products, including a proliferation of unverifiable or even misleading 'green' claims contributes to the risk that the transition to a circular economy may fail. To this end, integrating third-party verification or certification requirements for environmental claims is fundamental to protecting consumers and ensuring market transparency.[4] The growing attention to product life cycles—from design to disposal—necessitates the adoption of tools such as sustainability labelling and environmental footprint indicators.[5] These instruments would standardize information on key sustainability factors such as carbon footprint, energy efficiency, reparability, recyclability, and overall lifecycle impact. The implementation of harmonized EU rules would ensure that consumers can easily

[1] European Commission, COM(2019) 640 final.

[2] European Commission, COM(2020) 98 final.

[3] European Commission, COM(2020) 696 final.

[4] On this, see Directive (EU) 2024/825 of the European Parliament and of the Council of 28 February 2024 amending Directives 2005/29/EC and 2011/83/EU as regards empowering consumers for the green transition through better protection against unfair practices and through better information (ECD), OJ L, 2024/825, 6.3.2024. See also the Proposal for a Directive of the European Parliament and of the Council on substantiation and communication of explicit environmental claims (Green Claims Directive), COM(2023) 166.

[5] On this, see Regulation (EU) 2024/1781 of the European Parliament and of the Council of 13 June 2024 establishing a framework for the setting of ecodesign requirements for sustainable products, amending Directive (EU) 2020/1828 and Regulation (EU) 2023/1542 and repealing Directive 2009/125/EC, OJ L, 2024/1781, 28.6.2024.

compare products in terms of sustainability, facilitating informed purchasing decisions. The evolution of the Single Market framework must also leverage recent advancements in the digital sphere, where online platforms play a pivotal role in shaping consumer behaviour. The Digital Services Act (DSA)[6] and the Digital Markets Act (DMA)[7] are key regulatory instruments that, if effectively integrated into the Single Market framework, can significantly contribute to ensuring algorithmic transparency and allowing consumers to understand why certain products (or their related information) are more prominently displayed than others.[8]

It has been argued that the information requirements may lack effectiveness because consumers often do not read the information and, even if they do, it frequently fails to consider cognitive abilities and literacy levels. Even when consumers understand the information, they may not be willing or able to process it in a manner that is useful to them at the time it is provided. Therefore, attention must be drawn to the consumers' right to receive education on sustainable consumption and on the benefits of the transition towards a circular economy. In this context, the examination will also consider any measures that the EU intends to introduce, or requires Member States to introduce, to assist consumers in overcoming these barriers and better empower them to make informed, sustainable choices (Sect. 3).

Strengthening existing rights within the so-called *acquis communautaire* is important but cannot be sufficient. A true reconceptualization of consumer rights and business obligations through a sustainability lens is necessary (Sect. 4). The rights to product longevity and repairability will become fundamental consumer right in the transition from a linear to a circular economy. These rights will challenge traditional consumption patterns by imposing stricter obligations on businesses to design for longevity, recyclability, and minimal environmental impact. Recognizing these rights within the EU legal framework is essential to shifting liability, fostering sustainable consumption, and aligning market practices with the principles of circularity and environmental accountability.

---

[6] Regulation (EU) 2022/2065 of the European Parliament and of the Council of 19 October 2022 on a Single Market For Digital Services and amending Directive 2000/31/EC (Digital Services Act), OJ L 277, 27.10.2022, pp. 1–102.

[7] Regulation (EU) 2022/1925 of the European Parliament and of the Council of 14 September 2022 on contestable and fair markets in the digital sector and amending Directives (EU) 2019/1937 and (EU) 2020/1828 (Digital Markets Act), OJ L 265, 12.10.2022, pp. 1–66.

[8] Within this framework, the AI Act (Regulation (EU) 2024/1689 of the European Parliament and of the Council of 13 June 2024 laying down harmonised rules on artificial intelligence, OJ L, 2024/1689, 12.7.2024) does not add any additional specific obligations related to the operation of such algorithms if they do not directly affect areas protected by the 'high risk' criteria. Of course, this is not to say that there is no requirement for transparency where an AI system is deployed (see Article 50 AI Act); however, in the context of information on products' environmental performance, this is already well covered by regulations specific to digital services and the marketplace, and the imposition of additional technical and compliance burdens related to risk management for high-impact systems is generally not applicable. Only when, for specific platforms, AI features or algorithms are introduced that go beyond mere recommendation and directly affect critical decision-making processes, in such cases a framing as a high-risk system may be necessary, resulting in integrative AI Act obligations as well (see Article 9 and 13 AI Act).

The objective of this chapter, therefore, is to define and justify the (old and new) essential rights of consumers within the EU Single Market, highlighting how regulatory framework is going to evolve to support sustainable consumption and production models. This study aims to propose an integrated vision in which consumer powers and business obligations are redefined, according to the most recent pieces of EU legislation, to facilitate a transition toward a more sustainable, equitable, and responsible economic model, in which sustainable choices become the norm rather than the exception.

2 The Right to Information on Product Sustainability and Circularity

Consumer empowerment in the EU Single Market is intertwined with access to information.[9]

Extensive research has consistently demonstrated that, even with some flaws and limitations, transparent and accurate consumer information actually helps in shaping market dynamics.[10] Policymakers and legislators are even more enthusiastic about the 'power' of information.[11] The primary EU law reaffirms the centrality of the right to consumer information, a right that is instrumental both in promoting consumers' interests and in ensuring a high level of protection (in commercial relationships).[12] Consequently, secondary legislation must introduce the normative instruments needed to preserve this right, for example, setting out an extensive list of pre-contractual disclosure requirements,[13] or prohibiting misleading actions—which include information that is false or likely to deceive the consumer—and misleading omissions, where material information is either not provided[14] or it is 'hidden', 'unintelligible', 'ambiguous', or 'untimely'.[15] In other words, information

[9] On the international perspective of the right of access to information, considered as the backbone of consumer's power of choice, see Dal Monico, Chap. "Rethinking the Role of the Consumer in a Global Economy: The Power of Choice as a 'Human Right'?".

[10] Helleringer and Sibony (2017, pp. 607–646), Willett and Morgan-Taylor (2012, pp. 143–163), Howells (2005, pp. 349–370).

[11] Seizov et al. (2019, pp. 149–173).

[12] Article 169 TFEU.

[13] Cfr. Article 5 (Information requirements for contracts other than distance or off-premises contracts) and Article 6 (Information requirements for distance and off-premises contracts) Directive 2011/83/EU of the European Parliament and of the Council of 25 October 2011 on consumer rights (CRD), OJ L 304, 22.11.2011, pp. 64–88. Other relevant examples of directives containing explicit and mandatory information obligations were the E-commerce Directive (2000/31/EC), the Consumer Credit Directive (2008/48/EC), and the Services Directive (2006/123/EC).

[14] Article 7 (1) Directive 2005/29/EC of the European Parliament and of the Council of 11 May 2005 concerning unfair business-to-consumer commercial practices in the internal market (UCPD), OJ L 149, 11.6.2005, pp. 22–39.

[15] Article 7 (2) UCPD.

must be provided; it must be offered in a transparent, complete, or at least adequate manner;[16] and finally, it must be accurate and truthful.[17] Consumers should value such information so they can compare and reflect on the properties of products and understand the main elements of the contract before entering into a contractual relationship with the trader. The final outcome should be for the consumer to feel confident in exploiting the EU Single Market thanks to a high level of legal certainty.[18]

In the context of the transition towards a Sustainable Circular Economy (SCE), the consumer's right to receive clear and transparent information must be strongly protected, particularly with respect to the sustainability aspects of products. As highlighted in previous studies, information on the reparability and durability of products steers consumer choices towards more reparable and durable options.[19] On one hand, there is a clear appreciation for the usefulness of sustainability-related information; on the other hand, this usefulness is too often undermined by the generic, ambiguous, and even false nature of such information. A Commission study on environmental claims in the EU assessed 150 environmental claims and found that a significant share (53.3%) provided vague, misleading, or unfounded information on products' environmental characteristics across the EU and in a wide range of product groups (both in advertising and on the product).[20] As reported in a study commissioned by the European Parliament's Committee on the Internal Market and Consumer Protection, the analysis revealed that the credibility of almost half of the sustainability claims reviewed was doubtful, and that in around 60% of cases, traders did not provide sufficient information to allow consumers to assess the accuracy of the claims.[21]

This paragraph reconstructs the supranational regulatory framework by precisely outlining these aspects—that is, by identifying the informational obligations related to sustainability for businesses, the instruments that channel this information to consumers, and the control mechanisms in place to counteract commercial practices that distort or hinder genuinely informed sustainable consumption decisions.

[16] Schaub (2017, p. 38), says that 'This transparency requirement implies that the trader has to take into account the manner in which consumers read and process information when they provide the mandatory items of information'. See also Article 8(1) CRD.

[17] 'If they are to be properly empowered, consumers must be provided with clear, reliable and comparable information, and the tools to understand it'. European Commission, A European Consumer Agenda—Boosting confidence and growth, Brussels COM(2012)225 final, 9.

[18] Twigg-Flesner (2016, pp. 183–202).

[19] Cfr. European Commission, Directorate-General for Environment, (2021) Consumer study on the impact of reparability information formats on consumer understanding and purchase decisions: final report: followed by the executive summary. Publications Office, p. 5; European Commission, ConPolicy, Consumers, Health, Agriculture and Food Executive Agency (2018) Behavioural study on consumers' engagement in the circular economy: executive summary.

[20] European Commission, Directorate-General for Environment (2024) *Environmental claims in the EU—Inventory and reliability assessment—Final report*, Publications Office of the European Union.

[21] Collini et al. (2022).

Following this, the analysis reflects on the actual contribution of these measures to achieving the EU's objectives regarding the transition towards the SCE.

2.1 The Consumer's Right to Sustainable Information Before the Implementation of the Circular Economy Action Plan

Even before the recent wave of dedicated legislative acts, EU consumer law already included provisions that could support consumers' right to receive information on product sustainability.

The provisions of the CRD have significant potential in shaping a well-informed consumer capable of making responsible choices in terms of sustainability and circularity. First, the requirement concerning the 'main characteristics of goods or services'[22] is fundamental: although the text does not explicitly mention sustainability aspects, this element could also include information about the durability, repairability, and recyclability of products. If adequately specified, such data can guide consumers towards products designed for a longer lifecycle and promote reuse. Another crucial aspect is the information regarding after-sales services, commercial guarantees, and available complaint mechanisms.[23] These elements are essential to ensure that, in cases where products do not meet certain sustainability standards or exhibit defects related to their circularity, consumers have access to repairs, replacements, or returns. In a circular economy, the ability to repair or regenerate a product is at the heart of the model; therefore, clarity on these conditions is indispensable.[24] Additionally, information related to the duration of the contract and the conditions for its termination[25] assumes particular importance. In a circular system, a product's lifespan and maintenance directly affect its longevity and the efficiency of resource use. For example, such details could indicate warranty terms that favor repairability and the return of products that fail to meet sustainability criteria.

In order to strengthen consumer rights—particularly the right to information—in an exclusively digital context, the adoption of the DSA[26] and the DMA[27] has marked a significant milestone. Online platforms serve as a fundamental channel for disseminating product-related information, including data on sustainability, repairability, reuse, and other environmental aspects. As such, they play a strategic role not only as informational intermediaries but also as active agents in ensuring transparency and fairness toward consumers.

---

[22] See Art. 5(a) and Art. 6(a) CRD.

[23] See Art. 5(e) and Art. 6(m) CRD.

[24] For a more detailed discussion of the so-called 'right to repair', see Calabrese, Chap. "Right to Repair Between Intellectual Property and Servitization".

[25] See Art. 5 (f) and Art 6(o) and (p) CRD.

[26] See above, note 6.

[27] See above, note 7.

The DSA introduces transparency obligations that directly impact the consumer's right to receive clear and verifiable information.[28] Specifically, the DSA imposes requirements on transparency regarding advertising and sponsored content.[29] These obligations can be extended to the field of sustainability so that environmental claims (for example, those related to 'green claims') are accompanied by verifiable data and standardized indicators. Consequently, platforms may be required to remove or correct unverified or misleading information, thereby helping to ensure that consumers are not misled about the true environmental impact of a product.[30]

In contrast, the DMA focuses on regulating so-called 'gatekeepers', i.e. large, influential platforms that control access to numerous digital services, with the aim to prevent anticompetitive practices and promote equal treatment.[31] With regard to consumer rights within the context of the circular economy, the DMA provides equitable access to information based on a 'principle of technology neutrality'. It requires market operators with gatekeeping power to ensure that information is not unjustly favored, explicitly prohibiting practices such as self-preferencing,[32] which guarantees that platforms do not hinder the visibility of sustainable products or services offered by third parties. This is crucial for the circular economy, where innovative startups (e.g., producers of reusable packaging or repair services) might otherwise be marginalized by gatekeeper algorithms. In practical terms, it means that in the presence of search and recommendation algorithms, products or services cannot be promoted at the expense of providing accurate information about their sustainable characteristics, such as repairability indices or reuse data. Technology neutrality helps create an environment in which new companies offering circular solutions can more easily enter and compete with established operators. This aligns with the objectives of the forthcoming EU Circular Economy Act, which aims to standardize the use of secondary materials and reduce waste, thereby facilitating a more open and dynamic ecosystem.[33]

---

[28] Article 14, 15, 20, 22, 26, 28, 34, 39, 42 DSA.

[29] Maroni and Hillebrandt (2023, pp. 305–326), Duivenvoorde and Goanta (2023, pp. 1–14), Sevastianova (2023, pp. 1561–1589), Senftleben (2022, pp. 309–324).

[30] All this without prejudice to the forthcoming EU legislation on green claims, in particular the proposed Green Claims Directive currently under negotiation (see above, note 4).

[31] Witt (2023, pp. 625–666).

[32] Art. 6(5) DMA. For a deep analysis on this, see Höppner (2024). In this regard, see CJEU, case C-48/22 P, *Google and Alphabet v Commission*, ECLI:EU:C:2024:726, which provides a concrete example and a judicial interpretation of how self-preferencing practices may conflict with principles of fairness and technological neutrality, which underpin both the DMA and antitrust policies in general.

[33] See the EU Commissioner Roswall's keynote address at the event 'Towards a circular single market: Strengthening EU economic security and competitiveness', held in Brussels on 16 December 2024 (available at https://ec.europa.eu/commission/presscorner/detail/en/speech_24_6466). This initiative aims to stimulate market demand for recycled materials and establish a unified framework for waste management, with a particular focus on critical raw materials.

Despite these obligations providing a solid foundation, from a circular economy perspective there is still a notable gap: the explicit obligation to communicate detailed data regarding a product's environmental performance is missing. For instance, consumers are not currently required to receive detailed information on the environmental footprint, lifecycle, or materials used (all data that is essential to assess whether a product complies with sustainability and circularity principles).

Moreover, even though a study conducted by the European Union Agency for Fundamental Rights[34] highlighted that the wide scope of 'commercial practices' defined under the UCPD has allowed several Member States to tackle greenwashing even before the EU introduced specific legislation defining environmental claims, it also revealed notable inconsistencies among Member States in how unfair commercial practices rules are applied to greenwashing. These differences not only concern the interpretation of key terms but also the extent to which measures have been taken to combat greenwashing in the first place.

Another shortcoming is that the traditional approach to consumerism and consumer's rights in the DMA does not reflect the realities of digitalization and sustainability in the context of the circular economy.[35] The shift towards sustainable consumption increasingly relies on platforms that facilitate the reuse, repair, and exchange of second-hand goods, enabling consumers to act not only as buyers but also as 'prosumers', both providing and receiving products within circular business models. The outdated approach does not adequately capture these evolving roles, nor does it address the specific vulnerabilities and unique risks consumers face in digital marketplaces and second-hand markets,[36] such as unclear warranties, product reliability, liability gaps for used goods.[37]

Addressing these issues would have been essential for modernizing EU law to reflect digital realities and sustainability challenges. Therefore, the European Commission proposed to integrate the regulatory framework with specific rights and obligations, with a twofold desired outcome: reinforce the consumer's right to transparent and verified information and encourage businesses to design products that adhere to the principles of sustainability and circularity.

However, no initiative has been taken so far in order to amend the DMA according to the above-mentioned remark.

[34] European Union Agency for Fundamental Rights (2024).

[35] By referring to Article 2(2) P2B-Regulation (Regulation (EU) 2019/1150), Article 2(5) DMA defines an online intermediation service as meaning services which 'allow *business* users [emphasis added] to offer goods or services to consumers, with a view to facilitating the initiating of direct transactions between those business users and consumers, irrespective of where those transactions are ultimately concluded'.

[36] Moskal (2022, pp. 1113–1119).

[37] See Bergamini (Chap. "Dispute Resolution and Private International Law in the Context of Circular Economy: Effectiveness Beyond Alternatives") for a discussion of these issues from a private international law perspective.

2.2 *New Obligations on Sustainable Information and Environmental Claims*

Building on the European Union's commitment to sustainable development and consumer empowerment,[38] the policy tools and regulations developed under the Circular Economy Action Plan[39] are designed to ensure that consumers can make truly informed and responsible choices. Central to this effort was the proposal on empowering consumers for the green transition,[40] aimed at updating existing consumer law to ensure consumers are protected and can actively contribute to the green transition.

The recent Directive on Empowering Consumers for the Green Transition, to be transposed into Member States' national legal systems by 2026, mandates that the environmental attributes of products be communicated to consumers in clear, comparable, and accessible formats (whether on product labels, digital platforms, or within physical retail environments).[41]

First, the reform introduces significant modifications to the CRD, by incorporating new sustainability-related disclosure requirements.[42]

It is now mandatory to explicitly reminds consumers of the existence of the legal guarantee of conformity for goods,[43] with a minimum duration of two years,[44] and to communicate it in a prominent manner using a harmonised notice.[45] Additionally, if a producer offers a commercial guarantee of durability[46] beyond two years at no extra cost, this fact—along with the guarantee's duration and a reminder of the legal guarantee—must be prominently displayed using a harmonised label.[47] Similar

[38] In the European Green Deal (see above, note 1), whose normative value is examined by Harris (2024), the Commission made a commitment to ensure that consumers can make more informed choices and can actively participate in the ecological transition. In particular, the European Green Deal (at para. 2.1.3) aims to address false environmental claims by providing consumers with trustworthy, comparable and verifiable information, enabling them to make sustainable decisions and thereby reducing the risk of greenwashing.

[39] See above, note 2. According to the plan, the Commission should have proposed a revision of EU consumer law to ensure that consumers receive trustworthy and relevant information on products at the point of sale, including on their lifespan and on the availability of repair services, spare parts and repair manuals.

[40] European Commission, COM(2022) 143 final.

[41] See above, note 4. For a detailed analysis of the Directive, see Keirsbilck (2024, pp. 205–217).

[42] In essence, the changes affect Articles 5 and 6 CRD and add a new Article 22a.

[43] Article 5(1), point (e) CRD.

[44] As established by Directive (EU) 2019/771 of the European Parliament and of the Council of 20 May 2019 on certain aspects concerning contracts for the sale of goods (SGD), OJ L 136, 22.5.2019, pp. 28–50.

[45] As regulated by Article 22a.

[46] 'Durability' is 'the ability of the goods to maintain their required functions and performance through normal use', according to Article 2, point (13), of Directive 2019/771.

[47] Article 5(1), point (ea), CRD.

provisions apply for digital content, digital services, and for indicating the minimum period during which software updates will be provided for goods with digital elements.[48] Other new points focus on reparability and spare parts availability, as they require, where applicable, the communication of the reparability score of goods.[49] If such a score is not applicable, producers must provide information on the availability, estimated cost, and ordering procedure for spare parts essential to maintaining conformity, along with repair and maintenance instructions and any repair restrictions.[50]

The ECD also improves delivery and payment information, including in the CRD comprehensive details on payment arrangements, delivery—specifically mentioning environmentally friendly delivery options—performance timelines, and the trader's complaint handling policy.[51] A similar update concerns the inclusion of a prominent reminder of the legal guarantee of conformity.[52] Moreover, the new rules in this field replicate those already introduced in relation to commercial guarantees, digital content and services, software update periods, the reparability score, and the provision of information on spare parts and repair conditions.[53]

The Directive adds specific communication obligations in distance contracts, now specifically requiring that, prior to order placement, consumers are clearly and prominently informed about key aspects such as payment, delivery (including eco-friendly options), guarantee information, and other relevant points.[54]

In order to ease the understanding and processing of such a huge amount of information, while ensuring consistency for consumers across the EU, the Directive mandates the use of a harmonised notice for the information,[55] and a harmonised label for the information.[56] Nonetheless, while the aim is to enhance transparency, there is a risk that the proliferation of technical details on reparability scores, spare parts information, after-sales services and repair procedures, might overwhelm or confuse consumers, potentially diluting the intended clarity.[57]

However, the reform has the potential to enhance consumer confidence and support informed decision-making and responsible consumption. At the same time, by highlighting commercial durability guarantees, reparability scores, and the availability of spare parts as valuable product features, the regulatory framework creates market incentives for producers to design goods with longer lifespans and easier

[48] Article 5(1), points (eb) and (ed), CRD.

[49] Article 5(1) point (i) CRD. According to the amended version of Article 2, point (14d) CRD, 'reparability score' means a score expressing the capacity of a good to be repaired, based on harmonised requirements established at Union level.

[50] Article 5(1) point (j) CRD.

[51] Article 6(1), point (g), CRD.

[52] Article 6(1), point (l), CRD.

[53] Respectively, see Article 6(1), subpoints (la), (lb), and (lc), points (u) and (v), CRD.

[54] Article 8(2) CRD.

[55] Under Article 5(1)(e) and Article 6(1)(l), CRD.

[56] Under Article 5(1)(ea) and Article 6(1)(la), CRD.

[57] On this topic see Sect. 4 of this chapter.

maintenance, ideally steering consumer preferences towards such products and making them more commercially attractive.

The ECD also introduces changes to the UCPD, clarifying which commercial practices can be deemed misleading (and therefore prohibited) based on a case-by-case assessment.[58] Additionally, it identifies specific misleading practices that are considered unfair in all circumstances and are thus outright banned.[59] Among the targeted practices are greenwashing,[60] which misleads consumers about a product's environmental impact, and false claims regarding a product's durability when its actual lifespan is shorter than what a consumer could reasonably expect.[61]

The list of banned commercial practices now includes misleading claims based on greenhouse gas emissions offsetting. This means professionals are prohibited from declaring that a product has a neutral, reduced, or improved environmental impact if these claims are solely based on unverified offset programs. The text also clarifies that professionals are held accountable for providing accurate information—or for failing to do so—about design features that lead to premature obsolescence, unnecessary software updates, or the unjustified need to purchase original spare parts. However, this responsibility only applies if there is available information showing that the product was designed in a way that limits its longevity or forces additional costs.[62]

Considering that claiming to be 'green' and sustainable has become a competitiveness factor and that if goods and services purchased on the internal market are not as environmentally friendly as presented, this would mislead the consumers and prevent the reduction of negative environmental impacts, the EU Commission has

---

[58] Articles 6 and 7 UCPD.

[59] In doing so, the ECD amends Annex I UCPD.

[60] 'Greenwashing' refers to the practice of conveying false or misleading information about the environmental friendliness of a company's products. It involves using deceptive advertising or marketing tactics to convince the public that the company's products, goals and policies are environmentally sound. It can be found in advertising, sponsorship and public messaging in the media, including on social media. Examples of greenwashing can range from simply changing the name or label of a product to make it seem more natural, even if it contains harmful chemicals, to launching elaborate and expensive campaigns that portray highly polluting companies as committed to being eco-friendly. On this topic cfr. de Freitas Netto et al. (2020), Bernini and La Rosa (2024, pp. 405–444). According to recital 9 ECD, 'examples of generic environmental claims include 'environmentally friendly', 'eco-friendly', 'green', 'nature's friend', 'ecological', 'environmentally correct', 'climate friendly', 'gentle on the environment', 'carbon friendly', 'energy efficient', 'biodegradable', 'biobased' or similar statements that suggest or create the impression of excellent environmental performance'.

[61] The list now includes: (a) false information and other commercial practices that deceive or are likely to deceive the average consumer, even if the information is factually correct, in relation to (among others) 'environmental or social characteristics, accessories, circularity aspects, such as durability, reparability or recyclability, after-sale customer assistance'; (b) environmental claims related to future environmental performance without clear, objective, publicly available and verifiable commitments, where they cause or are likely to cause the average consumer to take a transactional decision that he would not have taken otherwise.

[62] Recital 19 ECD.

then published the Green Claims Directive Proposal.[63] This proposal requires that any environmental claims made by companies—whether used as part of mandatory disclosure in advertising or other forms of communication—be fully substantiated by robust scientific evidence and corroborated by comprehensive life cycle analyses. Only environmental claims that are reliable, comparable and verifiable, allow consumers to fully leverage their purchasing decisions to reward better environmental performance.

The Proposal aims at complementing the ECD as *lex specialis.*[64] The provisions establish a robust framework for environmental claims and labelling in the EU, requiring traders to conduct a thorough assessment using independent, peer-reviewed scientific evidence to substantiate explicit environmental claims, clearly indicating whether the claim applies to the whole product, parts of it, its life-cycle, or specific activities.[65] Explicit environmental claims may only cover environmental impacts, environmental aspects or environmental performance that are substantiated in accordance with the requirements set by the Proposal.[66] In doing so, the Green Claims Directive Proposal complements the requirements set out in the ECD by addressing specific aspects and requirements for explicit environmental claims. As a consequence, the requirements set out in the amended Directive 2005/29/EC with regard to those aspects are overridden by the requirements set out in Green Claims Directive Proposal.[67] Since at the moment there are over 200 environmental labels on the EU market,[68] each varying widely in transparency, criteria, revision frequency, and auditing rigor, the proposal mandates that environmental labels comply with rigorous requirements and be subject to verification, ensuring transparency and reliability.[69] Moreover, any new environmental labelling schemes introduced by public authorities or third countries must receive timely approval from the

[63] See above, note 4. At the time this chapter has been submitted, the future of the proposal appeared uncertain, due to the cancellation by the Polish Presidency of the EU Council of the third and final trilogue scheduled for 23 June 2025. The cancellation followed certain statements from the European Commission (later denied) suggesting the EU executive's intention to withdraw the proposal itself, also in response to an explicit request to that effect from the European Parliament's EPP and Conservative groups. In the meantime, the Council of the EU had adopted its 'general approach', with some very significant changes as regards scope and substance of the proposal. See Council, 'Proposal for a Directive of the European Parliament and of the Council on substantiation and communication of explicit environmental claims (Green Claims Directive)– General approach', 17 June 2024, 11,312/24. On the Commission proposal see Jung and Dowse (2024, pp. 11–23). The most important amendments adopted by the Council are presented in Evans (2024, pp. 174–187).

[64] See Recital 6 of the Proposal as amended by the European Parliament after its first reading. European Parliament, Legislative resolution on the proposal for a directive of the European Parliament and of the Council on substantiation and communication of explicit environmental claims (Green Claims Directive), 12 March 2024, P9_TA(2024)0131.

[65] Article 3 Green Claims Directive Proposal.

[66] Article 5 Green Claims Directive Proposal.

[67] Recital 14 Green Claims Directive Proposal.

[68] Recital 39 Green Claims Directive Proposal.

[69] Article 7 Green Claims Directive Proposal.

Commission before they enter the EU market, guaranteeing that such labels add real environmental value.[70]

Complementing these measures is the so-called 'Ecodesign Regulation',[71] which introduces detailed rules designed to enhance the environmental performance of products throughout their lifecycle. Companies are now obligated to assess key parameters—including repairability, durability, energy efficiency, and recyclability—during production processes. An innovative feature of the Regulation is the introduction of a Digital Product Passport (DPP),[72] a tool that allows for the continuous tracking of products from production to post-consumer use.[73] This passport provides consumers with essential information about a product's materials, environmental footprint, maintenance and repair instructions, and overall sustainability performance, thereby promoting transparency and informed decision-making.[74]

Retailers are obligated to make the DPP readily accessible, including through online channels.[75] Meanwhile, such obligations are extended to digital platforms,[76] which must adhere to the transparency and compliance standards established by the DSA.

Finally, the brand new EU Regulation on packaging and packaging waste,[77] not only requires clear, harmonized labeling on packaging and waste containers to inform consumers about recyclability and proper disposal locations. It establishes standardized symbols based on packaging materials to simplify waste sorting and recycling.[78] Moreover, the Regulation prohibits misleading labels or symbols that could confuse consumers about how to correctly dispose of packaging waste.[79]

By integrating these diverse policy instruments, the EU not only strengthens consumer protection and transparency but also fosters systemic changes in production and consumption patterns. Through the combination of clear information disclosure, scientifically backed environmental claims, and robust tracking mechanisms, the EU is paving the way for informed consumers and responsible businesses to work together in achieving the transition towards the circular economy.

---

[70] Article 8(4) Green Claims Directive Proposal.

[71] See above, note 5.

[72] Article 7, 9-15 Ecodesign Regulation. Furthermore, Article 9 underscores the mandatory nature of the DPP, ensuring that consumers and other stakeholders have reliable access to details regarding the origin, materials, and proper disposal methods of the product. On the DPP see Mittwoch (2024, pp. 62–67).

[73] Article 7(5) Ecodesign Regulation.

[74] The European Commission has the power to adopt delegated acts pursuant to Article 4 of the Regulation, in order to lay down further information requirements related to the product aspects.

[75] Article 31 Ecodesign Regulation.

[76] Article 35 Ecodesign Regulation.

[77] Regulation (EU) 2025/40 of the European Parliament and of the Council of 19 December 2024 on packaging and packaging waste, amending Regulation (EU) 2019/1020 and Directive (EU) 2019/904, and repealing Directive 94/62/EC, OJ L, 2025/40, 22.1.2025.

[78] See Recital 66, Article 12 and 13, Regulation on packaging and packaging waste.

[79] See Recital 71, Article 12(8), (9), (10), Regulation on packaging and packaging waste.

3 Is Information Enough? The Right to Education on Sustainable Consumption as a Necessary Complement to the Right to Information

The question of whether information is sufficient to effectively empower consumers is multifaceted and complex. Providing consumers with accurate and detailed information is a fundamental step in encouraging more informed choices and thus more sustainable behaviors. However, on the one hand, this alone is not sufficient to ensure that people actually modify their behavior in a sustainable way.[80] On the other hand, excessive or poorly structured information can have counterproductive effects from both a legal and socio-material perspective. The consumer may, in fact, be unable to manage such an influx of information in a way that is useful for the purposes for which it was provided. This is true also, and perhaps especially, in the context of the transition toward circular and sustainable consumption.

First, consider the issue of information overload and 'information fatigue'.[81] Consumers today are exposed to an ever-increasing amount of data regarding products: details about composition, origin, environmental impact, disposal methods, certifications, and more. Overly detailed or highly technical information can overwhelm the average consumer. Instead of facilitating informed decisions, an overload of data may result in confusion,[82] causing consumers to disregard the information altogether or to base their choices on superficial factors like price or reviews. From a legal standpoint, while EU legislation seeks to protect consumers from misleading omissions, an overload of complex information may paradoxically reduce market transparency, as discussed in relation to the Unfair Commercial Practices Directive.[83]

Moreover, poorly structured or excessive information can lead to 'choice paralysis', where consumers struggle to make decisions when faced with too many options or too many data points.[84] For example, if a sustainability label provides ten

---

[80] Howells (2005). This is also related to the so-called 'attitude-behaviour gap', a phenomenon well documented in psychology and social sciences. In practice, with regard to the role of consumers in the green transition, many people claim to support sustainability (positive attitude), but then fail to translate this belief into concrete actions (actual behaviour). The reasons for this gap can be numerous, including the higher cost of sustainable products, difficulties in accessing eco-friendly solutions, established habits, social and cultural influences, too much information, or conflicting messages that may lead consumers to doubt the effectiveness of their choices. On this topic, see Bray et al. (2010, pp. 597–608), Johnstone and Tan (2014, pp. 311–328).

[81] Cfr. Hwang and Lin (2016, pp. 213–218), Chernev et al. (2015, pp. 333–358), Hu and Krishen (2019, pp. 27–37).

[82] Better Regulation Executive and the National Consumer Council (2007) Warning: Too much information can harm (Interim Report). London: NCC

[83] Duivenvoorde (2015). The UCPD's benchmark is the 'average consumer', a consumer that is '*reasonably* [emphasis added] well-informed and *reasonably* [emphasis added] observant and circumspect'.

[84] Jacoby (1984, pp. 432–435).

different environmental parameters without indicating which ones are most critical, the consumer may either choose arbitrarily or ignore the label entirely. This phenomenon undermines the core purpose of consumer protection laws, such as the Consumer Rights Directive, which mandate transparency but do not necessarily ensure that information is presented in an accessible manner. The key issue is that the 'clarity' and 'comprehensibility' required of professionals under Articles 5 and 6 of the UCPD are relative concepts, not necessarily equivalent to 'usability' or 'effective communication'.[85]

An extended right to receive information, on the one hand, strengthens consumer awareness (which does not necessarily succeed in balancing the economic and commercial power of the seller or service provider); on the other hand, the diligent fulfillment of informational obligations by professionals leads to a redistribution of responsibility. In other words, a carefully and extensively informed consumer is expected to take greater responsibility for the actual impact of their choices and behaviors in the market.[86]

The risk is that the right to information and transparency may backfire on the consumer, who, no longer a vulnerable subject at the mercy of an information asymmetry favoring the professional, finds themselves as a mature and attentive 'commercial interlocutor' of the professional. This would be true if we assumed that an informed consumer is indeed an aware consumer, capable of processing and internalizing the information flow, transforming it into power that, if not necessarily advantageous over the counterpart, at least places them in a position of substantial parity. But this is almost never the case: the average consumer 'has a rough idea, but not necessarily a detailed knowledge, about the product or service in question'.[87] Additionally, consumers lack the literacy and knowledge to engage with relevant disclosure texts.[88]

As the transition to the SCE calls for the active engagement of 'responsible consumers', echoing the era in which the then-ECJ grounded the free movement of goods on the notion of a well-informed, critical, and attentive consumer within the Single Market,[89] it is inevitably necessary to invest in the right to sustainable education. The right to education, which was first laid out in a 1975 Council's Resolution[90] and more recently brought into direct relationship with the right to information in

[85] On this topic see Willett (2010, pp. 247–273). See also CJEU, case C-430/17, *Walbusch Walter Busch*, ECLI:EU:C:2019:47.

[86] In the context of financial services, see Stănescu (2019, pp. 49–67).

[87] Incardona and Poncibò (2007, p. 26).

[88] Mak (2012, pp. 254–263). On consumers' lack of knowledge and inability to differentiate between claims, labels, and other certification standards, see Janßen and Langen (2017).

[89] The development of the concept commenced with the landmark *Cassis de Dijon* judgement (ECJ, case 120/78, *Rewe-Zentral AG v Bundesmonopolverwaltung für Branntwein*, ECLI:EU:C:1979:42).

[90] Council Resolution of 14 April 1975 on a preliminary programme of the European Economic Community for a consumer protection and information policy, OJ C 92, 25.4.1975, pp. 1–1.

2020 by the New Consumer Agenda,[91] must be an essential corollary to the right of information in the SCE.

To truly empower all consumers, information must be complemented by accessible education initiatives and practical tools—such as standardized, intuitive labels or digital applications that offer layered information on demand—ensuring that every consumer, regardless of their background, can make choices aligned with sustainability and circular economy principles. Therefore, it is essential to acknowledge the social inequalities in accessing and interpreting complex information. Consumers with fewer economic or educational resources may not be able to benefit equally, thus widening the sustainability gap between different segments of the population.

Only through targeted training programs can consumers acquire the skills needed to process and internalize information, turning it into real decision-making power. Consumer education should not limited to providing basic knowledge about products and their impacts but should aims to develop the critical ability to independently and consciously evaluate technical and environmental information, such as sustainability, repairability, and reuse.

This educational dimension is essential to reducing the information asymmetry in favor of professionals, as it allows the consumer to move beyond the mere role of a passive subject and become an active and equal interlocutor in the commercial process. Education not only facilitates the understanding of environmental labels and certifications[92] but also encourages responsible consumption behaviors, contributing to a culture of sustainability that integrates into the circular economy model.[93]

This educational approach is particularly crucial in the digital era, where the quantity and complexity of information can easily lead to information overload and choice paralysis. The supranational instruments currently in place, such as the European Green Deal[94] and the Circular Economy Action Plan,[95] constitute important foundations for guiding change. Investing in educational programs and awareness campaigns, inspired by initiatives such as the European Commission's 'Learning for the Green Transition'[96] and the subsequent Recommendation issued

[91] See above, note 3. Although it is a non-binding communication, the New Consumer Agenda highlights the need to strengthen consumer empowerment through, among other measures, educational and informational actions to address the challenges posed by digitalization and sustainability.

[92] Grunert et al. (2014).

[93] As shown by Majer et al. (2022).

[94] Para. 2.2.4.

[95] Para. 5, where the Commission states that 'Further investment in education and training systems, lifelong learning, and social innovation will be promoted under the European Social Fund Plus'.

[96] See the Commission proposal of 14 January 2022 for a Council Recommendation on learning for environmental sustainability, COM(2022)11 final, and the Staff working document accompanying the proposal for a Council recommendation on learning for environmental sustainability, SWD/2022/3 final.

by the EU Council to Member States,[97] should enable citizens/consumers to develop the knowledge, skills, and attitudes necessary to promote sustainable consumption patterns, adopt more environmentally friendly lifestyles, and contribute—both individually and collectively—to the transformation of our societies.[98]

However, their effectiveness largely depends on the EU and Member States' ability to translate these tools into concrete actions, integrating targeted training programs and awareness campaigns with support tools. In this sense, complementing accessible education measures with practical tools (e.g., apps or QR codes) to provide in-depth information only to those who seek it—without overwhelming others—could help consumers who feel capable of handling such information apply the knowledge and skills they have acquired. Large online platforms themselves can become active allies of consumers by providing interactive tools such as sustainability search filters or repairability and reuse comparators, in line with the obligations laid down in the DSA and the DMA.[99]

Ultimately, consumer education emerges as a fundamental remedy to ensure that the right to information does not become a burden but instead becomes a true instrument of empowerment, capable of making the consumer a proactive actor in the transition toward the SCE. An integrated approach that leverages digital technologies and interactive tools can be helpful to make information more accessible and comprehensible to all segments of the population, an issue that, as scholarly literature indicates, remains particularly significant. This is essential to avoid the phenomenon of information overload, which risks making the consumer, despite the abundance of data, an inadequately informed interlocutor.

4 The Rights to Product Longevity and Repairability

In the context of the transition to a circular economy, qualities such as longevity and repairability have become increasingly prioritized in consumer goods.[100] As a result, the EU has recognized the need to impose obligations on producers and sellers to ensure that products placed on the market not only meet these standards but also that

[97] Council Recommendation of 16 June 2022 on learning for the green transition and sustainable development 2022/C 243/01.

[98] *Ibidem*, reccomendation no. 4(d).

[99] As seen above, under Sect. 2.1.

[100] Combination of longevity plus repairabilty and the right to sustainable disposal represents an emerging principle within EU environmental and consumer protection law. It encompasses two interrelated elements: ensuring that products are designed for a longer useful life–also thanks to their repairability–, and guaranteeing that, at the end of their lifecycle, they are disposed of in an environmentally responsible manner. This dual approach is fundamental to the EU's broader objective of fostering a circular economy, as outlined in the Circular Economy Action Plan and the European Green Deal. Sustainable disposal practices are regulated under the Waste Framework Directive (2008/98/EC), which sets out the principles for waste management and recycling, thereby ensuring that products at the end of their life are recovered and reused rather than discarded.

consumers receive clear and accurate information about these characteristics. This approach enables consumers to make well-informed choices, reinforcing their role in driving sustainable consumption.

However, as happened in the recent past within general consumer law, EU legislation on the circular economy should evolve beyond merely providing information to consumers and instead focus on actively empowering them. In this regard, it is essential to recognize a genuine right for consumers to access products that are both long-lasting and repairable. By doing so, the legislative framework would not only enhance transparency but also ensure that the goods available in the market truly support sustainable consumption, ultimately fostering a more resilient and environmentally responsible economy.

From a normative standpoint, product longevity is encouraged through legislation like the Ecodesign Regulation, which requires manufacturers to consider factors such as durability, reusability, repairability, and energy efficiency during the design phase.[101] At the same time, the recently adopted Right to Repair Directive[102] occupies a central position, addressing issues that are deemed critical not only by European institutions but also by citizens themselves.[103] Together, these initiatives mark a significant step forward in ensuring that products are designed for a longer lifespan and that consumers have the means to repair them, supporting a more sustainable and circular economic model.

4.1 *The Right to Product Longevity*

The European Union's approach to product sustainability is anchored in a comprehensive regulatory framework that integrates environmental performance with consumer protection. Historically, the Ecodesign Directive[104] served as the cornerstone for embedding environmental considerations into product design. However, in a significant policy shift, the new EU Ecodesign Regulation—effective from July 18,

[101] See Recital 16 and Article 5 Ecodesign Regulation.

[102] Directive (EU) 2024/1799 of the European Parliament and of the Council of 13 June 2024 on common rules promoting the repair of goods and amending Regulation (EU) 2017/2394 and Directives (EU) 2019/771 and (EU) 2020/1828 (R2RD), OJ L, 2024/1799, 10.7.2024. For a more detailed discussion of the Directive's scope, as well as issues related to intellectual property and servitization, see Calabrese, Chap. "Right to Repair Between Intellectual Property and Servitization".

[103] The outcome of the Conference on the Future of Europe also included a call for a right to repair. See Conference on the Future of Europe | Report on the final outcome, May 2022, notably proposal 5 (points 6 and 7) and 11 (point 2). Moreover, according to a Eurobarometer survey (Special Eurobarometer 503: Attitudes towards the impact of digitalisation on daily lives), 77% of EU citizens would rather repair their electrical equipment than throw it away.

[104] Directive 2009/125/EC of the European Parliament and of the Council of 21 October 2009 establishing a framework for the setting of ecodesign requirements for energy-related products (recast), OJ L 285, 31.10.2009, pp. 10–35.

2024—has replaced the Directive. This updated regulation not only reinforces but also expands the scope of ecodesign requirements, mandating that products achieve higher standards of durability, energy efficiency, repairability, and recyclability. The Regulation marks a substantial broadening of its applicability compared to the earlier Ecodesign Directive. Whereas the previous Directive focused solely on energy-related products like washing machines and refrigerators, the new framework now encompasses nearly all physical goods.[105]

At the core of the regulation is the principle that only products meeting specific ecodesign criteria can be placed on the market,[106] meaning that products are permitted free circulation only if they conform to the ecodesign requirements defined in the delegated acts.[107]

A pivotal element of the new Regulation is the imposition of improvements in 16 environmental aspects.[108] Among these, durability and repairability are prioritized. In particular, specific ecodesign requirements—based on the product parameters outlined in Annex I—are laid down to prevent planned (and premature) obsolescence.[109] This provision explicitly targets design practices that deliberately shorten a product's useful life. Such practices include using components that are significantly less robust than alternative options, impeding the disassembly of key components, withholding essential repair information or spare parts. Moreover, the Regulation addresses issues related to software obsolescence, such as software that ceases to function after an operating system update or when updates are no longer provided.[110]

Annex I of the Regulation details a comprehensive set of 20 product parameters that serve as benchmarks for durability and sustainability. These parameters cover multiple dimensions, which can be summarized as follows. The first one is durability and reliability, measured through the product's guaranteed lifetime, technical lifetime, mean time between failures, and resistance to stresses or aging mechanisms.[111] The second is ease of repair and maintenance, evaluated based on the availability, delivery time, and affordability of spare parts, as well as the simplicity

---

105 See Article 1(2) Ecodesign Regulation, for a list of the categories of goods excluded from the scope of the Regulation.

106 According to Article 3 Ecodesign Regulation.

107 Article 4 Ecodesign Regulation empowers the European Commission to adopt delegated acts (*ex* Article 290 TFEU) that lay down detailed requirements, including specific parameters for durability, repairability, and overall environmental impact. This delegation ensures that the regulatory framework remains adaptable, allowing for updates as technological and environmental standards evolve. According to Recital 49 of the same Regulation, 'the Commission should prioritise iron, steel, aluminium, textiles, in particular garments and footwear, furniture, including mattresses, tyres, detergents, paints, lubricants, chemicals, information and communication technology products and other electronics, and energy-related products for which ecodesign requirements are to be set for the first time or for which existing measures [...] are to be reviewed'.

108 Article 5 Ecodesign Regulation.

109 Article 5(2) Ecodesign Regulation.

110 *Ibidem*.

111 Parameters (a) and (s), Annex I.

of disassembly and reassembly, modularity, and the availability of repair instructions.[112] A third dimension is that of ease of upgrading, reuse, remanufacturing, and refurbishment, focused on modularity, the use of standard components, and conditions that allow non-destructive disassembly.[113] The other two dimensions are those of design for recycling and avoidance of detrimental technical solutions. The former emphasizes the use of easily recyclable materials, safe access to recyclable components, and the facilitation of high-purity material sorting,[114] while the latter ensures that design choices do not hinder reuse, repair, or recycling.[115]

These design criteria are not merely aspirational; they are enforceable and verifiable,[116] ensuring that manufacturers cannot employ anti-repair strategies such as incorporating incompatible software or making spare parts inaccessible.[117]

In addition, the Regulation delineates clear responsibilities for various market operators. Importers, for example, must ensure that products comply with these ecodesign requirements before they reach the market.[118]

By embedding these rigorous criteria into product standards, the Regulation seeks to shift manufacturing practices toward creating products that are not only more robust and repairable but also easier to upgrade and recycle, ultimately contributing to reduced waste and a more resource-efficient economy.

4.2 The Right to Product Repairability

Consumers are often discouraged from repairing damaged products due to a combination of economic, technical, and psychological barriers. High costs, anti-repair design choices, limited access to tools and spare parts, and ingrained habits that favor replacement over repair all contribute to this trend. Together, these barriers create a system in which repairing a product is often more expensive, difficult, or inconvenient than simply replacing it. Addressing these challenges is essential to

---

[112] Parameters (b) and (l), Annex I.

[113] Parameters (c) and (k), Annex I.

[114] Parameters (d), (h), (i), (j), (r), and (t), Annex I.

[115] Parameters (e), (f), (g), (m), (n), (o), (p), and (q), Annex I.

[116] Article 5(12), 8(g) and (i), 15, 39 Ecodesign Regulation.

[117] The main legal basis lies in Article 5(2) of the Regulation, which addresses obsolescence resulting from specific design choices made by manufacturers. The provision clearly indicates that any design strategy aimed at limiting repairability constitutes a breach of the principles of durability and sustainability underpinning the Regulation. Accordingly, the provision should not merely discourage, but in effect prohibit, manufacturers from adopting measures that intentionally make the maintenance and repair of products difficult or impossible, thereby directly countering anti-repair strategies.

[118] See Article 29 Ecodesign Regulation.

promoting a more sustainable approach to consumption and extending the lifespan of products.[119]

If the Ecodesign Regulation establishes technical requirements to enhance product repairability, only a genuine right to repair—legally enforceable—can effectively help reduce the environmental impact of consumption, ideally without compromising the quality of the products consumers purchase. Empowering consumers with greater ability to repair their devices ensures that the products they buy not only offer prolonged usability but also contribute to environmental sustainability throughout their entire lifecycle.

In the light of the above, the revision of the Ecodesign Regulation is complemented by the R2RD,[120] which amends the 'Sale of Goods Directive'[121] as part of the EU's sustainability strategy.

In general terms, under the SGD the seller is liable to the consumer for any lack of conformity which becomes apparent within a two-year span since the moment of delivery.[122] In the event of a lack of conformity, the consumer shall be entitled to have access to a list of alternative remedies, the first of which is having the goods brought into conformity.[123] In that context, 'bringing into conformity' either means to have the good repaired or replaced, unless the remedy chosen 'would be impossible or, compared to the other remedy, would impose costs on the seller that would be disproportionate'.[124]

While this general Directive rightly recognizes repair as a key remedy, promoting sustainability, it does not grant it priority over replacement. Instead, the European legislator leaves the decision between repair and replacement to the consumer, ensuring flexibility in addressing product defects.[125] Even where consumers choose repair over replacement, that could not be possible if the necessary spare parts and/or repair and maintenance information and/or any repair related tools are not made available by the manufacturers.

In the light of the above, special repair legislation can be a more effective solution,[126] in terms of circularity and sustainability, even beyond the scope and

---

[119] See extensively Perzanowski (2021).

[120] See above, note 102.

[121] See above, note 44.

[122] Article 10 SGD.

[123] Article 13(1) SGD.

[124] Article 13(2) SGD.

[125] Staudenmayer (2000, p. 554).

[126] See Terryn (2019, p. 867), on EU rules on the right to access to repair information in the vehicles industry.

impact of commercial guarantees,[127] including those on product durability.[128] Following this principle, the R2RD affirms that once the legal guarantee (automatically provided in all Member States under rules implementing the SGD) has come to an end, the manufacturer is now obligated to repair common products that are technically repairable according to EU law.

Repairers may provide consumers with a 'European Repair Information Form' before the consumer is bound by a contract for the provision of repair services.[129] Information on repair conditions and services helps consumers assess and compare repair options. Therefore, the repairer must provide complete and accurate information, in compliance with the following requirements: obligations regarding the key characteristics of the repair service, the identity and contact details of the repairer, the price, the methods, and the timeframe for performing the repair service.[130]

Additionally, a repair obligation is imposed on manufacturers at the simple request of the consumer, provided that the repair is not impossible,[131] and only for goods for which EU legislation establishes specific repairability requirements.[132] The repair must be carried out within a reasonable timeframe and either free of charge or at a reasonable cost, which may include the price of spare parts;[133] however, the cost of spare parts must not be set at a level that discourages repair.[134] Importantly, this repair obligation on manufacturers does not correspond to an obligation on consumers to turn exclusively to the manufacturer for repairs. On the contrary, the Directive expressly provides for the establishment of a European online repair platform to connect consumers with repairers, sellers of refurbished

---

[127] In addition to the conformity requirement and associated remedies, the SGD also contains a number of rules regarding 'commercial guarantees'. As better explained in Hawes and Twigg-Flesner (2018), they are voluntary undertakings given by a retailer or manufacturer in respect of the goods, that offers to reimburse the price paid or to replace, repair, or otherwise service the goods if they fail to meet the specifications or other non-conformity requirements set out in the guarantee statement or related advertising. This voluntary tool for repair supports product longevity and contributes to a more circular economy by reducing waste and extending the useful life of products. Article 6(1)(m) CRD, as is particularly clear from its wording, seeks to provide the consumer with pre-contractual information on the existence of such guarantees and the relevant conditions (CJEU, case C-179/21, *absoluts-bikes and more-GmbH & Co. KG*, ECLI:EU:C:2022:353, para. 57).

[128] Article 17 SGD.

[129] See again Article 10(1) and (2) SGD.

[130] Article 4 R2RD (recalling the relevant form as set out in Annex I).

[131] Article 5(1) R2RD.

[132] It mainly concerns certain household appliances, electronic displays, servers and data storage products, mobile phones and tablets, goods that incorporate batteries for light means of transport. For a detailed list, see Annex II of the R2RD (but the list of product categories can be extended over time).

[133] Article 5(2) R2RD.

[134] Article 5(4) R2RD.

goods, or buyers of defective goods for refurbishment purposes, as well as to inform them of community repair initiatives.[135]

Regarding products subject to the aforementioned sector-specific EU legislation, the exercise of the right to repair cannot be restricted or denied by manufacturers. Manufacturers cannot rely on legal mechanisms (such as contractual clauses) or technical barriers (such as hardware or software restrictions) to prevent the repair of covered goods,[136] unless justified by legitimate and objective factors, including the protection of intellectual property rights under EU and national law.[137] Similarly, manufacturers cannot prohibit the use of original or second-hand spare parts, compatible spare parts, or 3D-printed spare parts by independent repairers unless such parts fail to meet the requirements established by EU or national law, particularly regarding product safety and intellectual property protection.[138] The rationale behind this provision is to maintain competitive pressure on manufacturers, encouraging them to keep repair costs at levels acceptable to consumers.[139]

In addition, the R2RD introduces amendments to the general Sale of Goods Directive that significantly strengthen the consumer's right to repair within EU law.[140] One of the most important changes is the introduction of an additional 12-month liability period when a product is repaired to bring it into conformity.[141] This means that the consumer who opts for a repair rather than a replacement is not left unprotected once the standard liability period expires. Instead, the seller remains responsible for any lack of conformity that may arise for an extended period. This provision incentivizes businesses to ensure high-quality repairs, as they will remain accountable for the proper functioning of the repaired product. If a country chooses not to apply the 12-month extension, it must still guarantee that the seller's liability or the applicable limitation period for remedies after a repair lasts at least 3 years.[142] This ensures that consumers across the EU benefit from a solid legal guarantee when opting for repair instead of replacement.

---

[135] Article 7 R2RD.

[136] Article 5(6) R2RD.

[137] On the critical implications of this provision see Calabrese, Chap. "Right to Repair Between Intellectual Property and Servitization".

[138] See again Article 5(6) R2RD.

[139] Recital 16 R2RD.

[140] See Article 16 R2RD, amending Article 7 and 10 SGD.

[141] See the newly added para. (2)(a) of Article 10 SGD.

[142] See the newly added para. (2)(c) of Article 10 SGD.

5 Reshaping Consumer Powers and Responsibilities: What's There, and What's (Still) Missing?

The regulatory framework examined throughout this chapter demonstrates a significant evolution in the field of consumer protection within the European Union, particularly as it aligns with the transition toward a circular and sustainable economy. Recent legislative initiatives—including the Ecodesign Regulation, the Directive on Empowering Consumers for the Green Transition, and the Right to Repair Directive—have collectively enhanced transparency, encouraged the design of longer-lasting and more repairable products, and shifted responsibility towards producers. These instruments rely on detailed disclosure obligations, harmonized labeling systems, and digital tools to mitigate information asymmetries, ultimately aiming to transform consumers from passive recipients into active, well-informed market participants.

Nonetheless, the analysis allows to highlight a few notable regulatory gaps.

The first one is the absence of a specific legal framework addressing the right to return non-sustainable or 'green' products. The right to return—commonly associated with the 'cooling-off' period in distance selling or with defect-based returns—has traditionally been limited to circumstances where products are either defective or fail to match the description provided by the seller. In the evolving context of the SCE, the idea that consumers might have a right to return products when they no longer uphold their sustainability claims could be extremely useful. While the right to repair has been proposed as a mechanism to extend product lifespans, a formalized right to return non-sustainable products would mark a significant departure from existing consumer protection norms *and* align post-purchase consumer rights with sustainability benchmarks, thereby encouraging more responsible design and production practices. This innovative right would extend consumer protection beyond immediate safety concerns, addressing long-term environmental performance and quality. Nevertheless, implementing such a right poses several challenges, first of all the need for a clear legal definition of 'non-sustainable' that encompasses multiple dimensions such as resource efficiency, energy consumption, and environmental impact.

Another regulatory gap is related to the circumstance that the right to return, while a cornerstone of consumer protection, poses significant challenges to environmental sustainability within the framework of a circular economy. On one hand, this right empowers consumers by allowing them to return products that do not meet their expectations, thus fostering confidence in their purchasing decisions. However, its unrestricted application can inadvertently encourage over-purchasing and impulsive buying behaviors.

The critique here centers on the potential paradox that an overabundance of consumer rights might, in some cases, generate counterproductive outcomes for sustainability. Just like an overload of technical information can overwhelm consumers (as seen above), when the right to return is exercised without due consideration for environmental impacts, it may inadvertently foster a culture of disposability and wastefulness (not to mention higher transportation emissions, excess packaging waste, and additional energy consumption). Thus, the challenge for EU law is not solely to expand consumer rights but to calibrate them in a manner that integrates consumer empowerment with environmental stewardship. To reconcile the consumer benefits of the right to return with the imperatives of environmental sustainability, it is essential to reexamine and reshape this right through targeted regulatory and market-based reforms. One potential measure is the implementation of shorter return periods. By reducing the time frame during which returns are accepted, retailers could discourage impulsive and non-essential returns, ensuring that only genuinely defective or unsatisfactory products are sent back. This reduction in return volume would not only cut down on the carbon footprint associated with reverse logistics—such as transportation and repackaging—but also promote more thoughtful consumer purchasing decisions. Another strategy involves the introduction of restocking fees, which can serve as a financial deterrent to frivolous returns.

The future of EU consumer law may well depend on its ability to integrate mechanisms that not only inform and empower consumers but also actively discourage practices detrimental to environmental sustainability.

References

Bernini F, La Rosa F (2024) Research in the greenwashing field: concepts, theories, and potential impacts on economic and social value. J Manag Gov 28:405–444

Bray J, Johns N, Kilburn D (2010) An exploratory study into the factors impeding ethical consumption. J Bus Ethics 98:597–608

Chernev A, Böckenholt U, Goodman J (2015) Choice overload: a conceptual review and meta-analysis. J Consum Psychol 25:333–358

Collini L et al (2022) Analysis of the environmental footprint of online sales in the context of the circular economy. Publication for the Committee on Internal Market and Consumer Protection (IMCO), Policy Department for Economic, Scientific and Quality of Life Policies, European Parliament, Luxembourg

de Freitas Netto SV, Sobral MF, Ribeiro ARB et al (2020) Concepts and forms of greenwashing: a systematic review. Environ Sci Eur 32:19

Duivenvoorde B (2015) The consumer benchmarks in the unfair commercial practices directive. Springer, Cham

Duivenvoorde B, Goanta C (2023) The regulation of digital advertising under the DSA: a critical assessment. Comput Law Secur Rev 51:1–14

European Union Agency for Fundamental Rights (2024) Enforcing consumer rights to combat greenwashing

Evans L (2024) The green claims directive: the future legal framework for advertising with environmental claims. Eur Food Feed Law Rev 19(4):174–187

Grunert KG, Hieke S, Wills J (2014) Sustainability labels on food products: consumer motivation, understanding and use. Food Policy 44:177–189

Harris ME (2024) The normative values of the European green deal. Eurojus 2:116–133

Hawes C, Twigg-Flesner C (2018) Sales and guarantees. In: Howells G, Ramsay I, Wilhelmsson T (eds) Handbook of research on international consumer law, 2nd edn. Edward Elgar, Cheltenham, pp 172–201

Helleringer G, Sibony A (2017) European consumer protection through the behavioral lens. Colum J Eur Law 23:607–646
Höppner T (2024) Self-preferencing in online search: under Article 6(5) DMA, 1st edn. Nomos, Baden-Baden
Howells G (2005) The potential and limits of consumer empowerment by information. J Law Soc 32:349–370
Hu H, Krishen AS (2019) When is enough, enough? Investigating product reviews and information overload from a consumer empowerment perspective. J Bus Res 100:27–37
Hwang MI, Lin JW (2016) Information dimension, information overload and decision quality. J Inf Sci 25:213–218
Incardona R, Poncibò C (2007) The average consumer, the unfair commercial practices directive, and the cognitive revolution. J Consum Policy 30:21–38
Jacoby J (1984) Perspectives on information overload. J Consum Res 10:432–435
Janßen D, Langen N (2017) The bunch of sustainability labels: do consumers differentiate? J Clean Prod 143:1233–1245
Johnstone ML, Tan LP (2014) Exploring the gap between consumers' green rhetoric and purchasing behavior. J Bus Ethics 132:311–328
Jung S, Dowse M (2024) Key aspects of the green claims directive proposal. EuCML 13(1):11–23
Keirsbilck B (2024) Empowering consumers for the green transition: overview of directive (EU) 2024/825. J Eur Consum Market Law 13(5):205–217
Majer JM, Henscher HA, Reuber P, Fischer-Kreer D, Fischer D (2022) The effects of visual sustainability labels on consumer perception and behavior: a systematic review of the empirical literature. Sustain Prod Consum 33:1–14
Mak V (2012) The myth of the 'empowered consumer': lessons from financial literacy studies. Zeitschrift für Europäisches Unternehmens- und Verbraucherrecht 1(4):254–263
Maroni M, Hillebrandt M (2023) Mediated transparency: the digital services act and the legitimisation of platform power. In: Hillebrandt M, Leino-Sandberg P, Koivisto I (eds) (In)visible European government: critical approaches to transparency as an ideal and a practice. Routledge, Oxon, pp 305–326
Mittwoch AC (2024) The digital product passport of the ecodesign regulation—passport to a successful twin transformation in product law? Bus Law Rev 45(3):62–67
Moskal A (2022) Digital markets act (DMA): a consumer protection perspective. Eur Pap 7(3):1113–1119
Perzanowski A (2021) The right to repair: reclaiming the things we own. Cambridge University Press, Cambridge
Schaub MY (2017) How to make the best of mandatory information requirements in consumer law. Eur Rev Priv Law 25(1):25–44
Seizov O, Wulf A, Luzak J (2019) The transparent trap: a multidisciplinary perspective on the design of transparent online disclosures in the EU. J Consum Policy 42(1):149–173
Senftleben M (2022) Trademark law, AI-driven behavioural advertising and the digital services act—towards source and parameter transparency for consumers, brand owners and competitors. In: Abbott R (ed) Research handbook on intellectual property and artificial intelligence. Edward Elgar, Cheltenham, pp 309–324
Sevastianova VN (2023) Trademarks in the age of automated commerce: consumer choice and autonomy. IIC 54:1561–1589
Stănescu CG (2019) The responsible consumer in the digital age: on the conceptual shift from 'average' to 'responsible' consumer and the inadequacy of the 'information paradigm' in consumer financial protection. Tilburg Law Rev 24(1):49–67
Staudenmayer D (2000) The directive on the Sale of consumer goods and associated guarantees—a milestone in the European consumer and private law. Eur Rev Priv Law 2000:547–564
Terryn E (2019) A right to repair? Towards sustainable remedies in consumer law. Eur Rev Priv Law 27(4):851–873

Twigg-Flesner C (2016) The importance of law and harmonisation for the EU's confident consumer. In: Leczykiewicz D, Weatherill S (eds) The images of the consumer in EU law: legislation, free movement and competition law. Hart, Oxford, pp 183–202

Willett C (2010) Fairness and consumer decision making under the unfair commercial practices directive. J Consum Policy 33:247–273

Willett C, Morgan-Taylor M (2012) Recognising the limits of transparency in EU consumer law. In: Devenney J, Kenny M (eds) European consumer protection: theory and practice. Cambridge University Press, Cambridge, pp 143–163

Witt AC (2023) The digital markets act: regulating the wild west. Common Mark Law Rev 60(3):625–666

Dispute Resolution and Private International Law in the Context of Circular Economy: Effectiveness Beyond Alternatives

Elisabetta Bergamini

Abstract The paper focuses on the evaluation of the existing rules dealing with private international law (jurisdiction and conflict of law) and alternative dispute resolution in order to assess their application in the context of circular economy. In the first part of the paper, the focus is on the rules of the Brussels and Rome I and II regulations applying to consumer contracts, rules that are critically analysed in their application to the new scenario opened by the circular economy, in particular with regard to the selling from consumers to consumers using online platforms (and the relationship between consumers and platforms) and the rules related to product liability and intellectual property rights violation linked to the circular economy commerce opportunities. In the second part of the paper, the focus is on the alternative dispute resolutions systems offered by the same platforms and their effectiveness in dealing with the increase of C2C contracts and preventing the need to resort to judicial remedies. Finally, the author draws the consequences from the previous research and proposes new rights that should be implemented by the EU legislator while amending the existing legal framework in the field of private international law in order to tackle the existing outlined problems.

1 Introductory Remarks

This chapter moves from the substantive to the procedural realm, investigating the theme of dispute resolution for a sustainable circular economy in the EU. Namely, the EU single market represents the institutional system in which any economic relationship between business and individuals, as consumers-users-citizens, takes place: consequently, the EU legal order is the normative source entrusted to regulate in a harmonized way remedies and mechanisms available to individuals both from

E. Bergamini (✉)
University of Udine, Udine, Italy
e-mail: elisabetta.bergamini@uniud.it

B. Calabrese (ed.), *Legal Perspectives for a Sustainable Circular Economy*, European Union and its Neighbours in a Globalized World 30,
https://doi.org/10.1007/978-3-032-07795-0_9

the point of view of jurisdiction and alternative dispute resolution methods and of applicable law in cross-border situations.

In light of the current paradigm shift, a sustainable circular economy implies a human-centered approach also for dispute resolution, which constitutes a fundamental prerequisite for any form of citizens empowerment.[1] In this context, a rethinking of the EU system is offered, looking at classic issues of competent jurisdiction and applicable law, as well as at innovative channels of alternative dispute resolution, in order to make it fit for purpose and future-proof: in particular, it is emphasized the common need for any mechanism to allow effective and user-friendly remedies for EU individuals, especially in cross-border and digital contracts.

First of all, this essay will evaluate the traditional rules of private international law (from now on 'PIL') existing at EU level dealing with protection of the weaker party in the relationship in order to assess how such rules may apply in light of circular economy principles[2] (Sect. 2). After an interpretation of the EU PIL regulations dealing with contractual relationships (namely Rome I and Brussels I regulations),[3] a second focus will be devoted to the PIL rules on product liability (Rome II regulation),[4] that will need to be reinterpreted according to the circular economy paradigm in order to avoid the risk of rendering the new human centred approach ineffective.

Furthermore, the paper will deal with alternative dispute resolution ('ADR') mechanisms, known to offer greater protection to consumers, in order to better evaluate how circular economy values fit in the existing framework, especially in the case of selling platforms also meant for C2C contracts (Sect. 3).

Finally, a conclusion of general and systemic relevance will be put forth (Sect. 4).

2 Private International Law Rules and the Circular Economy: Are We in Need of a New Approach?

The traditional rules of PIL—i.e. norms of the Brussels I-bis and Rome I and II Regulations, which provide a framework for the protection of the weaker party in the relationship—remain the points of reference even if drafted in ah historical

[1] For the sociological framework related to such human-centred approach to circular economy see Marzulli (Chap. "'*Ubi societas ibi ius*': Centering a Sustainable Circular Economy from a Sociological Perspective").

[2] For a general comment on the use of Private International Law in order to protect the weaker contractual party, see Pocar (1984, p. 406), Sinay-Cytermann (2005, p. 737), Mahmoud (2005, p. 141).

[3] Regulation (EC) 593/2008 on the law applicable to contractual obligations ('Rome I') and Regulation (EU) 1215/2012 on jurisdiction and the recognition and enforcement of judgments in civil and commercial matters ('Brussels I').

[4] Regulation (EC) 864/2007 on the law applicable to non-contractual obligations ('Rome II'), p. 40.

moment when circular economy was not an aim at EU level.[5] However, cross-jurisdictional analysis cannot be neglected in legal studies on circular economy promotion as PIL is now recognised as a governance tool that can contribute to different aims related to sustainable development.[6] In particular the spread of the 'second-hand' markets—as an epitome of circular economy—raises doubts that are not easy to overcome from the point of view of private international law and consumer protection, under several profiles, and in particular: (i) the new role of the consumer-seller on e-platforms and the collective purchases; (ii) product liability. In this part of the research we will focus on how the existing rules may be applied in these new situations in order to evaluate the possible need for reform.

2.1 *The Contractual Relationships and the Consequences for Consumer PIL Rules in Platform Contracts and Group Buying*

Online reselling platforms—such as 'Vinted', 'eBay' and 'Etsy'—are one good example of instruments used by consumers in order to personally be part of a new, circular economy, approach; however the rules on applicable law and jurisdiction for similar consumer-to-consumer contracts are still in need of a specific framework.[7] The number of platforms potentially dealing with reselling by consumers is so relevant that it is almost impossible to do an extensive analysis of all the different terms and conditions. Therefore, in this research the focus has been put on the three above mentioned platforms as most relevant case studies dealing with direct selling by consumers in the EU market. National platforms, such as 'Subito.it' will not be evaluated as they only target a domestic market.[8] Other platforms, even if fostering the circular and green economy, will not be evaluated as the impact on PIL is less relevant (e.g. "Too Good to Go" which involves businesses selling surplus food to

[5] Traditionally, Brussels I and Rome I rules provide for a restrictive definition of consumer. For such an approach under Brussels I Regulation (in case of a person claiming the status of consumer but with an attitude that may give rise to the impression, on the part of the other contracting party, that he or she is acting for professional purposes) see recently CJEU, 9 March 2023, Case C-177/22, *JA v Wurth Automotive GmbH*, ECLI:EU:C:2023:185 and the case law referred to in the text of the judgement.

[6] See Ruiz Abou-Nigm and Sommerfeld (2024, p. 10), Salminen et al. (2024, p. 367).

[7] For a more extensive evaluation of platforms, even if restricted to the point of view of choice of court and choice of law, see Kunda (2026). On this issue see also Verstappen (2023, p. 321).

[8] As proved by the fact that they usually provide for application of Italian Law and use of Italian jurisdiction, avoiding cross border situations. See Article 15 of the Terms and conditions available at https://info.subito.it/policies/condizioni-generali.htm

consumers, for which cross-border situations are not so relevant due to the need to physically collect the goods in the business premises).[9]

In order to better understand the problems related to online platforms and users' protection it may be interesting to start with a reference to a specific case such as the one of the 'Vinted' platform, with which the European Commission had a recent dialogue[10] with the aim of improving the information on the application of prices on the platform in order to bring it more into line with EU consumer law. The European Commission and the Lithuanian Consumer Rights Protection Authority[11] started interacting with the platform in December 2021 and, after the entry into force of the EU Digital Services Act (DSA),[12] the platform changed its website to better inform consumers. However, no reference was made in this dialogue to private international law rules regarding applicable law or jurisdiction, not to alternative dispute resolutions instruments offered by the platform. This lack of specific dialogue on PIL may look like a lack of interest by the European Commission towards the topic, but it is probably linked to the need to properly address other more relevant and immediate problems leaving the private international law issue to a subsequent regulation. On the other side, the European Union has been addressing the new role of selling platforms from the point of view of their use by professionals through the so-called 'Platform to Business' Regulation (Regulation (EU) 2019/1150) that is mainly dealing with the relationship between platforms and professional sellers.[13] Thanks to this act the bigger online platform providers (employing more than 50 persons or achieving more than €10 millions turnover per year) must establish an internal system for handling complaints from professional users about non-compliance with the Regulation. However, no specific rules were introduced regarding applicable law or jurisdiction, even if a reference to the Rome I and Brussels I regulation is included only to the extent to define that the Platform to Business regulation should apply to business users or corporate website users that are directing

[9] In fact, terms and conditions for "Too Good To Go" in point 12.7 make limited reference to conflict of law rules by stating that "These Terms will be interpreted in accordance with the laws of the location you Pick-up your Surprise Bag regardless of conflict of laws rules unless laws applicable in your place of primary residence require other laws to apply. Claims must be brought in the location where you Pick-up the Surprise Bag unless laws applicable to you require another location". At the same time they have a reference to online dispute resolution for users in the EU with a link to the European Commission website. See Too Good To Go (2024) Terms and Conditions, https://www.toogoodtogo.com/terms-and-conditions-using-the-app

[10] See the relevant press release by European Commission, 18 June 2024, 'Dialogue with Commission and Consumer Authorities Brings Vinted to Improve Pricing Information and Transparency for Consumers', available at https://ec.europa.eu/commission/presscorner/detail/en/ip_24_3292

[11] Acting through the Consumer Protection Cooperation (CPC) Network, established by Regulation (EC) 2006/2004 on cooperation between national authorities responsible for the enforcement of consumer protection laws, as modified by Regulation (EU) 2017/2394 on cooperation between national authorities responsible for the enforcement of consumer protection laws.

[12] Regulation (EU) 2022/2065 on a Single Market For Digital Services (Digital Services Act).

[13] Regulation (EU) 2019/1150 on promoting fairness and transparency for business users of online intermediation services.

their activities to consumers located in one or more Member States:[14] a criterion that should be interpreted in accordance with the relevant case law of the Court of Justice of the European Union on 'directed activities'.[15] This means that the Regulation is indirectly meant to protect EU based consumers that are buying goods or services from professional users selling through platforms. The Regulation contains no specific rules on PIL except for a reference meant to qualify the Regulation itself as containing overriding mandatory provisions that should apply irrespective of the law otherwise applicable to a contract.

Switching the focus from the professional-seller to the consumer-seller role, we first of all need to reflect whether the consumer protection provisions of the Rome I and II and Brussels I-bis Regulations should not be reinterpreted to better tackle the new scenario created by online reselling platforms.[16] The concept of the consumer, questioned by the Court of Justice as an 'economically weaker and legally less experienced party'[17] who acts outside and independently of any activity or purpose of a professional nature, for the sole purpose of satisfying its own private consumption needs, needs to be brought into line with this new reality.[18]

In these new contexts, the seller may no longer be a professional—the strong party—against whom the consumer—the weak party—must be defended, especially in online commerce. We are faced with a reality in which sales contracts are no longer concluded mostly B2C, but also frequently C2C (even if thanks to the intermediary activity of a 'professional' subject: the platform that will conclude its own B2C services contracts in order to allow the consumer to use its services). B2C services offered by platforms themselves will be governed by the private international law provisions for consumer contracts. This means that if a consumer wants to present a claim towards the platform, he/she will be able to benefit from the consumer contracts rules of the Brussels and Rome regulations: i.e. the law of the habitual residence of the consumer will apply as long as the platform will be considered as directing its activity towards the place of habitual residence of the consumer, and any choice of law could not deprive the consumer of the protective mandatory rules

---

[14] See Recital 9, Regulation (EU) 2019/1150.

[15] For the case law related to direction of activities see CJEU, 7 December 2010, Joined Cases C-585/08 and C-144/09, *Peter Pammer v Reederei Karl Schlüter* and *Hotel Alpenhof GesmbH v Oliver Heller*, ECLI:EU:C:2010:740. For a critical evaluation of the consequences of that judgement see Svantesson (2011). On the new approach of the CJEU denying the need to link the conclusion of the contract with the existence of the website directing activities see CJEU, 17 October 2013, Case C-218/12, *Lokman Emrek v Vlado Sabranovic*, ECLI:EU:C:2013:666. For a comment see Boskovic (2014), Piroutek and Reinhold (2014).

[16] For a first evaluation of consumer online contracts see Farah (2008, p. 476), Cacha (2009, p. 476). For an approach considering consumer protection rules as not hindering free (electronic) commerce see Reich (2009, pp. 860–861). On the specific case of contracts conclude using a platform see Kunda (2026).

[17] CJEU, 17 September 2009, Case C-347/08, *Vorarlberger Gebietskrankenkasse v WGV-Schwäbische Allgemeine Versicherungs AG*, ECLI:EU:C:2009:561.

[18] For a reconstruction of this critical approach see Bergamini (2013, p. 277). More in general on the special provisions of the Brussels Regulation see Stone (2018, p. 177).

of the law of his/her habitual residence under Rome I Regulation.[19] At the same time, under Brussels I Regulation, consumer contracts are subject to limits to the possibility of choice of court agreements and the professional is allowed to sue a consumer only in the country of his/her domicile, while the consumer may take a professional to court in either country (the one where the consumer is domiciled or the one where the professional is domiciled).[20]

If this definite set of private international law rules does not specifically grant consumers the application of the highest level of protection offered by the different legal/judicial systems possibly linked to the contract they have entered into, such rules nonetheless grant consumers the chance to cut the cost of settling disputes by allowing to file their case in front of the judges of their country of domicile (or to be sued there)[21] and to have the contract regulated by the law of their residence or at least by its mandatory provisions. Unfortunately, this implies that the average consumer is expected to know the content of law of the country he/she is living in, which is not always the case. Moreover, special-jurisdiction rules will apply, thus derogating from the general principle basing jurisdiction on the domicile of the person being sued and on the other special rule for contracts linking jurisdiction to the place of performance of the obligation in question.[22] As recently confirmed by the CJEU, this kind of special-jurisdiction rules 'is designed to ensure that the weaker party who intends to bring an action against a stronger party can do so before a court of a Member State which is easily accessible'.[23]

If this is the legal framework that should apply to B2C contract involving the consumer and the platform, we need to stress that while some platforms (i.e. Vinted)[24] have in their own terms and condition the express reference to the law and jurisdiction of the place of habitual residence of the consumer or to some EU rules

[19] Art. 6, Regulation (EC) 593/2008; in general, on Rome I and consumer contracts see Ragno (2009, pp. 129–170), Ferrari and Ragno (2010). The general report by Fernández Arroyo is also published in Brown and Snyder (2012, p. 143).

[20] Respectively, Arts. 19 and 18, Regulation (EU) 1215/2012.

[21] Regarding this need to cut the costs for consumers, in CJEU, 29 July 2024, Case C-774/22, *JX v FTI Touristik GmbH*, ECLI:EU:C:2024:646, the Court of justice confirmed the Opinion of the Advocate General by declaring that jurisdiction rules should be applied to consumer contracts concluded for the purpose of a trip to a foreign country also if both consumer and business are domiciled in the same Member State. Justification for this choice is that 'the consumer being discouraged from enforcing his or her rights by the difficulties inherent in bringing proceedings against a supplier in a foreign country is clearly the *main* scenario that the legislature had in mind, it is not the *only one*' (see Opinion of Advocate General Emiliou, 7 March 2024, ECLI:EU:C:2024:219, para. 61, as confirmed by para. 45 of the judgement).

[22] See Arts. 17–19—compared to Arts. 4 and 7(1)—Regulation (EU) 1215/2012.

[23] With reference to Art. 18 Regulation (EU) 1215/2012, see CJEU, 29 July 2024, Case C-774/22, *JX v FTI Touristik GmbH*, ECLI:EU:C:2024:646.

[24] See point 20 of the Terms and conditions, https://www.vinted.it/terms_and_conditions

and principles, other (i.e. eBay, Etsy)[25] have rules on applicable law that do not comply with EU law making reference to applicable law, and sometimes also to jurisdiction, different from the one of the place of habitual residence of the consumer, even regarding the relationship between platform and final, non-professional, user.

If, instead, a consumer-buyer wants to address his/her complaint not to the platform but directly towards the consumer-seller, the case will be subject to the general rules, which means that the applicable law will be the one of the seller,[26] and jurisdiction will be held by the judge of the domicile of the defendant or by the judge of the place of performance of the obligation in question.[27] The possibility of making a choice of law or of court is almost irrelevant, because seller and buyer using the platform are probably unaware of such a possibility: and however they will have no chance to formalise a similar choice while entering the contractual relationship as they need to act using the rigid structure offered by the platform itself, without having the possibility (nor probably the legal knowledge) to draft a personalised selling contract.

Another profile to be considered is the possibility that behind the dress of a 'consumer' reselling a personal product, there is in fact a professional dealer who, in order to reach a new customer, pretends that its products are personal items and resells them. According to the Court of Justice, 'a person who publishes a number of sales advertisements on a website is not automatically a "trader"'.[28] This raises the question of what practices could be adopted to 'detect' real traders, and avoid the risk of abuse, therefore reactivating the typical B2C provisions of the EU regulations. Some platforms have special rules for professional sellers. For example, Vinted—in its 'Pro' terms and conditions (meant for professional users that want to sell items on the platform)—has an article that reads: 'This Agreement is governed

---

[25] See the User agreement, point 18 A, that contains a reference to the laws of the State of Utah as applicable law 'without regard to principles of conflict of laws' and the exclusive jurisdiction of the state or federal court located in Salt Lake County, Utah https://www.ebay.com/help/policies/member-behaviour-policies/user-agreement?id=4259. On the legal terms of use of Etsy see https://www.etsy.com/legal/terms-of-use?ref=ftr. Article 12 of this rules contains a reference to the European Commission's online dispute resolution platform for disputes 'Platform to Business'. From the point of view of applicable law however the reference is to New York Law and U.S. Federal law 'without regard to conflict-of-law rules'.

[26] Under the general rule, established in the Rome I framework as for applicable law in absence of choice, by Art. 4(1)(a) Regulation (EC) 593/2008.

[27] Art. 7(1) Regulation (EU) 1215/2012.

[28] CJEU, 4 October 2018, Case C-105/17, *Komisia za zashtita na potrebitelite v Evelina Kamenova*, ECLI:EU:C:2018:808. For a comment see Ho-Dac (2022); for an interesting parallel with EU trademark law, always related to this kind of platforms, see CJEU, 12 July 2011, Case C-324/09, *L'Oreal v eBay*, ECLI:EU:C:2011:474, where it is affirmed that 'when an individual sells a product bearing a trade mark through an online marketplace and the transaction does not take place in the context of a commercial activity, the proprietor of the trade mark cannot rely on his exclusive right [...]. If, however, owing to their volume, their frequency or other characteristics, the sales made on such a marketplace go beyond the realms of a private activity, the seller will be acting 'in the course of trade' within the meaning of those provisions' (para. 55).

by the laws of Lithuania and the European Union law directly applicable. You hereby expressly agree to submit to the exclusive personal jurisdiction of Lithuania any claims or dispute relating to this Agreement'.[29] These terms and conditions are relevant for the relationship between the professional seller and the platform: however, it seems that the decision to open a Pro account instead of a normal account is left to the choice of the seller and not made compulsory by the platform under certain conditions, nor is the platform checking if the seller is circumventing national obligations by not activating a professional account. Moreover, the Pro account rules of PIL only affect the relationship between Pro seller and the platform itself, and not between the Pro seller and consumers. Regarding this aspect, the general B2C rules will apply as long as the presence on the platform of the professional seller will prove the intention to direct the activities towards the place of residence of the consumer. It seems irrelevant that direction of activities is made by the professional seller using a platform and not directly through a personally owned website. The mere acceptance to sell using a platform makes it compulsory for the seller to accept that their activities are directed to all Member States from which the platform is accessible for consumers.[30] By the way, not all platforms have specific rules regarding professional sellers. Some of them have no distinction on rules for sellers based on their status as professional or non-professionals (i.e. eBay or Etsy[31]).

It is also worth expressing some thoughts on another different situation linked to circular economy: the case of consumers who are buying in a collective way, a situation that is not strictly linked to electronic commerce but may be concluded in traditional or electronic way. An example is the case of purchasing groups for fresh products collective buying, a practice strictly connected to the green economy as it is a way for consumers to benefit from a cost reduction while at the same time having a positive effect on the environment, in particular when privileging local producers. Group buying deprives consumers of the level of protection through PIL rules that they are expected to receive under the Brussels I and Rome I regulations, at least as long as we qualify them as a group and not as a single buyer for personal use. This is because the provisions of the Brussels I and Rome I Regulations have been created having in mind the consumer as a single person and not as a collective entity and could not be applied extensively. At the time being, there is no case law regarding the application of PIL rules to this phenomenon of consumers as a group and this is probably due to the situation not being statistically relevant from the point of view of cross-border situations. Collective buying is more frequently linked to national commerce due to the relevance for green economy principles, such as the

[29] Art. XIII, Annex II on Joint controllership agreement for Pro sellers (https://www.vinted.it/pro-terms-and-conditions)

[30] This paper will not tackle the details of the digital evolution regarding accessibility and directed activities. On the new scenario of geo-localisation, geo-blocking and use of VPN and how they could affect the application of the existing rules on private international law to consumer contracts see Bergamini (2026).

[31] For eBay User Agreement and for the Legal terms of Use on Etsy see above, note 24.

ideas of short chain transactions, like 'from farm to table' and "zero kilometer" purchases; all situations that being merely internal raise no PIL issue.

However, even if the standard PIL rules on contract will apply to similar situations, it will probably not affect much consumer groups. Actually, such groups will need to accept the application of different and less protective rules, due to the organized form that they decided to use for entering the contract as a collective subject, and therefore will need to accept the risk, in cross-border situations, to enter into a contract regulated by a national law different from the one of their residence, as well as to be under the jurisdiction of a foreign judge.

2.2 *Reselling and Non-contractual Obligations Arising Out of Tort or Delict in Private International Law*

Regarding product liability, the Brussels I Regulation makes it possible to sue a person domiciled in a Member State in another Member States in matters relating to torts, by virtue of the special jurisdiction criteria that is linked to the place where the harmful event occurred or may occur. This jurisdiction criteria for non-contractual liability has been interpreted as granting jurisdiction to the place where the product in question was manufactured, where a manufacturer faces a claim of liability for a defective product, being it the place of the event giving rise to the damage. No case law has made distinction between the case of a product purchased in person or online, the only relevant consideration being the fact that the CJEU has considered the criteria as linked to the interests of the proper administration of justice and specifically not designed to offer the weaker party (such as the consumer/final buyer) stronger protection.[32]

From the point of view of applicable law, instead, Rome II Regulation sets out different connecting factors for determining the relevant national legal framework in respect of this same situation.[33]

In fact, without prejudice to Art. 4.2 of the said Regulation under which 'where the person claimed to be liable and the person sustaining damage both have their habitual residence in the same country at the time when the damage occurs, the law of that country shall apply', Art. 5 considers as applicable:

[32] See, to that effect, CJEU, 16 January 2014, Case C-45/13, *Andreas Kainz v Pantherwerke AG*, ECLI:EU:C:2014:7, para. 31, and CJEU, 25 October 2012, Case C-133/11, *Folien Fischer AG and Fofitec AG v Ritrama SpA*, ECLI:EU:C:2012:664, para. 46.

[33] See Art. 5 Regulation (EC) 864/2007; on this norm see Huber and Illmer (2007, p. 31), Marongiu Bonaiuti (2013, p. 118). Product liability cases may also be subject to the 1973 Hague Convention on the Law Applicable to Products Liability, for the relationship between Rome II Regulation and the 1973 Convention see Kadner Graziano (2008, p. 425).

(a) the law of the country in which the person sustaining the damage had his or her habitual residence when the damage occurred, if the product was marketed in that country; or, failing that,
(b) the law of the country in which the product was acquired, if the product was marketed in that country; or, failing that,
(c) the law of the country in which the damage occurred, if the product was marketed in that country.

However, the law applicable shall be the law of the country in which the person claimed to be liable is habitually resident if he or she could not reasonably foresee the marketing of the product, or a product of the same type, in the country the law of which is applicable under (a), (b) or (c)'.[34]

With the exception of the case in which the tort is manifestly more closely connected with another country, this means that in order to identify the applicable law we first of all need to understand the notion of 'person claimed to be liable'. The Commission's Explanatory Memorandum to the Rome II Regulation states that:

'The expression "person claimed to be liable" does not necessarily mean the manufacturer of a finished product; it might also be the producer of a component or commodity, or even an intermediary or a retailer. Anybody who imports a product into the Community is considered in certain conditions to be responsible for the safety of the products in the same way as the producer'.[35]

The question therefore arises as to whether the situation we have evaluated above from the point of view of contractual obligations, i.e. the consumer who resells second-hand products, can lead to qualify him/her as a 'retailer' and therefore whether he/she can be subjected to the abovementioned rules on applicable law laid down by the Rome II Regulation in the case of damage caused by the buyer, who in this case is also a consumer.

In the absence of specific case law at EU level, it seems difficult to qualify the reseller as a retailer, except for the case he/she does it in a professional way, as we have seen in the previous Section in case of platforms used also by professional sellers.[36] A consumer occasionally selling products does not respect the organization and perseverance needed to qualify as retailer. A different approach might be

[34] The freedom of choice rules (Art. 14 Regulation (EC) 864/2007, allowing for an agreement even before the event giving rise to the damage in case all the parties are pursuing a commercial activity) will not be evaluated in this paper as they seem not relevant from the point of view of product liability for the non-professional seller.

[35] Proposal for a Regulation of the European Parliament and the Council on the law applicable to non-contractual obligations ('Rome II'), COM (2003) 427 final, p. 15.

[36] See European Commission (2021) where its Study on the Rome II Regulation (EC) 864/2007 on the law applicable to non-contractual obligations considers that 'the relatively small number of references for preliminary ruling on the interpretation of the Rome II Regulation received by the CJEU, and the limited number of cases reaching the decision stage, show that overall the Rome II Regulation has worked well in practice'. However, the lack of case law by the ECJ may also be the consequence of a not so relevant number of cross border cases on the more problematic provisions and there is certainly the possibility to improve some provisions in particular related to online violations.

applied in case of consumers who have a more stable and constant use of the selling platform. In my opinion, there should be a different approach from the one followed by the CJEU in qualifying consumer contracts. In case *Petruchová*,[37] the Court of Justice decided that a natural person entering a contract outside and independently of any professional activity should be considered a consumer, regardless of his/her possible knowledge or expertise in the field. In that case, the online contract (in the field of financial instruments) was entered into by a university student and part-time worker who clearly had a sound knowledge of the risk and benefits involved in such investments, as she was suing the business for not being timely enough in respecting her order, causing a significant economic loss. The CJEU stated that: 'the fact of considering that the status as a consumer of a contracting partner may depend on the knowledge and information he possesses in a given field, and not on whether or not the contract he has concluded is intended to satisfy his personal needs, would amount to referring to the subjective situation of that contracting partner. However [...] the status of a person as a "consumer" must be examined solely in the light of his position in a given contract, taking into account its nature and purpose'.[38]

It seems, therefore, that the individual conduct and personal situation of the consumer should not be considered relevant from the point of view of contractual obligations, as confirmed by the Court of justice also in the subsequent case *AU v. Reliantco Investments LTD*.[39]

However, if we change the subject to non-contractual obligations, it seems that the approach should be different. Moreover, in the situation we are examining the counterpart will be a weak part (a final user/consumer) and not a business, as was the case for *Petruchova*. Therefore, the individual conduct and personal situation might become relevant, consequently making it possible to apply Art. 5 of the Rome II Regulation.

Another relevant situation is connected to extra-contractual liability for intellectual property infringement in the platform economy.[40] Online trading of second-hand goods, as we have seen in the previous Section, may be the source of contractual liability but could also imply intellectual property violations that could lead to extra-contractual liability subject to the rules of the Rome II regulation. In similar situations, liability could also involve third parties (i.e. the platforms) aiding, enabling, or merely facilitating primary infringers' behaviour. While there are many

[37] CJEU, 3 October 2019, Case C-208/18, *Jana Petruchová v FIBO Group Holdings Limited,* ECLI:EU:C:2019:825. For a comment see Ho-Dac (2022).

[38] See again CJEU, 3 October 2019, Case C-208/18, *Jana Petruchová v FIBO Group Holdings Limited,* ECLI:EU:C:2019:825, para. 56.

[39] CJEU, 2 April 2020, Case C-500/18, *AU v Reliantco Investments LTD, Reliantco Investments LTD Limassol Sucursala București*, ECLI:EU:C:2020:264, in which the Court confirmed that for the purposes of the classification as consumer 'factors such as the fact that that person carried out a high volume of transactions within a relatively short period or that he or she invested significant sums in those transactions are, as such, in principle irrelevant' (para. 57).

[40] Frosio(2020) .

studies regarding direct violations of copyright law by online platforms,[41] the same attention is not devoted to secondary liability for violation of intellectual property rights made by platforms dealing with (counterfeit) second-hand products.[42] Nor is there any case law or harmonised regulation on secondary liability for intellectual property law infringement at EU level: this has relevant consequences at PIL level, meaning that the need to apply the Brussels I and Rome II regulations could lead to forum shopping and forum running as long as the interpretation of the connecting factors could lead to the application of different legal frameworks and different approaches.[43] With particular regard to applicable law, Rome II regulation considers the *lex loci protectionis* as applicable law for an infringement of an intellectual property right, unless in case of infringement of a unitary EU intellectual property right, for which the applicable law, for any question that is not governed by the relevant EU instrument, is 'the law of the country in which the act of infringement was committed'.[44] The margin of appreciation for the interpreter that shall apply this provision to a case of secondary liability is still in need of some guidelines, in particular in cases in which the violation is committed online. The same European Commission, in its recent Report,[45] suggests the need to targeted legislative adjustments of the Rome II regulation in particular 'in cases where the damage occurs simultaneously in many jurisdictions, leading to a possible application of multiple national laws to the non-contractual obligation (e.g. cases of collective redress and torts committed online, including infringements of IP rights online'. However, it seems that a recast Regulation addressing all the needed changes, also linked to the online scenario, will need further analysis and studies by the European Commission and will probably not be presented in a short time.

---

[41] See, for a more extensive evaluation, Angelopoulos (2017), Rosati (2021), Quintais et al. (2023) Geiger and Jütte (2021). See also Communication from the Commission, 'Guidance on Article 17 of Directive 2019/790 on Copyright in the Digital Single Market', COM(2021) 288 final, that evaluates the specific copyright authorization and liability regime for online content-sharing service providers that engage in copyright relevant acts in relation to the acts of their users.

[42] An exception can be seen for the violation of trademark rights by platforms acting not as mere intermediaries but more as sellers themselves: CJEU, 22 December 2022, Joined Cases C-148/21 and C-184/21, *Christian Louboutin v Amazon Europe Core Sàrl and Others*, ECLI:EU:C:2022:1016; for a comment see Rosati (2022) and Riis (2023).

[43] On the problematic interface between intellectual property rights and private international law see more broadly Kunda (2024).

[44] Art. 8 Regulation (EC) 864/2007.

[45] Report from the Commission on the application of Regulation (EC) No 864/2007 on the law applicable to non-contractual obligations (Rome II Regulation), COM(2025) 20 final. A special reference is made in this Report also to the issue of collective redress by consumers, also involving cases of product liability, or mass harm consumer cases, brought pursuant to the relatively recently adopted Directive (EU) 2020/1828 on representative actions for the protection of the collective interests of consumers.

3 Alternative Dispute Resolution and the Circular Economy: Is the Digital Market Approach Sufficient to Better Tackle the Problems Related to Consumer Contract in the Circular Economy?

This last Section of the paper deals with alternative dispute resolution ('ADR') mechanisms, meant to offer greater protection to consumers allowing them to avoid long and expensive in court procedures and to receive satisfaction in an easier and more efficient way. The digitalization of the consumer market, the complexity of the procedures and the lack of awareness call into question the current architecture of ADR, which is still seldom used by the average consumer and more in general by the platform users. The Proposal for a Directive in this field aims to simplify the current ADR schemes and adapt them to the digital market.[46] However, as the previous Directive (EU) 2013/11 on ADR, it is meant to apply only to B2C contracts[47] and therefore it will apply to the platform contracts entered into by consumers, as sellers or buyers, in their contractual or precontractual relationship with the platform, but will not be relevant for the C2C contracts concluded through platforms in the previously mentioned cases related to circular economy in which the consumer is selling second-hand goods.

A similar approach was used by the EU in the Regulation dealing with Online Dispute Resolution ('ODR'), creating a platform[48] maintained by the European Commission in order to regulate 'disputes concerning contractual obligations stemming from online sales or service contracts between a consumer resident in the Union and a trader established in the Union through the intervention of an ADR entity listed in accordance with Article 20(2) of Directive 2013/11/EU and which involves the use of the ODR platform'.[49] The ODR platform may also be used for the settlement of disputes 'initiated by a trader against a consumer, in so far as the legislation of the Member State where the consumer is habitually resident allows for such disputes to be resolved through the intervention of an ADR entity', but there is no specific rule regarding C2C disputes, even if the trader against consumer defini-

[46] Proposal for a Directive on alternative dispute resolution for consumer disputes, COM(2023) 649 final, still (March 2025) at the stage of first reading.

[47] In particular 'trader to consumer' contracts, covering disputes between EU consumers and EU and non-EU traders. The definition of trader in Art. 4(1)(b), Directive (EU) 2013/11 will remain unaltered as 'any natural persons, or any legal person irrespective of whether privately or publicly owned, who is acting, including through any person acting in his name or on his behalf, for purposes relating to his trade, business, craft or profession'. Art. 5 of the proposed amended Directive will further provide that 'Member States shall facilitate access by consumers to ADR procedures and shall ensure that disputes covered by this Directive and which involve a trader [...] can be submitted to an ADR entity which complies with the requirements set out in this Directive'.

[48] The ODR platform is available at https://ec.europa.eu/consumers/odr/main/?event=main.home2.show

[49] Art. 2, Regulation (EU) 524/2013 on online dispute resolution for consumer disputes (Regulation on consumer ODR).

tion may probably apply also to some C2C contracts.[50] However, in light of the proposed changes to the ADR Directive, the European ODR platform will be discontinued as of 20 July 2025.[51]

An interesting approach for the circular economy will come out from the idea in the new Directive Proposal to extend ADR to extra-contractual disputes, allowing consumers 'to seek redress for damages resulting from unfair commercial practices, including those related to misleading green claims',[52] thus contributing to achieving the goals of the European Green Deal strategy. Misleading pre-contractual information with regards to energy contracts or to environmental claims would also be subject, under the new Directive, to ADR claims.[53]

Outside the existing EU legal framework, we also need to remember that private online marketplaces (such as eBay),[54] after a first period in which they aimed to protect themselves as much as possible against liability, realized that they needed a way to maintain and extend their community of users and therefore started to offer their own online mechanism to solve disputes between sellers and buyers.[55] This internal ADR systems usually focus on improving the speed of communication and granting enforceability due to temporary 'holding' of the payments; they are usually applicable to all transactions, which means it is not relevant that the contract was entered into as B2C or C2C. However, not all platforms offer their own mechanism for dispute resolutions. Vinted for example makes a direct reference to the ODR system approved by the EU Regulation, with a link to the ODR platform, but as this system will be discontinued (and the last date to submit new complaints is 20 March 2025) it seems at least evidence of neglect that as of 16 March 2025 (last date the website was acceded for this research) no other information on ADR was provided in the general part of the website. More specific rules are suggested for disputes between buyers and 'Pro' sellers and between users (or 'Pro' users) and Vinted,

[50] Art. 2(2) Regulation (EU) 524/2013 (by the way, the relevant notion of trader defined under Art. 4(1)(a) is the same of Art. 4(1)(b), Directive (EU) 2013/11 as already mentioned in footnote above).

[51] See Regulation (EU) 2024/3228, with regard to the discontinuation of the European Online Dispute Resolution Platform, approving the termination of its operation.

[52] Proposal for a Directive on alternative dispute resolution for consumer disputes, COM(2023) 649 final (Impact Assessment).

[53] See again Proposal for a Directive on alternative dispute resolution for consumer disputes, COM(2023) 649 final (Impact Assessment).

[54] Katsh and Rabinovich-Einy (2017, p. 72) ('in establishing a dispute resolution process, the primary goal for a large e-commerce marketplace is actually not to resolve an exceptionally large number of disputes. The main goal is to maximize the number of successful transactions. Resolving disputes is essential to building trust and increasing that volume').

[55] See the eBay Resolution Centre https://resolutioncenter.ebay.com/. See also Commission Staff Working Document, Impact Assessment Report Accompanying the document 'Proposal for a Directive of the European Parliament and of the Council amending Directive 2013/11/EU on alternative dispute resolution for consumer disputes, as well as Directives (EU) 2015/2302, (EU) 2019/2161 and (EU) 2020/1828', SWD(2023) 335 final, para. 2.1. On the idea of community regarding ADR administered by online platforms and for the evolution of consumer ADR and ODR procedures see Bojin and Doroga (2026).

with a reference also to national Mediation Authorities depending on the State of the user, not providing Vinted for a specific internal ADR system. More relevant rules are proposed for dispute resolution on the Etsy platform,[56] which also still has a link to the ODR system that will be discontinued, but already suggests other possibilities included out-of-court dispute settlement bodies under the Digital Services Act (DSA).

Another important innovation is the European Commission's recommendation to bring dispute resolution systems in online marketplaces in line with European standards for fair and efficient alternative dispute resolution. In particular, the reform project of the ADR Directive aims to (i) extend the scope of the Directive to traders established in third countries, (ii) create incentives for businesses to participate and (iii) provide more assistance to consumers. As ADR and more specifically ODR are not yet able to satisfy all the needs for business/consumer disputes, as clearly evident from the Impact Assessment accompanying the Proposal for a new ADR Directive amending the existing framework,[57] the need for a reform seems to be relevant and would not be satisfied by the content of the actual Proposal. The challenge for the European Commission will be to oversee the new forms of ADR created by the platform economy actors and to further promote and encourage the circular economy by allowing all subjects involved to benefit from ADR procedures.

4 Final Remarks

The evaluation made in this chapter regarding the influence of PIL rules in the effective management of a sustainable circular economy approach leads to stress the need to outline and describe new consumers' rights that might (and should) in the future influence the evolution of the EU rules in the field.

First of all, EU citizens should be recognised a right to efficient PIL rules able to grant protection to platform users in C2C contracts. As we have seen, C2C contracts are much used in the platform economy each time a product is resold instead of

[56] Etsy terms and conditions just suggest the possibility, for disputes with other Etsy services' users, to participate in their case system (in which Etsy, however has no obligation to resolve or assist to resolve disputes). They also declare that they have an 'Informal Dispute Resolution' system, that also applies to European users, for which some minimal rules are listed in the Terms of Use.

[57] In this regard, the data reported in the abovementioned Commission Staff Working Document (Impact Assessment Report, SWD(2023) 335 final), are relevant. According to data transmitted by 23 competent national authorities, on average only 300,000 cases per year across the EU are considered suitable for resolution through an ADR procedure. For about half of them, no further action is taken because in most cases professionals are not required to participate, or the professional and the consumer agree to resolve the dispute before the ADR procedure is concluded, or they fail to reach an acceptable solution and decide to abandon the ADR procedure. Out of the 2,250,000 consumers interested in undergoing an ADR procedure, approximately 4.5% are involved in a dispute that currently falls outside the scope of the ADR directive and would therefore be inadmissible (100,000 disputes).

being thrown away, but the existing system has no specific rule to deal with the problems coming out from this situation each time the contract falls in a cross-border dimension. If we want to advocate the need to promote a human-centred circular economy, we also need for the EU to grant a solid and clear PIL framework dealing with jurisdiction and applicable law, i.e. EU mandatory provisions able to regulate in an uncontroversial and unambiguous way C2C online contracts.

A second right that should be granted to EU citizens is the one related to the creation of PIL rules in respect of damage caused by second-hand products purchased through online platforms. Reselling makes it difficult to establish a link with the liability of the producer and it has consequences from the point of view of applicable law and jurisdiction that deserve a more specific approach.[58] The lack of CJEU case-law on this issue (and on the problems related to intellectual property violation) is not sufficient to consider the Rome II Regulation as not in need of a reform to better tackle the specific situation.

Finally, the EU legislator should act in order to grant EU citizens and residents a right to effective and user-friendly remedies for all dispute resolution mechanisms. As we have seen above, the existing ADR legal framework seems not able to properly protect consumers who are acting using online platforms, neither if they are having as a counterpart other consumers, nor (even worst) if they are having as a counterpart professional sellers. The self-regulation by platforms that created their own ADR procedures cannot substitute the intervention by the EU, at least as a supervisor on the impartial and correct functioning of the procedures.

Moreover, this new approach towards consumers protection will not be enough to properly address the problems related to all the effects of PIL on circular economy as more generally linked to sustainability and to the need to promote a Green economy. In fact, more and more authors insist, for example, on the need for a reform of PIL rules in order to better capture adverse environmental impact of global value chains related issues.[59] Unfortunately, the corporate due diligence Directive (EU) 2024/1760, that could have provided for specific rules on jurisdiction and applicable law in order to grant the extraterritorial application of the relevant due diligence framework, was heavily criticized for the absence of specific provisions in the final text[60] (except for the mandatory overriding application of the

[58] For such an approach see also the new rules on product liability in case of repair, as recently provided by Directive (EU) 2024/2853 (see Recital 39): more broadly on so-called right to repair see Calabrese (Chap. "Right to Repair Between Intellectual Property and Servitization").

[59] Salminen and Rajavuori(2021, pp. 230–248). See also Directive (EU) 2024/1760 on corporate sustainability due diligence. For a comment from the PIL point of view see Boskovic (2024, p. 125), Bergamini and Ferrari (2024, p. 6).

[60] The need for a specific framework was requested in the Recommendation of the European Group for Private International Law (GEDIP) to the European Commission concerning the Private international law aspects of the future Instrument of the European Union on (Corporate Due Diligence and Corporate Accountability), 8 October 2021 (https://gedip-egpil.eu/wp-content/uploads/2021/02/Recommandation-GEDIP-Recommendation-EGPIL-final-1.pdf). For a comment see Van Loon (2022) and more recently Silva De Freitas and Kramer (2024).

provisions on civil liability of companies and the right to full compensation to be transposed in national law).[61]

It will be therefore up to the European Union, as long as it will decide to accept the role of promoter of a new human-centred approach in the evolution of the circular economy, to properly evaluate and introduce the amendments to the existing legal framework on private international law and ADR in order to better tackle the problems stemming from the new scenario we have presented in our research.

References

Angelopoulos C (2017) On online platforms and the commission's new proposal for a directive on copyright in the digital single market. Centre for Intellectual Property and Information Law (CIPIL), pp 19–33. University of Cambridge. https://juliareda.eu/wp-content/uploads/2017/03/angelopoulos_platforms_copyright_study.pdf

Bergamini E (2013) Evolution of consumer's role in international private law: the Brussels and Rome regimes. In: Bourgoignie T, Jovanic T (eds) Strengthening consumer protection in Serbia, Liber Amicorum Svetivlav Taboroši. University of Belgrade Law School, p 277

Bergamini E (forthcoming in 2026) EU private international law rules in the field of consumer protection and digital disruption: a real improvement for consumers or a framework still in need of intervention? In: Bergamini E, Willett C (eds) Consumer protection and the digital economy: a research companion. Edward Elgar

Bergamini E, Ferrari M (2024) La responsabilità civile delle società multinazionali quale strumento per promuovere la sostenibilità del mercato: l'applicazione della direttiva due diligence e i problemi derivanti dalle regole di diritto internazionale privato. In: Ruggieri L, Zuccarino S (eds) Persone e mercati nel prisma della sostenibilità. Edizioni Scientifiche Italiane, Naples, p 6

Bojin L, Doroga S (forthcoming in 2026) Digitalisation and consumer alternative dispute resolution. Despite (apparent) lack of success, Are there the germs of a new way of approaching disputes? In: Bergamini E, Willett C (eds) Consumer protection and the digital economy: A research companion. Edward Elgar, Cheltenham

Boskovic O (2014) Compétence en matière de contrats conclus par les consommateurs. Revue critique de droit international privé 2:633–639

Boskovic O (2024) Extraterritoriality and the proposed directive on corporate sustainability due diligence, a recap. J Priv Int Law 20:125–128

Cacha P (2009) Consumer contract in European private international law: the sphere of operation of the consumer contract rules in the Brussels I and Rome I regulations. Eur Law Rev 34(3):476

European Commission: British Institute of International and Comparative Law (BIICL), Civic Consulting, Directorate-General for Justice and Consumers, Migliorini S, Lein E et al (2021) Study on the Rome II regulation (EC) 864/2007 on the law applicable to non-contractual obligations. Publications Office of the European Union. https://data.europa.eu/doi/10.2838/399539

Farah Y (2008) Allocation of jurisdiction and the internet in EU law. Eur Law Rev 33(2):476

Fernández Arroyo DP (2012) Consumer protection in private international relationships. In: Brown KB, Snyder DV (eds) General reports of the XVIIIth Congress of the international academy of comparative law. Springer, New York, p 143

[61] See Art. 29(7), Directive (EU) 2024/1760; more broadly, about corporate due diligence in the context of corporate sustainability reporting see Genovese (Chap. "Corporate Sustainability Reporting and Commitments: Effectiveness and enforcEAbility from EU to National Law").

Ferrari F, Ragno F (2010) Consumer protection in international private relationships. European Union. In: Fernandez Arroyo DP (ed) Consumer protection in international private relationships—La protection des consommateurs dans les relations privées internationals. CEDEP, Asunción

Frosio G (2020) Intellectual property and extra-contractual liability. Handbook of intellectual property research: methods, lenses, and perspectives. Centre for International Intellectual Property Studies (CEIPI) Research Paper 2020-07. Available at SSRN https://ssrn.com/abstract=3726022 or https://doi.org/10.2139/ssrn.3726022

Geiger C, Jütte BJ (2021) Platform liability under Article 17 of the copyright in the digital single market directive, automated filtering and fundamental rights: an impossible match. GRUR Int 70(6):517

Ho-Dac M (2022) Du dialogue interprétatif entre droit (matériel) de la consommation et droit international privé de l'Union – L'exemple du « for du consommateur ». Revue critique de droit international privé 1:47–62

Huber P, Illmer M (2007) International product liability. A commentary on Article 5 of the Rome regulation. In: 2007's yearbook of private international law. European Law Publisher, Munich, p 31

Kadner Graziano T (2008) The Rome II regulation and the Hague conventions on traffic accidents and product liability—interaction, conflicts and future perspectives. Nederlands Internationaal Privaatrecht (NIPR), p 425

Katsh E, Rabinovich-Einy O (2017) Digital justice. Technology and the internet of disputes. Oxford University Press, Oxford, p 10

Kunda I (2024) IPL and PIL—exchanging glances over territoriality. IIC 55:1051–1054. https://doi.org/10.1007/s40319-024-01513-0

Kunda I (forthcoming in 2026) Choice-of-court and choice-of-law clauses in digital consumer contracts: current practices and compliance levels by online platforms. In: Bergamini E, Willett C (eds) Consumer protection and the digital economy: a research companion. Edward Elgar, Cheltenham

Mahmoud M (2005) Loi d'autonomie et méthodes de protection de la partie faible en droit international privé. Recueil des cours 315:141

Marongiu Bonaiuti F (2013) Le obbligazioni non contrattuali nel diritto internazionale privato. Giuffrè, Milan

Piroutek C, Reinhold S (2014) Wrong direction? - Causality between commercial activity and conclusion of contract in Art 15 Para 1 lic c Brussels I regulation. Zeitschrift für Europäisches Unternehmens- und Verbraucherrecht 3:41–46

Pocar F (1984) La protection de la partie faible en droit international privé. Recueil des cours 188:406

Quintais JP, De Gregorio G, Magalhães JC (2023) How platforms govern users' copyright-protected content: exploring the power of private ordering and its implications. Comput Law Secur Rev 48:105792

Ragno F (2009) The law applicable to consumer contracts under the Rome I regulation. In: Ferrari F, Leible S (eds) Rome I regulation: the law applicable to contractual obligations in Europe. Otto Schmidt/De Gruyter European Law Publishers, Munich, pp 129–170

Reich N (2009) Transnational consumer law—reality or fiction? Penn State Int Law Rev 27(3):860–861

Riis T (2023) Primary liability of intermediaries for trade mark infringement in light of the decision in joined cases Louboutin (C-148/21) and (C-184/21). EIPR 45(6):337–343

Rosati E (2021) Five considerations for the transposition and application of article 17 of the DSM directive. J Intellect Prop Law Pract 16(3):265–270

Rosati E (2022) The Louboutin/Amazon cases (C-148/21 and C-184/21) and primary liability under EU trade mark law. Eur Intellect Prop Rev 44(7):435–440

Ruiz Abou-Nigm V, Sommerfeld A (2024) Circular fashion and legal design: weaving circular economy threads into international contracts. Working Paper IE Law School. https://catedracervello.ie.edu/wp-content/uploads/sites/570/2024/12/AJ8-288-I.pdf?trk=public_post_comment-text

Salminen J, Rajavuori M (2021) Private international law, global value chains and the externalities of transnational production: towards alignment? Transnatl Leg Theory 12(2):230–248. https://doi.org/10.1080/20414005.2021.1970470
Salminen J, Rajavuori M, Eller KH (2024) Global value chains as regulatory proxy: transnationalising the internal market through EU law. In: Beckers A, Micklitz H-W, Vallejo R, Letto-Vanamo P (eds) The foundations of European transnational private law. Hart, Oxford, pp 367–397
Silva De Freitas E, Kramer X (2024) The corporate sustainability due diligence directive: PIL and litigation aspects. Conflict of Laws. https://conflictoflaws.net/2024/the-corporate-sustainability-due-diligence-directive-pil-and-litigation-aspects/
Sinay-Cytermann A (2005) La protection de la partie faible en droit international privé: les exemples du salarié et du consommateur. In: Jobard-Bachellier M-N, Mayer P (eds) Le droit international privé: esprit et méthodes: Mélanges en l'honneur de Paul Lagarde. Dalloz, Paris, p 737
Stone P (2018) Stone on private international law in the European Union. Edward Elgar, Cheltenham
Svantesson DJB (2011) Pammer and hotel Alpenhof—ECJ decision creates further uncertainty about when E-businesses "direct activities" to a consumer's state under the Brussels I regulation. Comput Law Secur Rev 3:298–304
Van Loon H (2022) GEDIP's recommendation on the proposal for a directive on corporate sustainability due diligence. EAPIL blog. https://eapil.org/2022/10/25/gedips-reccommendation-on-the-proposal-for-a-directive-on-corporate-sustainability-due-diligence/
Verstappen J (2023) Legal agreements on smart contract platforms in European systems of private law. Springer, Cham

The Constitutional Implications of a Sustainable Circular Economy at the European Union and National Levels

Alessia-Ottavia Cozzi

Abstract This chapter analyses the constitutional implications of the circular economy at the European Union and national levels. The chapter critically discusses the opinions that have emerged among the authors, according to which the circular economy has brought about a constitutional change in the European Union, reshaping the relationship between the single market and the environment, and compare them with national constitutional experiences. The Italian case is used as a case study, as the Italian Constitution has recently been amended to include environmental protection among the fundamental principles and as an explicit limit to the freedom of enterprise. The argument discussed in the chapter is that, at the level of the European Union, the circular economy affects the economic paradigm from within, while in the Italian constitution, as in other national constitutions, the environment is still perceived as an external limit to the economy and the market. However, the two perspectives are only apparently contradictory, because there has been a link of interdependence between the EU and national dimensions in environmental matters, so that changes at one level are reflected and inevitably influence the other.

1 Introduction

The aim of this chapter is to reflect on the implications of the circular economy for the constitutional dimension of the European Union (EU) and for the one of its Member States. In the EU's dimension, the circular economy represents a new way of reconciling the economy and environment. At the national level, many national constitutions contain provisions on environmental protection. The Italian Constitution was recently amended, moving in this direction: Constitutional Law no. 1/2022 has for the first time included environmental protection in the

A.-O. Cozzi (✉)
Università degli Studi di Udine, Udine, Italy
e-mail: alessiaottavia.cozzi@uniud.it

B. Calabrese (ed.), *Legal Perspectives for a Sustainable Circular Economy*, European Union and its Neighbours in a Globalized World 30,
https://doi.org/10.1007/978-3-032-07795-0_10

constitutional text, both in the fundamental principles and in relation to freedom of enterprise.

The present analysis aims at developing a comparison between the two levels, EU and national. The thesis it intends to discuss is that, although the two levels are structurally linked and interdependent, the approach on which the European framework on the circular economy and the Italian constitutional reform are based is different. In short, both level aim at a human-centred approach, placing the person, with his/her rights and obligations, at the centre of the legal construct, and both shift this approach in space and time, i.e. extending protection to future generations.[1] But the underlying scheme of the models seems to remain different. At the EU level, the circular economy aims to change the relationship between the economy and the environment from within, by reshaping production and consumption patterns. At the national (Italian) constitutional level, the constitutional reform is still anchored in a model that sees private enterprise and the environment as opposites, one limiting the other, assuming that they are in principle irreconcilable and that a balance must be found between them. In sum, at the EU level the concept of the environment acts 'within' the economy and generates an internal transformation. However, at the national constitutional level, in Italy as in the constitutional experience of many other Member States, the environment is still seen as an external limit to private enterprise.

This chapter is divided into three parts. The first part is devoted to the European Union level (Sect. 2). Some information is briefly provided on the European Union acts dedicated to the circular economy. Some views are discussed critically, that have emerged in legal literature, according to which the green transition would cause to an implicit change in the constitutional nature of the European Union. In fact, without amending the Treaties, the green transition would lead to a reinterpretation of the objectives of the European Union, which are set out in Art. 3(3) TEU, giving priority to the environment over the market.

The second part of the chapter is dedicated to the recent Italian constitutional reform (Sect. 3). Such a reform includes the environment and its components, biodiversity and ecosystems, among the constitutional goods that the Republic must protect in all its forms. The Italian case is used as a case study because it is a very recent reform and follows a model already present in many constitutions of Member States and also outside Europe.[2]

The third part is dedicated to a comparison between the two levels, European and national (Sect. 4). It discusses the mentioned argument: at the level of the Union, the environment, through the circular economy, determines a change 'from within' the production and consumption system. At the constitutional level, it seems to prevail the idea that the environment is still 'an external limit' to the production and consumption system.

---

[1] More broadly on this approach from a sociological perspective see Marzulli (Chap. "'*Ubi societas ibi ius*': Centering a Sustainable Circular Economy from a Sociological Perspective").

[2] Daly and May (2015).

2 The Circular Economy in the European Union and Its Constitutional Implications

It is well known that environmental protection was established as a primary objective of the European Communities long before it was codified in the Treaties with the Single European Act. Since the 1970s, the European Communities have acted through a variety of instruments. On the one hand, implicit powers have been used to adopt hard law acts, Regulations and Directives on sectoral aspects of environmental protection. Moreover, Member States have agreed to adopt the Commission's proposals of multiannual programmes containing objectives and periodic monitoring methods, allowing their flexible re-parameterisation in line with scientific knowledge and best available techniques.[3] On the other hand, it is well known that the Court of Justice of the European Union played a fundamental role in ensuring the effectiveness of European environment protection, both before and after its codification in the Treaties.[4]

Today the environment protection is one of the fundamental objectives of the Union under Art. 3(3) TEU.[5] Furthermore, Art. 4 TFEU regards environment as a shared competence between the Union and the Member States; Art. 11 TFEU establishes the principle of integration, according to which environmental protection requirements must be integrated in a transversal manner into the definition and implementation of all the Union's policies and activities, with a view to promoting sustainable development;[6] Art. 191 TFEU is specifically dedicated to environmental policy; Art. 191 TFEU contains the specific objectives, principles and criteria of EU environmental action and, in its second paragraph, has codified the main environmental principles derived from international law, thus making them legally binding in the Member States.[7] Moreover, among the primary sources, the transversal nature of environmental issues is confirmed by Art. 37 of the Charter of Fundamental Rights of the European Union, included in Title IV, Solidarity, which states that a high level of environmental protection and the improvement of the quality of the

---

[3] On EU environmental law, Krämer and Badger (2024), Jordan and Gravey (2021), Kingston et al. (2017), De Sadeleer (2014), Scott (2009), Kiss and Sheldon (1997).

[4] Peeters and Eliantonio (2020), Kramer (2009).

[5] Art. 3(3) TEU: 'The Union shall establish an internal market. It shall work for *the sustainable development* of Europe based on balanced economic growth and price stability, a highly competitive social market economy, aiming at full employment and social progress, and *a high level of protection and improvement of the quality of the environment*. It shall promote scientific and technological advance' (emphasis added).

[6] Art. 11 TFEU: 'Environmental protection requirements must be integrated into the definition and implementation of the Union's policies and activities, in particular with a view to promoting sustainable development'. See Sjåfjell (2015).

[7] Art. 191(2) TFEU: 'Union policy on the environment shall aim at a high level of protection taking into account the diversity of situations in the various regions of the Union. It shall be based on the precautionary principle and on the principles that preventive action should be taken, that environmental damage should as a priority be rectified at source and that the polluter should pay'.

environment must be integrated into the policies of the Union and ensured in accordance with the principle of sustainable development.[8]

The circular economy model, as pertaining to the wider paradigm of sustainability, sits at the intersection of the regulatory context concerning environment and the single market regulation.[9] The framework has evolved over time.[10] As is often the case with European policies, it consists of policy documents such as Commission communications,[11] multi-annual programs[12] and hard law.[13] We focus on the latest

[8] The Explanations to Art. 37 of the Charter clarify that the principles set out in this article have been based on Arts. 2, 6 and 174 of the EC Treaty, which have now been replaced by Art. 3(3) TEU and Arts. 11 and 191 TFEU, mentioned before; see Morgera and Gracia (2021).

[9] On the relationship between environmental protection and EU competition law Kingston (2010). About circular economy and the relevant role of EU in the international arena see Candelmo (Chap. "Global Sustainability in the International Arena Beyond the EU Policy Agenda").

[10] First references to the circular economy can be found in Communication from the Commission, 'Roadmap to a Resource Efficient Europe', COM(2011) 571 final. The Commission had already adopted the concept of the environmental life cycle of products, see Communication from the Commission, 'Integrated Product Policy Building on Environmental Life-Cycle Thinking', COM(2003) 302 final.

[11] Communication from the Commission, 'Closing the loop—An EU action plan for the Circular Economy' COM(2015) 614 final. The Action Plan is in turn composed of further policy documents, such as the Strategies. For example, as part of the 2018 Circular Economy Package related to the first Action Plan of 2015, see the Communication from the Commission, 'A European Strategy for Plastics in a Circular Economy' COM(2018) 28 final; recently, Communication from the Commission, 'Critical Raw Materials Resilience: Charting a Path towards greater Security and Sustainability' COM(2020) 474 final. In the literature, other Strategies are associated with policies strictly dedicated to the circular economy, because they are based on the same premises: the growth of the world's population, the increasing consumption of non-renewable natural resources, the structural limits of the Planet and its ecosystems, the need to develop different economic models; see de Leonardis (2023a). Concerning bio-economy, the circular economy is dedicated to inorganic products, while the bioeconomy is dedicated to organic products. See the Communication from the Commission, 'Innovating for Sustainable Growth: A Bioeconomy for Europe', COM(2012) 60 final, and the following Communication from the Commission, 'A sustainable Bioeconomy for Europe: Strengthening the connection between economy, society and the environment', COM(2018) 673 final. About biodiversity, Communication from the Commission, 'Our life insurance, our natural capital: an EU biodiversity strategy to 2020', COM(2011) 244 final; Communication from the Commission, 'Biodiversity Strategy for 2030 Bringing nature back into our lives' COM(2020) 380 final. In the agri-food sector, Communication from the Commission, 'A Farm to Fork Strategy for a fair, healthy and environmentally-friendly food system', COM(2020) 381 final. About industry, the most recent Communication from the Commission, 'A New Industrial Strategy for Europe', COM(2020) 102 final.

[12] References to sustainable production are frequent from the Sixth Community Environment Action Programme (2001–2010), as laid down by Decision (EC) 2002/1600, and with increasing intensity in the Seventh and the Eighth Programme, currently in progress; see respectively Decision (EU) 2013/1385 on a General Union Environment Action Programme to 2020 'Living well, within the limits of our planet', and Decision (EU) 2022/591 on a General Union Environment Action Programme to 2030.

[13] The Circular Economy Package of 2018 included four directives: Directive (EU) 2018/849 on end-of-life vehicles, on batteries and accumulators and waste batteries and accumulators, and on

developments, in particular the Circular Economy Action Plan, adopted in 2020.[14] This represents one of the key building blocks of the European Green Deal, Europe's new agenda for sustainable growth.[15] The Action Plan is one of the tools to achieve the EU's 2050 climate neutrality target and halt biodiversity loss. The aim of the EU's transition to a circular economy is to reduce pressure on natural resources and create sustainable growth and jobs. For these purposes, the Action Plan aims to regulate the entire life cycle of products: from the way products are designed, to circular economy processes, sustainable consumption, waste prevention and the promotion of re-use, so that resources are kept in the EU economy for as long as possible. The Action Plan focuses on sectors with high potential for circularity, such as electronics and ICT, batteries and vehicles, packaging, plastics, textiles, construction and buildings, food, water and nutrients. In summary, the Action Plan has put forward legislative and non-legislative measures targeting those areas where action at EU level could bring added value. The monitoring process in place since 2023 summarises these interventions in the following areas: production and consumption; waste management; secondary raw materials; competitiveness and innovation; global sustainability and resilience.

Other contributions in this volume analyse how these acts have led to a genuine re-conceptualisation of consumer rights and business obligations through the lens of sustainability.[16] In this chapter, we turn our attention to that part of legal doctrine which has hypothesised a change in the constitutional nature of the European Union brought about by the green transition.

Generally speaking, literature has demonstrated that EU environmental law has been the cradle of some principles that have subsequently become transversal to all areas of the Union's action, such as the principle of subsidiarity. From a legal point of view, therefore, the environment is a testing ground for experimenting with new regulatory systems and models for the relationship between the public and the private, to the point of touching the very foundations of the legal system, its fundamental principles, its essence.[17]

Following this line, recent green transition policies have been interpreted in some legal literature as a factor of constitutional transformation of the European Union, although the primary rules of the Treaties remain unchanged.[18] In fact, the green transition would not be an episodic moment in European policies and its

---

waste electrical and electronic equipment; Directive (EU) 2018/850 on the landfill of waste; Directive (EU) 2018/851 on waste; Directive (EU) 2018/852 on packaging and packaging waste.

[14] Communication from the Commission, 'A new Circular Economy Action Plan—For a cleaner and more competitive Europe', COM (2020)98 final.

[15] Communication from the Commission, 'The European Green Deal', COM(2019) 640 final.

[16] See, with regard to consumers' position, Deana (Chap. "Reshaping Consumer Powers and Responsibilities in the European Union's Transition to a Sustainable Circular Economy"), as well as, with regard to right to repair, Calabrese (Chap. "Right to Repair Between Intellectual Property and Servitization").

[17] Rossi (2021).

[18] Sikora (2020).

impact would go beyond the environmental sphere, reshaping the relationship between the environment and the economy as one of the fundamental objectives of the Union, thus touching on its constitutional nature.

This outcome has been achieved from different perspectives. One approach described the Green Deal as a constitutional process, in the sense that the green transition would integrate sustainability into pro-competitive regulation, causing a shift away from traditional economic regulation and, as a result, reshaping the substantive constitution of the Union.[19] Another approach focused on the environmental conditionality and argued in terms of a silent revolution.[20] The 'revolution' has been referred to the Next Generation EU, which, in response to the pandemic, has adopted the green transition, already foreseen in the Green Deal, as one of the fundamental missions of the Union. In particular, as part of the Next Generation Recovery Package, a requirement that an activity 'does not harm' any of the environmental objectives (DNHS principle) has been provided.[21] Accordingly, the European Semester-specific assessments have been supplemented by an environmental assessment to ensure that national measures implementing the recovery plans do not cause 'significant harm to environmental objectives'. In this way, the requirements of Regulation (EU) 2021/241 on the Recovery and Resilience Facility (RFF) make a significant part of the European budget subject to environmental conditionality for the first time.[22]

As mentioned, this constitutional transformation would been derived not only from the circular economy, but from the Green Deal as a whole, and its translation in the Next Generation EU packages. Nevertheless, some doctrines have pointed to

---

[19] Chiti (2022, 2024), who particularly emphasises the constitutional change produced by the Green Deal as a regulatory process; Monteduro (2022).

[20] De Sadeleer (2023, p. 25).

[21] Under the EU Next Generation Recovery Package, Regulation (EU) 2021/241 establishing the Recovery and Resilience Facility (RFF) is the main instrument for allocating funds to Member States. Recital 23 states: '[…] the measures supported by the Facility and included in recovery and resilience plans of the individual Member States should contribute to the green transition, including biodiversity, or to addressing the challenges resulting therefrom, and should account for an amount that represents at least 37% of the recovery and resilience plan's total allocation based on the methodology for climate tracking set out in an annex to this Regulation. […] The Facility should support activities that fully respect the climate and environmental standards and priorities of the Union and the principle of 'do no significant harm' within the meaning of Article 17 of Regulation (EU) 2020/852 of the European Parliament and of the Council (the principle of 'do no significant harm')'. The principle of 'do no significant harm' within the meaning of the RFF Regulation is defined in its Art. 2 as not supporting or carrying out economic activities that cause significant harm to any environmental objective. National plans must justify their compliance with this principle under Art. 18(4), and the Commission is responsible for the relative assessment under Art. 19(3). Moreover, Art. 17(1), Regulation (EU) 2020/852 provides detailed criteria for each of the environmental objectives to determine whether a particular economic activity can be considered to cause significant harm to these objectives.

[22] De Sadeleer (2023, p. 25). On the RRF conditionality in general, Fasone and Simoncini (2023), Cozzi and Grisostolo (2023), Baraggia (2023), Baraggia and Bonelli (2022). On the different meanings of conditionality, Pinelli (2013).

the circular economy as the engine of the implicit constitutional transformation resulting from the ecological transition. It has been argued that circular economy policies would make the European Union no longer 'secular' and 'neutral' towards the market. In fact, the circular economy would have established precise guidelines for public policies aimed at adapting and bending the system of production and consumption. In particular, the New Circular Economy Action Plan would have moved from an approach based on voluntary participation, which was considered insufficient in view of the seriousness of the environmental crisis, to a binding approach. Thus, the crucial point highlighted by this opinion is the adoption of a vision of an active and coercive policy, ready to give priority to the environment over the classical freedoms protected by EU law. Like the other opinions cited above, this opinion also argues for a change in the substance of the Union's constitution, which occurred without amending the Treaties.[23]

These doctrinal views, we believe, although different, have a common substrate. Environmental protection, made effective by the conditionality mechanism, is seen as a vehicle for the affirmation of human rights and thus of a human-centred perspective.[24] The basic idea is that the green transition would have shifted the objectives of the European Union in concrete terms, putting people at the centre and, through the environment, rediscovering the human-centred roots of European integration.[25] These views respond to a frequent criticism in legal literature, that, despite the formal statements of Art. 2 TEU, the protection of fundamental rights in the European Union has not been a value in itself, but rather a 'function' for the development of the market. These criticisms are old, but became much more acute during the economic crisis as a result of the European Union's austerity policy and the sacrifice of social rights in the Member States.[26] By setting limits to the unlimited development of the market, the green transition would have 'restored' the centrality of the human person, affirming that the market is an instrument for the development of the human being and not an end in itself. In this way, European construction would realign more strongly with the constitutions of the Member States, which, after the horrors of the Second World War, reject the functionalisation of the person for other goods or interests and put the personal development and wellbeing at the centre of any institutional and legal order.

---

[23] de Leonardis (2023a, pp. 81–83).

[24] In the distinct but related area of rule of law conditionality, the protection of the Union budget has led to the recognition of the binding nature of the values referred to in Art. 2 TEU, the very root of the Union's identity as a common legal order based on the principle of mutual trust, and a prerequisite for the autonomy of Union law in relation to national and international law (CJEU, 16 February 2022, Case C-157/21, *Republic of Poland v European Parliament and Council of the European Union*, ECLI:EU:C:2022:98, points 143–145); see Lupo (2023).

[25] The circular economy is discussed as a tool of distributional equity, affirmation of procedural rights and participation, especially for people marginalised by the dominant economic system, and therefore from a social justice perspective in Lesniewska and Steenmans (2023).

[26] Pinelli (2019), Kilpatrick (2015). Before the debt crisis, the conditional dimension of fundamental rights has led to accusations of asymmetry, with the Union imposing respect for rights externally that it is struggling to guarantee with equal intensity internally; see de Búrca (2011).

However, these theories, which argue for constitutional change, are not shared by all authors. On the contrary, there are those who believe that even in the context of green transition and environmental conditionality, market objectives prevail. Environmental conditionality would be a kind of 'greenwashing', without changing the priorities that the European Union has always given to the construction of the single market.[27] Concerning circular economy, the wording of EU acts and initiatives could lead to this conclusion. The information and active participation provided by the circular economy measures are aimed at the consumer and not at the person as such.[28] The focus is still on consumer rights, not personal rights or human rights. From this viewpoint, the Union's environmental policy would not be able to look beyond the purchase of goods and services, consumption and the market, whereas the current environmental and climate crisis requires a paradigm shift from a strictly market perspective.[29]

Another, different, criticism that can be raised against these opinions is that they confuse the level of policies and the level of constitutional transformations, which require stability and continuity of the interpretations adopted by the institutional actors. The fact that these transformations concern policies and not the constitutional structure can be seen in the recent European elections. The ongoing debate for a more conservative revision of the Green Deal shows that these are contingent political choices, linked to the physiological succession of majorities both in European institutions and Member States. So, while there is certainly a greater intensity of commitment to sustainable forms of production and consumption, this has not translated into a structural, constitutional change touching the Union's objectives.

Moreover, the absence of an implicit modification of the Treaties is demonstrated by some of the same opinions mentioned above, which, on the one hand, assume substantial constitutional changes and, on the other hand, suggest the need for a revision of the Treaties.[30] One of the authors mentioned above has interestingly shown that the word 'environment' appears 20 times in the TEU, the TFEU and the Charter of Fundamental Rights, while the words 'competition', 'market' and similar appear more than 150 times. According to this author, this is not a purely numerical fact, which in itself could be not significant, but the legacy of a different weight,

---

[27] Valerio (2023).

[28] For a further analysis of consumers powers and responsibilities within the new paradigm of Sustainable Circular Economy in EU framework see Deana (Chap. "Reshaping Consumer Powers and Responsibilities in the European Union's Transition to a Sustainable Circular Economy"), and also for a broader reconsideration of consumers' prerogatives and potential impact at the international level see Dal Monico (Chap. "Rethinking the Role of the Consumer in a Global Economy: The Power of Choice as a 'Human Right'?").

[29] For a wider reflection about the environment as the founding element of Sustainable Circular Economy see De Vido (Chap. "The International Dimension of the Environment as a Legal Entity: The Human Rights of the Sustainable Consumer in an Ecological Perspective").

[30] de Leonardis (2023a, pp. 126–129).

intensity and relevance of the respective areas in the primary norms.[31] This is why some of these doctrines have gone so far as to advocate a reform of the Treaties. But if a reform is necessary, it means that the changes brought about by the green transition, including the circular economy, have not already caused a substantial, albeit implicit, change in the order of objectives contained in Article 3(3) TEU.

Bearing in mind this unresolved debate on the implicit constitutional change, at the end of this Section we would like to highlight an aspect specifically related to the circular economy, and already pointed out, that allows us to move on to the dimension of national constitutions, particularly in the case of Italy. For the traditional approach to market economy regulation, the environment, albeit transversal, still represents an external limit to the free movement of goods, people and capital. On the contrary, as the above-mentioned doctrine has clearly shown, the circular economy has a direct impact on the regulation of the single market, involving competition law and consumer law. In this way, the circular economy brings the environment 'inside' the economic paradigm. From this point of view, the circular economy acts inside the economic paradigm itself, aiming to modify from within the 'highly competitive social market economy' to which Art. 3(3) TEU refers to. This approach is not entirely consistent with the vision found in many national constitutions, including the recent Italian constitutional reform of 2022. We will see in the next Section that this reform reflects in many respects the constitutional experiences already existing in the other Member States, which often see the environment as an external limit to private economic initiative.

3 The Italian Constitutional Reform on Environment of 2022

The Italian constitutional reform on the environment, approved in February 2022 by Constitutional Law no. 1/2022, has affected the text of the Italian Constitution in three points.[32] Firstly, a third paragraph has been added to Art. 9 of the Italian Constitution, that is part of the Fundamental Principles. The first two paragraphs of Art. 9, which remain unchanged, state that the Republic shall promote the development of culture and scientific and technical research, and that the Republic shall protect the landscape and the nation's historical and artistic heritage. The new third paragraph of Art. 9 now provides that the Republic 'protects the environment, biodiversity and ecosystems, also in the interest of future generations. State law shall regulate the ways and means of protecting animals'.

[31] Monteduro (2022, p. 246), excluding non-conferring expressions such as 'work environment', 'favourable environment', 'propitious environment', 'safe environment'.

[32] The Italian Constitution was approved by the Constituent Assembly on 22 December 1947, promulgated by the provisional Head of State on 27 December 1947 and entered into force on 1 January 1948. It is therefore one of the democratic constitutions of the second post-war period, after twenty years of fascism. It can be read in its English translation at www.senato.it/documenti/repository/istituzione/costituzione_inglese.pdf

The constitutional reform also affected Art. 41 of the Italian Constitution, contained in Part I, Rights and duties of citizens, Title II, Economic relations. Art. 41 is devoted to the freedom of enterprise. The first paragraph has not been amended and states that 'private economic initiative is free'. The second paragraph has been integrated, providing that private economic initiative: 'cannot be carried out contrary to social utility or in a way that could be harmful to *health, the environment*, safety, freedom or human dignity' (emphasis added). Health and the environment have thus become two explicit limits to the freedom of enterprise, whereas safety, freedom and human dignity already existed. Finally, the constitutional reform amended the third paragraph of Art. 41, devoted to public powers to direct and coordinate economic activity. The third paragraph now provides that 'the law shall establish the appropriate programmes and controls to direct and coordinate public and private economic activity for social *and environmental* purposes' (emphasis added). Environmental purposes have thus become a new explicit objective of the programmes and controls provided for by law to drive economic activity.

Article 41 of the Italian Constitution not only expresses an individual right, the freedom to engage in entrepreneurial activity, but also constitutes the first article of that part of the Constitution devoted to economic relations. For this reason, it has been interpreted as the opening clause of the so-called economic constitution, that is, the constitutional principles concerning the relationship between the individual, the market and the social dimension. For this reason, more than other provisions, Art. 41 has been influenced in its application by the European principles of free competition and access to the market.[33]

Looking at the structure of Art. 41 of the Italian Constitution, it must be immediately clarified that while the first two paragraphs have been considered as a kind of hendiadys in the Italian constitutional case-law, the third one, which refers to public programmes and controls, has been essentially silent for many years. The protection and, above all, the limits of entrepreneurial freedom have therefore been thoroughly analysed and the Italian Constitutional Court (hereinafter ItCC) has 'discovered' some implicit limits to the freedom of enterprise, health and the environment, long before their explicit formulation in the text of the Constitution in 2022. The third paragraph of Art. 41, on the other hand, has been largely absent from the case law of the ItCC. Public controls are a legacy of the period in which the Constitution was written. Those were years in which strong economic planning was envisaged and in which there were monopolies and numerous important companies all in public hands, for example in the oil, steel, mining and chemical sectors. The establishment of the free market, both as a result of economic development and, from a legal point of view, due to the influence of the European Communities, has severely limited the application of Art. 41(3) of the Italian Constitution. Due to the single market, the legal system has changed from an entrepreneurial role of the state to a so-called regulatory role of state, in which there is much less room for economic planning.[34]

[33] Cassetti (1997).

[34] Cassese (2021).

Back to the environmental dimension, before 2022 no constitutional provision explicitly referred to the environment, except for an insertion in 2001 concerning the legislative powers of the State and the Regions.[35] From this point of view, the Italian Constitution was a product of its time. In 1946–47, when it was written, there were already numerous ordinary laws on individual goods that we now consider to be part of the environment, such as water resources, parks, landscapes, but there was not yet a single legal concept of the environment, which was to emerge in international law in the 1970s.

Nevertheless, since the end of the 1980s, the environment has been considered by constitutional case law as a primary constitutional value, deriving it by interpretation from other explicitly protected constitutional goods, landscape in Art. 9 of the Constitution and health in Art. 32 of the Constitution.[36] Although not written down, the environment has thus been an existing and applied constitutional principle, used to interpret and, where necessary, overturn existing legislation.

From this point of view, the Italian case demonstrates that the terms used in the constitutional text are not sufficient to understand the constitutional structure of the legal system, which depends on the interpretation of constitutional principles and norms offered by political actors and jurisprudence. Although not formally written, for thirty-five years the environment has been a constitutional principle and value operating in the legal system.[37] During these years, a significant contribution to the

---

[35] Art. 117 of the Italian Constitution, as amended by Constitutional Law no 3/2001. On the Italian constitutional protection of the environment before the 2022 reform, see Del Signore (2022), Caravita and Morrone (2016), Grassi and Cecchetti (2002), Cecchetti (2000), Caravita (1999).

[36] ItCC, case 641/1987 qualified the environment as 'a unitary intangible asset, even if it is made up of various components, each of which can be the object of care and protection in isolation and separately'; in ItCC, case 67/1992, 'the integrity of the environment is a unitary asset that can be endangered even by minor interventions and must therefore be safeguarded in its entirety'; on the environment as a 'value' and at the same time as a unitary asset, ItCC, case 407/2002, interpreting for the first time Art. 117(2)(s) of the Italian Constitution on the protection of the environment, the ecosystem and the cultural heritage as a cross-cutting issue between the legislation of the State and the Regions, following the constitutional reform of 2001; ItCC, case 104/2008, on the environment as a 'system considered in its dynamic whole, as it really is, and not only from a static and abstract point of view', referring to the biosphere and the Stockholm Declaration of 1972; ItCC, case 12/2009, on the coexistence of goods having as their object components or aspects of the single good of the environment; ItCC, case 145/2013, on 'the environment in its entirety, as an organic entity', and thus ItCC, cases 246/2019 and 179/2019, on land use, according to the qualification given by the contested norms, as a 'non-renewable natural ecosystemic resource, essential for the purposes of environmental equilibrium, capable of expressing a social function and incorporating a plurality of collective interests and benefits, including those of an intergenerational nature', referring to the Commission Communication of 22 September 2006 'Thematic Strategy for Soil Protection' and to the Seventh Environmental Action Programme, already mentioned. References to the principles and acts of the European Union relating to the environment are very frequent in the case law of the ItCC (all the decisions of the ItCC can be read at www.cortecostituzionale.it, the most important in an official English translation; however, the quotations in this text are our translation).

[37] For a comparison with the French experience, where, on the contrary, the Constitutional Council had explicitly refused to derive environmental protection from the existing constitutional text

constitutional protection of the environment, also in constitutional case law, came from the acts of the Union, as interpreted by the Court of Justice. This influence was and remains decisive, if we consider that the entire Italian Environmental Code is an implementation of EU regulations.[38]

It is also worth noting that even before the constitutional reform, the ItCC clarified the relationship between individual freedom of enterprise, the environment, health and other constitutional rights, such as the right to work, in hard cases involving highly polluting industrial complexes. In a famous decision concerning the preventive seizure of one of the largest steelworks in Europe (Ilva in Taranto) for reasons of environmental pollution, the Court stated that no fundamental right has absolute priority over others, because otherwise there would be 'the unlimited extension of one right, which would become a 'tyrant' over the other protected constitutional rights', which 'as a whole are expressions of human dignity'; as to the Court, in the view of a systemic and non-fragmented constitutional protection, the qualification of the environment and health as 'primary values' does not imply a 'rigid hierarchy between fundamental rights', since the Italian Constitution, like other contemporary democratic and pluralist constitutions, requires a continuous and reciprocal balance between principles and fundamental rights.[39] Therefore, there is no rigid priority between constitutional rights and principles, nor is there an absolute prevalence of the environment or health over the right to work and, even though it did not emerge in this case, over private economic initiative, but each case requires a reasonable balance, entrusted to all the authorities involved and carried out according to the principles of participation and information, in compliance with the best available techniques.[40]

It is on the basis of this constitutional framework that we can now move on to the 2022 constitutional reform. The constitutional reform triggered a divisive debate in Italian academia.[41] Some authors have welcomed a long-awaited change to bring the Italian Constitution into line with many constitutions around the world.[42] In this positive sense, some authors consider that the constitutional amendments have an impact on the founding principles of the Republic, modifying the original pact: no longer the fight against social conflict and the function of distributive equality, but the fight against the climate and environmental crisis, for the survival of the planet

through interpretation before the formal adoption of the Environmental Charter in 2004, see Cozzi (2021).

[38] Del Signore (2022).

[39] ItCC, case 85/2013.

[40] In this sense, analyzing Workers' Buyout as a relevant model for 'regenerating' companies in crisis according to the paradigm of circular economy see Pasquariello (Chap. "Companies Regenerated with Workers' Buyout (WBO): A Human-Centric Tool for a Sustainable Circular Economy in Corporate Insolvency").

[41] The literature on the Italian constitutional reform of 2022 is extensive; for a general overview of the different positions Cecchetti et al. (2021), AA.VV. (2022), Sobrino and Imarisio (2022). Specifically regarding the amendments to Art. 41 It. Const., Cassetti (2022).

[42] Daly and May (2015).

and all forms of life.[43] Other authors, on the contrary, have considered the reform unnecessary because, as mentioned, the environment has already been a primary constitutional value in the case-law of the Italian Constitutional Court since the 1980s. Still others considered the reform to be even a dangerous precedent, regardless of the substantive norms introduced, because for the first time the Fundamental Principles of the Italian Constitution have been touched. This opinion, which is held by a minority, is the result of two factors. On the one hand, the fundamental principles express some of the basic norms on which the Italian constitutional order is based. On the other hand, in the Italian constitutional experience, there have been numerous attempts by the political majorities to modify, even profoundly, some parts of the Constitution, with the result that there is a widespread fear that a modification of the Fundamental Principles could open the way to divisive reforms, the expression of a populist or hardly democratic vision. However, these fears are not directly related to the environment, but rather to the historical context and the cultural and legal climate in Italy.

We agree with the first of these positions. The constitutional reform is positive, because it has completed a process already present in the national legal system and essentially based on the interpretative tools of the ItCC. It is not possible, in our opinion, to minimise the importance of the text as a constraint that crystallises a certain constitutional *acquis* and opens up new paths of interpretation.[44] Therefore, if it is true that the reform has had a 'recognising' significance of the existing,[45] it is also true that the writing in constitutional texts always has an innovative function, leading to the re-elaboration and development of existing concepts.

In any case, there are many fresh elements in the amended text. Firstly, Art. 9 of the Italian Constitution refers to some components of the general concept of the environment which deserve autonomous and specific attention: biodiversity and ecosystems. Secondly, it can be found for the first time an explicit reference to the interests of future generations. The interests of future generations were already present in the ItCC case law, but the fact that they are written in the normative formula gives rise to numerous potential applications, above all by the legislator when drawing up public policies. In fact, legal scholars have imagined that a form of impact assessment could be introduced for any policy that involves the consumption of resources, not only natural but also economic—for example the public debt—that will be passed on to future generations. There should be a mechanism, modelled on the principle of environmental integration, which sets out a procedural way of measuring the impact of any policy that creates burdens for the future.[46] Finally, the explicit inclusion of the environment as a limit to private economic initiative would seem to accentuate the limits of free competition, which, through the influence of

---

[43] Morrone (2023).

[44] Benvenuti (2023).

[45] Cecchetti (2020).

[46] Cozzi (2024) and the referenced bibliography.

the European Union, has had a major impact on the evolution of the internal legal system.

The reform is very recent. So far, the ItCC has only had to apply the new constitutional text once, in a case similar to the Ilva case mentioned above. This recent case concerned the preventive seizure, again for environmental reasons, of an industrial water treatment plant used in the one of the largest petrochemical complex in southern Europe, in Sicily, with a production capacity of one third of the national demand for oil. The Court confirmed the principles of the previous Ilva case, concerning production facilities of national strategic importance, on the need to strike a concrete balance, on a case-by-case basis, between the constitutional principles of private enterprise, health, the environment and work. In the light of the constitutional reform of 2022, the Court added that no measure could legitimately authorise a company to continue its activity in perpetuity, contrary to the prohibition on causing damage to health and the environment, as provided for in Art. 41(2) of the Constitution. The necessarily temporary measures to which the production activity is subject must therefore have a purpose that cannot be constitutionally circumvented, i.e. 'they must tend to achieve a rapid remedy of the situation of environmental degradation or potential damage to health caused by the activity of the seized companies'.[47] The constitutional reform has thus strengthened the positive obligation of the legislator to take charge of environmental protection, not in the sense of protection at all costs, but as an objective that can never be sacrificed or postponed *a priori*, to be pursued with concrete measures.

4 The Environment as an Internal Engine or as an External Limit to the Market Economy

In this last Section of the chapter, we can now try to compare the influence of the circular economy on the objectives of Art. 3(3) TEU, a highly competitive social market economy, aiming at full employment and social progress, and a high level of protection and improvement of the quality of the environment, with the Italian constitutional principles on the relationship between market and environment as resulting from the 2022 constitutional reform.[48]

As shown in the previous Sections, the circular economy aims to act on the production and consumption system from within, making the environment a structural component of the economic production model for the entire life cycle of products, from design to consumption, reuse and waste. The Italian constitutional reform, on the other hand, sees the environment as an external limit to the freedom of

[47] ItCC, case105/2024.

[48] A similar comparison, based on a partly different approach, is made by de Leonardis (2023b), arguing that there is an affinity between the Italian constitutional reform and the change of perspective in European policies brought about by the circular economy.

enterprise, an obstacle that reduces its operability. In the new text of Article 41(2) of the Italian Constitution, the environment is explicitly considered a limit to the freedom of enterprise, as it was in the previous case law of the ItCC. There seems to be a contradiction between the two models. The first, which is based on the circular economy, seems to be more advanced because it pursues the objective of a high-quality environment, as set out in Art. 3(3) TEU, 'through' the competitive market, also set out in Art. 3(3) TEU. An hendiadys, a fusion of the two objectives, would be achieved. Instead, the Italian constitutional reform would remain anchored in a more traditional vision of the relationship between the environment and the market, in which the protection of natural resources would constitute a limit to the market. The two factors would remain separate and opposed.

In our view, this is an apparent contradiction for several reasons.

Firstly, there is certainly nothing new about the need to consider the environmental, economic and social dimensions together. Their interaction is the defining feature of the concept of sustainable development, both in international law and in European Union law. In the same Art. 3(3) TEU, the two objectives of a highly competitive social market economy and a high quality and improvement of the environment are part of a single primary objective, the sustainable development of Europe.[49] From this point of view, the circular economy is one of the tools to achieve this interaction. Similarly, in the reform of the Italian Constitution of 2022, the concept of sustainable development emerged clearly in the preparatory work, as implicit in the protection of the environment, biodiversity and ecosystems, and is now explicit through the reference to the interests of future generations.[50]

Secondly, the circular economy is one of the components of the broader green transition. As mentioned, the circular economy is characterised by its impact on competition law and market regulation, but many other policies related to the green transition still see the environment as a limit to free enterprise, if we consider the protection of biodiversity or the reduction of land consumption, to name but a few examples. An inclusive model (the environment 'in' the economy) and an oppositional model (the environment 'as a limit' to the market) thus coexist and take on different consistencies, sometimes mixing, depending on the policies under consideration. The circular economy thus reflects a new model that fits into a more complex jigsaw puzzle in which the environment, the economy and, we can add, the social dimension, are mixed in different ways, without it being possible to absolutise a single scheme in the relationship between the objectives of Art. 3(3) TEU.

Thirdly, in connection with the previous point, it has already been said that it is not possible to interpret the constitutional structure of legal systems solely on the basis of the words of constitutional texts. This means that the interactions and interpretative schemes associated with primary norms, both at the European and national

---

[49] On ecological sustainability and sustainable development in the light of the Green Deal see Chiti and Giorgi (2024). About sustainability as a new goal of EU competition law see also Iacovides and Stylianou (2024).

[50] Cozzi (2021).

levels, are much more articulated and complex than a simple model of inclusion or opposition.

Fourthly, we must bear in mind that environmental protection is one of the material areas in which European and national regulations and policies have always been more closely linked. It has already been said that Italian environmental legislation is almost entirely dependent on EU regulations, as is the case in the other Member States. There is therefore a transfer of concepts, legal categories and balance models between the two levels, national and European. This transfer is very positive and to some extent inevitable, given the structurally transversal nature of environmental protection, which transcends national borders. From this point of view, as already mentioned, the norms of the Italian Constitution, in particular Art. 41, have always been strongly influenced by EU law on competition and the market. However, this is not a one-way street, from the EU to the Member States, but a two-way street. The history of environmental law amply demonstrates this. Some well-known instruments, such as environmental impact assessments, were originally introduced in some Member States and, based on these national experiences, were codified in European regulations and thus became mandatory for all Member States.

Therefore, in conclusion, if the circular economy would contribute to placing the human being at the centre of the legal construct, as the guiding element of the entire production and consumption system, it is a response that will be built together by the European level and the national systems, in the mutual exchange that has always constituted the distinctive fact of the European integration process.

References

AA.VV (2022) La riforma costituzionale in materia di ambiente. Atti del convegno 28 gennaio 2022. Editoriale Scientifica, Naples

Baraggia A (2023) La condizionalità come strumento di governo negli Stati compositi. Una comparazione tra Stati Uniti, Canada e Unione Europea. Giappichelli, Turin

Baraggia A, Bonelli M (2022) Linking money to values: the new rule of law conditionality regulation and its constitutional challenges. German Law J 23(2):131–156

Benvenuti M (2023) La revisione dell'articolo 41, commi 2 e 3, della Costituzione, i suoi destinatari e i suoi interpreti. Rivistaaic.it (2).

Caravita B (1999) Costituzione, principi costituzionali e tecniche di normazione. In: Grassi S, Cecchetti M, Andronio A (eds) Ambiente e diritto, vol 1. Olschki, Florence, pp 175–215

Caravita B, Morrone A (2016) Ambiente e Costituzione. In: Caravita B, Cassetti L, Morrone A (eds) Diritto dell'ambiente. Il Mulino, Bologna, pp 21–27

Cassese S (ed) (2021) La nuova Costituzione economica, 4th edn. Laterza, Roma-Bari

Cassetti L (1997) La cultura del mercato tra interpretazioni della Costituzione e principi comunitari. Giappichelli, Turin

Cassetti L (2022) La riforma dell'art. 41 della Costituzione: modello economico e tutela dell'ambiente. In: AA VV La riforma costituzionale in materia di ambiente. Atti del convegno 28 gennaio 2022. Editoriale Scientifica, Naples, pp 141–164

Cecchetti M (2000) Principi costituzionali per la tutela dell'ambiente. Giuffré, Milan

Cecchetti M (2020) Osservazioni e ipotesi per un intervento di revisione dell'art. 9 della Costituzione avente ad oggetto l'introduzione di una disciplina essenziale della tutela dell'ambiente tra i principi fondamentali dell'ordinamento costituzionale. Diritto pubblico europeo online 1:1–22

Cecchetti M, Ronchetti L, Bruti Liberati E (eds) (2021) Tutela dell'ambiente. Diritti e politiche. Editoriale Scientifica, Naples

Chiti E (2022) Managing the ecological transition of the EU: the European green deal as a regulatory process. CMLR 59(1):19–48

Chiti E (2024) Ecosystem restoration and EU law: an introduction to the symposium. Eur Law Open 3(1):175–179

Chiti E, Giorgi A (eds) (2024) Ecological sustainability and the law: the European green deal and the new frontiers of sustainability. Routledge-Giappichelli Studies in Law, Turin

Cozzi A-O (2021) La modifica degli artt. 9 e 41 Cost. in tema di ambiente: spunti dal dibattito francese sulla Carta dell'ambiente del 2004 tra diritti e principi. DPCE Online 49(4):3391–3430

Cozzi A-O (2024) Profili costituzionali delle proprietà pubbliche. Jovene editore, Naples

Cozzi A-O, Grisostolo FE (2023) Condizionalità europea e identità costituzionali. Un'introduzione. DPCE Online 61(4):3291–3303

Daly E, May JR (2015) Comparative environmental constitutionalism. Jindal Glob Law Rev 6(1):9–30

de Búrca G (2011) The road not taken: the European Union as a global human rights actor. Am J Int Law 105(4):649–693

de Leonardis F (2023a) Lo Stato ecologico. Approccio sistematico, economia, poteri pubblici e mercato. Giappichelli, Turin

de Leonardis F (2023b) Sustainable production as a driver for rewriting European treaties. Il diritto dell'economia 110(1):I–XVII

De Sadeleer N (2014) EU environmental law and the internal market. Oxford University Press, Oxford

De Sadeleer N (2023) Environmental law in the EU: a pathway toward the green transition. In: Garcia MDG, Cortês A (eds) Blue planet law, Sustainable development goals series. Springer, Cham, pp 22–35

Del Signore M (2022) voce Ambiente. In: Mattarella BG, Ramajoli M (eds) Enciclopedia del diritto. Vol. 3: Funzioni amministrative. Giuffré, Milan

Fasone C, Simoncini M (2023) The ambiguities of conditionality as an instrument of EU internal governance. In: Fasone C, Dirri A, Guerra Y (eds) Established EU rule of law instruments: state-of-the-art working paper. Luiss, pp 65–70

Grassi S, Cecchetti M (2002) Profili costituzionali della regolazione dell'ambiente nel diritto comunitario e nazionale. In: Rapisarda Sassoon C (ed) Manuale delle leggi ambientali. Giuffré, Milan, pp 7–102

Iacovides MC, Stylianou K (2024) The new goals of EU competition law: sustainability, labour rights, and privacy. Eur Law Open 3(3):587–616

Jordan A, Gravey V (eds) (2021) Environmental policy in the EU: actors, institutions and processes, 4th edn. Routledge, Oxon

Kilpatrick C (2015) On the rule of law and economic emergency: the degradation of basic legal values in Europe's bailouts. Oxf J Leg Stud 35(2):325–353

Kingston S (2010) Integrating environmental protection and EU competition law: why competition isn't special? Eur Law J 16(6):780–805

Kingston S, Heyvaert V, Čavoški A (2017) European environmental law. Cambridge University Press, Cambridge

Kiss AC, Sheldon D (1997) Manual of European environmental law. Cambridge University Press, Cambridge

Kramer L (2009) Environmental justice in the European court of justice. In: Ebbesson J, Okowa P (eds) Environmental law and justice in context. Cambridge University Press, Cambridge

Krämer L, Badger C (2024) Krämer's EU environmental law, 9th edn. Hart, Bloomsbury Academic

Lesniewska F, Steenmans K (2023) Circular economy and the law. Bringing justice into the frame. Routledge, Oxon

Lupo N (2023) The recovery and resilience facility and its effects on the rule of law conditionality: a (potentially) well-functioning connection. In: Fasone C, Dirri A, Guerra Y (eds) EU rule of law procedures at the test bench. Managing dissensus in the European constitutional landscape. Palgrave Macmillan, pp 243–260

Monteduro M (2022) Riflessioni sulla "primazia ecologica" nel moto del diritto europeo (anche alla luce della riforma costituzionale italiana in materia ambientale). In AA VV La riforma costituzionale in materia di ambiente. Atti del convegno 28 gennaio 2022. Editoriale Scientifica, Naples, pp 221–260
Morgera E, Gracia M-D (2021) Commentary to article 37—environmental protection. In: Peers S, Hervey T, Kenner J, Ward A (eds) Commentary on the EU charter of fundamental rights, 2nd edn. Hart, Bloomsbury Academic
Morrone A (2023) "Ambiente" fondamento della Costituzione repubblicana. In: Rescigno F, Giorgini Pignatiello G (eds) One earth-one health. Giappichelli, Turin, pp 5–11
Peeters M, Eliantonio M (2020) On regulatory power, compliance, and the role of the court of justice in EU environmental law. In: Peeters M, Eliantonio M (eds) . Research handbook on EU environmental law, Edward Elgar, pp 475–499
Pinelli C (2013) Conditionality. In: Max Planck Encyclopedia of public international law. Oxford Public International Law. https://opil.ouplaw.com/display/10.1093/law:epil/9780199231690/law-9780199231690-e1383
Pinelli C (2019) Conditionality and economic constitutionalism in the Eurozone. Ital J Public Law 1:22–42
Rossi G (ed) (2021) Diritto dell'ambiente. Aggiornamento a cura di Andrea Farì. Giappichelli, Turin
Scott J (ed) (2009) Environmental protection: European law and governance. Oxford University Press, Oxford
Sikora A (2020) Constitutionalisation of environmental protection in EU law. Europa Law, Groeningen
Sjåfjell B (2015) The legal significance of Article 11 TFEU for EU institutions and member states. In: Sjåfjell B, Wiesbrock A (eds) The greening of European business under EU law: taking article 11 TFEU seriously. Routledge, Oxon, pp 51–72
Sobrino G, Imarisio L (2022) La riforma degli artt. 9 e 41 della Costituzione e le sue implicazioni: un primo confronto. Atti del seminario svoltosi a Cuneo il 29 aprile 2022. Università degli studi di Torino. Giappichelli, Turin
Valerio P (2023) Il dialogo tra condizionalità ambientale, tutele costituzionali e libertà economiche nel contesto della crisi naturale e climatica. DPCE Online 61(4):3401–3415

Global Sustainability in the International Arena Beyond the EU Policy Agenda

Claudia Candelmo

Abstract In the last decade, the EU has become a champion in the promotion of sustainability, especially in the paradigmatic terms of a Sustainable Circular Economy (SCE), but what does the landscape of the international scene look like? The chapter explores the promotion of SCE worldwide and thus addresses the question of whether the EU is a frontrunner in the transition from linear to circular economy or its role needs to be rescaled to one player among the many others that populate the international community. In fact, while the EU is surely one of the most prominent actors in this respect, it does not act in a vacuum. Many other actors took an interest the achievement of sustainability in general and in SCE in particular, and have become drivers of progressive change, in their respective geographical areas and fields of competence. The research shows that, while the EU is endowed with considerable power to influence and drive the legislative and policy agenda of Member States, other actors are, in their field of competence, promoting sustainable circular economy, consequently giving rise to a truly international and global effort from a linear economic system to a circular one.

1 Introduction

A Sustainable Circular Economy ('SCE'), as a 'new' economic model that departs from the 'old' linear one, is gaining momentum in the international community, with a crucial role being played by the European Union (EU).

Currently, there is no internationally agreed upon definition of this concept.[1] The United Nations Environment Programme (UNEP) has referred to circular economy

[1] Castro de Hallgren et al. (n.d.).

C. Candelmo (✉)
Università degli Studi di Udine, Udine, Italy
e-mail: claudia.candelmo@uniud.it

B. Calabrese (ed.), *Legal Perspectives for a Sustainable Circular Economy*, European Union and its Neighbours in a Globalized World 30,
https://doi.org/10.1007/978-3-032-07795-0_11

as an economic model in which 'products and materials are designed in such a way that they can be reused, remanufactured recycled or recovered and thus maintained in the economy for as long as possible',[2] thereby limiting or avoiding waste and greenhouse gasses. UNEP has thus provided some key elements that help the identification of what circular economy is, but such elements are not contained in an international agreement on the topic, which would be binding on States Parties.

Nevertheless, this does not mean that there are no actions in the international community to advance the transition to circular economy. Many actors (States, international organisations, networks and NGOs) took an interest in this concept in recent years and have become drivers for significant change. Key initiatives are being carried out at the international level, both within universal and in regional organisations around the globe. Furthermore, such organisations do not merely act individually, but also tend to collaborate, creating networks of international cooperation on the matter, whose actions are crucial to achieve sustainability.

There is, in other words, global attention on this topic, which pushes for the transition to more sustainable patterns of consumption and production, through circular economy.

Such data is relevant for at least two, interconnected, reasons.

First, the implementation of the new SCE should not concern exclusively some parts of the globe. The progressive pressure put on the environment, which derives from the exasperation of the linear model of economy,[3] cannot be obviously tackled in a single State or in a few, selected States. It seems reasonable to affirm that common features should be shared on the international plane, in order to maximise the relieving effect that the new SCE can have on the environment. In fact, without agreeing on minimum common standards, the impact of national or regional initiatives is necessarily limited.[4]

Indeed, this is not an easy endeavor. Challenges to a global common approach to sustainability may include differences in the economic, political and institutional systems, heterogeneity in the legal cultures and systems as well as the needs of local economic producers that must adjust their production to accommodate requirements of circular economy, including with more extended responsibilities in terms of prolonged lifespan, reparation and recycling of products.[5]

Second, the fact that international organisations and States worldwide are promoting autonomously a progressive transition to SCE shows that the intention to implement this new economic model is not a prerogative of few States. Rather, as it shall be seen, environmental protection and the effort to achieve sustainability are

[2] UNEP/EA.4/Res.1, Innovative pathways to achieve sustainable consumption and production (2019), p. 2.

[3] European Investment Bank, The EIB Circular Economy Guide. Supporting the Circular Transition (2020), p. 6.

[4] This is expressly recognized in the Circular Economy Action Plan adopted by the European Commission in 2020, in particular at p. 18.

[5] Maitre-Ekern (2021). In this connection, support from public authorities can be crucial and act as an incentive to help producers convert to more sustainable production patterns.

values promoted, at different levels, on the global scene. In this context, circularity is not an objective inspired or compelled by external sources or policies, but often derives from values that are shared and rooted in many States, for example in indigenous cultures, whose principles should not only be taken into account but also respected and included in the new economic model.

Upon this background, the chapter will explore international initiatives carried out to promote and implement the transition to circular economy, in order to assess whether the EU is effectively a frontrunner on this issue or, rather, its role should be rescaled to 'one among the others'.

To do so, a brief look will be given to the main features of EU action on circular economy (Sect. 2), exclusively with a view of identifying its key components and better contextualise initiatives promoted by other international actors. Then, some privileged actors will be specifically assessed, that is first of all international organisations and other networks of international cooperation, both of a universal (the United Nations: Sect. 3) and of a regional character (distinctly in Africa, America, Asia and the Pacific: respectively, Sects. 4, 5, 6, and 7).[6] Actually, the positions expressed by individual States within such organisations can also be relevant in order to assess the consensus that is forming around certain concepts related to circular economy, but individual States' actions will not be analysed. Rather, the role of the relevant organisations in which States aggregate and cooperate is taken into account, employing a possibly inclusive approach that does not disregard any region of the world. Furthermore, international agreements will be relevant as well: in particular, a look will be given to Multilateral Environmental Agreements ('MEAs') that bear (or can potentially bear) significance for the promotion of circular economy (Sect. 8), in the absence of a comprehensive agreement on SCE (Sect. 9). Finally, conclusive remarks on such international arena and the respective role of the EU therein will be drawn (Sect. 10).

2 The Privileged Position of the EU on Circular Economy

According to Art. 3(3) TEU, sustainable development is one of the aims of the European Union. The EU is thus one of the most powerful actors in the promotion of sustainability, both in Member States and with a view to supporting its achievement internationally, beyond the EU itself.[7] In this context, the attainment of sustainability informs the action of the EU in the global sphere and its choices

[6] A limited look may include also NGOs, as a means to convey the instances of the public and to understand whether they are taken into account in order to shape the position of the relevant organizations, but will not form a substantial part of the analysis.

[7] The Union sets as its objectives the work for the sustainable development of Europe (Art. 3(3) TEU) as well as the contribution to sustainable development 'in its relations with the wider world' (Art. 3(5) TEU). More specifically, in its external action, the Union shall work to improve the sustainable management of global natural resources (Art. 21(2)(f) TEU).

internationally, but the coherence between internal and external action is also a distinctive feature of EU activities in this field and both are essential to the achievement of the objective of sustainability. In fact, on the one hand, sustainability and sustainable development are intended to be fundamental features of the environmental action of the EU;[8] on the other, the overall journey through sustainable development includes action to target climate change worldwide.[9] Its effects and efforts, therefore, are international and global in nature.

Furthermore, on environmental matters, the EU is provided with an overall competence that is shared with Member States,[10] which results in the participation of Member States in the adoption of international agreements on the topic.[11] Nevertheless, other areas may be called into action that may entrust the EU with an exclusive competence: notably the adoption of an act using as a legal basis the definition of competition rules for the functioning of the internal market, a competence that is exclusively of the Union.[12]

The EU is, also, characterized by a unique feature that puts it in a privileged position and entrusts it with powers often unknown to other international organisations: its action can be particularly pervasive not only in light of its significant competences, but especially in light of its institutional and legal framework, which provides it with the ability to enter into legal orders of Member States. Sometimes, the Union does so directly, through regulations, while sometimes it proceeds through indirect legislation, namely directives. After all, regulations and directives are the main instruments that the EU has been using in this field, with the recent legislative reforms being some of the most ambitious transformations and developments of the EU policy on sustainability in general and circular economy in particular,[13] having

[8] In the present contribution, the term sustainability is preferred, with a view of stressing the condition of sustainability, intended as the ultimate objective to achieve, in order to ensure compatibility of everyone's conduct, lifestyle and more generally action with the limited resources of the planet. Sustainable development, on the other hand, puts the stress on the need to ensure development without impairing the resources of the planet. The overlapping or rather different meaning of the two terms, as well as the usefulness of any distinction is extensively discussed by Washington (2015).

[9] The UN 2030 Agenda for Sustainable Development specifically dedicates Goal 13 to address climate change (Goal 13 Climate Action). Furthermore, the preamble of the Agenda recalls that one of the key areas of work relates to the protection of the planet, by solemnly affirming that "We are determined to protect the planet from degradation, including through sustainable consumption and production, sustainably managing its natural resources and taking urgent action on climate change, so that it can support the needs of the present and future generations". See A/RES/70/1, Transforming our world: the 2030 Agenda for Sustainable Development (2015).

[10] Art. 4 b TFEU.

[11] Vedder (2012, p. 19).

[12] Art. 3 b TFEU.

[13] For example, Regulation (EU) 2024/1781 establishing a framework for the setting of ecodesign requirements for sustainable products, or Directive (EU) 2024/1799 on common rules promoting the repair of goods, as well as Directive (EU) 2022/2464 as regards corporate sustainability reporting: on such legislative acts, see respectively Deana (Chap. "Reshaping Consumer Powers and Responsibilities in the European Union's Transition to a Sustainable Circular Economy"), Calabrese (Chap. "Right to Repair Between Intellectual Property and Servitization") and Genovese

affirmed the specific relevance of the transition to circularity to achieve a sustainable future.[14]

However, the Union's efforts will be successful, only if they are accompanied by comprehensive action at the global level, and resource use as well as the environmental impact of human activities remain within the limits that the planet allows. The perspective of other regions of the world, in particular through the lens of international organisations, is thus essential and allows us to understand the position of both actors. On the one hand, it allows us to discern whether the EU should be effectively considered a frontrunner in the global transition to circular economy. On the other, it allows a more conscious look at the efforts promoted at various levels of the international community. In fact, international organisations generally have a more limited outreach and, at best, set rules or targets that must be implemented by States in their national legal orders to display effects at the national level. Often, thus, much more discretion is left to Member States to implement eventual commitments taken at the international level, if compared to EU legal acts. Furthermore, it is not rare that international organisations take action through acts, such as guidelines or declarations of principle, that lack binding effects. Nonetheless, such documents can act as political incentives to boost action in certain fields, such as sustainability.

3 The United Nations

Consideration of SCE by the United Nations is not a recent phenomenon. Early, indirect, reference to the model of circular economy can be traced back to the Brundtland Report (1987)[15] and to the Rio Declaration (1992), which underlined, in principle 8, that 'States should eliminate unsustainable patterns of production and consumption'.[16] This objective was reiterated and further elaborated in the Johannesburg Plan of Implementation (2002), which declared that 'fundamental changes in the way societies produce and consume are indispensable for achieving

(Chap. "Corporate Sustainability Reporting and Commitments: Effectiveness and Enforceability from EU to National Law").

[14] Communication from the Commission to the European Parliament, the Council, the European Economic and Social Committee and the Committee of the Regions empty, 'Fit for 55': delivering the EU's 2030 Climate Target on the way to climate neutrality, COM(2021) 550. The relevance of circular economy is also indirectly recognized by the Sustainable Development Goals that, by requiring responsible consumption and production patterns, as well as reducing waste generation through prevention, reduction, recycling and reuse (Target 12.5), also require policies that aim at "promoting circular economy practices and supporting sustainable procurement policies".

[15] Chapter 8 of the Report was entitled 'Producing more with less' and focused among the need to reduce the impact of the industrial sector on the environment in particular by taking into account the need to ensure development while, at the same time. See Report of the WCED, Our Common Future (1987).

[16] A/CONF.151/26 (Vol. I), Rio Declaration on Environment and Development (1992), Principle 8.

global sustainable development'.[17] The plan highlighted, in particular, that changes would be needed in order to prevent and minimize waste, while maximizing reuse and recycling, as well as the production of reusable goods and biodegradable products.[18] Such change could be intended as a need to shift from the most popular linear model to a circular one, encouraging reusing and repairing as positive patterns that would later become pillars of SCE.

The existence of such references shows that the acknowledgment of the need to change production and consumption patterns was already clear at the beginning of the Nineties and would develop in the following years, with initiatives being discussed and taken directly at the international level.[19] Indeed, the Rio Declaration is a soft law document and, as such, it does not have a binding character. Furthermore, its above-cited principle 8 cannot be considered mandatory as a matter of customary law,[20] therefore its effectiveness in terms of pure bindingness is rather limited. Nevertheless, its political relevance should not be underestimated: the need to ensure more sustainable patterns of production and consumption became a key principle, specifically linked to SCE.

Attention to SCE grew within the UN together with attention to global warming and climate change. Soon, the two issues were linked to an understanding that, as recalled even recently, the transition to circular economy is crucial to address climate concerns.[21] Circular economy, in fact, has a clear impact on the well-being of the environment and on preserving resources as well as limiting pollution from waste.

In 2003, the Marrakech Process on Sustainable Consumption and Production was launched, with the aim of assisting countries in their efforts to make their economies more sustainable, help corporations develop greener business models and encourage consumers to adopt more sustainable lifestyles.[22] One of the aims of the Process was the elaboration of a 10-Year Framework of Programmes ('10YFP'), to support countries to implement sustainable consumption and production policies and patterns.

A particularly relevant forum for discussion of topics related to sustainability and circular economy was the Environment Assembly ('EA'). This body, instituted

[17] A/CONF.199/20, Report of the World Summit on Sustainable Development, Annex Plan of Implementation of the World Summit on Sustainable Development (2002), para. 14.

[18] See again A/CONF.199/20, para. 22.

[19] Early, scholarly research on circular economy date back to the Sixties, however the term first appeared in the work by Pearce and Turner (1990). See, on the point, Andrade et al. (2021). The focus here is, however, on international initiatives taken by States and other international actors to implement in their policy, which would appear at a later stage.

[20] Voigt (2015).

[21] See, in the context of COP29 as presented shortly after, Multilateral Development Banks' Circular Economy Working Group (2024). Circular Economy, in particular, is seen as key to addressing the triple climate planetary crisis (climate change, pollution and biodiversity loss).

[22] Takase (2005, p. 404).

within the UNEP, was provided with universal membership in 2012,[23] and took its current denomination to better reflect its membership, as opposed to the former Governing Council, which only counted 54 Members.[24] It meets periodically in Nairobi to discuss key issues to promote the protection of the environment. As it shall be seen, the EA has been engaging in the promotion of circular economy, but notably the efforts stayed at a level of intergovernmental cooperation with the adoption of decisions that, while showing the commitment of States on the topic, remain limited in their impact. The Assembly noted the importance of circular economy originally in 2019,[25] and more recently adopted a resolution where it invited Member States to 'integrate circular economy approaches into national and regional strategies action plans, including those related to relevant multilateral environmental agreements […]'[26] and to favour product lifetime extension, repair, re-use and easier recycling.[27]

The resolution is relevant at least for two reasons. First, it promotes an integration between the approach to circular economy and MEAs. In other words, while there are no multilateral agreement specifically designed to promote an international transition to SCE, considerations on this approach can (and should) be integrated in the implementation of MEAs that deal with similar or other topics. The integration between the two allows MEAs to act as a tow for stronger commitments on circular economy, for example through the integration of SCE in action plans that are, formally, devoted to implement other agreements. Second, the resolution also denotes an alignment in terms of what the transition to a circular economy entails. It focuses on the reuse, reparation and recycling of materials and products as much as possible, in order to reduce waste and the impact of human production on the environment. This also explains why the implementation of SCE is clearly linked to the implementation of MEAs, especially those that promote responsible management of waste, reduction of pollutants or other agreements related to sustainable production and consumption.

But 2012 was a key year for UN action on the environment. At the Rio + 20 United Nations Conference on Sustainable Development, the outcome was the adoption of the landmark document 'The future we want', endorsed by the General Assembly,[28] in which a whole subheading was dedicated to 'sustainable consump-

[23] A/RES/66/288, The future we want (2012), para. 88, adopted at the Rio+20 Conference. For a critical analysis of the limited impact of this Conference on the specific subject of the green economy, see Bratspies (2013).

[24] UNEP/GC.27/17, Decision 27/2, Implementation of 88 of the outcome document of the United Nations Conference on Sustainable Development (2016), suggesting the GA to change the name of the body (para. 21).

[25] UNEP/EA.4/Res.1, Innovative pathways to achieve sustainable consumption and production (2019).

[26] UNEP/EA.5/Res.11, Enhancing circular economy as a contribution to achieving sustainable consumption and production (2022) para. 1.

[27] See again UNEP/EA.5/Res.11, para. 2.

[28] A/RES/66/288, The future we want (2012).

tion and production'. The conference recognized that 'fundamental changes in the way societies consume and produce are indispensable for achieving global sustainable development'[29] and adopted simultaneously the 10-Year Framework of Programmes on sustainable consumption,[30] envisaged in the Marrakech Process. The Framework is interesting in that it underlines the principle of common but differentiated responsibilities in connection with more responsible patterns of consumption and production[31] and affirms the need to integrate sustainable consumption and production 'in decision-making at all levels, taking into account its cross-cutting nature, for example through strategic planning and policymaking'.[32]

Along with the creation of the UNEA, the Partnership for Action on Green Economy was launched, bringing together five key UN agencies dedicated to environment and sustainable development to provide support and assist partner countries in the transition toward an Inclusive Green Economy ('IGE').

The circular economy also received special attention during UNFCCC COPs.[33] As it is well known, the COP is the forum where all States Parties of the Framework Convention on Climate Change ('UNFCCC') meet, on an annual basis, to discuss the status of its implementation. Addressing the topic within the COP further strengthened the understanding of the inextricable link between climate change and the transition to a circular economy, also emphasizing the importance of forum of cooperation dedicated to the protection of the environment in the absence of specific ones to address SCE.

The circular economy theme is not new to COPs. It had been first addressed at COP25, but during COP28 attention to SCE was significantly reinforced, with numerous sessions dedicated to it.[34] Furthermore, on this occasion, the emblematic result of having SCE included for the first time in the text of the negotiating outcome was reached. States Parties noted 'the importance of transitioning to sustainable lifestyles and sustainable patterns of consumption and production in efforts to address climate change, including through circular economy approaches, and

---

[29] Again, A/RES/66/288, para. 224.

[30] A/CONF.216/5, Annex to the letter dated 18 June 2012 from the Permanent Representative of Brazil to the United Nations addressed to the Secretary-General of the United Nations Conference on Sustainable Development. A 10-year framework of programmes on sustainable consumption and production patterns (2012).

[31] See again A/CONF.216/5, para. 1: 'All countries should promote sustainable consumption and production patterns, with the developed countries taking the lead and with all countries benefitting from the process […]'.

[32] See again A/CONF.216/5, para. 3(d).

[33] Many NGOs, including the Ellen MacArthur Foundation, the Climate Works Foundation and the National Centre for Climate Change Strategy and International Cooperation, worked to highlight how the circular economy can contribute to combating climate change and achieving the goals of the 2030 Agenda.

[34] 'Circular Economy: A path to climate solutions and sustainable development', 'How the circular economy can support China's carbon emissions reduction', 'The fashion industry on the race to zero: circular economy and why it matters for fashion'

encourages efforts in this regard'.[35] Finally, during the latest COP (COP 29, Azerbaijan), Multilateral Development Banks presented their joint report on circular economy,[36] where, through the presentation of case studies, they provided a picture of actions taken to support key actors in circular economy, both State and non-state entities.

All the documents that have been surveyed so far bear a similar feature: they are intergovernmental initiatives, mostly characterized by non-binding character. The significant number of initiatives must surely be praised but it is also important to explore if any international agreement, that is thus binding on States Parties (excluding the UNFCCC, within which the COPs are carried out) may be relevant to foster circular economy beyond the mere policy intention.

In fact, while the developments sketched out so far highlight a global recognition of the relevance of circular economy within the UN, they fall short of defining international, binding, standards on the advancement towards its implementation. Intergovernmental initiatives have been conducive to the adoption of multilateral environmental conventions and treaties, revealing a normative impact that has gone beyond the mere 'wishful thinking' expressed by soft-law documents, but this has not happened for circular economy specifically.

In terms of international agreements, the Convention on Biological Diversity is of undoubted international importance. Signed in 1992 at the Rio Earth Summit, now has 196 States Parties. It acknowledged that biological diversity must be protected, preserved and its sustainable use ensured. This Convention is relevant in that the protection of biological diversity is inextricably linked with a reduction of pollutants that may affect the life of micro-organisms, plants, animals and humans, therefore impacting on their protection. The Convention on Biological Diversity requires States to protect sites that are rich in biological diversity, including eventual policies of recovery for threatened species.[37] This Convention could be an example of how circular economy can be brought into the picture of the implementation of a MEA, for example by enriching plans that protect biological diversity with attention to SCE. By reducing considerably waste and pollutants brought into the environment, in fact, SCE supports the preservation of biological diversity, threatened by such agents.

In a similar fashion, the Basel Convention on the Control of Transboundary Movements of Hazardous Wastes and their Disposal is relevant in that it not only intends to control the movement of hazardous wastes and their disposal, as would be evident from the title of the Convention itself, but also aims at minimizing their generation, thus requiring States to take appropriate measures to reduce the creation of hazardous wastes and other wastes to a minimum (including through

[35] FCCC/PA/CMA/2023/L.17, First global Stocktake (2023), para. 36.

[36] Multilateral Development Banks' Circular Economy Working Group (2024). The report was prepared jointly by a number of MDBs, in particular the African Development Bank, the Asian Development Bank, the European Bank for Reconstruction and Development, the European Investment Bank, the Inter-American Development Bank, IDB Invest and the World Bank Group.

[37] See, in particular, Arts. 8 and 9, Convention on Biological Diversity (1992).

international cooperation).[38] This is another example of how SCE approaches could be integrated in MEAs: being clear that one of the key pillars of the SCE is the reduction of waste, SCE could be fostered through the tool of the Basel Convention.

Finally, the developments promoted by UNECE (United Nations Economic Commission for Europe) must be recalled. Not only has it established a platform, 'Circular Step', to facilitate the exchange of experiences, share best practices and engage stakeholders in the transition to a circular economy, UNECE has also adopted a number of binding regulations, requiring specific products to abide by more sustainable requirements, including enhanced recyclability and reduced aptitude to obsolescence.[39]

These normative and political achievements within the United Nations are surely very significant. They show a global commitment to promoting SCE. The absence of an international convention on circular economy should not be thus considered a justification for States to avoid taking steps towards this transition, which can be carried out through a number of other tools, including by using other MEAs as a point of departure to integrate SCE approaches.

Beside the United Nations, the international community is populated by several regional entities, to whose activity the next Sections are dedicated.

4 The African Continent and Sustainable Circular Economy

The African region is prominently working to promote the implementation of circular economy, at different levels.[40] This continent may present specific challenges, such as resistance of developing economies that heavily rely on exports of raw materials in their economies and thus antagonize the reduction of such exports in favour of recycled materials,[41] but at the same time also presents specific potentials. In particular, it has been noted that key principles of circularity, which is often considered a modern concept of western derivation, are in fact rooted in many indigenous cultures,[42] which advocate existence in complete harmony with nature, a fea-

[38] See, in particular, Arts, 4 and 10, Basel Convention on the Control of Transboundary Movements of Hazardous Wastes and their Disposal (1989).

[39] See, in particular, Addendum 132—Regulation No. 133, Annex to the 1958 Agreement (Concerning the Adoption of Uniform Technical Prescriptions for Wheeled Vehicles, Equipment and Parts which can be Fitted and/or be Used on Wheeled Vehicles and the Conditions for Reciprocal Recognition of Approvals Granted on the Basis of these Prescriptions), Uniform provisions concerning the approval of motor vehicles with regard to their reusability, recyclability and recoverability. See, on the point, Mandizvidza and Makhanda (2024), Käsner et al. (2024).

[40] These include both intergovernmental initiatives and civil society organisations' activities, such as the African Circular Economy Network, that promotes and supports projects aimed at implementing circular economy at the local level.

[41] Castro de Hallgren et al. (n.d.).

[42] Arkin and Diggs (2022), Going back to move forward. By adopting zero waste systems, cities can redress historic injustices and cool the climate, Earth Island Journal, 2022, 55–57.

ture that—as shall be shown also in the following Sections—is equally relevant for indigenous peoples living in other continents, too. For example, circular economy promotes minimization and reuse of waste and regeneration of nature, in harmony with nature's rhythms and cycles, and this is true in several African communities.[43] In a similar way, indigenous people often live a special relationship with the land (and, thus, the nature) that goes well beyond the exploitation of its resources to encompass connections of a spiritual nature,[44] and thus specifically value its protection and preservation.[45] This aspect should not be underestimated. The embedding of indigenous principles and knowledge in initiatives of circular economy promoted at the regional level may be particularly helpful. Reconciling circular economy with indigenous principles could be essential and support the implementation of circular economy even in small businesses and especially in areas where indigenous peoples are particularly present.

In terms of institutional organisations' initiatives, the African Union has developed the Agenda 2063, which prioritises sustainable development and prosperity, also with a view of mitigating climate change, affecting disproportionately most vulnerable people in the region.[46] Furthermore, the African Union, in 2018, established the African Continental Free Trade Area (AfCFTA), which can be a powerful channel to promote the implementation of sustainable circular economy. The AfCFTA agreement identifies as general objectives the creation of a single, liberalized market among Member States of the African Union, but also the promotion of sustainable and inclusive socio-economic development,[47] while specific objectives include the progressive elimination of any barrier to trade in goods as well as cooperation on investments and all trade-related areas.[48] Such objectives make it one of the ideal *fora* to promote circularity among the Members, since the economic character of the agreement allows for the identification of shared standards of production that could be used as mutually accepted standards for the circulation of goods around the FTA.

At the governmental level, also more specific initiatives bear relevance. The Durban Declaration on taking action for environmental sustainability and prosperity in Africa was adopted in 2019 by the African Ministerial Conference on the Environment.[49] The Conference was founded in 1985 with the aim of enhancing environmental protection in the African continent and most recently Governments have also identified as a priority of their action the transition from a linear to a circular economy. This was recognized explicitly in the Durban Declaration which,

---

[43] Taremwa et al. (2024).

[44] Göcke (2013).

[45] United Nations Declaration on the Rights of Indigenous Peoples, 2007, Art. 25.

[46] African Union (2013), Agenda 2063, The Africa We Want, Aspiration 1, para. 16.

[47] Art. 3(a) and (e), African Continental Free Trade Area (AfCFTA) Agreement (2018).

[48] See again Art. 4(a), (c) and (d), African Continental Free Trade Area (AfCFTA) Agreement (2018).

[49] African Ministerial Conference on the Environment (2019), Durban Declaration on taking action for environmental sustainability and prosperity in Africa.

having highlighted the value of circular economy, crystallised the commitment of States to 'replicating, scaling up and using circular economy approaches as part of our region's transformation efforts as contained in Agenda 2063 of the African Union'[50] and encouraged non-state entities to do the same, while also underlying the importance of 'circular economy approach in Africa to assist with reducing the dependence on natural resources and reducing pollution in Africa'.[51]

The adoption of the Declaration is relevant for a number of reasons. On the one hand, it promoted an integrated approach with the Agenda 2063 of the African Union, thus showing that this is not an isolated initiative, but rather one of the many that are being implemented in the continent. On the other, it recognized the link between circular economy and the reduction of pollution, which plagues African countries.[52]

This is further confirmed by the creation of a dedicated intergovernmental network, devoted to the promotion of circular economy in Africa. The African Circular Economy Alliance (ACEA) is an alliance of African governments, focused on the transition to the circular economy as a future economic model to invest in, to generate new jobs, economic growth and positive environmental impacts. The secretariat of the Alliance is hosted by the African Development Bank (AfDB) and supported by the Africa Circular Economy Facility (ACEF), a multi-donor trust fund, administered by the AfDB, which provides assistance in three key areas to implement circular economy, namely the creation of an enabling policy environment, the promotion of a circular business model and the sharing of knowledge and best practices. Grants are assigned to Member States of the AfDB, NGOs and research institutions to further the implementation of circular economy in Member States.

5 The American Continent and Sustainable Circular Economy

With a view of achieving sustainable development, circular economy initiatives have become popular in the American continent as well. The Organization of American States (OAS), which has its own Department of Sustainable Development, has promoted the 'CircularAmericas' initiative, directed at OAS Member States, which intends to assist Governments in the formulation of policies of transition to circular economy and promote awareness and understanding on this new economic model.[53] The initiative is in line with a long-standing effort to promote circular economy in the region which saw as one of the main outcomes the adoption of the

[50] See the just above-cited Durban Declaration, para. 7.

[51] See again Durban Declaration, para. 9.

[52] On pollution in Africa see, among the others, Health Effects Institute (2022), Blaauw (2021), Darwish (2021).

[53] More information on the initiative are available online, in particular at www.oas.org

Declaration of Santo Domingo for the Sustainable Development of the Americas, whereby the Ministers and High-Level Authorities responsible for the sustainable development of the Americas decided to promote 'sustainable production and consumption patterns'.[54] Therefore, despite falling short of referring explicitly to circular economy, the OAS, already in 2010, regionally recognized the need to switch to more sustainable patterns of production and consumption with a view of preserving the resources of the planet.

Another organisation that deals generally with environmental issues and specifically with the transition to circular economy, despite not having been created for that exact purpose, is the Permanent Commission of the South Pacific. This is one of the oldest organisations of the continent (born in 1952) and is composed of the States of the American Continent that have access to the Pacific shore, specifically Chile, Colombia, Ecuador and Peru.[55]

More specifically on circular economy, the Latin America and Caribbean Circular Economy Coalition was established. The Coalition is an intergovernmental initiative, where government representatives cooperate together with permanent strategic partners (which include private foundations as well as institutional partners) in a steering committee.[56] Its purpose is to build a common regional vision on sustainable production and consumption, promote knowledge on the topic and increase dialogue as well as access financing for innovation and circular economy both by governments and the private sector.

During the last meeting of the Forum of Ministers of Environment of Latin America and the Caribbean, held in Panama City in 2023, the Ministers adopted 'Decision 2' on sustainable consumption and production and circular economy, whereby they committed to accelerating regional policies to contrast unsustainable consumption and production.[57] During the same meeting, in the Ministerial Segment of the Forum, the San Jose Declaration was adopted, too.[58] This Declaration recognised the need to promote 'an inclusive circular economy approach as one of the available models to achieve sustainable consumption and production practices and environmentally sound waste management'[59] and reaffirmed the need to take measures with a view of implementing sustainable production, including circular econ-

[54] OEA/Ser.K/XVIII.2, Declaration of Santo Domingo for the Sustainable Development of the Americas (2010), para. 31.

[55] Convenio Sobre Organizaci6n de la Comisi6n Permanente de la Conferencia Sobre Explotaci6n y Conservación de las Riquezas Marítimas del Pacífico Sur (1952).

[56] Currently—and until October 2025—the Steering Committee is composed of Peru, Costa Rica, Dominican Republic, Colombia, Ecuador, Brazil, plus the UNEP as coordinator and the eight strategic partners (Decision 2 on Sustainable Consumption and Production and Circular Economy, taken at the XXIII Meeting of the Forum of Ministers of Environment of Latin America and the Caribbean, para. 21).

[57] Forum of Ministers of Environment of Latin America and the Caribbean (2023), Decision 2, para. 2.

[58] Forum of Ministers of Environment of Latin America and the Caribbean, The San Jose Declaration (2023).

[59] See the just above-cited San Jose Declaration, para. 31.

omy models.[60] Being adopted in the framework of an intergovernmental forum of cooperation, these initiatives underscore the commitment of Latin American and Caribbean States to transition to a sustainable circular economic model.

On a different note, which, for the reasons mentioned above, is particularly significant, the same Declaration expressly recognised the role of indigenous people and knowledge, underscoring their 'invaluable contribution [...] for the conservation and sustainable use of natural ecosystems',[61] treasuring traditional, local and indigenous peoples' knowledge in the discourse concerning sustainability and promotion of circular economy.[62] The relevance of indigenous knowledge is furthermore significant in light of the numerous indigenous communities living in the region, which amount to around 42 million people.[63] Also in this case, it is particularly important that the transition to circular economy takes into account indigenous practices and knowledge, especially because, as seen above, indigenous knowledge, far from contrasting circularity, promotes it and can be of invaluable help to support the transition to circular economy, especially, but not exclusively, among indigenous people.

6 The Asian Continent and Sustainable Circular Economy

The Asian region is characterised by very big economies (such as China and India), whose involvement in the transition to circular economy is fundamental. Despite sometimes being seen as more reluctant to abide by standards of cleaner production and consumption, the region is very active in promoting this transition.

The Association of South-East Asian Nations (ASEAN) has created the ASEAN Circular Economy Stakeholder Platform, which supports Member States to progress in the transition to SCE and is part of the EU-ASEAN Partnership on Circular Economy. Furthermore, recently, ASEAN also adopted the Framework for Circular Economy for the ASEAN Economic Community, which provided stakeholders with a structured pathway to support their transition to circular economy and identified key priorities for ASEAN Member States to implement.[64] Also, ASEAN has created the ASEAN Circular Economy Business Alliance (ACEBA), which promotes innovation and responsible business practices, in particular pushing member organisations to commit to take action on circular economy and concretely foster the transition.

Most recently, roots were laid to adopt a regional plan for the implementation of circular economy in the Member States of the Economic Cooperation Organization

[60] See again San Jose Declaration, para. 41.

[61] San Jose Declaration, para. 22.

[62] San Jose Declaration, para. 31.

[63] World Bank Group, Indigenous Latin America in the Twenty-First Century. The First Decade (2015), p. 10.

[64] ASEAN, Framework for Circular Economy for the ASEAN Economic Community (2021).

(ECO), who belong primarily to Central and East Asia, after a consultation meeting was held in January 2025 between ECO and ESCAP (United Nations Economic and Social Commission for Asia and the Pacific). The ECO has also drafted a Regional Initiative on Resource Efficiency, Sustainability and Circular Economy (RESCUE), in which the Organization espoused the benefits of circular economy and recognised the need for 'a cohesive approach to accelerate the adoption of circularity as a paradigm and at a systemic level'.[65] The initiative was launched during the ECO Ministerial Meeting on circular economy, on the same days in which the COP29 was taking place in Baku, under the Presidency of Azerbaijan.

Finally, specific action is being taken in the area (and beyond) to end plastic pollution and improve the management of plastic waste, in particular through the Alliance to End Plastic Waste,[66] whose headquarters are located in Singapore. The Alliance benefits from partnerships in the business sector and has activated several projects worldwide in order to increase recycling and improve waste management,[67] while working for the reduction of plastic waste. Furthermore, the Alliance promotes the principles of circular economy, recognizing that the pathway to reducing plastic waste passes through a circular economy for plastic and this requires governmental and non-State entities to collaborate.

7 The Pacific Region and Sustainable Circular Economy

The Pacific region is here intended as encompassing States, Islands and other territories located in the Pacific Ocean, beside the States of the Asian Continent, which have been separately addressed before.

The region is extremely vital with initiatives that aim at furthering the implementation of circular economy. This must not come with a surprise: the region is mostly composed of territories that are disproportionately affected by climate change, being largely islands which are very low on sea level and for which the rising levels of the sea constitute a very tangible existential threat. Proof of this situation is the extraordinary efforts of these States to promote international initiatives in the hope that bigger States, whose action can have a much more extended impact on the environment, take concrete action to protect the environment and contrast climate change.[68]

---

[65] ECO, Regional Initiative on Resource Efficiency, Sustainability and Circular Economy in the ECO Region (RESCUE) (2023), p. 1.

[66] Poor management of plastic waste is a particularly harsh phenomenon in Asia, considering that '[…] according to the study *Stemming the Tide*, 60% of the plastic waste entering the oceans comes from five Asian countries: the People's Republic of China, Indonesia, the Philippines, Thailand, and Viet Nam (Ocean Conservancy 2015)'; in these terms see Sachdeva and Srivastava (2022).

[67] Kolesch et al. (2022).

[68] Among the most recent and relevant initiatives, see the creation of the Commission of Small Island States on Climate Change and International Law, in 2021, and the consequent Request for

In this area, the South Pacific Regional Environment Programme (SPREP) was established in 1993, following up to the Conference on the Human Environment in the South Pacific in 1982 to establish the program as a separate entity within the South Pacific Commission. It is an intergovernmental organisation based in Samoa, whose objectives include the protection of the environment and 'to ensure sustainable development for present and future generations'.[69] The Convention established also the SPREP Secretariat, which also serves as Secretariat of the Noumea, Waigani and Apia Conventions,[70] and is mandated with the implementation of the activities of the organization,[71] as well as the SPREP Meeting, which is the Plenary body of the Organization and adopts periodic Action Plans (named Strategic Plans).[72]

The latest Strategic Plan, prepared by the Secretariat and endorsed by the Meeting in 2016,[73] covers the decade 2017–2026 and, albeit not referring explicitly to circular economy, promotes activities that are entirely in line with the idea of reducing the impact of production and consumption, with a view of protecting the extraordinary environment located in the area.

In particular, this Plan aims at minimising adverse impact of waste and strengthen waste management, in particular by increasing recycling and recovery in order to reduce waste.[74] The effort made by the SPREP is also in line with the 'Cleaner Pacific 2025', the Pacific Regional Waste and Pollution Management Strategy and its implementation plan,[75] adopted by the same organisation, aimed at reducing the enormous impact of waste on the territories and maritime zones of the States belonging to the SPREP, whose increased pollution is a threat to life in the sea and beyond.[76] The first guiding principle identified by the Strategy goes under the name of 'Reduce, Reuse, Recycle, Return (3Rs + Return)', which mirrors the principles underlying circular economy, and aims, equally, at preventing and minimising the

an Advisory Opinion submitted by the Commission of Small Island States on Climate Change and International Law on 12 December 2022 (available at www.itlos.org) as well as the Australia-Tuvalu Falepili Union Treaty, signed on 9 November 2023 and entered into force on 28 August 2024.

[69] Art. 3, Agreement establishing the SPREP—South Pacific Regional Environment Programme (1993).

[70] Namely, the 'Noumea' Convention for the Protection of Natural Resources and Environment of the South Pacific Region (which is also enriched by two Protocols, the first on the prevention of pollution of the South Pacific Region by dumping and the second concerning cooperation in combating Pollution Emergencies in the South Pacific Region) of 1986, the 'Waigani' Convention to Ban the importation into Forum Island Countries of Hazardous and Radioactive Wastes and to Control the Transboundary Movement of Hazardous Wastes within the South Pacific Region of 1995, and the 'Apia' Convention on Conservation of Nature in the South Pacific of 1976.

[71] Art. 7, Agreement establishing the SPREP (1993) .

[72] See again Art. 3, Agreement establishing the SPREP (1993).

[73] See Twenty Seventh SPREP Meeting, Agenda Item 6.8: SPREP Strategic Plan (2016).

[74] See again the just above-cited SPREP Strategic Plan (2016), Regional Goal 3, Objectives 3.1, 3.2 and 3.3.

[75] SPREP, Cleaner Pacific 2025. Pacific Regional Waste and Pollution Management Strategy 2016–2025 (2016).

[76] See further SPREP, Cleaner Pacific 2025, principle 1.

generation of waste,[77] building on the Regional 3R Forum in Asia and Pacific Islands (created in 2009).[78] It is true that the strategy heavily relies on recycling and puts a more limited attention on the importance of reusing, thus prolonging the life of products before going into recycling, but for an area dramatically affected by poor waste management, the effort to ensure that first of all recycling is prioritised should still be commended as positive progress. Furthermore, the Strategy acknowledges that 'in prescribing waste management interventions, the preference shall be to reduce the generation of waste and pollutants; to reuse if appropriate and safe to do so'.[79]

Taking stock of the Cleaner Pacific 2025, recognized as the region's framework to address waste and pollution,[80] the 2050 Strategy of the South Pacific Forum Implementation Plan 2023–2030 goes even one step further and proposes as Regional Collective Actions the review of the framework and other regional policies, 'to ensure a regional approach to support and monitor Safe Circular Economy including Sustainable consumption (and Production)'.[81] The Strategy, thus, brought circular economy into the realm of policies on sustainability adopted in the region, which is also enriched with the unique perspective of the peoples of the region, deeply connected with their natural environment, and the related resources, livelihoods, faiths, values and traditional knowledge.[82] This unique perspective, far from decreasing the effectiveness of the circularity approach, seems to be, again, the keystone to develop and implement shared principles, while taking into due account the extraordinary rich cultural background of the region. The same approach could, and should, be promoted also in other areas where the local—including indigenous—knowledge, should not be excluded from the equation, but rather embedded in it.

[77] See SPREP, Cleaner Pacific 2025, principle 6.

[78] The Tokyo 3R Statement Towards the Establishment of Regional 3R Forum in Asia (2005). The Statement originally created a forum for cooperation among Asian countries, later extended also to Pacific countries, which now covers the whole Asia-Pacific region. The Forum also adopted the Ha Noi 3R Declaration—Sustainable 3R Goals for Asia and the Pacific for 2013–2023 (2013), a non-binding declaration in which signatories resolved to "develop, introduce, and implement policy options, programmes, and projects towards realizing the following sustainable 3R goals in the region, with an ultimate goal of achieving a resource-efficient and resilient society and transitioning to green economy".

[79] P. 41 of the Strategy.

[80] Pacific Islands Forum, 2050 Strategy for the Blue Pacific Continent (2022), p. 27.

[81] SPREP, 2050 Strategy Implementation Plan 2023–2030, Phase I - 2050 Strategy for the Blue Pacific Continent Setting the Foundations Towards Transformational Change (2022), p. 29.

[82] Pacific Islands Forum, 2050 Strategy for the Blue Pacific Continent (2022), p. 6.

8 International Cooperation

Apart from initiatives taken at the regional level or within the United Nations, sustainability has given rise to a significant effort of cooperation among different regions and organisations (as well as between States). This is an aspect that not only merits consideration, but on which particular focus should be put, since international cooperation is key to addressing the global challenge of sustainability, especially with a view of limiting climate change.

Events of global reach include the creation of the World Circular Economy Forum, which brings together key stakeholders, including representatives of the UN and the EU agencies, on a yearly basis, to discuss and lead businesses in their transition to circular economy models.

Among the numerous initiatives, the Global Alliance on Circular Economy and Resource Efficiency ('GACERE') should be surely recalled. The Alliance was launched by the EU and UNEP in February 2021, at the fifth United Nations Environment Assembly.[83] This is an alliance of national governments willing to join forces at the global level to achieve a fair circular economy, with the aim of developing sustainable production and consumption models and more sustainable management of natural resources. The Alliance counts Members from Asia, Africa and America while, for Europe, the European Union is a (founding) Member.[84] Its unique feature is that, beside Member States, it includes also other networks and organisations and has a global reach, trying to fulfil the aim of a global transition to circular economy, including a more sustainable management of natural resources. It aims, more specifically, at enhancing sectoral, bilateral and/or regional partnerships and identify gaps and best practices on circular economy worldwide.[85] However, it must be noted that GACERE still has only a few Members, albeit distributed around the world. Membership should be expanded if the alliance intends to have any significant impact.

Beside international efforts of cooperation, also other efforts to promote SCE are being conducted, for example through bilateral actions. In this context, the Memorandum of Understanding concluded between EU and China on the topic was signed in 2018.[86]

---

[83] The Alliance is the result of a joint effort by the European Commission and the United Nations Environment Programme (UNEP), in coordination with the United Nations Industrial Development Organisation (UNIDO).

[84] To date (20 March 2025), GACERE members include the EU, Canada, Chile, Colombia, Ecuador, India, Japan, Kenya, Morocco, New Zealand, Nigeria, Norway, Peru, South Korea, Rwanda, South Africa and Switzerland, as well as Mexico and Singapore as observers.

[85] Concept Note, Global Alliance on Circular Economy and Resource Efficiency (GACERE) Towards Just Transitions (2021).

[86] Commission Decision on the conclusion of a Memorandum Of Understanding on circular economy between the European Commission and the National Development and Reform Commission of the People's Republic of China, C(2018) 4382 final.

Also, at the latest meeting of the Regional 3R and Circular Economy Forum in Asia and the Pacific, the Jaipur Declaration was adopted by Member States, who shared they common vision on circularity and sustainability.[87]

Finally, within the World Economic Forum, the Platform for Accelerating the Circular Economy ('PACE') was launched. The Platform engages with key stakeholders and experts on topics identified as 'underserved and that presents an opportunity to deliver a public good',[88] in order to identify recommendations for action.

9 The Missing Piece: An International Treaty on Sustainable Circular Economy

The review just carried out has shown that, if considerable activity exists at the level of political, intergovernmental cooperation, international agreements on SCE are still lacking. At the moment, there is no international comprehensive treaty on circular economy nor has it been tabled within the United Nations.

Furthermore, the process of concluding sectoral agreements has been difficult, too. In this last respect, it is worth mentioning the disappointing progress made on the text of the global plastic pollution treaty, during the fifth session of the Intergovernmental Negotiating Committee in November 2024. During the latest negotiations, negotiators could not find a deal on some of the most delicate aspects of the treaty, such as 'a possible target of reducing the production of primary plastic polymers, bans and restrictions of chemicals of concern in plastic products, as well as problematic and avoidable plastic products'.[89]

Consequently, mechanisms to monitor whether facts follow from solemn declarations and voluntary pledges made by States or by and within international organisations are almost non-existent. In this framework, and in light of the triple planetary crisis in action, an important step forward would surely be the adoption of a global treaty on SCE, but several obstacles should be borne in mind, in this respect.

For example, the fact that the legitimacy of certain MEAs, which are already in force, has been occasionally challenged by some key States:[90] this makes it difficult

[87] Jaipur Declaration on 3R and Circular Economy. Sustainable 3R and Circular Economy Goals for Achieving Resource Efficient, Clean, Resilient, Sound Material Cycle and Low-Carbon Society in Asia and the Pacific (2025–2035).

[88] Platform for Accelerating the Circular Economy (PACE), Purpose Statement, 6 (https://pacecircular.org/sites/default/files/2023-11/Purpose_Statement.pdf).

[89] Directorate-General for Environment, 'EU regrets lack of conclusion on global plastics agreement', 2 December 2024 (https://environment.ec.europa.eu/news/eu-regrets-inconclusive-global-plastics-treaty-2024-12-02_en#:~:text="I%20strongly%20regret%20that%20there,to%20finding%20a%20global%20solution.).

[90] Most recently, the United States have notified their intention to withdraw from the Paris Agreement. See Executive Order no. 14162, Putting America First in International Environmental Agreements, 20 January 2025 (https://www.federalregister.gov/documents/2025/01/30/2025-02010/putting-america-first-in-international-environmental-agreements#page-).

to envisage the possibility of further commitments by those States who express willingness not to increase but rather to reduce their environmental commitments. The risk would be that the conclusion of such agreement takes place only among few States, thus decreasing its potential impact. Another possible difficulty could be linked to the fact that any comprehensive agreement on SCE would necessarily have to take into account the role that non-state entities play in the process, thus adding a further layer of complexity. In this connection, both producers (distinctly, as duty-bearers) and consumers, both as duty-bearers (in particular by adopting more conscious, environment-friendly practices), and as ultimate beneficiaries, together with all human-beings, of the new model of SCE, should be addressed. Such a model, in fact, would be adopted for the ultimate benefit of individuals and for the environment itself, inextricably linked to human beings and all living creatures.[91]

Nevertheless, such an agreement could, if properly drafted and implemented, bring with it several benefits: for example, it could identify minimum international legal standard that States must implement in their economies; it could contain minimum obligations for producers and connected monitoring systems; it could identify international rights of consumers and in this way, it could fill the gaps of a proper, international protection for consumers and individuals involved in the process of global transition to SCE. In this respect, such an agreement could, eventually, include detailed provisions on, for example, consumer information as well as minimum product requirements, at the same time ensuring that monitoring mechanisms, in order to strengthen compliance with the standards agreed, are put in place while, at the same time, supporting States in the shift to circularity. Such monitoring mechanisms could include, for example, periodic reports that States would have to submit to a committee of experts, to check the progress made in the implementation of the treaty. At the same time, given the active role of natural and legal persons in the transition to circular economy (producers as well as consumers), it would also be fundamental to include the possibility of individual communications. Such means would allow natural and legal persons to refer to monitoring committees cases of non-implementation of the obligations contained in the said treaty, which impinges on individuals' (especially consumers') rights. Monitoring mechanisms could be based, with due caution and with due distinctions, on models now well-settled in human rights treaties that enhance the role of individuals as beneficiaries and empower them with tools to protect their rights in case of violations.[92]

---

[91] For a sociological reconstruction of the human-centred approach at the basis of this paradigm shift see Marzulli (Chap. "'*Ubi societas ibi ius*': Centering a Sustainable Circular Economy from a Sociological Perspective"), while for an even more wide consideration of such 'human' nature as indeed implying and therefore encompassing the 'living' environment itself see De Vido (Chap. "The International Dimension of the Environment as a Legal Entity: The Human Rights of the Sustainable Consumer in an Ecological Perspective").

[92] For a contextualization of consumers' right in such an international framework see Dal Monico (Chap. "Rethinking the Role of the Consumer in a Global Economy: The Power of Choice as a 'Human Right'?").

10 Concluding Remarks: The Role of the EU, Frontrunner or One Among the Others?

As the present chapter has tried to show, circular economy has become progressively popular in recent years across the globe. Awareness of the new circular economy model is expanding internationally, and this is not limited to the European continent but goes well beyond it, with local, regional and international initiatives being autonomously carried out in all regions of the world. This feature includes intergovernmental but also private-led, informal and networking activities. The picture that results is in line with the understanding that the transition from a linear model to a circular one is not perceived as an option but as the only possible model that must be implemented in order to reach the objective of a sustainable future. Furthermore, SCE is significantly more in line with a form of development that does not see nature as a mere source to be used but rather as a relevant 'partner' that must be respected, protected and, where possible, restored.

As seen above, much progress has been made, and the circular economy is effectively now a familiar concept in all areas of the world. However, notwithstanding this positive note, there is still a long way to go to achieve a complete transition and effectively implement a circular economy. Such implementation includes the development of specific obligations incumbent on producers worldwide but also the development of new, specific rights of consumers, intended as conscious users, that are aware of their rights and have tools to have them respected. In particular, the lack of international treaties on the topic, with wide membership, shows that, on the one hand, States are still reluctant to commit to binding standards and, on the other, regional initiatives around the world still largely remain at the political level.

Furthermore, lack of coordination at the global level includes not only absence of a global treaty on circular economy, but also slow progress in some sectoral agreements (such as the plastic pollution treaty). In this framework, a partial way out of this impasse could be to bring the SCE approach into already existing MEAs or to address circularity obligations within bilateral or regional treaties, in particular by introducing provisions on SCE, as the EU has done recently.[93] While more feasible, especially if the EU is a Party to the agreement, however, this option would not address the problem of identifying internationally agreed standards on SCE, and would therefore fall short of regulating globally the phenomenon. If SCE is to become the new economic model worldwide, and it appears that, in one way or another, all areas of the world tend to agree that this is the case, international binding standards should be agreed upon. Such standards should be shared worldwide and should necessarily include big economies of the world, otherwise the risk could be that of leaving out States that mostly impact on the environment with unsustainable economic practices.

In this complex international scenario, the EU is indeed at the forefront of the promotion of SCE, having adopted very advanced rules that promote circularity,

[93] Bellmann and Sell (2021, pp. 2–3).

both among its Member States and worldwide, not only through its autonomous action but also through coordination with other international organisations and Third States. And, while internationally, stringent standards as those imposed by the EU are still lacking, this may be attributable to the more recent awareness of the relevance of this new economic model in such areas. With increased consciousness of the benefits of SCE and of the impossibility to keep the linear model worldwide,[94] stricter commitments and plans are (hopefully) to come also internationally.

This, however, should now become a priority for those countries that still lack such standards, if the transition is to become truly global. The conclusion of an international treaty on circular economy could be the first step that, while paying due attention to the peculiarities of each region, including local and indigenous knowledge, identifies binding standards that States should respect in order to achieve SCE worldwide and adequately protects the rights of individuals (as consumers, if not even as citizens) all around the globe.

References

Agreement Establishing the South Pacific Regional Environment Programme (SPREP) (1993).

Andrade C, Selosse S, Maïzi N (2021) Thirty years since the circular economy concept emerged: has it reached a consensus [research report] working paper

Arkin C, Diggs C (2022) Going back to move forward. By adopting zero waste systems, cities can redress historic injustices and cool the climate. Earth Island J 2022:55–57

Bellmann C, Sell B (2021) Options to incorporate circular economy provisions in regional trade agreements. IISD Report

Blaauw M (2021) Status of soil pollution in sub-Saharan Africa. In: FAO and UNEP, global assessment of soil pollution: report. https://doi.org/10.4060/cb4894en

Bonafe S (2020) The importance of the circular economy model. Accelerating the transition to a circular economy model is not an option, but a mandatory decision. In: Eisenriegler S (ed) The circular economy in the European Union. An interim review. Springer, Cham, pp 55–56

Bratspies RM (2013) The green economy will not build the rule of law for nature. In: Voigt C (ed) Rule of law for nature. New dimensions and ideas in environmental law. Cambridge University Press, Cambridge, pp 295–311

Castro de Hallgren S, et al (n.d.) New economics for sustainable development. Circular economy. In: New economics for sustainable development. Available via United Nations Economist Network. https://www.un.org/sites/un2.un.org/files/circular_economy_14_march.pdf

Darwish T (2021) Status of soil pollution in near east and North Africa. In: FAO and UNEP, global assessment of soil pollution: report. https://doi.org/10.4060/cb4894en

Göcke K (2013) Indigenous peoples in international law. In: Hauser-Schäublin B (ed) Adat and indigeneity in Indonesia. Göttingen University Press, Göttingen, pp 17–29

Health Effects Institute. (2022). The State of Air Quality and Health Impacts in Africa. A Report from the State of Global Air Initiative. Boston, MA:Health Effects Institute.

Käsner S-A et al (2024) Circular economy transitions in Africa: a policy perspective. In: Passaro R et al (eds) Circular economy for social transformation: multiple paths to achieve circularity. ACEN, pp 265–278

[94] Bonafe (2020).

Kolesch N et al (2022) Closing the "circularity gaps": practical strategies to address key challenges undermining the collective goal of a global circular economy of plastics. In: Prospects for transitioning from a linear to circular economy in developing Asia. Asian Development Bank Institute, pp 63–77

Maitre-Ekern E (2021) Re-thinking producer responsibility for a sustainable circular economy from extended producer responsibility to pre-market producer responsibility. J Clean Prod 286:1–11

Mandizvidza C, Makhanda R (2024) Circular Economy (CE) in African countries. In: Passaro R et al (eds) Circular economy for social transformation: multiple paths to achieve circularity. SEERC, pp 248–264

Pearce DW, Turner KR (1990) Economics of natural resources and environment. Johns Hopkins University Press

Sachdeva A, Srivastava A (2022) Extended producer responsibility: lessons for realizing and implementing a circular economy for plastics in Asia. In: Prospects for transitioning from a linear to circular economy in developing Asia. Asian Development Bank Institute, pp 93–109

Takase C (2005) Changing consumption and production patterns—the Marrakech process. Nat Res Forum 29:404–407

Taremwa NK et al (2024) Indigenous knowledge and circular agro-economy: universities as co-creation partners for sustainable agriculture in Rwanda. In: Filho Leal W et al (eds) University initiatives on climate change education and research. Springer, Cham, pp 1–25

Vedder H (2012) The formalities and substance of EU external environmental competence: stuck between climate change and competitiveness. In: Morgera E (ed) The external environmental policy of the European Union. EU and international law perspectives. Cambridge University Press, Cambridge, pp 11–32

Voigt V (2015) Sustainable patterns of production and consumption and demographic policies. In: Viuales J (ed) The Rio declaration on environment and development a commentary. Oxford University Press, Oxford, pp 245–268

Washington H (2015) Is 'sustainability' the same as 'sustainable development'? In: Kopnina H, Shoreman-Ouimet E (eds) Sustainability key issues. Routledge, London, pp 359–376

Rethinking the Role of the Consumer in a Global Economy: The Power of Choice as a 'Human Right'?

Sara Dal Monico

Abstract The purpose of this chapter is to reconsider the role of consumers as 'sustainable' consumers (or even 'sustainable' users) in a global economy. The premise upon which the chapter is built is that both the digital and environmental challenges have imposed a shift in the way in which individuals approach consumption. In a circular economy-oriented model, the very notion of consumers seems outdated, as this economic model strives towards the recycling and reuse of goods, challenging the consumeristic approach which has so far characterized most economic models, including the European one. At the same time, said challenges have, in some ways, strengthened the position of consumers and the power that they hold. Indeed, consumers' attention towards the sustainability of certain products, their interest towards the protection of the environment can have an important impact on businesses' compliance with sustainability rules. The power of choice which consumers have can greatly influence and contribute to shifting towards a circular economy model focused on sustainability and environmental protection. Starting from this assumption, the chapter tries to pin-point how consumer protection is (if at all) approached at the international legal level. It reflects on whether it is possible to talk about global consumer law at all, and whether the intersection between consumer rights, the environment, and sustainability has been acknowledged by international legal instruments. The chapter will delve into consumer rights as an innovative way of conceptualising human rights and will try to evaluate whether it is possible to talk about consumer rights as human rights. In this context, particular attention will be devoted to the right of access to information, considered as the backbone of consumers' power of choice. Furthermore, the contribution will try to move a step further and propose a conceptualization of consumer rights which is not only human-centric, rather eco-centric, thus approached in a holistic way, with consumer rights being instrumental in achieving environmental protection and sustainability.

S. Dal Monico (✉)
Università Ca' Foscari, Venice, Italy
e-mail: sara.dalmonico@unive.it

B. Calabrese (ed.), *Legal Perspectives for a Sustainable Circular Economy*, European Union and its Neighbours in a Globalized World 30,
https://doi.org/10.1007/978-3-032-07795-0_12

1 Introduction

The purpose of this chapter is to rethink the role of consumers as 'sustainable' consumers (or even sustainable 'users') in a global economy by looking at the human rights dimension related to consumerism. The contribution investigates an issue which is crucial within the broader context of a sustainable circular economy: is it possible to talk about consumers' human rights? In establishing whether it is indeed possible to assess the emergence of new human rights specifically safeguarding the individual as a consumer, the contribution reflects on that set of rights and, eventually, on whether a right to free, informed, and sustainable choice exists in its own legitimacy, in an attempt to propose the conceptualization of a new catalogue of rights of consumers.

The premise upon which the chapter is built is that both the digital and environmental challenges have imposed a shift in the way in which individuals approach consumption. The very notion of 'consumer' is to be challenged, especially if a change towards a circular economy is to be fostered and promoted. In a circular economy-oriented model, the concept of *consumers* should be considered outdated, as this economic model strives towards the recycling, repair and reuse of goods, challenging the consumeristic approach which has so far characterized most economic linear models, tossing aside the outdated "buy, use, toss" model typical of many economic systems, including the European one.[1] At the same time, said challenges have in some way strengthened the position of consumers and the power that they hold. Indeed, consumers' attention towards the sustainability of certain products, their interest towards the protection of the environment and of non-human animals can have an important impact on businesses' compliance with sustainability rules. The power of choice which consumers have can influence greatly and contribute to shifting towards a circular economy model focused on sustainability and environmental protection.[2] But does that power correspond to an established right?

Starting from the assumption that the very notion of consumer should be challenged in a circular economy-oriented model, the chapter first tries to pin-point how consumer protection is (if at all) approached at the international legal level. It reflects on whether it is possible to talk about global consumer law at all, and whether the intersection between consumer rights, the environment, and sustainability has been acknowledged by international legal instruments. Secondly, the chapter will delve into consumer rights as an innovative way of conceptualising human rights and will try to evaluate whether it is possible to talk about consumer rights as human rights. In this context, particular attention will be devoted to the

[1] In this sense, more in depth about the so-called 'right to repair' see Calabrese (Chap. "Right to Repair Between Intellectual Property and Servitization").

[2] In the same paradigmatic context, for a specific analysis of consumers' powers and responsibilities under EU law see Deana (Chap. "Reshaping Consumer Powers and Responsibilities in the European Union's Transition to a Sustainable Circular Economy"). On the close connection between circular economy, sustainability and environmental protection, see: Backes (2017), Ferrara (2018); Wright and others (2019); Ellen MacArthur Foundation (2021).

right of access to information, considered as the backbone of consumer's power of choice. Disinformation and greenwashing practices, in this sense, constitute obstacles to be overcome and to be tackled with a restrictive approach, though the challenge on a global scale is not to be underestimated. Lastly, the chapter will try to move past the anthropocentric conceptualization of law and human rights, proposing a conceptualization of consumer rights which is not only human-centric, but also eco-centric, thus approached in a holistic way, with consumer rights being instrumental in achieving environmental protection and sustainability and which need to be read in light of the human right to a healthy environment.[3] In doing so, it will focus on the notion of the consumer itself as contradictory in the context of sustainable circular economy.

2 Global Consumer Law: Myth or Evolving Reality?

The global scale and international dimension of consumerism are an apparent fact. The globalisation and digitalization of commerce, leading to an easy access to the international market, in an interconnected world, has enlarged the boundaries of what consumers can reach to the global level, and consequently brought about the issue of their protection as the weaker party as opposed to traders, internationally.[4] Moreover, some recent global consumer law scandals, such as the Apple and Dieselgate cases,[5] urge to reflect on the significance and relevance of consumer protection on a global level, as well as to picture consumer protection more broadly. Notwithstanding the international dimension within which consumers move, the legal response to this issue has been lacking. Other fields, such as economics and political studies, have been more responsive to the phenomenon, but as far as (public) international law goes, the matter has not received the attention it deserves. This becomes even more pressing from a circular economy perspective, which aims at changing the economic model in a contemporary world still heavily anchored to linear logics of consumerism.

Despite the scattered and unharmonized tendency to develop supranational rules for consumer protection, attempts have been more regional than international, with the European Union at the forefront in terms of consumer protection rules,[6] and soft

---

[3] More broadly in this perspective see De Vido (Chap. "The International Dimension of the Environment as a Legal Entity: The Human Rights of the Sustainable Consumer in an Ecological Perspective").

[4] Durovic and Micklitz (2017, p. 1), see also: Lima Marques (2020).

[5] As reported by Durovic (2020, p. 126).

[6] In addition to Deana (Chap. "Reshaping Consumer Powers and Responsibilities in the European Union's Transition to a Sustainable Circular Economy"), see the specific reconstruction of private international law by Bergamini (Chap. "Dispute Resolution and Private International Law in the Context of Circular Economy: Effectiveness Beyond Alternatives"). See also: Lima Marques (2020).

law attempts at the international level, the most relevant of which is the United Nations (UN) Guidelines for Consumer Protection (hereinafter 'UN Guidelines').[7] This set of principles, which aims at establishing 'the main characteristics of effective consumer protection legislation, enforcement institutions and redress systems',[8] was developed by the UN Conference on Trade and Development (UNCTAD). The Guidelines apply to business-to-consumer (B2C) transactions, including amongst businesses also State-owned enterprises, and from the very beginning, in laying out the objectives, the edited version of 2016 established the close link between consumer protection and sustainability, alongside environmental protection.[9] They also underline the necessity to protect consumers due to the imbalance of power, information, and economic power as opposed to businesses.[10]

As guidelines, the instrument has a non-binding character; they set out standards and good practices to follow, but do not provide legally binding solutions concerning consumer protection. Despite being a soft law instrument, the adoption of the UN Guidelines has helped to generate a consensus around minimum standards of protection for consumers and have been adopted (though on a voluntary basis) by corporations world-wide, probably due to their voluntary commitment basis, as businesses may feel more inclined to decide which practices to follow instead of undergoing their enforcement.[11] The noteworthy role of the UN Guidelines is exemplified by their wide implementation by UNCTAD Member States,[12] not to mention their unanimous adoption,[13] as well as by their attempt at harmonizing practices in an extremely scattered scenario, though some scholars point to the fact that their drafting was framed around other, more advanced regimes—such as the European one—becoming a model to be extensively used worldwide.[14] However, their lack of bindingness is a double-edged sword, with positive implications on one side (indeed, a voluntary basis can enhance implementation) and negative ones, such as the

[7] United Nations Guidelines for Consumer Protection (2016), UNCTAD/DITC/CPLP/MISC/2016/1 (https://unctad.org/system/files/official-document/ditccplpmisc2016d1_en.pdf)

[8] UN Guidelines for Consumer Protection (2016, p. 3).

[9] When first drafted in 1985, the UN Guidelines for Consumer Protection did not include sustainability references or provisions dedicated to sustainable consumption. Such modifications were first added in the 1999 revision, during which sustainable consumption was introduced, and later in a second revision in 2016, which added good practices concerning business conduct in B2C relations, as well as provisions concerning dispute resolution and consumer redress. See: Durovic and Micklitz (2017, p. 6).

[10] UN Guidelines for Consumer Protection (2016), secs. I and II (respectively, 'Objectives' and 'Scope').

[11] Durovic (2020, p. 129).

[12] UNCTAD, Report of the Eighth United Nations Conference to Review All Aspects of the Set of Multilaterally Agreed Equitable Principles and Rules for the Control of Restrictive Business Practices (2020), TD/RBP/CONF.9/2, para. 1.

[13] De Melo (2020, p. 3).

[14] Durovic (2020, p. 129).

problematic aspect of the enforcement of the standards and principles set out by the UN Guidelines.[15]

As per the scope of the UN Guidelines, the establishment of a common and minimum benchmark for consumer protection was indicated, an attempt in harmonizing standards (which is not a mandatory obligation, though), below which the Member States (MS) should not descend.[16] This benchmark can be found within the 'General Principles' (Sect. 3), that outline the 'legitimate needs which the guidelines are intended to meet',[17] to which corresponds a set of rights of consumers, such as: the right to access to essential goods and services; the right to dispute resolution and redress; the right to privacy and the right to consumer education; and, particularly relevant for the purposes of this contribution, the right to access to adequate information to make informed choices. The principle of promotion of sustainable patterns of consumption is also mentioned by the UN Guidelines, as per the revision they underwent in 2016.[18] With the rights comes also a set of principles for good business practices (Sect. 4), directly targeting businesses' conducts, as opposed to the general principles mentioned above targeting States' behaviour. Such principles include: the fair and equitable treatment of consumers; legal, non-discriminatory and ethical business conduct; disclosure and transparency; education and awareness raising; privacy protection; and easy access to dispute resolution for consumers' complaints.[19]

Alongside the UN Guidelines and the role of the UNCTAD in promoting standards and practices relevant to consumer protection, the role of the Organization for Economic Cooperation and Development (OECD) is noteworthy. The role of the organization has been that of developing policy papers and briefs aimed at supporting the MS in implementing and improving their consumer law provisions, working on issues such as consumer vulnerability[20] and the digital dimension of consumerism.[21] An intergovernmental forum addressing a broad range of consumer issues, the Committee on Consumer Policy (CCP), was also established under the OECD, with a mandate aimed at promoting consumer welfare, particularly focusing on empowering consumers to make well-informed decisions as well as protecting them from misleading, deceptive, fraudulent, and unfair practices. The OECD has also adopted declarations (again non-binding) on consumer issues, such as the 'Declaration on Protecting and Empowering Consumers in the Digital and Green Transitions', where MS of the organization have committed to take action to reduce digital harms targeting consumers (particularly vulnerable ones) and to encourage businesses to act in good faith, paying due regard to consumers interests; as well as

[15] Durovic (2020, p. 130).

[16] Durovic (2020, p. 131).

[17] UN Guidelines for Consumer Protection (2016), sec. III, para. 5.

[18] UN Guidelines for Consumer Protection (2016), sec. III, para. 5(a)–(k).

[19] UN Guidelines for Consumer Protection (2016), sec. IV, para. 11(a)–(f).

[20] OECD (2023).

[21] OECD (2022).

strengthening consumer protection against deceptive and misleading environmental claims; empowering consumers' access to accessible information; and strengthening cooperation amongst the MS to address such issues.[22] However, the outreach of the CCP and of the OECD more in general has been rather limited due to the fact that the organization counts 38 Member States, mostly developed country, hence attracting some criticism for lacking a 'proper global representative character'.[23]

Notwithstanding the initiatives undertaken at the international level by the UN, and by organizations such as the OECD, which, despite a global vocation, have more of a regional focus, it is yet too early to discuss about the existence of an actual global consumer law. Indeed, such attempts comprise mostly (if not only) soft law instruments lacking binding character, which results in different legal regimes applicable to consumers worldwide. Though it was argued that 'the focus of international consumer law should not be on the development of unified substantive rules on consumer protection, but on the securement of adequate enforcement of consumer law',[24] the international legal system has yet to produce a harmonized and uniform system of enforceable rules of consumer law, thus leaving an important legal void in the international legal framework. The need to fill such void became necessary with the development of the international market and the continuously growing interconnection among economic systems, yet it becomes even more apparent and urgent in light of the need to shift the linear economic model to a circular one, as well as of the growing environmental concerns.

3 Human Rights Law as a Possible Avenue to Enhance Consumer Rights?

Despite some noteworthy soft law attempts to tackle the issue, up until the date in which this chapter is being drafted, the legal efforts expressly dedicated to consumer rights are clearly of regional vocation, with the European Union being at the forefront of the matter. Thus, it is not yet possible to draw the contours of an international legal framework for consumer rights. The lacking framework at the international level generates a legal void concerning consumer protection, which could potentially be addressed by human rights. However, in this regard, two sets of questions arise: can consumer rights be construed as human rights? If so, is it worthwhile?

[22] OECD (2024).

[23] Durovic (2020, p. 129).

[24] Durovic (2020, p. 140).

3.1 *Consumer Rights as Emerging Human Rights?*

Conceptualising consumer rights as human rights has sparked a lively debate in legal scholarship, which saw some initial contributions already in the 1990s,[25] with several scholars arguing in favour of the recognition of a human rights dimension for consumers, not only to ensure legal protection, but essentially because the 'consumer dimension' is a feature characterising everyone living in the twenty-first century.[26] According to De Melo, consumption should be characterised as a universal necessity, thus consumer protection would be 'crucial to achieve and maintain human dignity'.[27] At the international level, human rights do offer a possible framework for the protection of consumers. Indeed, the peculiar aspect of human rights is their justiciability: the possibility to invoke such rights in front of international human rights courts offers a way through which consumer protection can be approached. The question remains as to whether consumer rights can be effectively conceptualized as human rights, if it is possible to conceive a new generation of human rights dealing specifically with consumer rights or if, on the other hand, consumer rights must be anchored to other already existing human rights. In Deutsch's conceptualization,[28] two sets of issues contribute to furthering this argument: a political one and a strictly legal one, which intertwine. Moving from Deutsch's argument, the following paragraphs will retrace and add to the debate concerning consumers' human rights in light of the shift towards a sustainable circular economy.

3.2 *The Political Argument*

From the political perspective—which also interweaves with socio-economic considerations[29]—protecting consumers on a broader level is essential for the functioning of modern societies. For the purposes of this contribution, it is posited that the protection of consumers is essential not only for the enhancement of the linear model, but even more so for the shift towards a circular economy oriented model.

[25] Deutch (1994), who spoke of consumer rights as *soft* human rights, focusing on their non-binding character (since at the time the author recognised that it was still too premature to infer that a formal recognition of consumer rights as human rights had been established).

[26] See: Benöhr (2013), De Melo (2020), Lesniewska and Steenmans (2023), Tambussi (2014), Ukwueze (2015), Wacinkiewicz (2013). In particular, De Melo (2020, pp. 11–15) offers philosophical insights as to why consumer rights should be regarded as human rights, aside from the legal arguments in favour of such recognition.

[27] De Melo (2020, p. 3).

[28] Deutch (1994).

[29] For the relevance of a sociological contextualization of the research topics at hand see Marzulli (Chap. "'*Ubi societas ibi ius*': Centering a Sustainable Circular Economy from a Sociological Perspective").

Consumers (or rather 'users' in a circular economy) would be one of the key instruments through which such shift can be achieved, by educating them at orienting their preferences towards goods and services enhancing circularity and sustainability. Moreover, it is possible to argue that being a consumer is a feature that characterizes the lives of a large number of individuals worldwide, not necessarily only those living in Western societies.[30] Notwithstanding the neoliberal and westernized approach to consumption and more specifically towards consumerism, being a consumer is a feature which belongs to every individual as an actor in the economic market(s), thus also displaying the element characterising human rights in general.[31] Therefore, protecting individuals in a specific moment of their lives—when they become involved in consumption choices, approaching the economic market(s)—is a necessity which should not be overlooked. This becomes more pressing when considering the proposed shift towards circularity, which can be enhanced by protecting consumers' rights to make sustainable choices oriented towards a circular economy.

3.3 *The Legal Argument*

From a strictly legal perspective, having established the universal character of consumer rights, it still remains to be settled, on the one hand, what is the value being protected by recognising consumer rights as human rights, and on the other, if and how consumer rights can be defined as human rights. One of the critiques advanced in this debate is that consumer rights need not be protected as human rights, since the latter are aimed at protecting fundamental values which may be undermined if their boundaries are stretched too far. Yet, it is widely recognised that human rights

[30] Although it can undoubtedly be argued that consumerism is a Westernized concept, which has evolved in Western societies and has been shaped by them, it is also undeniable that this activity affects most individuals living in a globalized society. However, it is necessary to stress that the way in which consumerism has been approached, conceptualized, and enacted is the product of a Western mindset, following the logic of the "take-make-dispose" model, also described as "extract-transform-dispose" if the colonial perspective is added. The logic behind consumerism is, therefore, to be criticized and revisited to foster a change towards a circular economy-oriented model, which approaches consumption in a decolonized, eco-centric, and inclusive way. In addition to De Vido (Chap. "The International Dimension of the Environment as a Legal Entity: The Human Rights of the Sustainable Consumer in an Ecological Perspective"), see Cabrales Salazar et al. (2021).

[31] In support of the universality of consumer protection and, consequently, of their rights, it should be highlighted that the UN Guidelines state within their objectives that such measures are to be enacted 'taking into account the interests and needs of consumers in all Member States, *particularly in developing ones*' (emphasis added: UN Guidelines for Consumer Protection (2016), sec. I, para. 1). Thus, despite the Westernized conceptualization of consumer rights, the UN has recognized that this feature belongs to all individuals, even in developing countries, who may be consumers from time to time, thus underscoring the universal component of consumer rights and protection. See Deutch (1994), Wacinkiewicz (2013), Benöhr (2013).

are not set in stone,[32] and that they are bound to evolve according to how societies themselves evolve and change, with the range of interests protected possibly expanding. Some recent examples can be found in the emergence of a human right to a healthy environment, recognised both at the UN level[33] and by legal scholarship;[34] as well as, for instance, the set of human rights connected to the digital age, such as the right to privacy in the digital age.[35] Whereas some are more linked and find their legitimacy within other previously existing rights, such as the right to privacy in the digital age, the example of the human right to a healthy environment clearly has emerged in its own legitimacy, despite being connected to several others—right to life, right to health, right an adequate standard of living, right to food.

As for their value, consumer rights are inextricably linked with human dignity.[36] This view is shared also by who posits that, in a consumer society, the protection of the individual in their feature as a consumer is 'part of maintaining human dignity. If not given the right to fair trade, the right to a fair contract, and the right of access to courts, a person's dignity is disregarded. At the end of the day, these rights are no less important than other human rights'.[37] To this argument, which dates back to 1994, we would argue that in light of the purpose of shifting away from linear economic models favouring a more sustainable and circular approach to economy, from the consumer to the user, ensuring such protection is pivotal and even more entrenched in dignity. Recognising that consumer rights as human rights ultimately safeguard individuals' dignity meets, according to such line of reasoning, the substantive test for human rights, providing additional support to the theory.[38]

The substantive test alone cannot support the theory; hence, further legal considerations need to and can be advanced to further the human rights dimension of consumer rights. Such proposals revolve around the already mentioned justiciability of human rights and the rebalancing of unequal powers between consumers and corporations. As for the first aspect, the lack of an international legal framework ensuring consumer protection has been mentioned. However, it should be noticed that, as far as activities carried out by consumers having a transnational component

[32] On the matter, see among others: Buergenthal (2006), Charlesworth and Chinkin (2000), Ruggie (2007), Gros Espiell (1979).

[33] HRC (2021), A/HRC/RES/48/13; UNGA (2022), A/RES/76/300. See also the reports by the Special Rapporteur on the human right to a healthy environment (https://www.ohchr.org/en/documents-listing?field_content_category_target_id%5B186%5D=186&field_entity_target_id%5B1281%5D=1281)

[34] See among others: Giorgetta (2002), Boyd (2011), Knox (2020), Knox and Pejan (2018), Cima (2022). Moreover, within the research perspective at hand, see De Vido (Chap. "The International Dimension of the Environment as a Legal Entity: The Human rights of the Sustainable Consumer in an Ecological Perspective").

[35] HRC (2018b).

[36] As highlighted by De Melo (2020).

[37] Deutch (1994, p. 552).

[38] Deutch (1994, pp. 551–554).

go, the field of private international law may fit into the picture.[39] Yet, this instrument is not incompatible with the recognition of consumer rights as human rights, as this offers a further level of protection, which should therefore be developed alongside other instruments for protection. Indeed, access to remedies at the international level and the justiciability of consumer rights in front of human rights courts would allow further safeguarding of consumer rights in cases in which national legal systems fail to do so. In regard to the latter consideration, namely that conceptualizing consumer rights as human rights would allow a rebalancing of powers in a clearly unbalanced position of the subjects involved, a parallel has been drawn between the way in which human rights ultimately aim at protecting individuals from the arbitrary infringements by governments and the relation between consumers and corporations.[40] There is a clear imbalance between the position of consumers and that of corporations (as there is between individuals and governments), and the underlying scope of consumer rights is that of rebalancing such unequal positions, thus adding the equity criterion to support the theory.

Aside from the substantive test, there is also a procedural test for human rights,[41] namely if such rights have been recognised in any legal document. At the international level, as established, there is no formal recognition of consumer rights as human rights, not even within the UN Guidelines, which nonetheless set rights for consumers to ensure their enjoyment of the right to 'just, equitable and sustainable economic and social development'.[42] Moreover, the adoption of the UN Guidelines themselves, though a soft law instrument, does attest to a formal recognition at the international level that consumer protection is not a matter relating to domestic systems only, rather an issue deserving attention at the international level as well.[43]

UNCTAD's Manual for Consumer Protection[44] reports that by 2018, 24 countries provided consumer protection within their constitutions, as well as underscored that 'in many cases, consumer protection has been constitutionally enshrined, and some countries have recognised consumer rights as human rights'.[45] Within the European Union, consumer protection is provided for at Article 169 TFEU, which states that: 'in order to promote the interests of consumers and to ensure a high level

[39] Due to space constraints, the contribution will not venture into detailing the pros and cons of the private international law field in the context of consumer protection, which has been duly acknowledged by legal scholarship. On the matter, in addition to the specific analysis put forward in this research context by Bergamini (Chap. "Dispute Resolution and Private International Law in the Context of Circular Economy: Effectiveness Beyond Alternatives"), see: Lima Marques (2006), Schu (1997), Arroyo (2012).

[40] Deutch (1994, p. 552).

[41] Deutch (1994, p. 557).

[42] UN Guidelines for Consumer Protection (2016), sec. I, para. 1.

[43] See again Deutch (1994).

[44] UN Manual on Consumer Protection (2017), UNCTAD/DITC/CPLP/2017/1, p. 17

[45] Ibid. Mexico, El Salvador, Egypt, Poland and Switzerland are among the countries which have recognized a human rights dimension to consumer rights, though significant differences can be highlighted in terms of content.

of consumer protection, the Union shall contribute to protecting the health, safety and economic interests of consumers, as well as to promoting their right to information, education and to organise themselves in order to safeguard their interests',[46] which is to be read together with Article 12 TFEU, stating that in defining policies and activities the EU must take into account consumer protection.[47] Consumer protection is also mentioned within the European Charter of Fundamental Rights, at Article 38, under the Chapter dedicated to 'solidarity', which sets out the requirement for a high level of consumer protection.[48] A growing trend toward the recognition of consumer rights at the constitutional level can be noticed, denoting their acceptance as fundamental rights.

In terms of the positioning of consumer rights as human rights, scholars have posited that they may be considered a special category of human rights;[49] a new (or third)[50] generation of human rights,[51] or simply as new and emerging human rights. The argument advanced for conceptualizing consumer rights as a special category lies in the assumption that they complement the general category of human rights by strengthening the legal protection granted to individuals in their capacity as actors approaching the market(s).[52] However, the 'speciality' argument does not find resonance in legal scholarship, as there are no recognised special categories of human rights. Considering consumer rights as special would attach more of a moral value to them, rather than being a legal attribute. Furthermore, being consumer rights a category in-between economic, social and cultural rights and civil and political rights, it seems that attaching a special attribute to them privileges the feature of the individual as an actor of the market, thus deserving special protection because they are consumers, rather than protecting the individual itself.

As for the argument concerning the generations of human rights, we welcome and share the critique that the 'generational metaphor in human rights law is controversial'.[53] Indeed, fitting human rights neatly into categories is rather challenging, considering that the interconnectedness and link among human rights have been recognised by scholars as well as in the jurisprudence of human rights Courts. To further such an argument, the example of the right to freedom of thought, con-

[46] Blanke and Mangiameli (2021).

[47] Blanke and Mangiameli (2021).

[48] In this regard see also Benöhr (2013).

[49] Wacinkiewicz (2013).

[50] The characterization of consumer rights as a third generation of human rights was rendered by Deutch (1994), at a time in which there were only two recognized generations of human rights, with some others still forming. For instance, less than a decade later, Charlesworth and Chinkin (2000) described the third generation of human rights as the rights of peoples or collective rights, which include for instance the right to self-determination and the right to development. These were rights which were not yet enshrined in legally binding documents (with the exception of the right to self-determination) but rather within soft law instruments..

[51] Deutch (1994), Benöhr (2013).

[52] Wacinkiewicz (2013).

[53] Charlesworth and Chinkin (2000, p. 204).

science, and religion is proposed, which has classically been positioned within civil rights as a 'quintessential individual civil right'.[54] Nonetheless, individuals form their thoughts and beliefs according to their culture, through education, and expresses them through their language, all of which are defined as economic, social, and cultural rights. Digging deeper, culture and education can only be fully enjoyed through an adequate standard of living and health, all of which are, once again, associated with economic, cultural, and social rights.[55] The close connection and interrelation among different human rights are somehow diminished by a neat categorization into different generations.

A similar reasoning can be applied to consumer rights, which furthers the notion that considering them as a new generation of human rights would be detrimental, rather than conceptualizing them simply as emerging human rights. If one were to contemplate the rights which have emerged as a consequence of the principles expressed within the UN Guidelines, such as the right of access to essential goods and services, the right to dispute resolution and redress, and the right to consumer education,[56] as well as the list proposed by Wacinkiewic of possible consumer human rights, such as the right to be informed, the right to safety and health, the right to choose, and the right to a healthy environment,[57] the connection with other already legally recognized human rights becomes apparent. What becomes even more apparent is the difficulty in clearly separating consumer rights from other human rights and placing them into neat and distinct categories.

Having met both the substantive and procedural tests, it is possible to infer that consumer rights may be considered human rights. Though they have not been recognised as such in binding documents at the international level, State practice of providing constitutional protection to consumer rights, as well as the recognition at the UN level and regionally at the EU level of consumer protection, seems to support the trend of recognition of the human rights dimension of consumer rights. This becomes even more necessary if entered into the larger picture of the shift towards a sustainable circular economy, and a human rights-based approach becomes decisive in light of the fact that the consumer may refer to different groups according to their age, their social and cultural background, which may, through an intersectional lens, exacerbate vulnerability conditions in their role as consumers.[58]

---

[54] Charlesworth and Chinkin (2000, p. 206).

[55] Again, Charlesworth and Chinkin (2000, p. 206).

[56] UN Guidelines for Consumer Protection (2016).

[57] Wacinkiewicz (2013).

[58] See: Federico (2024), OECD (2023). The definition of vulnerable consumer has been offered by a European Commission (2016), in the context of a study which defined the vulnerable consumer as 'a consumer, who, as a result of socio-demographic characteristics, behavioural characteristics, personal situation, or market environment: (1) Is at higher risk of experiencing negative outcomes in the market; (2) Has limited ability to maximise their well-being; (3) Has difficulty in obtaining or assimilating information; (4) Is less able to buy, choose or access suitable products; or (5) Is more susceptible to certain marketing practices'. Along the same line see OECD (2024).

4 The Right to Free, Informed, and Sustainable Choice in Sustainable Consumption

The aim of this contribution is, aside from establishing that consumers' rights can be considered human rights, to assess how the sustainable circular economy dimension affects, if at all, consumers' human rights and whether it is possible to establish that a human right to free, informed, and sustainable choice exists. It was already established that it is difficult and counterproductive to neatly separate human rights into different categories, and this can be found also in the context of consumers' rights, especially if the issue is approached from an eco-centric perspective. Indeed, in order to foster a change which is truly sustainable, consumers' rights need to be thought of with a broader conceptualization, beyond the only-human dimension, and by enhancing a perspective which takes into account the environment as an entity which encompasses also (but not only) humans.[59]

The right to free, informed, and sustainable choice could be located at the intersection of the right to access to information, the right to a healthy environment, and the right to sustainable development. It needs to be established whether such a right has emerged as having its own legal standing or if it has to be derived from one of the aforementioned rights. In order to do that, this Section will first provide a framework for the existence of the right to free, informed, and sustainable choice in the context of circular economy, to later reflect on the pieces of legislation which support its conceptualization.

The right to free, informed, and sustainable choices in sustainable consumption is crucial in circular economy, not only as a catalyst to foster change but also as a pillar of the new economic model and of the protection of the environment. Being able to make decisions which are free, informed, and sustainable is determinant in empowering consumers for the transition to a sustainable circular economy.[60] More specifically, decisions that are: free, i.e. not the result of manipulated, greenwashed, and false information, and made on a voluntary basis; informed, i.e. meaning that the information is accessible, easy to understand, and that the consumer is aware and educated about the implications of that choice, not only economically but also environmentally and socially;[61] and sustainable, i.e. in accordance with the principles of a sustainable, circular economy.

[59] See more specifically De Vido (Chap. "The International Dimension of the Environment as a Legal Entity: The Human Rights of the Sustainable Consumer in an Ecological Perspective").

[60] OECD (2024). See also: Geissdoerfer and others (2017), Lesniewska and Steenmans (2023), Thomas (2020).

[61] In particular, OECD (2024, p. 7), recognized that among the risks faced by consumers, especially in the digital world, there are: 'manipulative, coercive, deceptive, or addictive online design techniques; fake reviews; exploitative personalisation; pervasive and extensive data collection, tracking and sharing; the exploitation of behavioural biases and information asymmetries; algorithmic discrimination; fraud; sophisticated scams; counterfeit goods; and access to unsafe products'. See also: Lesniewska and Steenmans (2023).

In addition, OECD Member States recognised expressly that 'consumers have the power to collectively influence businesses conduct' and that 'evidence indicates that many consumers globally would like to make more sustainable choices to mitigate the pace and gravity of climate change, depletion of natural resources, biodiversity loss, pollution, and other environmental harms, but often face a number of obstacles that prevent them from acting on their preferences and undermine consumer choice'.[62] The necessity to empower consumers for the green transition clearly emerges: the green transition and circular economy go hand in hand, with consumer empowerment and the circular economy serving as both pillars and catalysts for the green transition. In short, one cannot be achieved without the other. Consumers' choices weigh not only in terms of the inner workings of international and internal markets, but also in terms of fostering chances. For instance, consumption is among the leading causes of biodiversity loss, habitat fragmentation, deforestations, and non-human animals' extinctions.[63] Changing consumers' habits, empowering their ability to make sustainable choices is not only a necessity concerning circular economy, but an environmental urgency.

To empower consumers to make those decisions, the European Union adopted Directive (EU) 2024/825, amending Directive (EC) 2005/29 on empowering consumers for the green transition. Within the Impact Assessment Report which accompanied the proposal, the Commission highlighted how supplying reliable information for consumers to facilitate buying environmentally sustainable products was an important concern addressed by the proposal, alongside their protection against unfair commercial practices.[64] Indeed, the specific aims of this Directive are to enable informed purchasing decisions by consumers to foster sustainable consumption by providing better information, and, on the other hand, to eliminate misleading practices, guaranteeing better protection against unfair conducts. All in all, what these two aims entail is the protection of the right to make choices in consumption.[65] Free, informed, and, in the context of the green transition, sustainable choices. The same underlying goal of protecting consumers' right to choose is enshrined in Directive (EU) 2011/83, also known as Consumer Rights Directive.[66]

Within the EU Framework, which, as mentioned, is at the forefront in terms of protection of consumers, it is also in the final phases of negotiation the so-called 'Green Claims Directive',[67] a piece of legislation whose overall aim is to protect consumers from further aspects of greenwashing.[68] The underlying goal of this proposal too is the protection of consumers' choices, of their ability to make free

---

[62] OECD (2024, p. 5).

[63] Shoreman-Ouimet and Kopnina (2015), Ellen MacArthur Foundation (2021).

[64] European Commission (2022).

[65] See again European Commission (2022); see also Caterina (2012).

[66] Directive (EU) 2011/83 on consumer rights.

[67] Proposal for a Directive of the European Parliament and of the Council on substantiation and communication of explicit environmental claims, (COM) 2023 166 final.

[68] On this perspective, see Nemes et al. (2022).

choices which are not manipulated by unfair practices or unreliable or false information. This proposal would not only protect consumers in their purchasing choices but would also foster their education as sustainable consumers, since information should be accessible and verifiable, thus allowing for the creation of the appropriate conditions for them to understand and decide on their own terms.

In a 2020 resolution concerning the European Green Deal, the European Parliament had stressed the importance of empowering consumers to act as well-informed consumers, in an effort to enhance the shift towards a green and sustainable economy, and also to ensure that 'consumers are provided with transparent, comparable, and harmonised product information, including the labelling of products, based on solid data and consumer research, to help them make healthier and more sustainable choices'.[69] Accessing information is therefore key to the protection of consumers' choices. In this sense, it can be affirmed that the right to information is a human right which assumes significant relevance in the context of consumer rights and the circular economy. The right to information is the backbone of consumer protection, aimed at rebalancing the inherent vulnerability of consumers and the asymmetry between consumers and market operators.[70]

The right to information is also a pillar in the context of environmental protection. The UNECE Convention on access to information, public participation in decision-making and access to justice in environmental matters of 1998 (Aarhus Convention)[71] enshrines such right and encapsulates the significance of having access to information—reliable and verifiable—when it comes to environmental matters. Worthy of notice is that within the Preamble of the Convention 'the importance of adequate product information being provided to consumers to enable them to make informed environmental choices' is recalled, and that, when dealing with the collection and dissemination of environmental information, it is provided for Parties to 'develop mechanisms with a view to ensuring that sufficient product information is made available to the public in a manner which enables consumers to make informed environmental *choices*'.[72]

The crucial role of accessing environmental information is also recalled at UN level within the Framework Principles elaborated by the Special Rapporteur on the human right to a safe, clean, healthy, and sustainable environment in 2018.[73] The aim of the report was to provide guiding principles concerning the human right to a healthy environment, setting out State's obligations under human rights law in relation to the enjoyment of a safe, clean, healthy, and sustainable environment.[74] Specifically, Framework Principle Number 7 states that 'States should provide pub-

[69] European Parliament Resolution of 15 January 2020 on the European Green Deal, 2019/2956/(RSP). See also the relevant Briefing by European Parliament (2024).

[70] Benöhr (2013, p. 157).

[71] Further on this Convention see De Vido (Chap. "The International Dimension of the Environment as a Legal Entity: The Human Rights of the Sustainable Consumer in an Ecological Perspective").

[72] Art. 5(8) Aarhus Convention (emphasis added).

[73] HRC (2018a).

[74] HRC (2018a), para 7.

lic access to environmental information by collecting and disseminating information and by providing affordable, effective and timely access to information to any person upon request'.[75] State parties are therefore required not only to collect information, which is reliable, but also to share it in a manner which is accessible both in terms of costs and of understandability, while also being time efficient. Receiving such information is fundamental for individuals to be able to make informed decisions about their lives and to be aware of their rights and how environmental decisions may impact them. At the basis of this framework principle lies the necessity to protect individuals' ability to make choices: not any choice, but informed and free choices.

Despite the existence of the aforementioned legal documents enshrining those rights, which at their core entail the protection of individual's choices, it seems premature to state that a right to make free, informed, and sustainable choices in sustainable consumption exists on its own. This stems from the fact that the existence of this right has not emerged expressly within pieces of legislation, even though, as mentioned, it is possible to infer that the safeguarding of the right to choose in consumption is at the core of the relevant Directives at the EU level. Furthermore, advancing the argument that this right has emerged as custom, even a regional one, is a difficult task as well, one which cannot easily be solved within these pages, but which would deserve some deeper considerations. Surely, Member States of the EU, by adopting said Directives, had to comply with the obligations and regulate their conduct to favour and safeguard consumers' choices; yet, it seems hazardous to state with clarity that such conduct was followed by *opinio juris* in that regard.

However, the interconnectedness of human rights is well established: human rights reinforce one another and can integrate one another. Hence, the right to free, informed, and sustainable choice could be derived from other existing rights, starting from the right to information in the context of consumer's rights, if read in light of the already existing rights to sustainable development and the right to a healthy environment. The protection of free, informed, and sustainable choices is also crucial for the enjoyment of the right to a healthy environment, given the profound impact that consumption choices have on the environment.[76] It is also a catalyst for the right to sustainable development,[77] in light of the weight that consumption choices have on economies, markets, and societies.

[75] HRC (2018a), paras 17–19.

[76] See further De Vido (Chap. "The International Dimension of the Environment as a Legal Entity: The Human Rights of the Sustainable Consumer in an Ecological Perspective"). See also Ellen MacArthur Foundation (2021).

[77] On the existence of the right to sustainable development, see: Moellendorf (2011), Sengupta (2001), Uvin (2007), Singh (1987).

5 The Elephant in the Room: Sustainable Consumers, a Legal Oxymoron?

The transition towards a sustainable circular economy is a process that exceeds law. Though changes in legislation at the national, regional, and international levels are necessary to promote and enhance such transition, they are but a starting point. What is needed, aside from legal changes, is a shift in paradigm in terms of how we approach, behave, and shape our consumption patterns. This is why consumer education and measures aimed at raising awareness are crucial and should be considered as obligations for States stemming from the right to free, informed, and sustainable choice.

Moving towards conclusions, a crucial point deserving further reflection, alongside legal considerations, is the role of the consumer itself. The interrelation between consumers, sustainability, and the circular economy has been a *leitmotiv* within these pages. This, however, begs the question of whether, for the purpose of shifting towards a sustainable circular economy, it is still possible and even useful to frame individuals within such an economic model as 'consumers'. Furthermore, the 'merely human' dimension also needs to be questioned in the effort to shift towards a sustainable circular economy.[78]

The image of the consumer is not anchored to a fixed concept. In light of the emergence of online platforms for trade, scholars proposed the notion of 'prosumer', a conflation of the terms 'producer' and 'consumer', which refers to those 'natural persons not acting in the course of a business or profession' who 'can move to the supply side of the market',[79] thus becoming so-called prosumers. Furthermore, bringing sustainability within the economic models' discourse has necessarily challenged not only the way in which economic models themselves are conceived, but also the actors who approach them, i.e. individuals. To that extent, authors began discussing about the responsible consumer,[80] who is able to make sustainable choices because they are informed and because asymmetries and imbalances in information gathering are addressed and lowered; while others have proposed the concept of the sustainable consumer,[81] a key figure in the shift towards sustainable consumption. Furthermore, the figure of 'the ethical consumer' was put forth in order to explore the behaviour, discourses, and narratives surrounding the concept of ethical (and unethical) consumption, and how, if at all, ethical consumers actions have an impact on their social and political contexts.[82]

[78] For complementary critical appraisals in this sense see Marzulli (Chap. "'*Ubi societas ibi ius*': Centering a Sustainable Circular Economy from a Sociological Perspective") and De Vido (Chap. "The International Dimension of the Environment as a Legal Entity: The Human Rights of the Sustainable Consumer in an Ecological Perspective").

[79] Mak (2022).

[80] Menghini et al. (2013).

[81] Zoboli (2021), Kostadinova (2016), Mak (2022).

[82] Harrison et al. (2005).

The notion of sustainable consumption was proposed a few years after the adoption of the Brundtland Report which defined the concept of sustainable development.[83] It was elaborated in 1994 at Oslo Symposium on Sustainable Consumption as 'the *use* of services and related products which respond to basic needs and bring a better quality of life while minimizing the use of natural resources and toxic materials as well as emissions of waste and pollutants over the life cycle of the service or product so as not to jeopardize the needs of future generations'.[84] Worthy of notice here is the choice of the term 'use'. Sustainability seems to strive in the direction of *using* rather than *consuming*, the latter entailing the handling of a product which, after a certain period, will no longer be used and hence disposed of, i.e. consumed, in a 'buy-use-toss' logic, which is at the basis of the consumption-linear economic model.

Therefore, in light of the need to move towards a sustainable and circular economic model, which sets aside the logic of 'buy-use-toss' and 'consumerism', the term 'sustainable consumer' seems to be contradictory, as well as conflicting with the purpose of the sustainable circular economy altogether. Rather, the term 'user' could be applied and preferred to underscore the need to set aside consumeristic logic and favour a more responsible, informed, and sustainable approach towards purchases. This would be a first step in changing individuals' behaviours, which are crucial for a sustainable circular economy, and even more so for a broader approach which is not only focused on the individual and which does not view nature only as a resource to be turned into a product. Indeed:

'Circular economy strategies are decisive for restructuring the take-make-dispose model through the active participation of all actors of supply chains and consumers. To achieve this purpose, it is necessary to review the Western model of take-make-dispose, and the negative effects caused by the current economic model based on "extract, transform, and disposing" and the consumer market trends threaten the stability of the economies and the integrity of natural ecosystems, [...] it becomes essential to activate the transition toward a new productive model that reduces pressure on the environment, and that is capable of transforming economic and social development focused on consumption and waste. Hence, a critical understanding of the Western way of life is necessary. One which, in terms of decolonial thinking, implies looking deeply at reality and the possibility of developing a pedagogy that harmonizes the being, knowledge and doing of man oriented towards preservation and conservation environmental care'.[85]

---

[83] WCED (1987), Report 'Our Common Future' (http://www.un-documents.net/our-common-future.pdf) was the first to formulate the notion of sustainable development as meeting the needs of the present without comprising those of future generations, which in its original conceptualization did not focus only on economic terms.

[84] See (with emphasis added) Roy (2021); for a comment see Kostadinova (2016).

[85] Cabrales Salazar et al. (2021).

6 Conclusion

In his report of 2018 on the human rights obligations relating to a safe, clean, healthy, and sustainable environment, the HRC Special Rapporteur David Boyd quoted, in turn, the worldwide-known French author Victor Hugo, who said 'it is impossible to resist an idea whose time has come'.[86] Boyd continued: 'The interdependence of human rights and the environment is an idea whose time is here'.[87] Building on this consideration, we would further expand this concept also to sustainability, circular economy, the environment, and human rights and their interdependence. To foster change that is effective, the circular economy discourse cannot be approached with a monolithic and narrow perspective, but rather it must take into account that changing the economic model at the basis of our society implies—and goes hand in hand with—changes in law and in societies, which affect humans, non-human animals, and the natural environment alike.

This contribution has tried to offer a possible avenue to promote change at the international level, so far lagging behind both in terms of a shift towards a circular economy and the protection of consumers' rights, by suggesting that consumers' rights could be considered as human rights. This would allow access to remedies at the international level as well as promote a human rights-based approach in the shift towards a sustainable circular economy.

References

Arroyo DPF (2012) Consumer protection in private international relationships. In: Brown K, Snyder D (eds) General reports of the XVIIIth Congress of the International Academy of Comparative Law/Rapports généraux du XVIIIème Congrès de l'Académie Internationale de Droit Comparé. Springer, Dordrecht. https://doi.org/10.1007/978-94-007-2354-2_7

Backes C (2017) Law for a circular economy. Eleven International, The Hague

Benöhr I (2013) EU consumer law and human rights. Oxford University Press, New York

Blanke H, Mangiameli S (2021) Treaty on the functioning of the European Union—a commentary. Springer Nature, Cham

Boyd D (2011) The implicit constitutional right to a healthy environment. Rev Eur Commun Int Environ Law 20(2):171–179

Buergenthal T (2006) The evolving international human rights system. Am J Int Law 100(4):783–807. https://doi.org/10.1017/S0002930000031894

Cabrales Salazar O, Márquez Vargas F, Garzón Pascagaza E (2021) Circular economy and reducing consumption from a decolonial approach. Cuad Adm 37(70):e5110905. https://doi.org/10.25100/cdea.v37i70.10905

Caterina R (2012) Architettura delle scelte e tutela del consumatore. Consumatori, Diritti e Mercato 2012:73–80

Charlesworth H, Chinkin C (2000) The boundaries of international law: a feminist analysis. Manchester University Press, Manchester

86 HRC (2018a), para 20.

87 HRC (2018a), para 20.

Cima E (2022) The right to a healthy environment: reconceptualizing human rights in the face of climate change. In: Tignino M, Mbengue MM (eds) Special issue: human rights and the climate change crisis, vol 31. Wiley, pp 38–49. https://doi.org/10.1111/reel.12430
De Melo ÉR (2020) Consumer rights as human rights: legal and philosophical considerations. Rev Rep Derecho V:1–26
Deutch S (1994) Are consumer rights human rights? Osgoode Hall Law J 32(3):537–579. https://doi.org/10.60082/2817-5069.1668
Durovic M (2020) International consumer law: what is it all about? J Consum Policy 43:125–143. https://doi.org/10.1007/s10603-019-09438-9
Durovic M, Micklitz HW (2017) Internationalization of consumer law: a game changer. Springer, Cham. https://doi.org/10.1007/978-3-319-45312-5
Ellen MacArthur Foundation (2021) The nature imperative: How the circular economy tackles biodiversity loss. https://www.ellenmacarthurfoundation.org/biodiversity-report
European Commission (2022) Impact assessment report, accompanying the document proposal for a directive of the European Parliament and of the Council. https://eur-lex.europa.eu/legal-content/EN/TXT/PDF/?uri=CELEX:52022SC0085
European Commission: Consumers, Health, Agriculture and Food Executive Agency (2016) Consumer vulnerability across key markets in the European Union—Executive summary. https://data.europa.eu/doi/10.2818/165625
European Parliament (2024) Briefing: 'green claims' directive protecting consumers from greenwashing. https://www.europarl.europa.eu/RegData/etudes/BRIE/2023/753958/EPRS_BRI(2023)753958_EN.pdf
Federico M (2024) Protezione dei dati personali e tutela collettiva: Itinerari di comparazione tra Europa e Stati Uniti, Collana del Dipartimento di Economia. Centro Studi giuridici. Ca' Foscari. Giappichelli
Ferrara R (2018) Brown economy, green economy, blue economy: L'economia circolare e il diritto dell'ambiente. Il Piemonte delle Autonomie V(2)
Geissdoerfer M, Savaget P, Bocken NMP, Hultink EJ (2017) The circular economy—a new sustainability paradigm? J Clean Prod 143:757–768. https://doi.org/10.1016/j.jclepro.2016.12.048
Giorgetta S (2002) The right to a healthy environment, human rights and sustainable development. Int Environ Agreem Politics Law Econ 2:171–192. https://doi.org/10.1023/A:1020938009559
Gros Espiell H (1979) The evolving concept of human rights: western, socialist and third world approaches. In: Ramcharan BG (ed) Human rights: thirty years after the universal declaration. Brill | Nijhoff, Leiden. https://doi.org/10.1163/9789004638075_006
Harrison R, Newholm T, Shaw D (2005) The ethical consumer. Sage, London
HRC (2018a) Report of the Special Rapporteur on the issue of human rights obligations relating to the enjoyment of a safe, clean, healthy and sustainable environment, A/HRC/37/59. https://docs.un.org/en/A/HRC/37/59
HRC (2018b) The right to privacy in the digital age - report of the United Nations High Commissioner for Human Rights, A/HRC/39/29. https://www.ohchr.org/en/documents/thematic-reports/ahrc3929-right-privacy-digital-age-report-united-nations-high
HRC (2021) The human right to a clean, healthy and sustainable environment, A/HRC/RES/48/13. https://docs.un.org/en/A/HRC/Res/48/13
Knox JH (2020) Constructing the human right to a healthy environment. Annu Rev Law Soc Sci 16:79–95. https://doi.org/10.1146/annurev-lawsocsci-031720-074856
Knox JH, Pejan R (eds) (2018) The human right to a healthy environment. Cambridge University Press
Kostadinova E (2016) Sustainable consumer behaviour: a literature review. Econ Alternat 2:224–234
Lesniewska F, Steenmans K (2023) Circular economy and the law: bringing justice into the frame. Routledge, New York
Lima Marques C (2006) Consumer protection in private international law rules: The need for an Inter-American convention on the law applicable to some consumer contracts and con-

sumer transactions (CIDIP). Cad Prog Pós-Grad Dir – PPGDir/UFRGS 5:41–73. https://doi.org/10.22456/2317-8558.51111
Lima Marques C (2020) International protection of consumers as a global or a regional policy. J Consum Policy 43(1):57–75. https://doi.org/10.1007/s10603-019-09434-z
Mak V (2022) A primavera for European consumer law: re-birth of the consumer image in the light of digitalisation and sustainability. J Eur Consum Mark Law 11(3):77–80
Menghini S, Marinelli N, Alampi Sottini V, Fabbrizzi S (2013) Il consumatore responsabile. Sostenibilità ambientale, sociale ed economica della filiera vitivinicola
Moellendorf D (2011) A right to sustainable development. Monist 94(3):433–452
Nemes N et al (2022) An integrated framework to assess greenwashing. Sustainability 14(8):4431. https://doi.org/10.3390/su14084431
OECD (2022) The role of online marketplaces in protecting and empowering consumers: country and business survey findings. OECD Digital Economy Papers No. 329. OECD, Paris. https://doi.org/10.1787/9d8cc586-en
OECD (2023) Consumer vulnerability in the digital age. OECD Digital Economy Papers No. 355. OECD, Paris. https://doi.org/10.1787/4d013cc5-en
OECD (2024) Declaration on protecting and empowering consumers in the digital and green transitions. https://legalinstruments.oecd.org/en/instruments/OECD-LEGAL-0504
Roy M (2021) Sustainable development strategies: engineering, culture and economics. Elsevier, Oxford
Ruggie JG (2007) Business and human rights: the evolving international agenda. KSG Working Paper No. RWP07-029. shttps://doi.org/10.2139/ssrn.976547
Schu R (1997) The applicable law to consumer contracts made over the internet: consumer protection through private international law? Int J Law Inf Technol 5(2):192–229. https://doi.org/10.1093/ijlit/5.2.192
Sengupta A (2001) Right to development as a human right. Econ Polit Wkly 36(27):2527–2536
Shoreman-Ouimet E, Kopnina H (2015) Culture and conservation: beyond anthropocentrism. Routledge, London. https://doi.org/10.4324/9781315858630
Singh N (1987) Right to environment and sustainable development as a principle of international law. J Indian Law Inst 29(3):289–320
Tambussi CE (2014) Los derechos de usuarios y consumidores son derechos humanos. Lex 12(13):VII 1–VII 15. https://doi.org/10.21503/lex.v12i13.38
Thomas S (2020) Law and the circular economy. J Bus Law 1:62–83
Ukwueze FO (2015) Elevating consumer rights to human rights. Niger Jurid Rev 13:131–156
Uvin P (2007) From the right to development to the rights-based approach: how "human rights" entered development. Dev Pract 17(4/5):597–606
UNGA (2022) The human right to a clean, healthy and sustainable environment, A/RES/76/300. https://docs.un.org/en/A/RES/76/300
Wacinkiewicz EC (2013) Consumer's rights as a special category of human rights. Int J Consum Law Pract 1
WCED (1987) Report of the World Commission on Environment and Development: Our Common Future, A/42/427. https://digitallibrary.un.org/record/139811?v=pdf
Wright CY, Godfrey L, Armiento G, Haywood LK, Inglesi-Lotz R, Lyne K, Schwerdtle PN (2019) Circular economy and environmental health in low- and middle-income countries. Glob Health 15. https://doi.org/10.1186/s12992-019-0501-y
Zoboli R (2021) Consumi e consumatori sostenibili: idee e problemi aperti. In: Zoboli R (ed) Consumi e consumatori sostenibili. Valori, responsabilità, incertezze. Vita e Pensiero, Milan, pp 11–29

The International Dimension of the Environment as a Legal Entity: The Human Rights of the Sustainable Consumer in an Ecological Perspective

Sara De Vido

Abstract The chapter focuses on the environment as the foundation of a Sustainable Circular Economy. In this sense, it is argued that the environment, meant as 'us', including humanity, non-human animals, and natural objects, is not only an element of sustainability as it has been traditionally conceived, but constitutes, in itself, the foundation of sustainability and therefore of a Sustainable Circular Economy. Such a paradigm transition implies rethinking the relationship between economy and environment, entailing a reflection about the human role and its relevant impact on nature. In this reflection, the right to a healthy environment, which opens a new perspective that construes environment not as a mere resource but as an autonomous legal entity, is particularly relevant. Some examples will be provided in that respect: from the recognition of a right to a healthy environment in constitutions and policies, to the elaboration of a theory on 'blue planet law'. The chapter will reflect on the right to a healthy environment that is more than a human right, and that recognizes the schemes of oppression of a part of humanity on natural elements. The consumers in Western societies have contributed to the exploitation of nature through the activities of transnational corporations, but also through overconsumption, lack of awareness of the importance of recycling and waste reduction, the impact of the exploitative animal agriculture, and replicated a model of oppression that should be read through a post-colonial perspective. Consumers are not a monolithic category but rather a category that changes according to time and space. Human rights law can be read in an ecological perspective to understand that the rights of the consumers are both contextualised and universal and must be considered in their relation to nature. The chapter conceptualises the idea of a sustainable consumer, that is well informed of the effects of his/her behaviour on humanity, non-human animals and nature.

S. De Vido (✉)
Università Ca' Foscari, Venice, Italy
e-mail: sara.devido@unive.it

B. Calabrese (ed.), *Legal Perspectives for a Sustainable Circular Economy*, European Union and its Neighbours in a Globalized World 30,
https://doi.org/10.1007/978-3-032-07795-0_13

1 Introduction

The chapter focuses on the environment as the foundation of a Sustainable Circular Economy. In this sense, it is argued that the environment, meant as 'us', including humanity, non-human animals, and natural objects, is not only an element of sustainability as it has been traditionally conceived but constitutes, in itself, the foundation of sustainability and therefore of a Sustainable Circular Economy. Such a paradigm transition implies rethinking the relationship between economy and environment, entailing a reflection about the human role and its relevant impact on nature.[1] In this reflection, the right to a healthy environment, which opens a new perspective that construes environment not as a mere resource but as an autonomous legal entity, is particularly relevant. Some examples will be provided in that respect: from the recognition of a right to a healthy environment in constitutions and policies, to the elaboration of a theory on 'blue planet law'.

The chapter will reflect on the right to a healthy environment that is more than a human right, and that recognizes the schemes of oppression of a part of humanity on natural elements. The consumers in Western societies have contributed to the exploitation of nature through the activities of transnational corporations, but also through overconsumption, lack of awareness of the importance of recycling and waste reduction, impact of the exploitative animal agriculture, and replicated a model of oppression that should be read through a post-colonial perspective. Consumers are not a monolithic category but rather a category that changes according to time and space. Human rights law can be read in an ecological perspective to understand that the rights of the consumers are both contextualised and universal and must be considered in their relation to nature. The chapter conceptualises the idea of a sustainable consumer, that is well informed of the effects of his/her behaviour on humanity, non-human animals and nature. Hence, for example, the sustainable consumer's right to information is the right to know the effects of the economy on the environment, at both local and at the international level. Ecolabels are an example of information, but they often represent more a declaration of intent rather than determine a change in consumers' behaviours. A sustainable consumer is one that does not stop at the label, but actively takes information that are useful to elaborate an unbiased opinion. The consumer has also the right to restoration of nature, which is a right of the environment, of which both the consumer and natural objects are entitled. The right to restoration of nature should be read in an ecological and non-anthropocentric way, that is why the chapter will critically examine the EU regulation on the restoration of nature.

The change of perspective from a pure (Western) consumer-oriented approach to a more consumer-as-part-of-the-environment approach leads to raising awareness of the paucity of the resources and the effects on present and future generations of

[1] For a sociological perspective on the concept of sustainable circular economy, see Marzulli (Chap. "'*Ubi societas ibi ius*': Centering a Sustainable Circular Economy from a Sociological Perspective").

both human and non-human beings. As a method of analysis, this chapter will use legal ecofeminism as thought that disrupts patterns of discrimination within and across species.

2 A Feminist Critique of the Concept of Sustainable Development

Sustainable development has been defined by the World Commission on Environment and Development, the so-called Brundtland Commission, as a development that 'meets the needs of the present without compromising the ability of future generations to meet their own needs'.[2] This definition is particularly vague when analyzed from the perspective of international law. It is not the purpose of this chapter to delve into the academic debates surrounding the concept: whether it is a political objective, an 'interstitial norm',[3] or whether it has normativity,[4] the concept of sustainable development has permeated the environmental legal discourse and has incorporated numerous principles that are essential to its realization, like the right to access to information, which is also relevant to our discussion.[5] The purpose of this part of the chapter is rather to reflect on the feminist critique of the concepts of 'sustainable development' and 'sustainable consumer' looking at the Agenda 2030 of the United Nations and at the newly adopted Directive (EU) 2024/825.[6] It will be argued that the concepts, as they stand, reproduce models of production and consumption that have not put into question inequalities both intra species and inter species.

As it is well known, the Agenda 2030 is composed of 17 goals and 169 targets, it is a soft law instrument addressed to all countries in the world, integrating the economic, social and environmental dimensions in the concept of development.[7] Among the goals, gender equality (no. 5) aims at ending all forms of discrimination against women and girls everywhere, all forms of violence against women and girls, and all harmful practices; ensuring universal access to sexual and reproductive health and reproductive rights; ensuring 'women's full and effective participation and equal opportunities for leadership at all levels of decision-making in political, economic and public life'; reducing (and redistributing to a limited extent) unpaid

[2] WCED, Report 'Our Common Future' (1987), para. 51 (http://www.un-documents.net/our-common-future.pdf).

[3] Lowe (1999, p. 19).

[4] Barral (2012, p. 398). See, *inter alia*, Boyle and Freestone (1999), Lang (1995), Voigt (2009).

[5] Sands (1994, pp. 338–348).

[6] Directive (EU) 2024/825 as regards empowering consumers for the green transition through better protection against unfair practices and through better information.

[7] United Nations, Transforming Our World: the 2030 Agenda for Sustainable Development (2015), A/RES/70/1 (https://sdgs.un.org/publications/transforming-our-world-2030-agenda-sustainable-development-17981).

care and domestic work; and undertaking 'reforms to give women equal rights to economic resources, as well as access to ownership and control over land and other forms of property, financial services, inheritance and natural resources, in accordance with national laws'. Goal 12 is particularly relevant to this chapter because it aims at ensuring sustainable consumption and production patterns, and it is articulated into 12 different targets, among which the achievement by 2030 of the sustainable management and efficient use of natural resources; the halving per capita global food waste at the retail and consumer levels and the reduction of food losses along production and supply chains; the substantial reduction of waste generation through prevention, reduction, recycling and reuse; the encouragement of companies to adopt sustainable practices and to integrate sustainability information into their reporting cycle; the access to relevant information for people everywhere and awareness for sustainable development and lifestyles in harmony with nature; the support to developing countries to strengthen their scientific and technological capacity to move towards sustainable patterns of consumption and production.

A feminist analysis, which develops ecological and postcolonial concerns, will highlight the fact that the concept of sustainable development is anthropocentric and androcentric, it does not affect the dynamics of power—men, women, and non-binary people; human and non-human; developed and developing countries—and encourages a model of growth that is compatible with the persistence of structural inequalities. For example, the Agenda 2030 considers gender equality as synonym of equality of opportunity between women and men: however, this understanding of equality does not affect power relations and does not change the subordinate position of women, especially those at the intersection of different grounds of discrimination, in societies.[8] Esquivel argued indeed that 'power relations are the big elephant in the room of Agenda 2030'.[9] Cheryl McEwan, using a postcolonial lens, contends that 'development is about power', and that it is crucial to contemporary development study policies to reflect on relations of power.[10] The Agenda 2030 does not explicitly recognize the link between women's rights, gender equality, exploitation of the environment, global economic governance. It fails to grasp the interconnections between the different Agenda 2030's goals and to understand the impact of humanity, particularly that of a part of humanity, on non-human beings. Sustainable development requires the conservation of plants and animals, but assuming that generations refer to 'human'; as in the context of the Brundtland report, the anthropocentric focus of the definition is clearly discernible in the complete neglect of non-human interests and the preponderant emphasis related to meeting the needs of humanity.[11] With regard to the Agenda 2030, although negotiations had opened to eco-centric perspectives, 'weak' anthropocentrism, thus tempered by commitments to environmental protection, was favored, reinforcing an agenda that is of purely

[8] Esquivel (2016).

[9] Esquivel (2016, p. 12).

[10] McEwan (2001). See also Struckmann (2018).

[11] Kotzé and French (2018b, p. 20). See also Kiss (1996, p. 24).

'human'—and only a part of humanity—sustainable development.[12] As it was argued, sustainable development 'has failed to meaningfully change the human behavior that created the Anthropocene'.[13] Non-human animals are also excluded from the concept of sustainable development, in particular from the components of intergenerational and intragenerational equity. However, it should also be acknowledged that in 2019 the UN Global Sustainable Development Report recognized for the first time that animal welfare is a key issue missing from the 2030 Agenda.[14]

One author, referring to the body of international law related to climate change, analyzed the convergence over the years between the concepts of sustainable development and 'ecological modernization' as dominant paradigms, revealing their anthropocentric (human) and androcentric (male) nature.[15] As early as the 1980s, these concepts were in fact based on the idea that 'care for nonhuman nature can be internalized into existing political, social and economic institutions'.[16] MacGregor encouraged the incorporation of feminist and ecological concerns into a 'more inclusive definition of sustainability that has the potential to address more completely the interrelationships between social equity and environmental destruction'.[17] She identified some conditions of the so-called 'feminist sustainability', including 'an ethical perspective that is based on solidarity, reciprocity, and non-hierarchical and non-violent relationships among and within human societies and between humans, non-humans, and the ecosystem; [...] the equitable distribution of paid and unpaid among men and women; [...] socio-political arrangements that foster cultural and political diversity, based on an expanded notion of citizenship as well as the notion of multiple publics; and non-sexist sustainable cities that take the different identities, abilities, needs, and experiences of diverse publics into account—this entails a de-gendering of urban space and a re-claiming of the urban commons'.[18] Among feminist theories, ecofeminism, on which this article will further reflect below, has been highly critical of ecological modernization precisely because it is based on 'underlying conceptual, structural and institutional barriers that reinforce the marginalization of women, non-human nature and other disadvantaged groups'.[19] As it was pointed out, sustainability should refer to something that we owe to other humans and non-human communities as well.[20] This chapter will add some

[12] Kotzé and French (2018b, p. 27 ss).

[13] Craig and Benson (2013, p. 843). Kotzé (2017, p. 266): 'sustainable development has been used as the ethical justification for the legal creation of deeply embedded anthropocentric human demands on dwindling resources.'

[14] *Global sustainable report 2019: The future is now—science for achieving sustainable development*, p. 117. See also Van Hoorick and Verniers (2024, pp. 228–229).

[15] Wilkinson Cross (2023).

[16] Wilkinson Cross (2023, p. 44).

[17] MacGregor (2003).

[18] MacGregor (2003).

[19] MacGregor (2003).

[20] Weinhues (2020).

considerations to these concerns by working on the concept of 'sustainable consumer' from a feminist and ecofeminist perspective.

3 What Is a 'Sustainable Consumer'? A Critical Appraisal

The consumer perspective in the circular economy is fundamental, and, as stated by the European Commission, this is linked to 'elements such as the optimal lifetime and durability of products and the easy repair, upgrade, disassemble and recycling of products'.[21] The newly-adopted Directive (EU) 2024/825, empowering consumers for the green transition through better protection against unfair practices and through better information, is surely an important step in ensuring that a sustainable consumer 'knows' and is aware of his/her/their behavior. For example, in the preamble, Recital 3 stresses how consumers must be empowered 'to take better-informed decisions and thus stimulate the demand for, and the supply of, more sustainable goods, they should not be misled about a product's environmental or social characteristics or circularity aspects, such as durability, reparability or recyclability'. The Directive protects the consumer from misleading messages, such as labels that include environmental claims ('environmentally friendly', 'eco-friendly'), unless supported by an excellent and demonstrated environmental performance, as declared under Recital 9. This outcome within the EU legal system is fundamental and empowers consumers to make the best choices to protect the environment.[22]

However, using an ecofeminist lens, this outcome is not completely satisfactory. First of all: what kind of consumer? Are consumers a unique entity? There is an increasing research on consumers' behavior and climate change, 'gradually improving our understanding of the most effective way to mobilize consumers to mitigate climate change'.[23] Research has focused on 'specific carbon-intensive behaviours, mostly investigating consumers' willingness to change to a less carbon intensive substitute (such as a diet with less meat), but sometimes just cutting down on a carbon intensive behaviour that is viewed as a luxury (such as vacation air traveling) or

[21] See the European Commission webpage 'Sustainable Consumption' (https://commission.europa.eu/live-work-travel-eu/consumer-rights-and-complaints/sustainable-consumption_en#circular-economy); on the issue of product repairability see Calabrese (Chap. "Right to Repair Between Intellectual Property and Servitization").

[22] More broadly about the position of consumers in this paradigm transition within EU law see Deana (Chap. "Reshaping Consumer Powers and Responsibilities in the European Union's Transition to a Sustainable Circular Economy"), and also from the point of view of private international law see Bergamini (Chap. "Dispute Resolution and Private International Law in the Context of Circular Economy: Effectiveness Beyond Alternatives"); while for a wider international perspective about consumers and human rights see Dal Monico (Chap. "Rethinking the Role of the Consumer in a Global Economy: The Power of Choice as a 'Human Right'?"), and Candelmo (Chap. "Global sustainability in the international arena beyond the EU policy agenda").

[23] Thøgersen (2021, p. 12).

waste'.[24] With regard to food safety, it should also be acknowledged that 'the EU has gone well beyond empowerment through information', by adopting legislation that prohibits unsafe food and extensive substantive regulation of matters such as biocides, product traceability, novel product approval, ingredients, contamination rules, hygiene in manufacturing, irradiation, packaging materials, animal health, and genetically modified organism.[25] The concepts of sustainable consumer and of green transition have developed responding to concerns that stemmed from consumers themselves and civil society more generally. However, the approach has always been very anthropocentric, stuck in the present, centered around the humans—or, better, the so-called 'Global North'—and devoid of any acknowledgment of the interconnections among species. For example, despite the growing number of studies on the benefits stemming from plant-based food, little has been incorporated in the legislation, apart from very important but still very anthropocentric measures on 'animal welfare'.[26] The idea of consumer conveyed in legal instruments, including Directive (EU) 2024/825, is also monolithic, but consumers are not a collective entity or the mere sum of individuals: they differ because of their gender, gender identity, social and economic conditions, education, geographic location, among others.[27] Ecolabelling in itself, if correctly informing the consumers, is a good instrument to raise awareness of environmental issues in consumer behavior. However, it does not take into account power dynamics in our societies and patterns of discrimination within and among species.[28] With regard to the action on climate change, for example, MacGregor unravels the problems surrounding the focus on the individual and the private sphere as areas of action to counter climate change: 'people in the affluent world have internalized the idea that the best way to tackle climate change is through lifestyle change. Not only is the word "citizen" typically absent from the climate discourse [...], but both governments and popular environmental campaigns emphasize the role of individuals to do their bit by conserving energy, taking public transit, recycling waste, growing food, and foregoing flights'.[29] This reasoning is relevant to the debate on sustainability as well. It is not that the individual behaviour is unimportant, but there are two correlated issues: first, the focus on the private sphere sets aside the impact of a growing militarization of the environment on the one hand, and the feminisation of the private sphere, on the other. Focusing on the latter, given the responsibility for household management in most cultures, 'making it a site for environmental action poses particular threats for women and for feminist politics'; it means, in other words, 'more unpaid work for women—work that may divert time and attention away from other kinds of citizenly

[24] Thøgersen (2021, p. 11).

[25] Gokani (2024, p. 275).

[26] In the treaties, Article 13 Treaty of the Functioning of the EU. The newly confirmed European Commission has for the first time in history a Commissioner on Health and Animal Welfare.

[27] The lower the socioeconomic position of the consumer, the more likely they are to be negatively affected by unhealthy diets and diet-related diseases. See Drewnowski (2009).

[28] See, already in the 1990s, the work by Bristor and Fischer (1993).

[29] MacGregor (2014, p. 624).

environmental action in the public sphere'.[30] The author finds it troubling to 'observe the emergence of a particular kind of self-identified women's climate change activism that connects feminine domestic expertise with saving the planet from the apocalypse'.[31]

The second aspect concerns the emphasis on environment and ecology (eco-friendly, environmentally friendly among the most common labels that are used). The question is: what environment? Is the environment close to 'us' (us as Europeans)? Is the environment including non-human animals? These two points lead us to a reflection on the right to a healthy environment as both a human and non-human right and how new methods of legal analysis might help in shifting the legal paradigm.

4 Sustainable Consumption and the Right to a Healthy Environment

A former Special Rapporteur on human rights and the environment acknowledged, in his 2019 report, that the right to a healthy environment had already been recognized by a majority of States in their constitutions, legislations and various regional treaties to which they are party.[32] He also recognized that, in spite of this achievement, the right to a healthy environment has not yet been recognized as such at the global level.[33] Within the UN system, absent a general normative framework on the human right to a healthy environment, there have been several attempts to integrate the dimensions of human rights and the environment, which culminated in the adoption of the Human Rights Council 2021 Resolution formally recognizing that having a clean, healthy and sustainable environment is a human right.[34] Despite being non-binding, the resolution has been welcomed as a milestone in the process of consolidating a practice that, coupled with the *opinio juris*, leads to the formation of an international custom. One year later, the UN General Assembly formally recognized that access and enjoyment of a clean, healthy and sustainable environment is

[30] MacGregor (2014, p. 625).

[31] MacGregor (2014, p. 625). The author encourages political acts of citizenship.

[32] Human Rights Council, Issue of human rights obligations relating to the enjoyment of a safe, clean, healthy and sustainable environment A/HRC/40/55 (2019), para. 13.

[33] Ibid. It is possible to find references to the right to a healthy environment in the 1972 Stockholm Declaration, in the African Charter of human and peoples' rights (Article 24, right to a satisfactory environment), in Additional Protocol to the American Convention on Human Rights in the Area of Economic, Social and Cultural Rights (Protocol of San Salvador, Article 11: right to live in a healthy environment), and in the Convention on Access to information, public information, public participation in decision-making and access to justice in environmental matters (preamble, right to a healthy environment).

[34] A/HRC/48/L.23/Rev.1 (2021). See the evolution of the right to a healthy environment in Zhang (2024, p. 39).

a universal human right, and called upon States and non-State actors, including businesses, to 'scale up efforts' in order to ensure this newly recognized right.[35] This UNGA Resolution was adopted with a great majority, no vote against and four abstentions (China, Russia, India and Japan). The soft law nature of the act does not diminish its importance, because the UNGA Resolution paved the way for further commitments by States and other stakeholders to accelerate the action at the international level for the implementation of this right. The UNGA Resolution was also a landmark because it acknowledged in its preamble the disproportionate impact of environmental damage on 'women and girls and those segments of the population that are already in vulnerable situations, including indigenous peoples, children, older persons and persons with disabilities'. The choice of the words 'clean', 'healthy', and 'sustainable' is important because it identifies the elements of the environment that allow the enjoyment of all human rights. Additionally, the inequality dimension could have been better stressed as *trait d'union* between the environmental and the human rights dimensions.[36]

Outstanding authors have commented on the possibility of conceptualizing a right to a decent environment and of locating it within the corpus of economic, social, and cultural rights. According to Boyle, 'clarifying the existence of such a right would entail giving greater weight to the global public interest in protecting the environment and promoting sustainable development' and 'the further elaboration of procedural rights [...] would facilitate the implementation of such a right'.[37] Boyle further argued that 'a right to a decent environment has to address the environment as a public good, in which form it bears little resemblance to the accepted catalogue of civil and political rights, a catalogue which for good reasons there is great reluctance to expand'.[38]

The missing point is the interconnection among the elements of the environment, which was firstly provided by the Inter-American Court of Human Rights (IACHR) that, in its Advisory opinion of 15 November 2017, recognized the existence of a right to a healthy environment as an autonomous right, presenting an individual and a collective dimension. In its collective dimension, it constitutes an 'universal interest' that must be granted to both present and future generations. In its individual dimension, its violation might directly or indirectly affect other rights, such as the rights to health, to personal integrity, to life, among others. The Court recognized that the degradation of the environment can cause irreparable damages to all human beings, with the consequence that the right to a healthy environment is fundamental for the existence of humankind.[39] The approach followed by the Inter-American

[35] UNGA, A/RES/76/300, The human right to a clean, healthy and sustainable environment (2022).

[36] See the reflection in Atrey (2023, p. 26).

[37] Boyle (2015).

[38] Boyle (2015, p. 221).

[39] IACHR, *Opinión Consultiva* OC-23-17 (2017), 59; Peña Chacón (2019). Even though this chapter is not aimed at the analysis of the IACHR jurisprudence, the case *Lhaka Honhat (nuestra tierra) v. Argentina* [2020], IACHR, Ser. C No. 400 is worth mentioning. The Court concluded, for the first time, that a State had violated the right to a healthy environment and highlighted that the rights

Court of Human Rights drives a further shift of paradigm, from a mere anthropocentric to a more ecocentric approach. If we consider the *human* right to a healthy environment, the lens through which we view it is strictly anthropocentric. It is a right belonging to *human beings*. However, the existence of human beings depends on the existence of the flora and the environment. As Stone argued even before environmental law had started to develop at the international level, 'because the health and well-being of [human]kind depend upon the health of the environment, these goals will often be so mutually supportive that one can avoid deciding whether our rationale is to advance "us" or a new "us" that includes the environment'.[40] We might indeed wonder whether a purely anthropocentric approach is still appropriate in light of the ongoing environmental crisis. This was precisely the point caught by the IACHR in the aforementioned opinion, which emphasized how, compared to other human rights, the right to a healthy environment protects nature, even in the absence of evidence of potential risks for human beings, because of its importance for the rest of living beings, which deserve protection.[41] It is precisely the 'us' including the environment envisaged by Stone; an environment which must be conceived as embracing both flora and fauna. It follows that human beings bear the responsibility to protect this value and, through their actions, to develop an environmental consciousness.[42] Francioni contended that a 'more advanced jurisprudence in the field of human rights which recognizes the collective dimension of the right to a decent and sustainable environment as an indispensable condition of human security and human welfare' is necessary, and that 'it does not make much sense to engage human rights language to combat environmental degradation only when such degradation affects the rights to life, property, and the privacy of certain directly affected individuals'.[43] As stressed by the Special Rapporteur Boyd, 'the loss of global biodiversity is having and will continue to have devastating effects on a wide range of human rights for decades to come. [...] we can simply not enjoy our basic human rights to life, health, food and safe water without a healthy environment'.[44]

The question is: 'why not requalify nature as a rights-holder itself instead of basing environmental statutes on the premise that humans need a healthy

of vulnerable groups are disproportionally harmed by environmental damage. See Jiménez Guanipa and Barraco (2024). More recently, the Court adopted the *Opinión Consultiva* 31 (2025) on climate emergency and human rights.

[40] Stone (1972).

[41] IACHR, Opinión Consultiva OC-23-17 (2017), p. 180.

[42] Iovino (2008, p. 83).

[43] Francioni (2010).

[44] See at https://www.ohchr.org/en/press-releases/2019/06/failing-protect-biodiversity-can-be-human-rights-violation-un-experts?LangID=E&NewsID=24738

environment for their own purposes?'[45] The idea of granting legal personhood to natural elements and non-human animals is not relevant to our discussion and would require a much deeper analysis; however, what is interesting is to appreciate the intrinsic value of nature, irrespective of the human benefits derived from any action in support of the environment.[46] There are several missing points in the legal debate, to the point of reflecting, on the one hand, on the right to a healthy environment as a human right, and on the other hand, on the rights of nature and the rights to which non-human animals should be entitled. However, apart from the recognition of rights for non-human entities, what is missing is the idea that we need to change our lens of analysis and produce a paradigmatic shift in legal reasoning—which is not unrelated to recent jurisprudence—that has to emphasize the interconnections between elements of the environment and the need to decentralize humans for the benefit of all species across generations. The right to a healthy environment is therefore an expression of human rights, but also of the rights of nature, which incorporates, as well said by an Ecuadorian court, non-human animals' rights.[47] Meant in this holistic way, the human and non-human right to a healthy environment opens a new perspective that construes the environment not as a mere resource, but as the constitutive element of a Sustainable Circular Economy. According to a proposal for a EU Charter of the Fundamental Rights of Nature, five pillars can be identified: the rule of non-regression; the rule of resilience evaluation; *in dubio pro natura* (and now *pro clima*) criterion; the rule of sustainable democratic methods; the rule of five responsibilities towards Nature, with reversal of the burden of proof.[48] This shift of paradigm disrupts the dichotomy market/environment by advocating an understanding of the interconnectedness of all human, non-human, and natural elements. This is not a utopia in jurisprudence. Hence, for example, the Ecuadorian constitutional court in *Los Cedros* case revoked in 2021 two mining concessions, arguing that there was a risk of severe and irreversible damage to nature, and that a precautionary approach must prevail.[49] In the view of the drafters of a EU Charter of the Fundamental Rights of Nature, the rule of responsibility towards Nature, 'with reversal of the burden of proof, allows ecological damage to be taken into account even in case of legal provisions legitimizing the environmental harm'.[50]

---

[45] Schoukens (2024, p. 184).

[46] Schoukens (2024, p. 190).

[47] Ecuador Constitutional Court, 27 January 2022, Case no. 253–20-JH/22 ('Mona Estrellita').

[48] Carducci et al. (2020).

[49] Ecuador Constitutional Court, 10 November 2021, Case no. 1149–19-JP/21 ('Los Cedros'). About this decision see Prieto Munoz (2021).

[50] Carducci et al. (2020). A critical view in Petersmann (2024).

5 Why We Need More Blue than Green in Our Transition: Blue Planet Law

The European Union has worked extensively on a green transition, through the European Green Deal, which is described as 'Europe's new growth strategy' to 'transform the Union into a modern, resource-efficient and competitive economy'.[51] The green transition responds to 'political, economic, and security needs', and requires, within the system of the 27 Member States, a 'complex normative process', which involves 'institutions with divergent, if not antagonist, interests'.[52] It is not the purpose of a legal analysis to delve into the economics of green technologies,[53] but rather to discuss whether the traditional way in which law is conceived is sufficient to address current challenges, and which methodological alternatives might be useful.

A new kind of law has indeed emerged that shifts the focus from a mere action of 'greening' legal provisions to incorporating environmental concerns into a 'blue planet law', that 'does not renounce economic and technological development, but gives sufficient consideration to sustainability standards and human responsibility for the future of the "Earth's Ecosystem", the future of this Blue Planet where humankind lives in communion with other forms of life, other living species'.[54] Blue is indeed the color that prevails when the Earth is seen from the outer space, and it also stresses the key aquatic component of life on Earth. As it was interestingly argued, in the sustainable development model—involving economic, social and environmental development—economic growth has generally prevailed, but 'sustainable development does not exist without robust and multiform legal protection of the environment on which human food, life and health depend'.[55] Blue planet law endorses an intergenerational perspective and consecrates the 'duty of care for the environment'.[56] This duty of care has been conceptualized in the Draft Global Pact for the Environment, which was launched in 2017 as initiative to conclude a legally binding international instrument under the United Nations that would synthesize the principles outlined in several documents, including the World Charter of Nature, the Rio declaration and the IUCN World Declaration on the Environmental Rule of law. The UNGA adopted Resolution 72/277 "Towards a Global Pact for the Environment" on 10 May 2018.[57] The Pact aims at becoming binding law, including consolidated principles of international law and progressively developing the law to

[51] See the European Commission webpage 'Green Transition' (https://reform-support.ec.europa.eu/what-we-do/green-transition_en).

[52] De Sadeleer (2023, p. 26).

[53] On the 'utopian soul of the modern techno-scientific revolution' see Soromenho-Marques and Magalhães (2023, p. 38).

[54] Cortês (2023, p. 5).

[55] Cortês (2023, p. 10).

[56] Cortês (2023, p. 11).

[57] UNGA, A/RES/72/277, Towards a Global Pact for the Environment (2018).

provide a right to an ecologically sound environment. The relevant Draft includes the right to an ecologically sound environment (Article 1), which is however acknowledged as a human right only—'every person'—and the duty to take care of the environment (Article 2). Article 3 is devoted to integration and sustainable development, identifying the obligations that States (and not clearly non-State actors such as transnational corporations) must abide by, in particular the integration of the requirements of environmental protection into the planning and implementation of policies and national and international activities. The Draft also enshrines the principles of precaution and intergenerational equity, as well as other related human rights, such as right of access to environmental information held by public authorities.[58] With regard to the precautionary principle, it imposes the burden of proof on potentially damaging economic activities and technologies in favour of environmental protection (*in dubio pro natura*).[59]

Despite the reference to remediation of environmental damages (Article 7), which is not related to human well-being, and the reference to gender equality in the preamble, the draft is inherently anthropocentric. Kotzé and French contented that the Pact should adopt a more ecological approach, and that the word 'Earth' should be used to replace 'environment'.[60] They argued that 'from a legal perspective, this would lead one to begin to talk about Earth system law, moving towards a *Lex Anthropocenae*, which hints at a transformed type of law, grounded in and focused on the entire Earth, while promoting positive notions of the rule of ecological law, a transformed sense of global democracy, global ecological citizenship and the rights of nature'.[61]

This perspective is very fascinating and highlights the importance of a change in the paradigm and a disruption of mechanisms of exploitation of nature. The Draft is still a draft and has not turned into a binding legal instrument, which pays the difficulties of a lengthy negotiating process and an even more complex ratification procedure. Considering the international political resistance to binding environmental law—for example the US recently withdrawing from the Paris Agreement—it seems that the draft will either remain as it is or become an ineffective legal instrument. However, even at this stage, the Draft can show the incipient formation of customary law or the evolution of the law, as *lex necessitatis* which corresponds to the values of the international community as a whole. Compared to Kotzé and French, Cortês considers that the Draft has already shown a shift toward an ecological approach, by referring in the preamble to the interdependence of humanity with the entire natural world.[62] Using a blue planet law perspective, Cortês contends that economic and technological developments have to acquire a new direction: 'we need ecologically sustainable policies, economies and technologies,' and 'a

---

[58] See further below.

[59] On the *in dubio pro natura* principle, see Baldin and De Vido (2022).

[60] Kotzé and French (2018a).

[61] Kotzé and French (2018a).

[62] Cortês (2023, p. 15).

sustainable development informed by a holistic, intergenerational and precautionary approach'.[63]

6 How Ecofeminism in Circular Economy Translates into Law: Expanding Rights and Not Merely Greening them

What blue planet law misses, as well as a pure ecological approach, is the understanding that sustainable development and so a Sustainable Circular Economy cannot be achieved without reducing the inequalities that are present in our societies and across species: poverty, food insecurity, gender inequalities. Pollution, for example, is the largest environmental cause of death in the world,[64] but the effects of pollution are unequally distributed, with minorities and the most vulnerable people being more affected than the average population.[65] Abandoning a contaminated area and relocating elsewhere is 'only possible when the environmental victims have the economic capacity to leave their homes', with the consequence that the most disadvantaged are those who not only bear the most direct effects of pollution but also the long-term consequences.[66] The shift this chapter proposes is from an anthropocentric and androcentric understanding of Sustainable Circular Economy to an ecofeminist reading of the law of circular economy, that takes into consideration that the environment must be considered, for the sake of the future of both human and non-human beings, as a holistic entity characterized by the interconnection among all the elements.

Ecofeminism has rarely been explored in law, and never included among 'the' methods of international legal analysis. It is a method that unravels dynamics of power and oppression within and between different species, expanding the view of these dynamics beyond humans. Ecofeminism expresses great potential for application as a legal method of international law because it questions monolithic legal categories and reconsiders them in light of the interdependence among all species (human and non-human) and with nature, prioritizing the needs of communities whose voice have never been effectively heard and that are most affected by climate change and, as this book argues, by environmental chronic emergencies. Feminist theories put into question dichotomies such as male/female, reason/emotion, white/coloured, transcendent/material, culture/nature, mind/body, human/animal, which are gendered in the sense that the first word is associated with maleness and masculinity, while the second, subordinate one, is associated with women and femininity. One of ecofeminism's point of strength is 'subjected to the subordinating process of dualism, that nature is perhaps the ultimate "Other" upon which the human self gets

[63] Cortês (2023, p. 17).

[64] Das and Horton (2018).

[65] EEA (2018).

[66] Pintado and Aragão (2023, p. 95). See also Nixon (2011).

constructed'.[67] Ecofeminism, in other words, rejects 'false binaries and dualisms such as the human/nature dualism [...], as well as a refusal to privilege "ecological" concerns over so-called "humanist"'.[68] Karen Morrow argued that 'when ecofeminism is pursued in an international context, its goal is to import this paradigm shifting approach to accommodating alternative/additional procedural and substantive expertise and experience, from the periphery to the mainstream'.[69] Since international law 'embraces and even embeds dualism at its very core, with entrenched power holders enjoying the advantages of othering non-privileged humans and the environment,' an ecofeminist approach 'could offer a corrective [...] entailing at base a radical, relational process of (re)connection—as humans with one another and as humans with the non-human environment'.[70] Ecofeminism, focusing on the processes through which gender, racial, and ecological oppression are connected, is 'not merely conceptual': it shows 'how these ideological connections are dialectically entangled with the material condition of women and other oppressed groups'.[71] An ecofeminist method to law guarantees environmental justice by recognizing the ways in which 'systems of oppression (such as racism, gender discrimination, and environmental degradation) are interconnected and mutually reinforcing'.[72] It can be used to avoid, for example, the inequitable allocation of environmental harms.

It seems almost impossible, at first sight, to connect this view with the idea of a sustainable consumer and a Sustainable Circular Economy. However, it is not. A sustainable consumer of the Global North is sustainable not only if they/he/she is not misled by imprecise labels, but also if the consumer has the skills to search for adequate information about the origin of a product—considering social and environmental aspects, and taking into consideration the disproportionate impact of economic activities on the most disadvantaged people and on nature—and the management of waste (see following Sect. 6.1). An ecofeminist reading of the newly adopted Directive (EU) 2024/825 will put into question the anthropocentric nature of the EU system.[73] A sustainable consumer has also the right to the restoration of nature, which is a right belonging to humans, non-human beings and natural objects (see following Sect. 6.2).

[67] Mallory (2013, p. 254).

[68] Mallory (2013).

[69] Morrow (2023, p. 194).

[70] Morrow (2023, p. 194). See the discussion of ecofeminism in private international law in De Vido (2024).

[71] Mallory (2013, p. 255).

[72] Mallory (2013, p. 253).

[73] Hovden (2018, p. 281).

6.1 Right of Access to Information

In a Sustainable Circular Economy, consumers should be aware of their ecological impact.[74] This awareness is possible if consumers—the category that we described above—enjoy the right of access to information that allows them to make an informed decision. The right of access to information is enshrined in the UNECE Convention on access to information, public participation in decision-making and access to justice in environmental matters of 1998 (Aarhus Convention). Under Article 1, 'in order to contribute to the protection of the right of every person of present and future generations to live in an environment adequate to his or her health and well-being, each Party shall guarantee the rights of access to information, public participation in decision-making, and access to justice in environmental matters'. The right of access to environmental information has a specific provision, Article 4, which must be read in conjunction with the definition of 'environmental information' under Article 2(3), which means the following: 'the state of elements of the environment, such as air and atmosphere, water, soil, land, landscape and natural sites, biological diversity and its components, including genetically modified organisms, and the interaction among these elements; factors, such as substances, energy, noise and radiation, and activities or measures, including administrative measures, environmental agreements, policies, legislation, plans, and programmes, affecting or likely to affect the elements of the environment; the state of human health and safety, conditions of human life, cultural sites and built structures, inasmuch as they are or may be affected by the state of the elements of the environment'. The approach of the Aarhus Convention is focused on humans, overlooking the intersection between the quality of the environment and the enjoyment of such as the right to food.

In recent years, ecolabelling has developed to provide clear and easy-to-use information on products, including food. In the European Union, the Community eco-label was launched more than 30 years ago, becoming the largest and best-known scheme used across Member States.[75] It is a voluntary scheme, designed to be 'part of the sustainable consumption and production policy of the Community, which aims at reducing the negative impact of consumption and production on the environment, health, climate and natural resources'.[76] In terms of access to information, the current Regulation stresses that it is necessary to 'inform the public and to raise public awareness of the EU Ecolabel through promotion actions, information and education campaigns, at local, national and Community levels, in order to make consumers aware of the meaning of the EU Ecolabel and to enable them to make informed choices'.[77] In addition, the recent Directive (EU) 2024/825, amending the

---

[74] De Sadeleer (2023, p. 32).

[75] See originally Regulation (EEC) 880/92 on a Community eco-label award scheme, and now the consolidated version of Regulation (EC) 66/2010 on the EU Ecolabel

[76] Recital 5, Regulation (EC) 66/2010.

[77] Recital 13, Regulation (EC) 66/2010.

previous legislation on unfair business-to-consumer commercial practices, intervenes in this field in order to protect consumers and ensure that general ecolabels are reliable and transparent. The legal instruments differentiate between environmental claims, where the product or brand declares that it has a positive or zero impact on the environment, or is less damaging than other products; generic environmental claims, made in written or oral form, without further specifying the details of the claim; sustainability label, meaning 'any voluntary trust mark, quality mark or equivalent, either public or private, that aims to set apart and promote a product, a process or a business by reference to its environmental or social characteristics, or both, and excludes any mandatory label required under Union or national law'.[78]

Despite these positive steps, and bearing in mind that the impact of this Directive cannot be assessed at the moment, the level of transparent and clear information is very low.

The possibility to have access to all possible information online is positive on the one hand, but it makes it very difficult to obtain reliable and accurate information. Ecolabels are crucial and have proven to be effective,[79] but they are voluntary schemes, and they are based on the willingness of the producers to be transparent.[80] It should also be acknowledged that regulations and schemes on ecolabels do not refer to the right to a healthy and clean environment, nor do they take into account the intersecting grounds of discrimination existing in the society in which the products are advertised. This is also the missing point in Directive (EU) 2024/825: its failure to acknowledge that it is important to overcome the dichotomy market/environment and promote legislation that is capable of 'listening' to not only producers—especially small-scale ones, that are commonly disregarded—and civil society, but also the environment, because what is a sustainable good for us—Europeans—might not be such if we look at the raw materials that are used to produce it. As it was pointed out, 'companies produce information to sell their products and services and increase their profits, banks produce information to sell financial services and increase their portfolio [...] as is typical in the post-truth era, none of these discourses is false; they are all based on facts, but they are also brand-centered narratives and, in some way, marketing-oriented'.[81] We need environmental literacy, ecological literacy, and ecoliteracy.[82]

Research on these aspects is extensive, but the impact has been limited. This chapter suggests a paradigmatic shift in the legal discipline, taking into account ecofeminist concerns. We need to move toward a society which is consumer-oriented, not only in the sense that consumers must be protected against actions of greenwashing, but also in the sense that they can be game-changers and influence

[78] Art. 1, Directive (EU) 2024/825.

[79] Englandar et al. (2023).

[80] See also Mogyoros (2025).

[81] Tavares da Silva and Gomes Martins (2023, p. 147).

[82] McBride et al. (2013).

the way in which ecolabeling is promoted and realized. It also means to consider the dynamics of power in our societies, which are characterized by the disproportionate impact of certain decisions on part of humanity and on nature—the 'environment as us'. For example, it means to (at least) put into question the sustainability of meat and dairy products, which is the result of oppression in intensive animal farming.[83] The legal reasoning surrounding animal welfare should be, though it rarely is, informed by these considerations. With regard to renewable energy, any reflection 'must also consider its "dark side", that is, its negative impact on the environment'.[84] Other examples taken from fisheries[85] and the flower market[86]—just to mention two cases—suggest that the dominant ecolabel schemes cannot grasp realities that are 'kind' to and respectful of the environment, a concept encompassing both human and non-humans.

With regard to plastics, in particular single-use plastics, the information should not be limited to how to recycle plastics or the percentage of recycled materials in it, but should rather be focused on the process, which starts from the origin: how to reduce single-use plastic and how to develop 'good practices in collaboration with consumers, producers, farmers and other waste generators'.[87] According to some research, green consumption behaviors are shaped by gender and gender identity, but, as we said, consumers also have different social and economic conditions.[88] The right to access to information should evolve and be interpreted in a way that takes into consideration all these concerns and incorporates the right to a healthy environment, as described in the previous pages.

6.2 Right to Restoration of Nature

In its Constitution, Ecuador acknowledges that nature has the right to be restored.[89] Hence, the proposal for a right to restoration of nature is not particularly innovative. What is innovative is its connection with the concept of Sustainable Circular Economy. In the EU system, such a right is not enshrined in the founding treaties, and an imperative of restoration has manifested itself more in the case law of the Court of Justice rather than in the text of secondary law, such as the Habitats

[83] Deckha (2022).

[84] Tavares da Silva and Gomes Martins (2023, p. 149).

[85] Højrup and Ounanian (2022). The Danish state-sponsored eco-label precluded small-scale fishers due to the particularities of stock assessment for certain fisheries targeted by these fishers and an alternative based on the concept of care was suggested.

[86] Craig (2014).

[87] Pintado and Aragão (2023, p. 94).

[88] Zhao et al. (2021).

[89] Article 72, which also provides that this restoration shall be apart from the obligation of the State and natural persons or legal entities to compensate individuals and communities that depend on affected natural systems.

Directive, that is more focused on conservation.[90] For example, the Court has interpreted the Habitats Directive in a way that requires Member States to include degraded areas with ecological potential in the Natura 2000 Network.[91]

More recently, however, the EU has achieved the important Regulation (EU) 2024/1991, amending Regulation (EU) 2022/869, which, despite not recognizing any right—either human or non-human—to restoration and maintaining a highly anthropocentric structure, identifies legal obligations Member States must abide by.[92] The proposal, presented by the European Commission in 2022,[93] was much more advanced than the final text, which is the outcome of a very complex negotiation process within the Parliament and the Council. For example, the text in force provides that restoration should take place not for all ecosystems, but only for 'degraded' ecosystems which implies a purely anthropocentric assessment of the level of degradation.[94] Furthermore, some derogations from the general restoration objectives are indicated: the disputed paragraph—originally providing that 'Member States shall ensure that areas that host habitat types listed in Annex I are not deteriorated'—has been 'softened' and EU Member States now must only *endevour* to put in place measures with the aim of preventing significant deterioration of areas where the habitat types listed in Annex I to the Regulation occur.[95] Compared to the proposal, derogations also include now 'a plan or project of overriding public interest for which no less damaging alternative solutions are available, to be determined on a case by case basis'.[96]

With such a human-oriented provision, which paves the way for anthropocentric evaluation of 'cases', the possibility is only a judicial ecological interpretation, such as the one endorsed by the Ecuadorian Constitutional Court in *Los Cedros*, to shift the weighing up of nature's interests and economic considerations that does not automatically lead to the prevalence of the latter. It refers to an interpretation that contests 'vested rights that are often attached to ongoing activities, such as unsustainable agriculture practices'.[97]

It is time for European institutions to take a step further towards the realization of a human (and non-human) right to a healthy environment. In this sense, the Directive on single-use plastics has been criticized not so much for its laudable goal or even for the ways in which that goal is to be achieved, but for the absence of reference to the ultimate goal: safeguarding a right (not only human) to a healthy

[90] Directive (EEC) 92/43 on the conservation of natural habitats and of wild fauna and flora.

[91] Schoukens (2024, p. 209), referring to C-281/16, 2017, ECLI:EU:C:2017:774.

[92] Regulation (EU) 2024/1991 on nature restoration.

[93] European Commission, Proposal for a regulation on nature restoration, COM (2022) 304 final.

[94] Article 1(1)(a), Regulation (EU) 2024/1991.

[95] Article 4(12), Regulation (EU) 2024/1991.

[96] Article 4(14)(c), Regulation (EU) 2024/1991.

[97] Schoukens (2024, p. 209).

environment.[98] The link to the Plastics Directive is also entirely absent from the preamble to the Nature Restoration Regulation: is it not the presence of single-use plastics in nature that has prompted Union action on the subject aimed at reducing them? One scholar, arguing in favor of 'environmental justice', pointed out the two-fold cause of social injustice: on the one hand, the lack of awareness of the physical, chemical and biological links that exist in ecosystems; on the other hand, the absence of genuine solidarity that extends to the whole of humanity, both present and future.[99] This chapter adds a layer to this analysis: a concept of environment that includes both human and non-human species, and that takes into account structural discrimination and inequalities.

7 Conclusions

A sustainable economic development protects the environment and prevents pollution, and must be based on some actions, such as reduction, reuse, recovery, and recycling of materials and energy. The responsibility that humanity—*rectius,* the part of humanity that mainly overexploits natural resources—has stretched across time and space. This chapter provided a legal critique of the concepts of sustainable development and sustainable consumer to reflect on the inherent anthropocentrism and androcentrism of the law, including EU law, as it stands. It used important insights from blue planet law and ecofeminism not to provide one irrefutable truth, but to suggest that we must encourage a shift in paradigm and in the *forma mentis* of lawyers and judges, who must be open to the challenges of environmental degradation.[100] The legal (r)evolution required to achieve a 'blue planet law' aware of the dynamics of power in our societies (an 'ecofeminist' law), both in the domestic—but one should have in mind the open-minded Ecuadorian Constitutional Court decision in *Los Cedros*—and EU systems, might seem *prima facie* utopian. However, it is the *sive necessitatis* response to a drift that affects not only human rights as traditionally conceived, but also the right to a healthy environment, that should be recognized for both humans and non-humans alike.

---

[98] De Vido (2020). Directive (EU) 2019/904 on the reduction of the impact of certain plastic products on the environment.

[99] Belaïdi (2014).

[100] On the new concept of environmental chronic emergencies, see De Vido et al. (2025).

References

Atrey S (2023) The inequality of climate change and the difference it makes. In: Albertyn C, Campbell M, Alvair Grarcia H, Fredman S, Rodriguez de Assis Machado M (eds) Feminist frontiers in climate justice: gender equality, climate change and rights. Edward Elgar, Cheltenham, pp 17–39. https://doi.org/10.4337/9781803923796.00006

Baldin S, De Vido S (2022) The in dubio pro natura principle: an attempt of a comprehensive legal reconstruction. Rev Gen Derecho Público Comparado 32:168–199. https://doi.org/10.2139/ssrn.4313438

Barral V (2012) Sustainable development in international law: nature and operation of an evolutive legal norm. Eur J Int Law 23(2):377–400. https://doi.org/10.1093/ejil/chs016

Belaïdi N (2014) Identité et perspectives d'un ordre public écologique. Droit Cult 68(2):15–49. https://doi.org/10.4000/droitcultures.3401

Boyle A (2015) Human rights and the environment: where next? In: Boer B (ed) Environmental law dimensions of human rights. Oxford University Press, Oxford, pp 201–239. https://doi.org/10.1093/acprof:oso/9780198736141.003.0008

Boyle A, Freestone D (eds) (1999) International law and sustainable development: past achievements and future challenges. Oxford University Press, New York

Bristor JM, Fischer E (1993) Feminist thought: implications for consumer research. J Consum Res 19(4):518–536. https://doi.org/10.1086/209320

Carducci M, Montini M, Mumta I, Lorubbio V, Barreca A, Di Francesco MC, Musarò E, Spinks L, Powlesland P, Bagni S (2020) Towards an EU charter of the fundamental rights of nature. European Economic and Social Committee, Brussels. https://data.europa.eu/doi/10.2864/25113

Cortês A (2023) Blue planet law and ecological sustainability in the twenty-first century. In: Garcia MG, Cortês A (eds) Blue planet law. Sustainable development goals series. Springer, Cham, pp 3–19. https://doi.org/10.1007/978-3-031-24888-7_1

Craig L (2014) Thinking flowers? As black eco-feminist activism. Feminist Rev 108(1):71–80. https://doi.org/10.1057/fr.2014.21

Craig RK, Benson MH (2013) Replacing Sustainability. Akron Law Rev 46(4):841–880

Das P, Horton R (2018) Pollution, health, and the planet: time for decisive action. Lancet 391(10119):407–408. https://doi.org/10.1016/S0140-6736(17)32588-6

De Sadeleer N (2023) Environmental law in the EU: a pathway toward the green transition. In: Garcia MG, Cortês A (eds) Blue planet law, Sustainable development goals series. Springer, Cham, pp 21–33. https://doi.org/10.1007/978-3-031-24888-7_2

De Vido S (2020) La direttiva UE sulla plastica monouso alla luce del diritto umano ad un ambiente salubre. SIE 15(1):133–146

De Vido S (2024) The privatisation of climate change litigation: current developments in conflict of laws. Jus Cogens 6(1):65–88. https://doi.org/10.1007/s42439-023-00084-x

De Vido S, Russo D, Tramontana E (eds) (2025) Gendering international legal responses to environmental chronic emergencies. Edward Elgar, Cheltenham

Deckha M (2022) The one health initiative and a deeper engagement with animal health and well-being: moving away from animal agriculture. In: Braverman I (ed) More-than-one health: humans, animals, and the environment post-COVID, 1st edn. Routledge, London, pp 157–170

Drewnowski A (2009) Obesity, diets, and social inequalities. Nutr Rev 67(s1):S36–S39. https://doi.org/10.1111/j.1753-4887.2009.00157.x

Englandar G, Stevens AW, Taylor RLC, Villas-Boas SB (2023) The impact of ecolabels and green taxes on market outcomes. In: Garcia MDG, Cortês A (eds) Blue planet law, Sustainable development goals series. Springer, Cham, pp 159–171. https://doi.org/10.1007/978-3-031-24888-7_13

Esquivel V (2016) Power and the sustainable development goals: a feminist analysis. Gend Dev 24:9–23. https://doi.org/10.1080/13552074.2016.1147872

European Environment Agency (2018) Unequal exposure and unequal impacts: social vulnerability to air pollution, noise and extreme temperatures in Europe. Report 22/2018. https://www.eea.europa.eu/publications/unequal-exposure-and-unequal-impacts

Francioni F (2010) International human rights in an environmental horizon. Eur J Int Law 21(1):41–55. https://doi.org/10.1093/ejil/chq019
Gokani N (2024) Healthier food choices from consumer information to consumer empowerment in EU law. J Consum Policy 47(2):271–296. https://doi.org/10.1007/s10603-024-09563-0
Højrup M, Ounanian K (2022) 'It's how you catch the fish': debates on ecolabelling, yield thinking, and care in Denmark. Gend Place Cult 29(10):1399–1422. https://doi.org/10.1080/0966369X.2021.1975101
Hovden K (2018) The best is not good enough. Ecological (il)literacy and the rights of nature in the European Union. J Eur Environ Plan Law 15(3–4):281–308. https://doi.org/10.1163/18760104-01503004
Iovino S (2008) Filosofie dell'ambiente: natura, etica, società. Carocci, Rome
Jiménez Guanipa H, Barraco M (2024) The inter-American human rights system's impact on the protection of the right to a healthy environment. In: von Bogdandy A, Piovesan F, Ferrer Macgregor E, Morales Antoniazzi M (eds) The impact of the inter-American human rights system: transformations on the ground. Oxford University Press, New York, pp 237–253. https://doi.org/10.1093/oso/9780197744161.003.0013
Kiss A (1996) The rights and interests of future generations and the precautionary principle. In: Freestone D, Hey E (eds) The precautionary principle and international law: the challenge of implementation, International environmental law and policy, vol 31. Kluwer Law International, The Hague, pp 19–28
Kotzé LJ (2017) Global environmental constitutionalism in the Anthropocene. In: Kotzé LJ (ed) Environmental law and governance for the Anthropocene. Bloomsbury, London
Kotzé LJ, French D (2018a) A critique of the global pact for the environment: a stillborn initiative or the foundation for Lex Anthropocenae? Int Environ Agreements 18:811–838. https://doi.org/10.1007/s10784-018-9417-x
Kotzé LJ, French D (2018b) The anthropocentric ontology of international environmental law and the sustainable development goals: towards an ecocentric rule of law in the Anthropocene. Glob J Comp Law 7(1):5–36. https://doi.org/10.1163/2211906X-00701002
Lang W (ed) (1995) Sustainable development and international law. International environmental law and policy. Graham and Trotman/Martinus Nijhoff, London/Boston
Lowe V (1999) Sustainable development and unsustainable arguments. In: Boyle A, Freestone D (eds) International law and sustainable development: past achievements and future challenges. Oxford University Press, New York, pp 19–37. https://doi.org/10.1093/acprof:oso/9780198298076.003.0002
MacGregor S (2003) Feminist perspectives on sustainability. In: Bell DVJ, Cheung A (eds) UNESCO encyclopedia of life support systems: introduction to sustainable development. Eolss Publishers, Oxford, pp 467–492
MacGregor S (2014) Only resist: feminist ecological citizenship and the post-politics of climate change. Hypatia 29(3):617–633. https://doi.org/10.1111/hypa.12065
Mallory C (2013) Environmental justice, ecofeminism, and power. In: Rozzi R, Pickett S, Palmer C, Armesto J, Callicott J (eds) Linking ecology and ethics for a changing world: values, philosophy, and action, Ecology and ethics, vol 1. Springer, Dordrecht, pp 251–258. https://doi.org/10.1007/978-94-007-7470-4_21
McBride BB, Brewer CA, Berkowitz AR, Borrie WT (2013) Environmental literacy, ecological literacy, ecoliteracy: what do we mean and how did we get here? Ecosphere 4(5):67. https://doi.org/10.1890/ES13-00075.1
McEwan C (2001) Postcolonialism, feminism and development: intersections and dilemmas. Prog Dev Stud 1(2):93–111. https://doi.org/10.1177/146499340100100201
Mogyoros A (2025) The inconsistent reality of certifying trade marks: how certification marks are failing their truth ideals. IIC 56:91–114
Morrow K (2023) Towards an ecofeminist critique of international law? In: Chapaux V, Mégret F, Natarajan U (eds) The Routledge handbook of international law and anthropocentrism, 1st edn. Routledge, London, pp 183–197. https://doi.org/10.4324/9781003201120-12

Nixon R (2011) Slow violence and the environmentalism of the poor. Harvard University Press, Cambridge. https://doi.org/10.2307/j.ctt2jbsgw

Peña Chacón M (2019) Derecho humano a un ambiente sano, un derecho humano sui generis. ACODI. https://www.acodicr.org/single-post/2019/07/29/derecho-humano-a-un-ambiente-sano-un-derecho-humano-sui-generis

Petersmann MC (2024) The EU charter on rights of nature—colliding cosmovisions on non/human relations. In: Alvarez-Nakagawa A, Douzinas C (eds) Non-human rights: critical perspectives. Edward Elgar, Cheltenham, pp 141–163. https://doi.org/10.4337/9781802208528.00012

Pintado M, Aragão A (2023) Pollution and law. In: Garcia MG, Cortês A (eds) Blue planet law, Sustainable development goals series. Springer, Cham, pp 85–97. https://doi.org/10.1007/978-3-031-24888-7_7

Prieto Munoz JG (2021) The Los Cedros Forest has rights: the Ecuadorian constitutional court affirms the rights of nature. Verfassungsblog: On Matters Constitutional. https://doi.org/10.17176/20211211-064222-0

Sands P (1994) International law in the field of sustainable development. Br Yearb Int Law 64:303–381. https://doi.org/10.1093/bybil/65.1.303

Schoukens H (2024) Rights of nature in the European Union: a rights-based approach as an inevitable outcome of increased environmental protection in the Anthropocene? In: Schoukens H, Bouquelle F (eds) The right to a healthy environment in and beyond the Anthropocene: a European perspective. Edward Elgar, Cheltenham, pp 184–226. https://doi.org/10.4337/9781035300426.00017

Soromenho-Marques V, Magalhães P (2023) Our blue planet at the crossroads: between the Hobbesian nightmare and a new culture of the commons. In: Garcia MG, Cortês A (eds) Blue planet law, Sustainable development goals series. Springer, Cham, pp 35–47. https://doi.org/10.1007/978-3-031-24888-7_3

Stone C (1972) Should trees have standing? Towards legal rights for natural objects. South Calif Law Rev 45:450–501

Struckmann C (2018) A postcolonial feminist critique of the 2030 agenda for sustainable development: a south African application. Agenda 32:12–24. https://doi.org/10.1080/10130950.2018.1433362

Tavares da Silva S, Gomes Martins A (2023) Renewable energies, sustainability and law. In: Garcia MG, Cortês A (eds) Blue planet law, Sustainable development goals series. Springer, Cham, pp 145–158. https://doi.org/10.1007/978-3-031-24888-7_1

Thøgersen J (2021) Consumer behavior and climate change: consumers need considerable assistance. Curr Opin Behav Sci 42:9–14. https://doi.org/10.1016/j.cobeha.2021.02.008

Van Hoorick G, Verniers E (2024) Some explorations about extending the right to a healthy environment to future generations and animals. In: Schoukens H, Bouquelle F (eds) The right to a healthy environment in and beyond the Anthropocene: a European perspective. Edward Elgar, Cheltenham, pp 227–245. https://doi.org/10.4337/9781035300426.00018

Voigt C (2009) Sustainable development as a principle of international law: resolving conflicts between climate measures and WTO law. Legal aspects of sustainable development, vol 2. Nijhoff, Leiden. https://doi.org/10.1163/ej.9789004166974.i-428

Weinhues A (2020) Ecological justice and the extinction crisis: giving living beings their due. Bristol University Press, Bristol

Wilkinson Cross K (2023) A critical evaluation of inter-generational equity and its application in the climate change context. In: Albertyn C, Campbell M, Alvair Grarcia H, Fredman S, Rodriguez de Assis Machado M (eds) Feminist frontiers in climate justice: gender equality, climate change and rights. Edward Elgar, Cheltenham, pp 40–67. https://doi.org/10.4337/9781803923796.00007

Zhang M (2024) A half-century journey of human rights and the environment in the international arena: from separation to integration. In: Schoukens H, Bouquelle F (eds) The right to a healthy environment in and beyond the Anthropocene: a European perspective. Edward Elgar, Cheltenham, pp 34–52. https://doi.org/10.4337/9781035300426.00008

Zhao Z, Gong Y, Li Y, Zhang L, Sun Y (2021) Gender-related beliefs, norms, and the link with green consumption. Front Psychol 12:710239. https://doi.org/10.3389/fpsyg.2021.710239

Afterword

Christopher Willet

This collection contains a range of carefully argued chapters that highlight and critique existing regulatory initiatives and their fitness for purpose in promoting sustainability and the circular economy; and that imagine the role that might be played by alternative regulatory initiatives. The numerous extremely insightful arguments make their own important contributions to the scholarship. However, it is the far-sightedness and cohesiveness of the overall collection—the overall conceptualisation—that is perhaps the most valuable attribute of the book. I would use the analogy of sports, where we often contrast what can be achieved by a set of very good individual performances; with what can be achieved by a genuinely 'team performance': a team that is built to function with an overall goal in mind, understanding the complex and changing range of challenges that may arise, and built to work cohesively and consistently as a collective to continue to meet these challenges.

One often reads essay collections that contain plenty of excellent individual contributions, which are for sure a 'whole' at least in the sense that they deal with the same area of law, and which clearly cover important contemporary issues within the field. However, the chapters could work better as a collective—as a team.

The key to the excellent teamwork in this collection lies in the recognition that the creation of a dynamic circular economy that can promote sustainability, not perfectly but reasonably effectively, requires reflection and adjustment across a range of traditional legal fields (e.g. corporate governance, consumer law, intellectual property law, constitutional law, private international law, human rights), as well as contributions from other disciplines such as sociology.

A vital starting point in this approach comes with the recognition in Bernardo Calabrese's Introduction that 'we cannot rely exclusively on economic rationales and techno-science, in their fallacious promise of infinite progress, but we must

C. Willet (✉)
University of Essex, Colchester, UK
e-mail: cwillett@essex.ac.uk

B. Calabrese (ed.), *Legal Perspectives for a Sustainable Circular Economy*,
European Union and its Neighbours in a Globalized World 30,
https://doi.org/10.1007/978-3-032-07795-0_14

look to humanity to fairly orient the evolution of society'. We cannot create a sustainable circular economy without understanding humans and human nature. This makes it indispensable to include a foundational chapter providing a sociological analysis of the challenges, which aims to present the relevant framework by means of the analysis of its key concepts, issues and actors. This chapter by Michele Marzulli demonstrated the social complexity that arises in regulating for circularity and sustainability, including in particular the complex partnership required between individual and collective intervention. As Bernardo Calabrese points out in the Introduction, this raises huge challenges in selecting appropriate measures, which in turn explain in part why environmental strategy is in a state of crisis. Perhaps a key challenge going forward—for politicians, sociologists and civil society—is to work out how to develop a reasonably common view as to which individuals, firms, governments must do more or less—what is a fair distribution of the burden?

Corporate governance-company-law is clearly a key part of the picture, and there are several important chapters on this. Anna Genovese considered corporate sustainability reporting, highlighting, *inter alia*, the need for further evidence as to the effectiveness of information disclosure as a regulatory tool to discipline the circular economy, and also for further work on achieving management compliance. These insights should in my view be direct us to the need for future (non-legal) contributions to the field: including in particular further behavioral psychology and behavioral economics work on the scope and limits of information obligations, and from the discipline of business management on compliance theory and practice.

Andrea Caprara considered the role of citizens as stakeholders in corporate governance. Of course, this adds to a long-term broader debate as to the role of the corporate entity in society and the extent to which its governance is a matter of interest beyond those with an (economic) shareholder interest. The case for wider involvement is arguably made even more pressing given the universality of the environmental interests now at stake. Again, though, going forward, we should not restrict ourselves to traditional legal scholarship in understanding how to achieve such wider engagement, but look, e.g. to sociological work on social systems, political science work on participatory democracy, and business management and other work on organisational theory.

Francesca Bianconi explored what development of the circular economy might mean for the way in which the law constitutes the duties of company directors. Can sustainability be transformed into a concrete and workable legal management obligation? This is a key question, as obviously it is very hard to see how companies can contribute to the broader circular economy without the directors having obligations within the company that are in congruence with this broader goal. So the perennial broader debate as to the role of directors (and companies) in balancing profit with broader social goals, becomes crystallized specifically in relation to environmental sustainability: what are the particular challenges and opportunities in striking this balance in this context? What lessons are there from the broader debate beyond the environmental context? What can other disciplines such as business management teach on this challenge?

Federica Pasquariello focused again on the corporate governance field but from the fascinating angle of insolvency rules. How can insolvency regimes foster sustainability and contribute to the circular economy, e.g. by facilitating employee buy-outs or other solutions that aim to prevent resources being wasted? This is an intriguing angle, raising questions about re-balancing insolvency law, perhaps reducing the extent to which it favors large financial creditors such as banks. Notwithstanding that there are some real challenges here, it is surely an issue that must be part of a genuinely holistic approach to developing the circular economy. After all, with increasingly unstable national and international economies, insolvency and the waste it can produce, are likely to continue to be significant problems.

Bernardo Calabrese's chapter took us beyond corporate governance to how commercial law may re-shape legal rights and steer market transactions such as to promote sustainability and the circular economy. A key example here is the notion, taking hold in European law, of a right to have products repaired, the obvious point being to avoid the wastage involved in discarding the product. Another example is so called 'servitization', the move to customers paying for a service, e.g. air conditioning, cleaning, driving; rather than buying the equipment themselves. This can reduce waste and promote decarbonisation. Nevertheless, there are questions as to how the law best facilitates such approaches, and Calabrese's chapter explores in particular some intellectual property law challenges.

Francesco Deana continued the focus on how customers, especially consumers, can shape the circular economy by the sorts of transactions they enter. The argument made is for consumer law to recalibrate to empower consumers to make informed and sustainable decisions. However, it is recognised that information provision is not in itself a panacea, especially given so called 'information overload' and the complexity of environmental data. Consumer education also has a key role to play. Moreover, it is recognised that genuine consumer empowerment will also require more substantive interventions in terms of what consumers can expect, e.g., rights to product longevity and repair.

Of course a serious perennial challenge for consumer law, and this continues in consumer law being asked to play a role in building the circular economy, is the enforcement challenge. In many areas of consumer law that are vital to promotion of the circular economy enforcement is problematic. Take, for instance, regimes on unfair commercial practices, necessary to control misleading environmental claims and aggressive practices which push consumers into purchases they do not need; or regimes on unfair contract terms which control terms that excludes liability for such misleading or aggressive practices, or which exclude 'environmentally friendly' rights such as rights to repair. These regimes do not generally intervene at the earliest stages by pre-vetting and not allowing unfair terms and practices onto the market in the first place. Generally they only come into play when the terms and practices are spotted on the market, and this is often in such huge numbers that they are difficult to detect. Now AI based enforcement is increasingly being vaunted as a much faster way of detecting such problems. However, this raises a dilemma given that there are serious questions as to the amount of energy used by AI.

A further set of enforcement issues was dealt with in Elisabetta Bergamini's chapter. Private international law has always faced the incredibly tricky challenge of balancing various competing interests in deciding which laws and which courts should decide disputes that arise across borders. However, this chapter demonstrated the new challenges posed for pre-existing conflicts rules when they must be applied to the increasingly common peer to peer transactions which are facilitated by online platforms, and which undoubtedly have at least some dimensions that can be viewed as circular. Further on the enforcement theme the chapter considered how circular economy-friendly alternative dispute resolution can be fostered by applying innovative solutions to the schemes run by platforms. Going forward, cross-border and less formal redress will continue to be very significant issues in building the circular economy. It will be important to continue to develop the sort of ideas presented in this chapter, and also to look to empirical studies which give the best sense of what is happening and working in practice.

A further important part of the jigsaw has been provided by Alessia-Ottavia Cozzi 's chapter. It explored the constitutional foundations of the circular economy and sustainability, in particular focusing on the relationship between governance at EU and national levels. Using Italy as a case study, it was argued that there is a significant degree of similarity and integration between the national and EU approach. It will be important going forward to continue to develop theoretical frameworks for assessing constitutional foundations at national and EU level, and to continue to test the degree of integration as the needs of the circular economy develop and change and as we see perhaps changes in political and economic priorities.

The chapter by Claudia Candelmo provided a broader international analysis, making comparisons between EU approaches and other regimes. The broad picture emerging is of the EU model being something of a frontrunner in providing an effective legal framework for a circular economy, a framework being followed to a degree by other regimes. Similarly to immediately above, it will be important to work further on developing theoretical frameworks to assess the effectiveness of systems, comparisons between them, and how similarities and differences develop.

The chapter by Sara Dal Monico also took a global approach and brings the conversation back to the role of consumers in a circular economy. This time the focus was on the concept of 'sustainable' consumers and in particular the extent to which consumer rights may be viewed as human rights. A key suggested application of this is the notion that consumers could be viewed as having a (human) right to access to information; helping to empower consumers to make informed sustainable choices that discipline the market to produce sustainable offerings. This role for consumers in driving development of the circular economy is clearly important. Key for future work will be to continue to work on the potential and limits of information in empowering consumers, especially here drawing on the findings of behavioral science; and exploring whether or not a human rights (over a traditional consumer law) approach has the potential to enhance the potential of information to empower consumers.

The final chapter by Sara De Vido argued for an approach that is underpinned by a notion of ‘human nature’ embracing the whole of the rest of the natural world. The logic then appears to be to use this as the foundation to view the environment as more than resource, but rather as an autonomous legal entity, an entity that has special rights that can more effectively battle for supremacy with purely selfish economic interests. In some ways this is the most radical and ambitious reform suggested in the book. It will be fascinating to see how this sort of analysis can be developed in future work, and the extent to which it can incorporate and/or integrate with other analyses in this book and elsewhere.

Overall, this book demonstrates the breadth of the challenge in regulating to develop the circular economy: a challenge that not only requires reflection and analysis across a very significant range of traditional legal categories, but also requires interaction with other disciplines including but not limited to sociology, politics, economics, management and behavioral science.

MIX
Papier aus verantwortungsvollen Quellen
Paper from responsible sources
FSC® C105338

If you have any concerns about our products,
you can contact us on
ProductSafety@springernature.com

In case Publisher is established outside the EU,
the EU authorized representative is:
Springer Nature Customer Service Center GmbH
Europaplatz 3, 69115 Heidelberg, Germany

Printed by Libri Plureos GmbH
in Hamburg, Germany